the Pajama Diaries

Déjà To-Do

To Julie...
Hope you enjoy!
All the best,
Terri

TJStudios
LTD

Printed by Laserwave Graphics - www.Laserwave.com

The Pajama Diaries is distributed internationally by King Features Syndicate, Inc. For information, write King Features Syndicate, Inc., 300 W. 57th Street, New York, NY 10019

ISBN: 978-0-9833272-0-2

Library of Congress Control Number: 2011924739

See **www.pajamadiaries.com** for latest news, samples and more.

If you would like your local paper to carry *The Pajama Diaries*, please contact the newspaper editor and request that they add it to their lineup!

With love to my incredible, complying family:
Mike, Mollie and Nikki.

In 2004, between the kids' naps and my intermittent crying jags, I managed to squeeze in some reading time. There was a growing emergence of literature and blogs written by moms who were overwhelmed with their frenzied lives. I realized then that there were no mainstream *comics* that reflected this new reality.

I am part of the generation of women who were taught we could grow up to do anything we wanted. We partook in higher education, but we never took that "Motherhood 101" course that taught us how to be a million different things to everyone in our lives.

If I knew then what I know now...well, I probably wouldn't have done things much differently. **But** I would have been more prepared. And that's why I created "The Pajama Diaries." It's my way of reaching out to other parents to let them know that they are not alone in this absurd work/parenthood journey.

And maybe, just maybe, I could provide them with a few laughs along the way.

-Terri Libenson, 2011

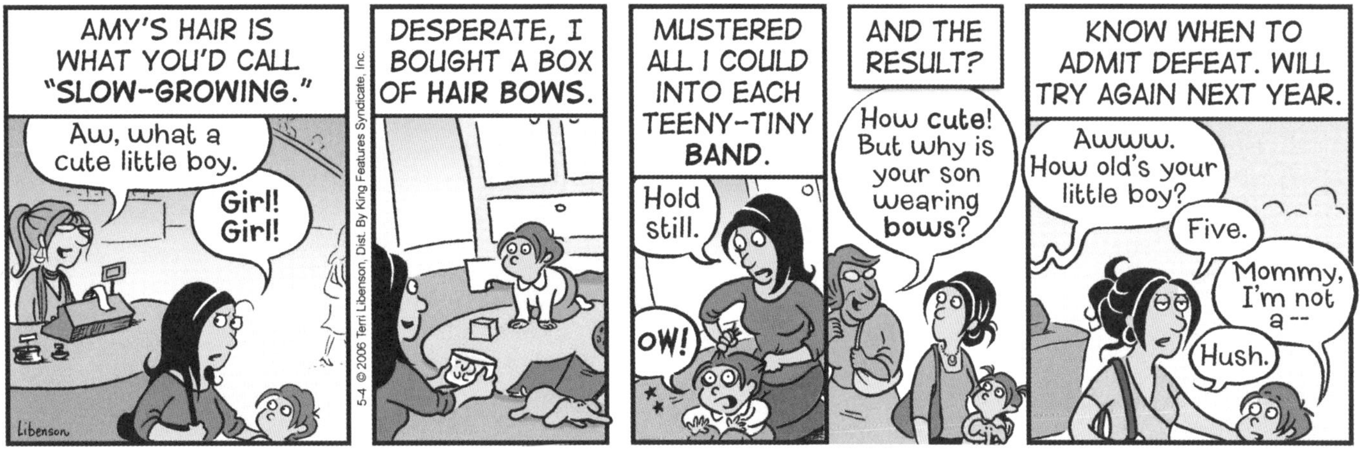
AMY'S HAIR IS WHAT YOU'D CALL "SLOW-GROWING."
Aw, what a cute little boy.
Girl! Girl!
Libenson
5-4 © 2006 Terri Libenson, Dist. By King Features Syndicate, Inc.
DESPERATE, I BOUGHT A BOX OF HAIR BOWS.
MUSTERED ALL I COULD INTO EACH TEENY-TINY BAND.
Hold still.
OW!
AND THE RESULT?
How cute! But why is your son wearing bows?
KNOW WHEN TO ADMIT DEFEAT. WILL TRY AGAIN NEXT YEAR.
Awww. How old's your little boy?
Five.
Mommy, I'm not a --
Hush.

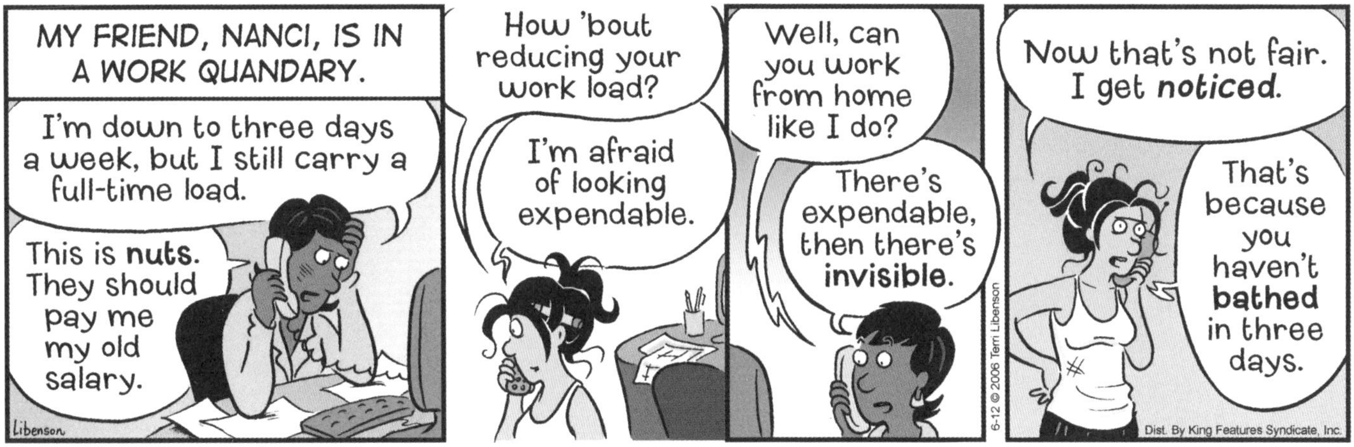
MY FRIEND, NANCI, IS IN A WORK QUANDARY.
I'm down to three days a week, but I still carry a full-time load.
This is nuts. They should pay me my old salary.
Libenson
How 'bout reducing your work load?
I'm afraid of looking expendable.
Well, can you work from home like I do?
There's expendable, then there's invisible.
6-12 © 2006 Terri Libenson
Now that's not fair. I get noticed.
That's because you haven't bathed in three days.
Dist. By King Features Syndicate, Inc.

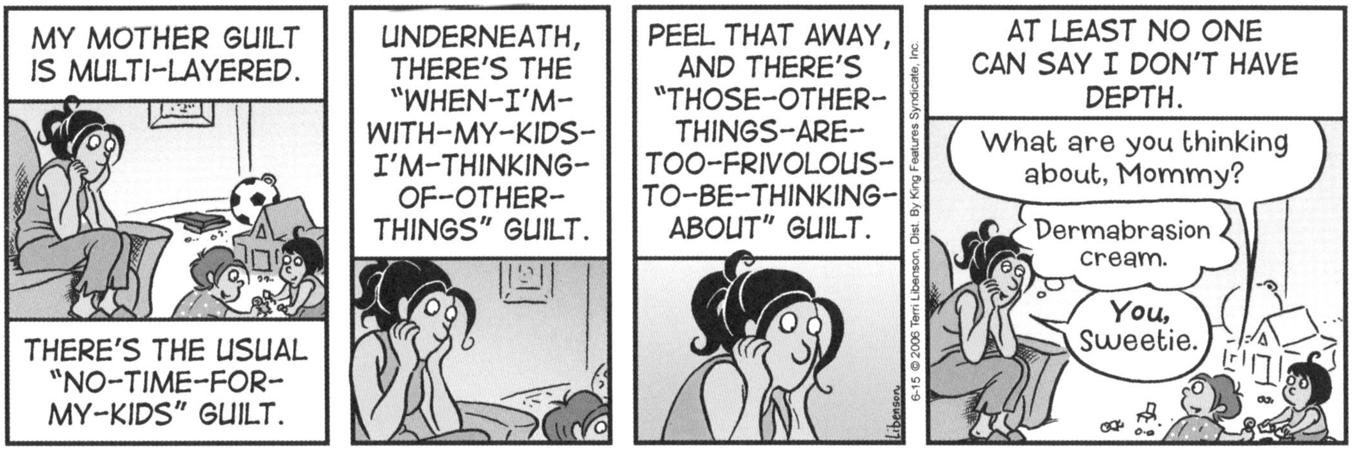
MY MOTHER GUILT IS MULTI-LAYERED.
THERE'S THE USUAL "NO-TIME-FOR-MY-KIDS" GUILT.
UNDERNEATH, THERE'S THE "WHEN-I'M-WITH-MY-KIDS-I'M-THINKING-OF-OTHER-THINGS" GUILT.
PEEL THAT AWAY, AND THERE'S "THOSE-OTHER-THINGS-ARE-TOO-FRIVOLOUS-TO-BE-THINKING-ABOUT" GUILT.
Libenson
6-15 © 2006 Terri Libenson, Dist. By King Features Syndicate, Inc.
AT LEAST NO ONE CAN SAY I DON'T HAVE DEPTH.
What are you thinking about, Mommy?
Dermabrasion cream.
You, Sweetie.

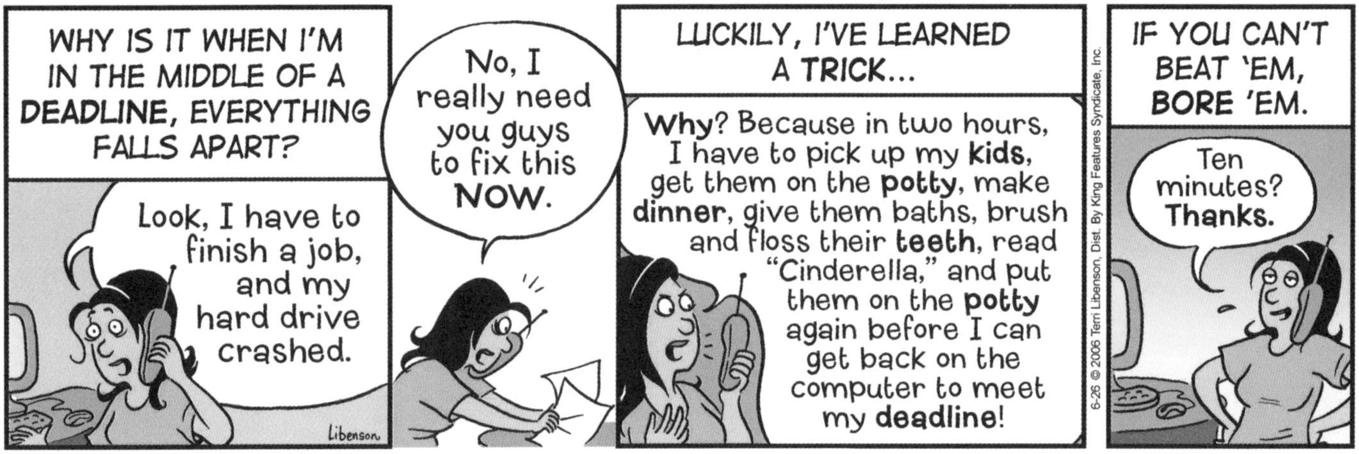
WHY IS IT WHEN I'M IN THE MIDDLE OF A DEADLINE, EVERYTHING FALLS APART?
Look, I have to finish a job, and my hard drive crashed.
Libenson
No, I really need you guys to fix this NOW.
LUCKILY, I'VE LEARNED A TRICK...
Why? Because in two hours, I have to pick up my kids, get them on the potty, make dinner, give them baths, brush and floss their teeth, read "Cinderella," and put them on the potty again before I can get back on the computer to meet my deadline!
6-26 © 2006 Terri Libenson, Dist. By King Features Syndicate, Inc.
IF YOU CAN'T BEAT 'EM, BORE 'EM.
Ten minutes? Thanks.

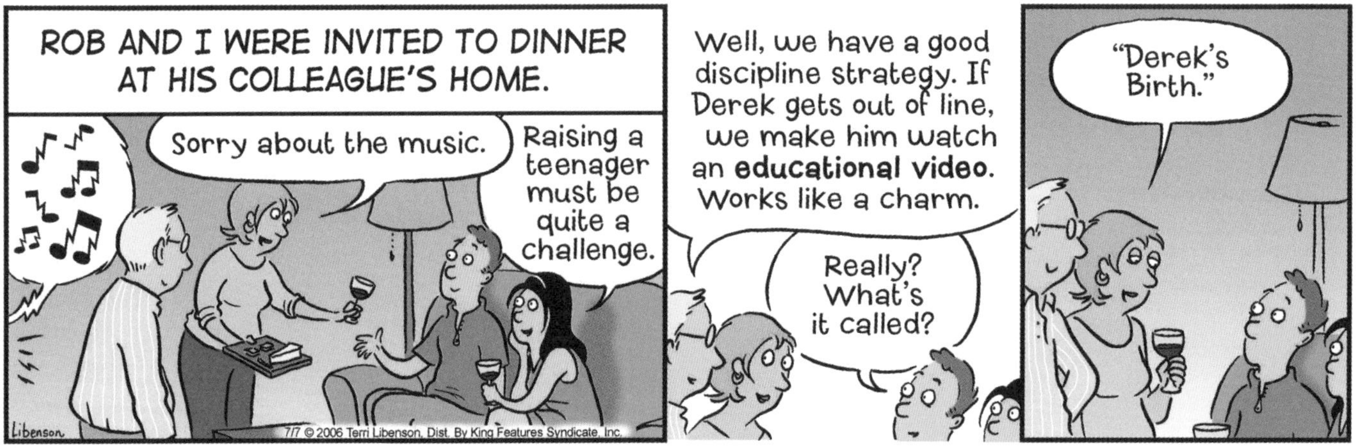
ROB AND I WERE INVITED TO DINNER AT HIS COLLEAGUE'S HOME.
Sorry about the music.
Raising a teenager must be quite a challenge.
Libenson
7/7 © 2006 Terri Libenson, Dist. By King Features Syndicate, Inc.
Well, we have a good discipline strategy. If Derek gets out of line, we make him watch an educational video. Works like a charm.
Really? What's it called?
"Derek's Birth."

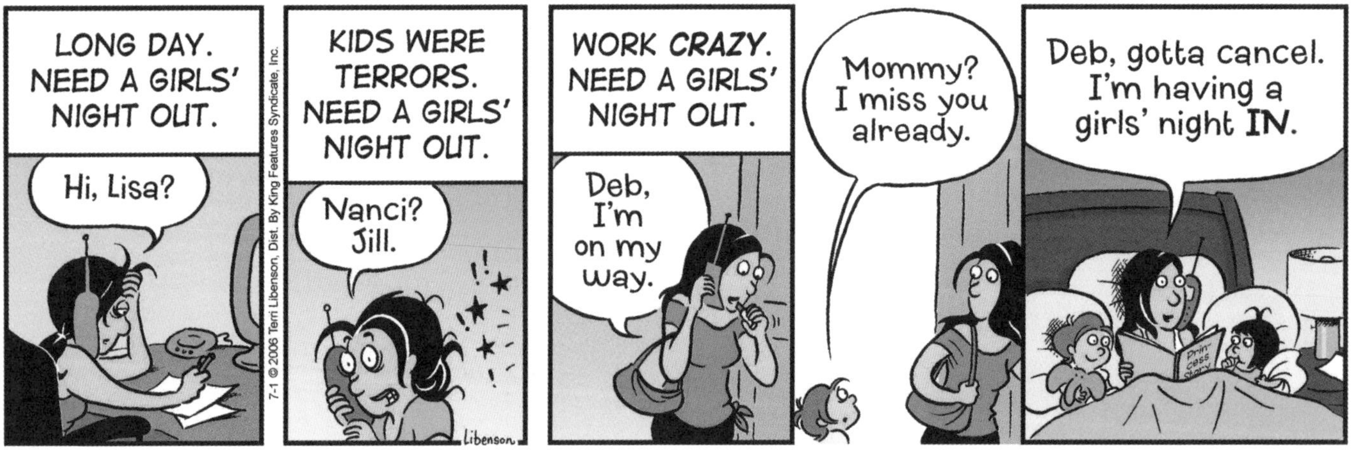
LONG DAY. NEED A GIRLS' NIGHT OUT.
Hi, Lisa?
7-1 © 2006 Terri Libenson, Dist. By King Features Syndicate, Inc.
KIDS WERE TERRORS. NEED A GIRLS' NIGHT OUT.
Nanci? Jill.
Libenson
WORK CRAZY. NEED A GIRLS' NIGHT OUT.
Deb, I'm on my way.
Mommy? I miss you already.
Deb, gotta cancel. I'm having a girls' night IN.

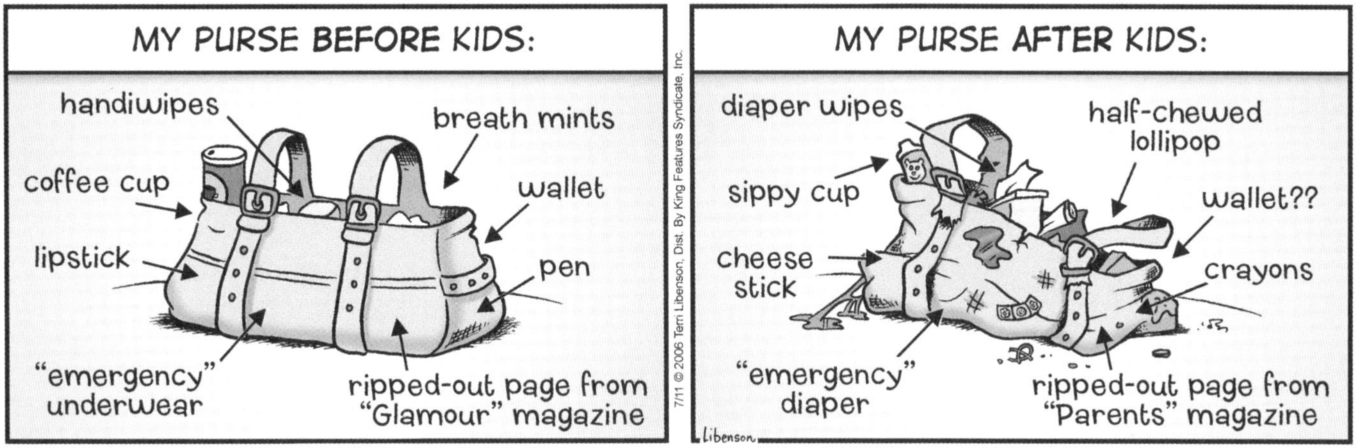
MY PURSE BEFORE KIDS:
handiwipes
breath mints
coffee cup
wallet
lipstick
pen
"emergency" underwear
ripped-out page from "Glamour" magazine
7/11 © 2006 Terri Libenson, Dist. By King Features Syndicate, Inc.
MY PURSE AFTER KIDS:
diaper wipes
half-chewed lollipop
sippy cup
wallet??
cheese stick
crayons
"emergency" diaper
ripped-out page from "Parents" magazine
Libenson

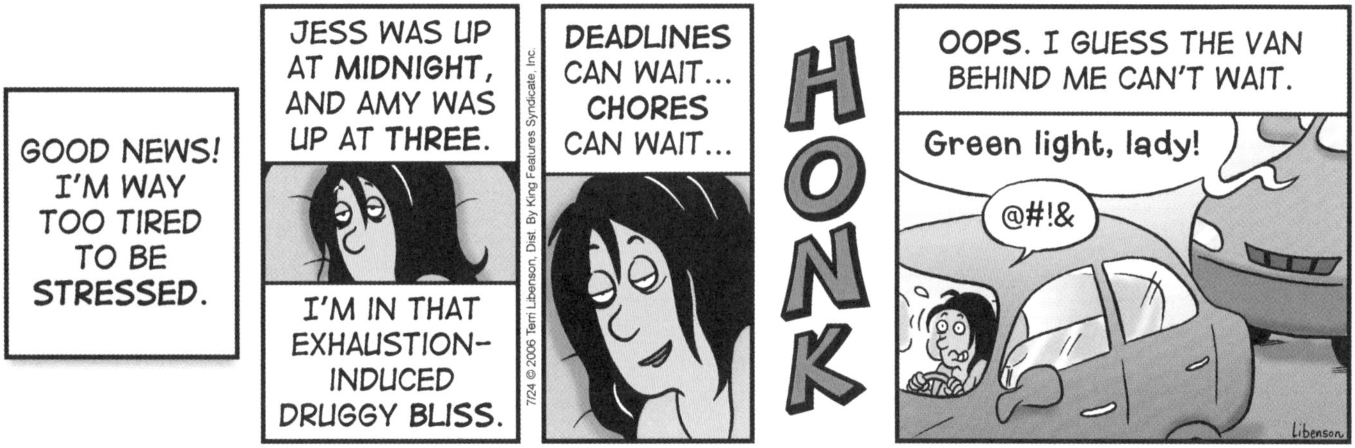
GOOD NEWS! I'M WAY TOO TIRED TO BE STRESSED.
JESS WAS UP AT MIDNIGHT, AND AMY WAS UP AT THREE.
I'M IN THAT EXHAUSTION-INDUCED DRUGGY BLISS.
7/24 © 2006 Terri Libenson, Dist. By King Features Syndicate, Inc.
DEADLINES CAN WAIT... CHORES CAN WAIT...
HONK
OOPS. I GUESS THE VAN BEHIND ME CAN'T WAIT.
Green light, lady!
@#!&
Libenson

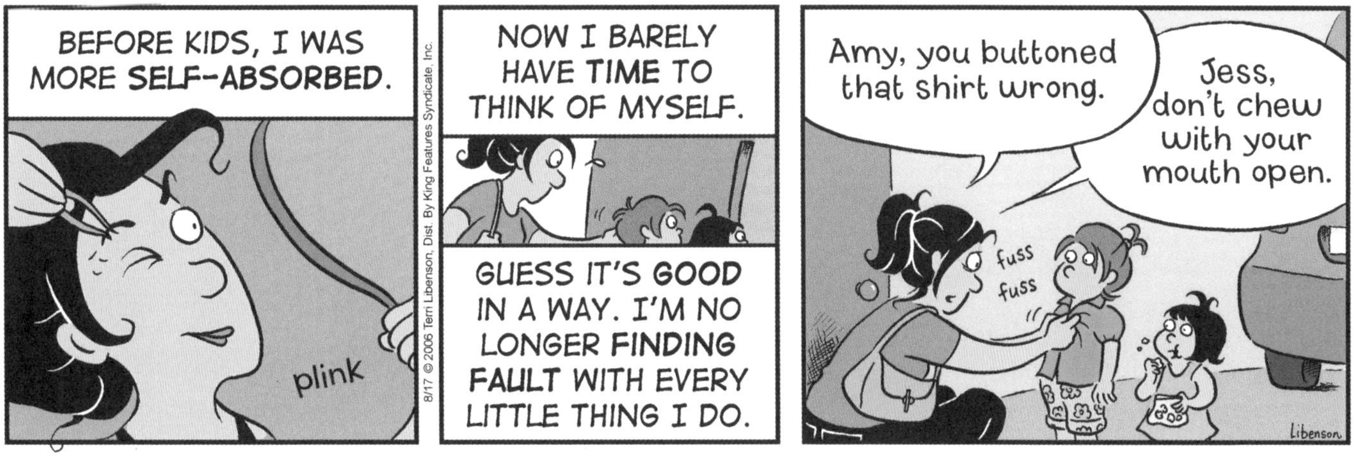
BEFORE KIDS, I WAS MORE SELF-ABSORBED.
plink
8/17 © 2006 Terri Libenson, Dist. By King Features Syndicate, Inc.
NOW I BARELY HAVE TIME TO THINK OF MYSELF.
GUESS IT'S GOOD IN A WAY. I'M NO LONGER FINDING FAULT WITH EVERY LITTLE THING I DO.
Amy, you buttoned that shirt wrong.
Jess, don't chew with your mouth open.
fuss fuss
Libenson

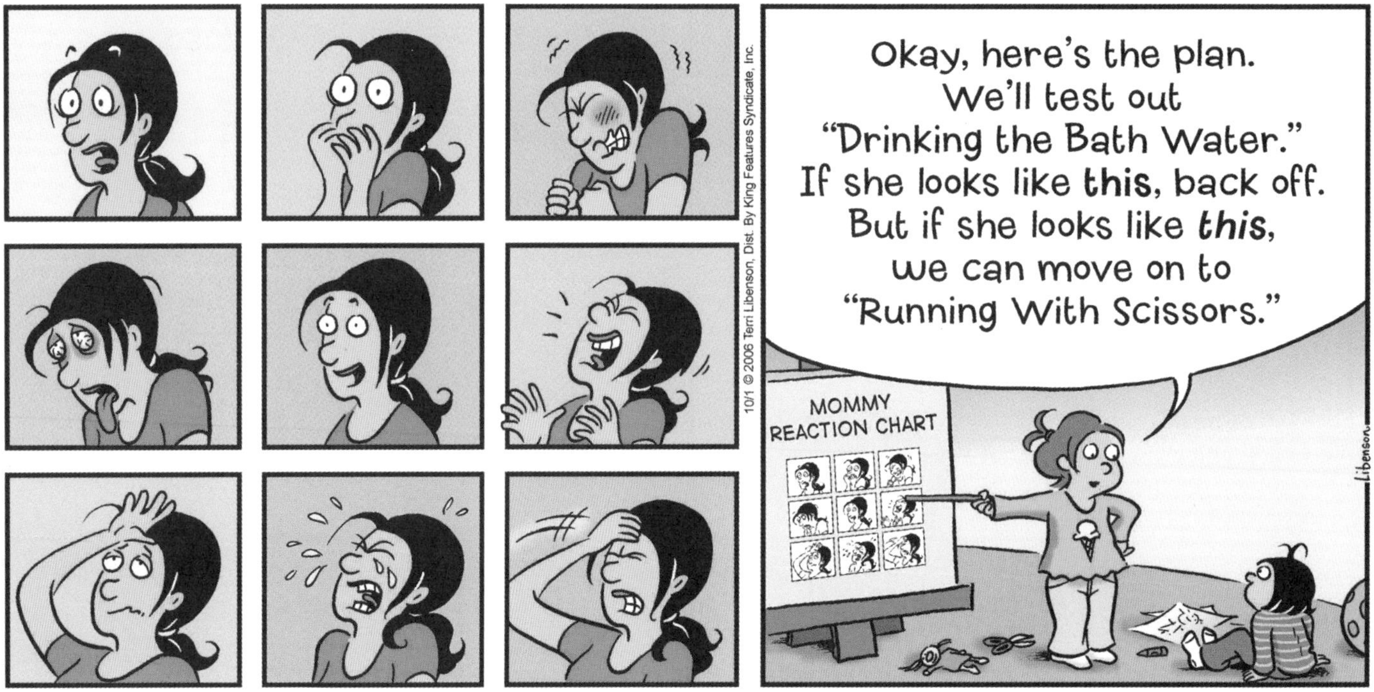
10/1 © 2006 Terri Libenson, Dist. By King Features Syndicate, Inc.
Okay, here's the plan. We'll test out "Drinking the Bath Water." If she looks like **this**, back off. But if she looks like ***this***, we can move on to "Running With Scissors."
MOMMY REACTION CHART
Libenson

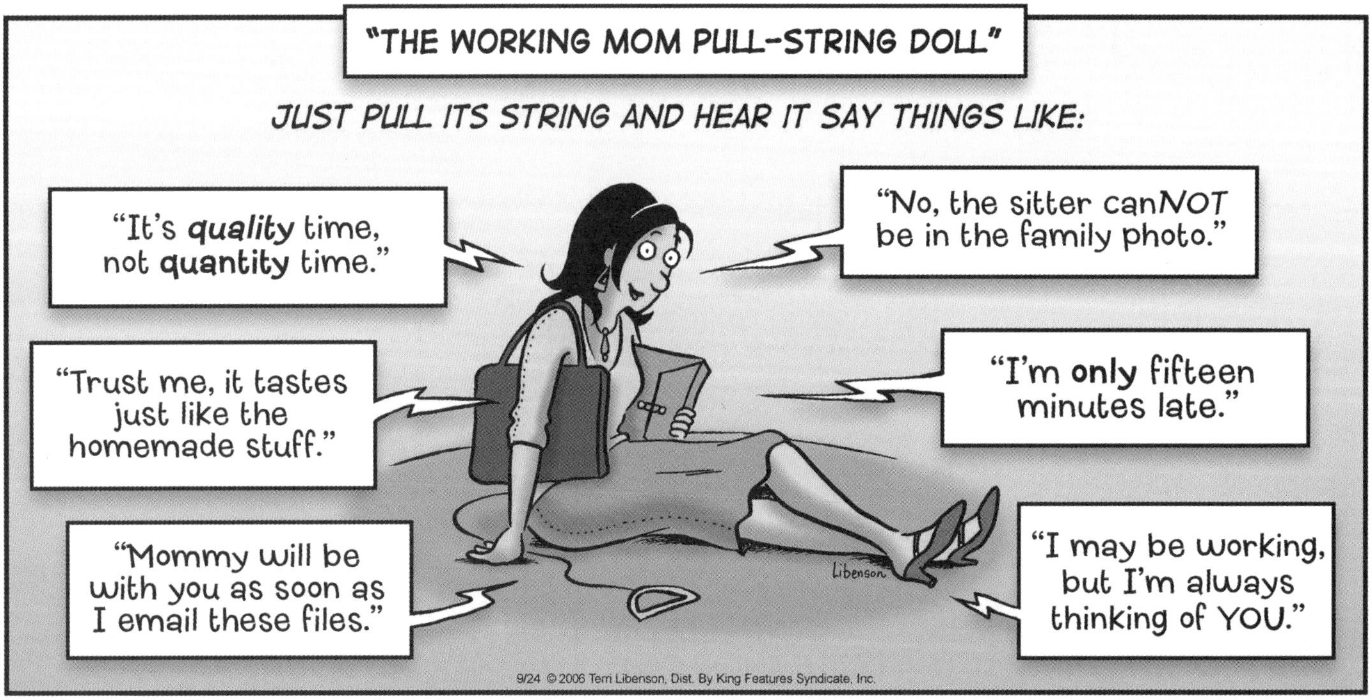
"THE WORKING MOM PULL-STRING DOLL"
JUST PULL ITS STRING AND HEAR IT SAY THINGS LIKE:
"It's ***quality*** time, not **quantity** time."
"No, the sitter can*NOT* be in the family photo."
"Trust me, it tastes just like the homemade stuff."
"I'm **only** fifteen minutes late."
"Mommy will be with you as soon as I email these files."
"I may be working, but I'm always thinking of YOU."
Libenson
9/24 © 2006 Terri Libenson, Dist. By King Features Syndicate, Inc.

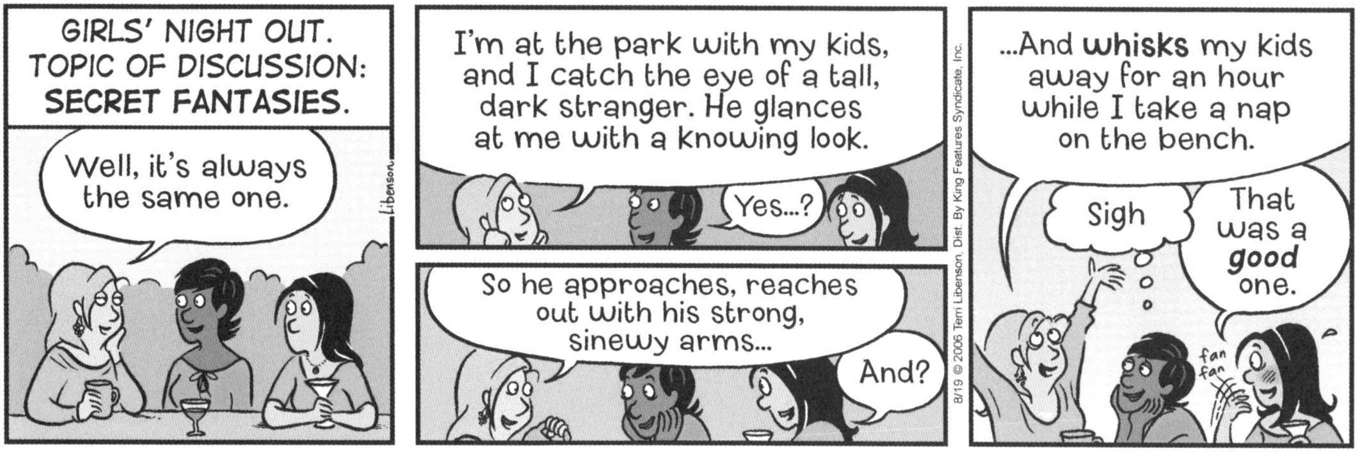
GIRLS' NIGHT OUT. TOPIC OF DISCUSSION: **SECRET FANTASIES.**
Well, it's always the same one.
Libenson
I'm at the park with my kids, and I catch the eye of a tall, dark stranger. He glances at me with a knowing look.
Yes...?
So he approaches, reaches out with his strong, sinewy arms...
And?
8/19 © 2006 Terri Libenson, Dist. By King Features Syndicate, Inc.
...And **whisks** my kids away for an hour while I take a nap on the bench.
Sigh
That was a ***good*** one.
fan fan

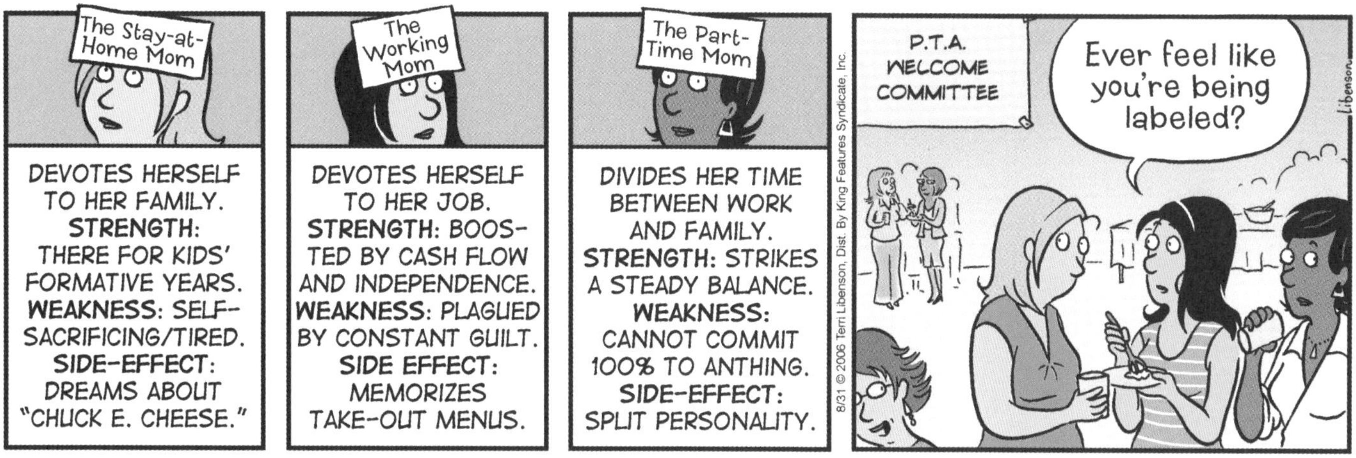
The Stay-at-Home Mom
DEVOTES HERSELF TO HER FAMILY. **STRENGTH**: THERE FOR KIDS' FORMATIVE YEARS. **WEAKNESS**: SELF-SACRIFICING/TIRED. **SIDE-EFFECT**: DREAMS ABOUT "CHUCK E. CHEESE."
The Working Mom
DEVOTES HERSELF TO HER JOB. **STRENGTH**: BOOSTED BY CASH FLOW AND INDEPENDENCE. **WEAKNESS**: PLAGUED BY CONSTANT GUILT. **SIDE EFFECT**: MEMORIZES TAKE-OUT MENUS.
The Part-Time Mom
DIVIDES HER TIME BETWEEN WORK AND FAMILY. **STRENGTH**: STRIKES A STEADY BALANCE. **WEAKNESS**: CANNOT COMMIT 100% TO ANTHING. **SIDE-EFFECT**: SPLIT PERSONALITY.
8/31 © 2006 Terri Libenson, Dist. By King Features Syndicate, Inc.
P.T.A. WELCOME COMMITTEE
Ever feel like you're being labeled?
Libenson

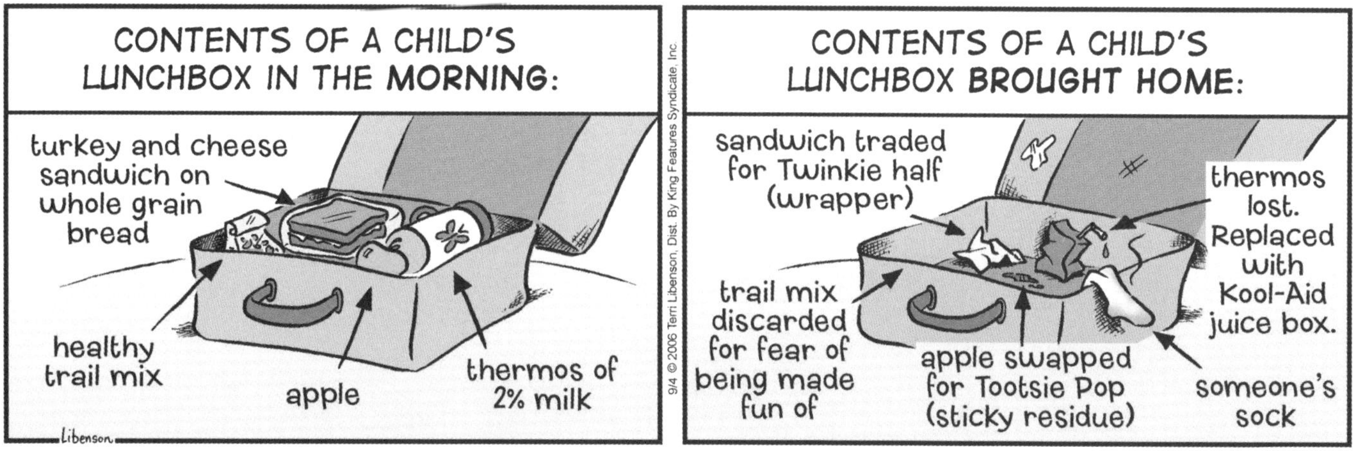
CONTENTS OF A CHILD'S LUNCHBOX IN THE **MORNING**:
turkey and cheese sandwich on whole grain bread
healthy trail mix
apple
thermos of 2% milk
Libenson
9/4 © 2006 Terri Libenson, Dist. By King Features Syndicate, Inc.
CONTENTS OF A CHILD'S LUNCHBOX **BROUGHT HOME**:
sandwich traded for Twinkie half (wrapper)
thermos lost. Replaced with Kool-Aid juice box.
trail mix discarded for fear of being made fun of
apple swapped for Tootsie Pop (sticky residue)
someone's sock

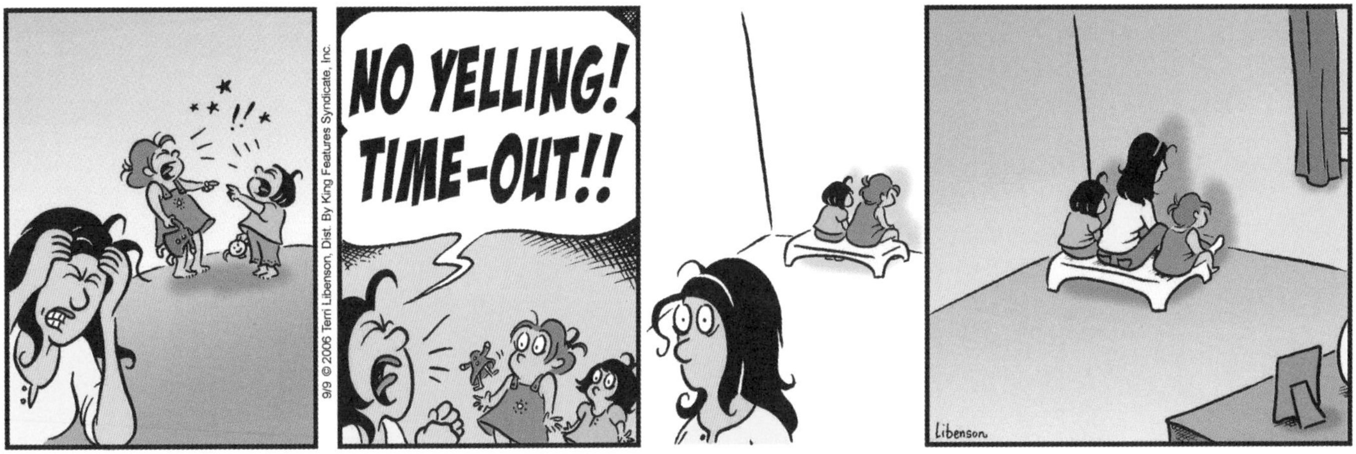
9/9 © 2006 Terri Libenson, Dist. By King Features Syndicate, Inc.
NO YELLING! TIME-OUT!!
Libenson

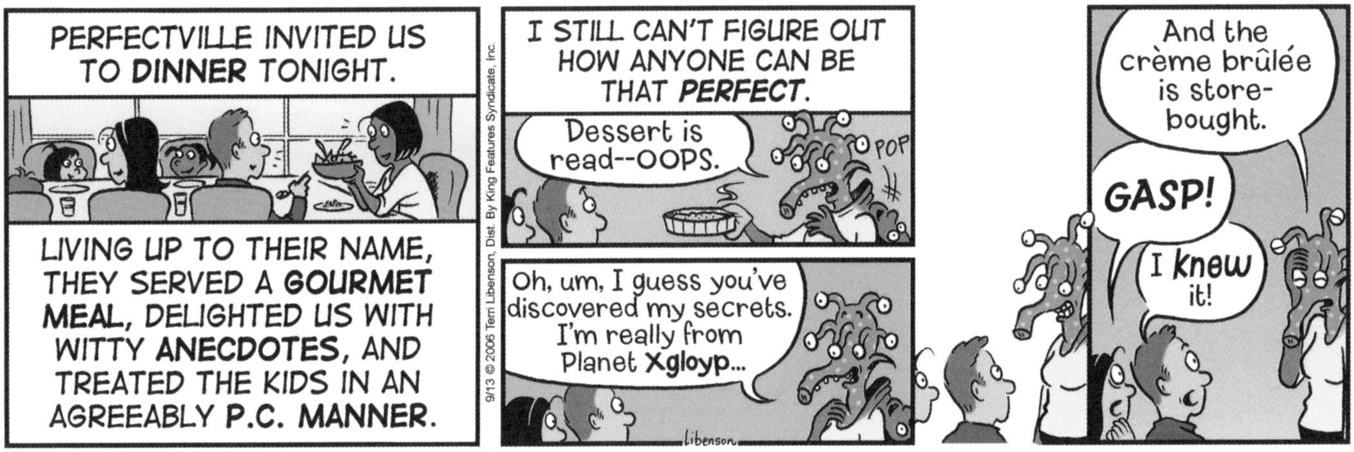
PERFECTVILLE INVITED US TO DINNER TONIGHT.
LIVING UP TO THEIR NAME, THEY SERVED A GOURMET MEAL, DELIGHTED US WITH WITTY ANECDOTES, AND TREATED THE KIDS IN AN AGREEABLY P.C. MANNER.
9/13 © 2006 Terri Libenson, Dist. By King Features Syndicate, Inc.
I STILL CAN'T FIGURE OUT HOW ANYONE CAN BE THAT PERFECT.
Dessert is read--OOPS.
POP
Oh, um, I guess you've discovered my secrets. I'm really from Planet Xgloyp...
Libenson
And the crème brûlée is store-bought.
GASP!
I knew it!

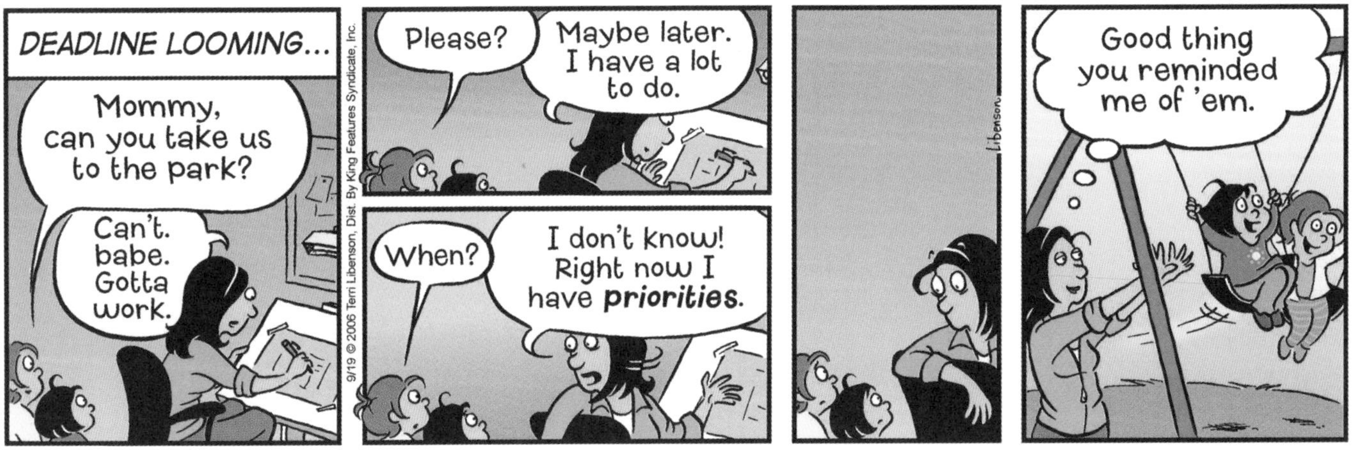
DEADLINE LOOMING...
Mommy, can you take us to the park?
Can't. babe. Gotta work.
9/19 © 2006 Terri Libenson, Dist. By King Features Syndicate, Inc.
Please?
Maybe later. I have a lot to do.
When?
I don't know! Right now I have priorities.
Libenson
Good thing you reminded me of 'em.

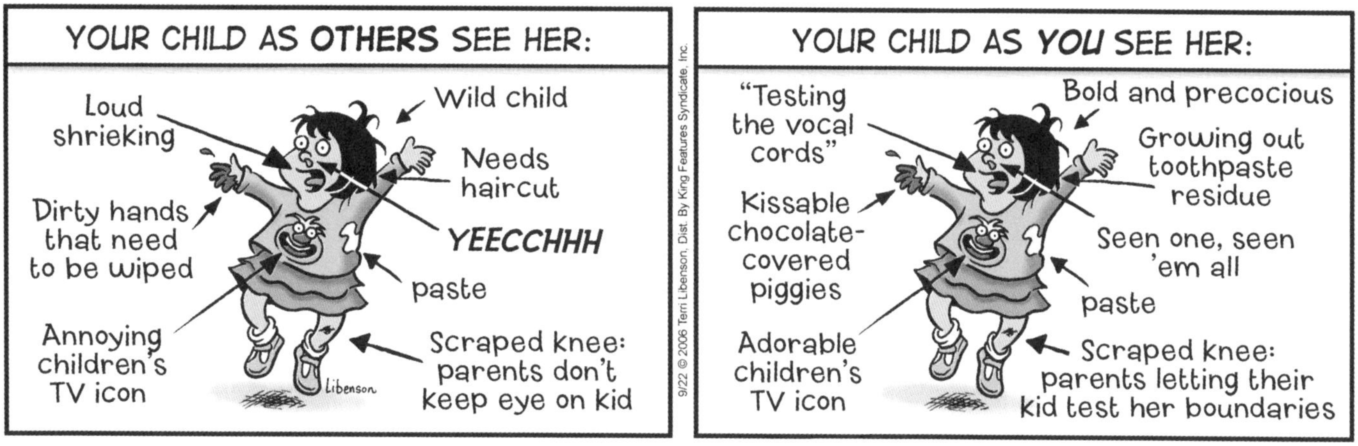
YOUR CHILD AS **OTHERS** SEE HER:
Loud shrieking
Wild child
Needs haircut
Dirty hands that need to be wiped
YEECCHHH
paste
Annoying children's TV icon
Scraped knee: parents don't keep eye on kid
Libenson
9/22 © 2006 Terri Libenson, Dist. By King Features Syndicate, Inc.
YOUR CHILD AS ***YOU*** SEE HER:
"Testing the vocal cords"
Bold and precocious
Growing out toothpaste residue
Kissable chocolate-covered piggies
Seen one, seen 'em all
paste
Adorable children's TV icon
Scraped knee: parents letting their kid test her boundaries

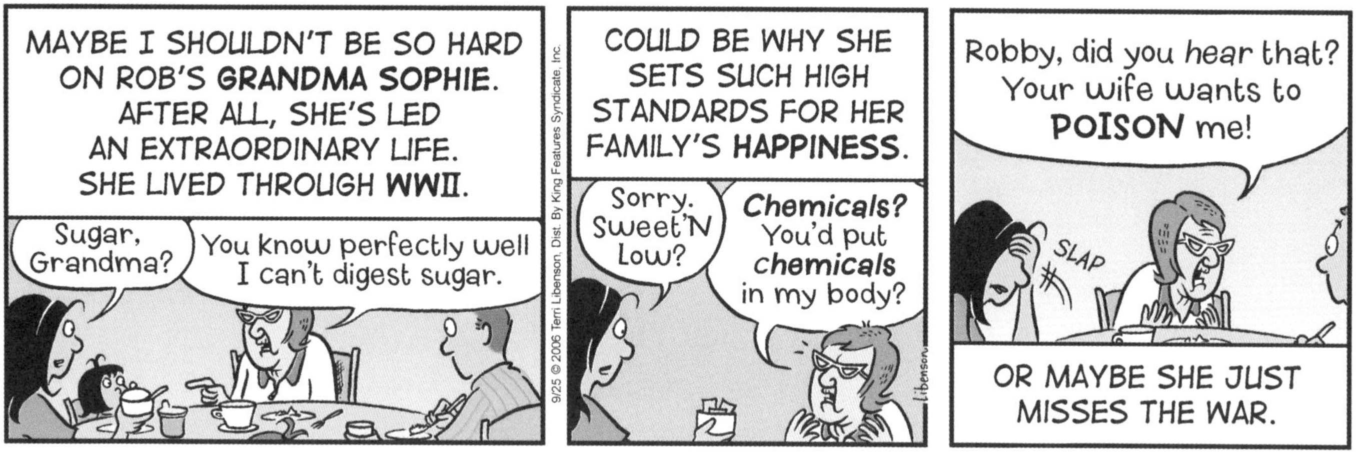
MAYBE I SHOULDN'T BE SO HARD ON ROB'S **GRANDMA SOPHIE**. AFTER ALL, SHE'S LED AN EXTRAORDINARY LIFE. SHE LIVED THROUGH **WWII**.
Sugar, Grandma?
You know perfectly well I can't digest sugar.
9/25 © 2006 Terri Libenson, Dist. By King Features Syndicate, Inc.
COULD BE WHY SHE SETS SUCH HIGH STANDARDS FOR HER FAMILY'S **HAPPINESS**.
Sorry. Sweet'N Low?
Chemicals? You'd put ***chemicals*** in my body?
Libenson
Robby, did you *hear* that? Your wife wants to **POISON** me!
SLAP
OR MAYBE SHE JUST MISSES THE WAR.

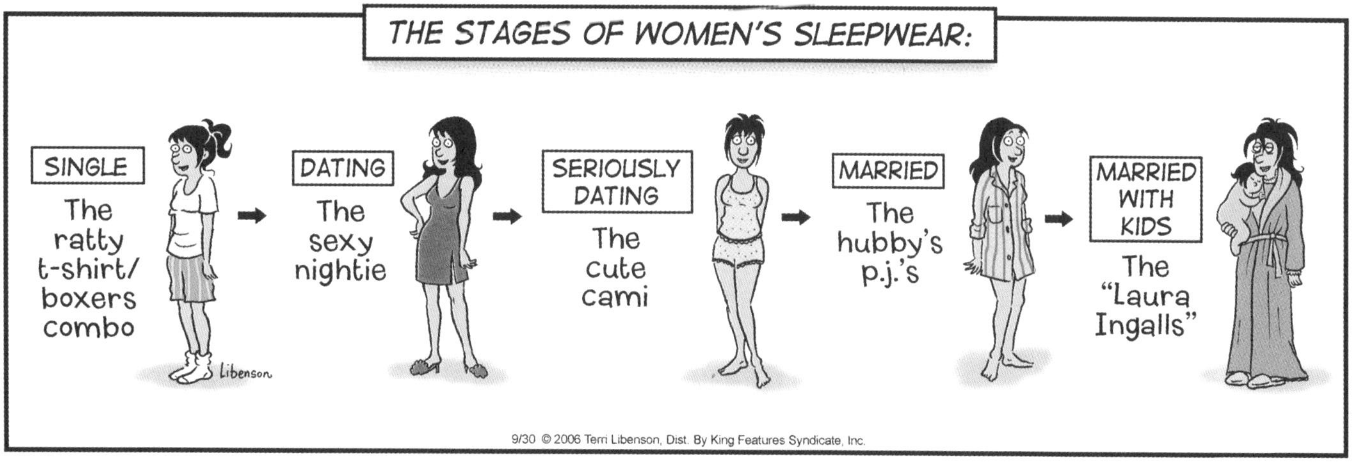
THE STAGES OF WOMEN'S SLEEPWEAR:
SINGLE
The ratty t-shirt/boxers combo
DATING
The sexy nightie
SERIOUSLY DATING
The cute cami
MARRIED
The hubby's p.j.'s
MARRIED WITH KIDS
The "Laura Ingalls"
Libenson
9/30 © 2006 Terri Libenson, Dist. By King Features Syndicate, Inc.

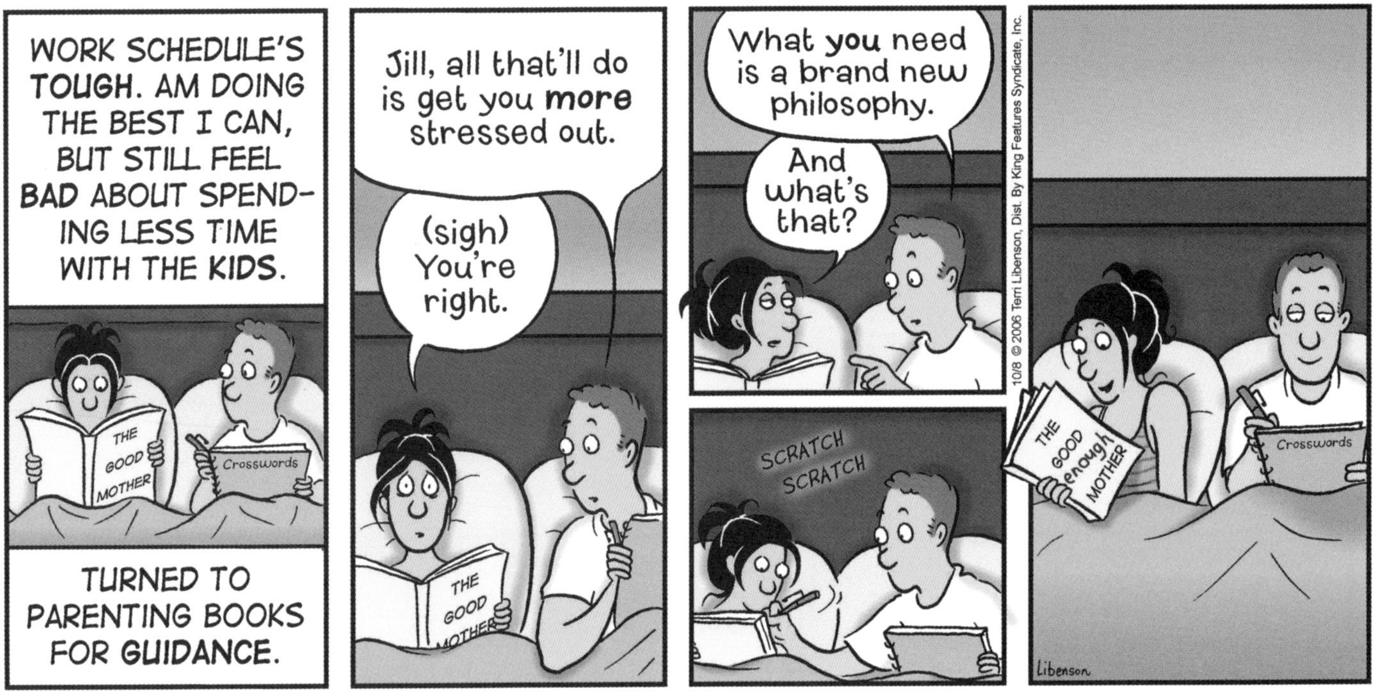

WORK SCHEDULE'S TOUGH. AM DOING THE BEST I CAN, BUT STILL FEEL BAD ABOUT SPENDING LESS TIME WITH THE KIDS.
THE GOOD MOTHER
Crosswords
TURNED TO PARENTING BOOKS FOR GUIDANCE.
Jill, all that'll do is get you more stressed out.
(sigh) You're right.
THE GOOD MOTHER
What you need is a brand new philosophy.
And what's that?
10/8 © 2006 Terri Libenson, Dist. By King Features Syndicate, Inc.
SCRATCH SCRATCH
THE GOOD enough MOTHER
Crosswords
Libenson

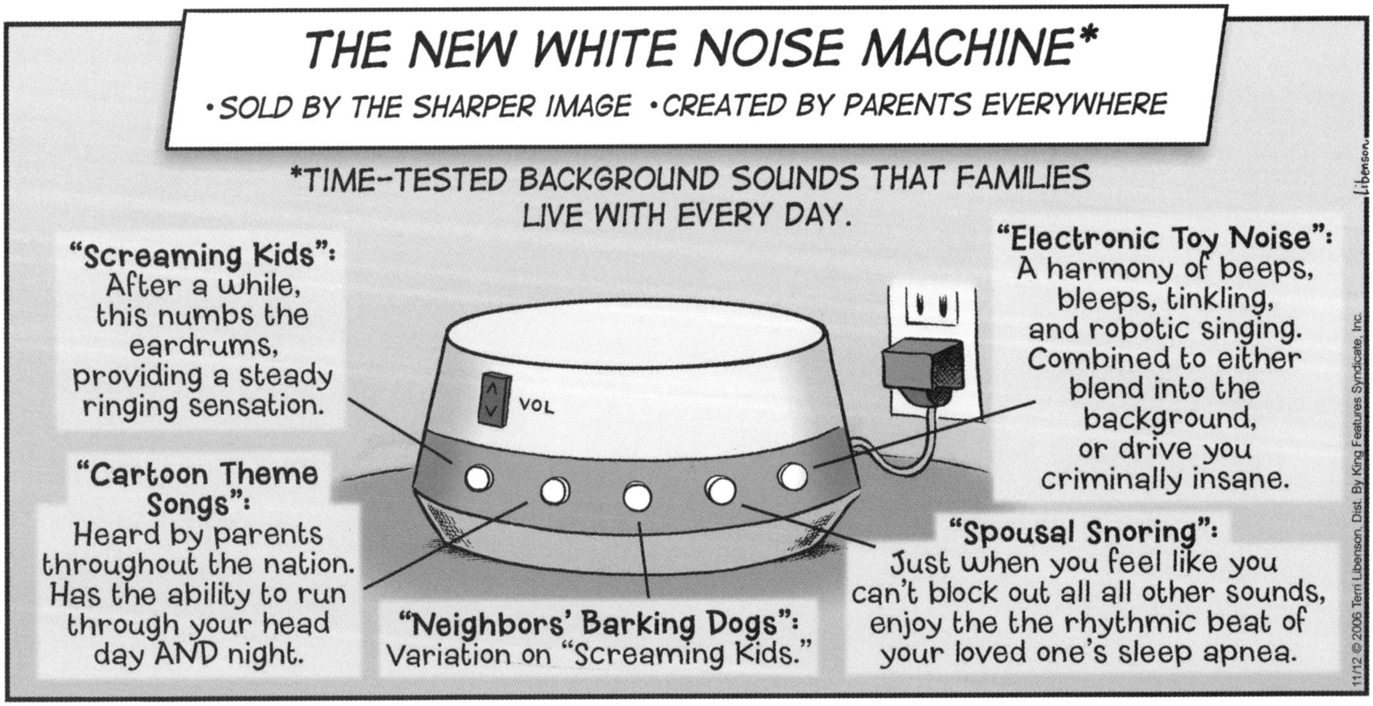

THE NEW WHITE NOISE MACHINE*
•SOLD BY THE SHARPER IMAGE •CREATED BY PARENTS EVERYWHERE
*TIME-TESTED BACKGROUND SOUNDS THAT FAMILIES LIVE WITH EVERY DAY.
Libenson
"Screaming Kids": After a while, this numbs the eardrums, providing a steady ringing sensation.
"Electronic Toy Noise": A harmony of beeps, bleeps, tinkling, and robotic singing. Combined to either blend into the background, or drive you criminally insane.
VOL
"Cartoon Theme Songs": Heard by parents throughout the nation. Has the ability to run through your head day AND night.
"Neighbors' Barking Dogs": Variation on "Screaming Kids."
"Spousal Snoring": Just when you feel like you can't block out all all other sounds, enjoy the the rhythmic beat of your loved one's sleep apnea.
11/12 © 2006 Terri Libenson, Dist. By King Features Syndicate, Inc.

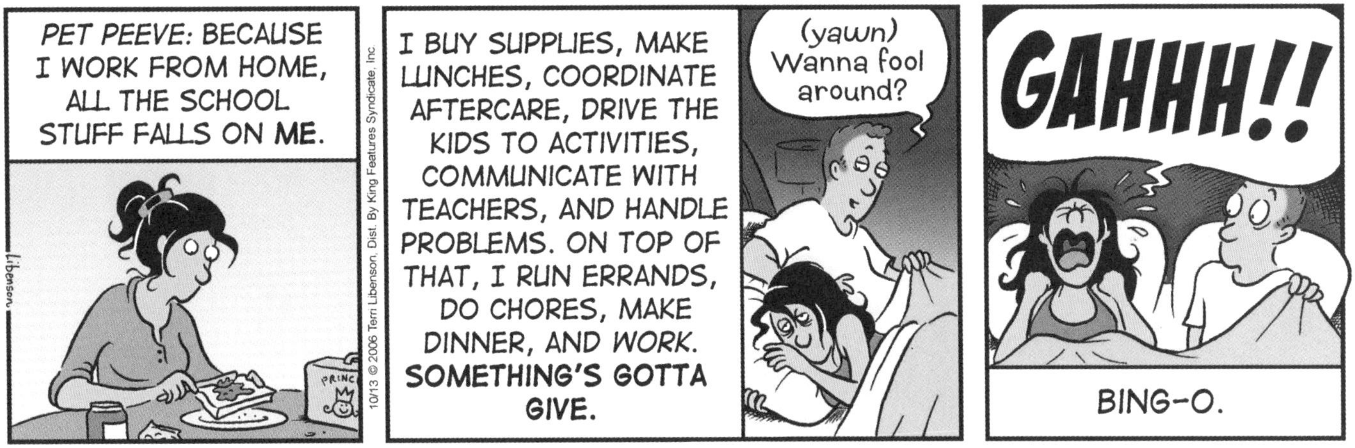
PET PEEVE: BECAUSE I WORK FROM HOME, ALL THE SCHOOL STUFF FALLS ON ME.
Libenson
PRINC
10/13 © 2006 Terri Libenson, Dist. By King Features Syndicate, Inc.
I BUY SUPPLIES, MAKE LUNCHES, COORDINATE AFTERCARE, DRIVE THE KIDS TO ACTIVITIES, COMMUNICATE WITH TEACHERS, AND HANDLE PROBLEMS. ON TOP OF THAT, I RUN ERRANDS, DO CHORES, MAKE DINNER, AND WORK. SOMETHING'S GOTTA GIVE.
(yawn) Wanna fool around?
GAHHH!!
BING-O.

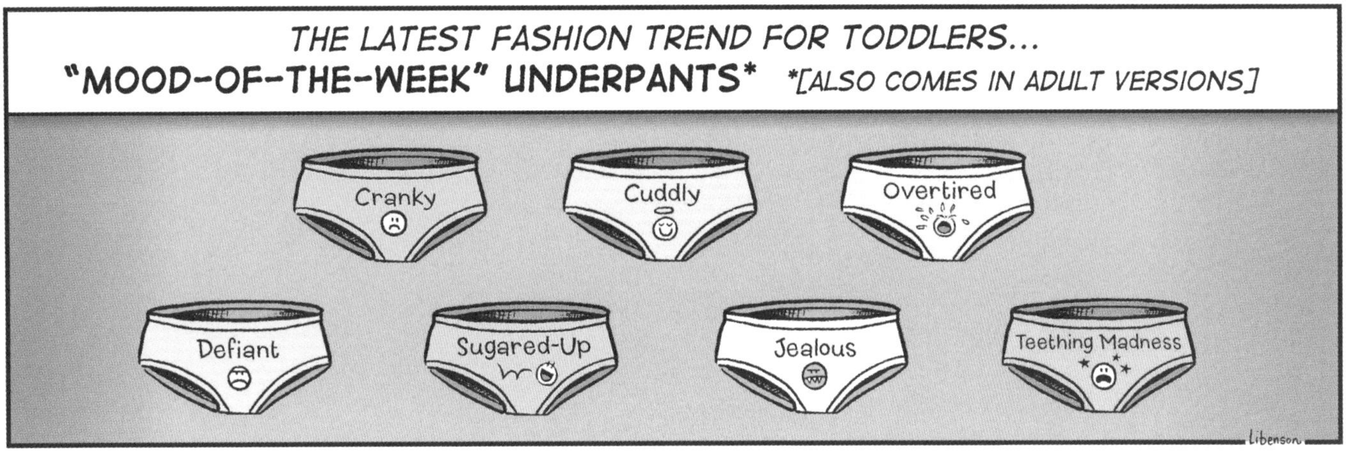
THE LATEST FASHION TREND FOR TODDLERS...
"MOOD-OF-THE-WEEK" UNDERPANTS* *[ALSO COMES IN ADULT VERSIONS]
Cranky
Cuddly
Overtired
Defiant
Sugared-Up
Jealous
Teething Madness
Libenson

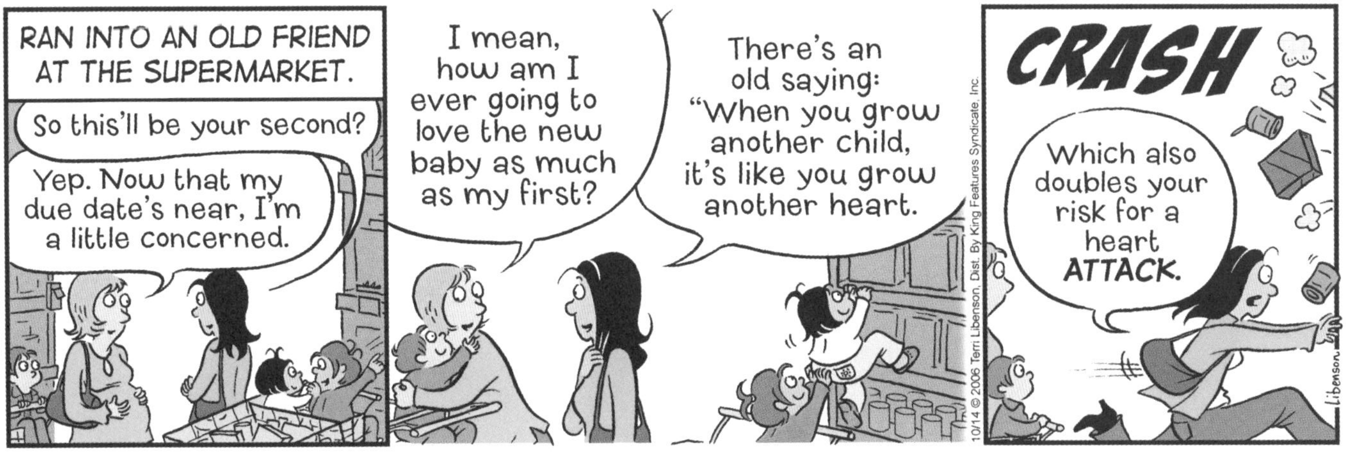
RAN INTO AN OLD FRIEND AT THE SUPERMARKET.
So this'll be your second?
Yep. Now that my due date's near, I'm a little concerned.
I mean, how am I ever going to love the new baby as much as my first?
There's an old saying: "When you grow another child, it's like you grow another heart.
10/14 © 2006 Terri Libenson, Dist. By King Features Syndicate, Inc.
CRASH
Which also doubles your risk for a heart ATTACK.
Libenson

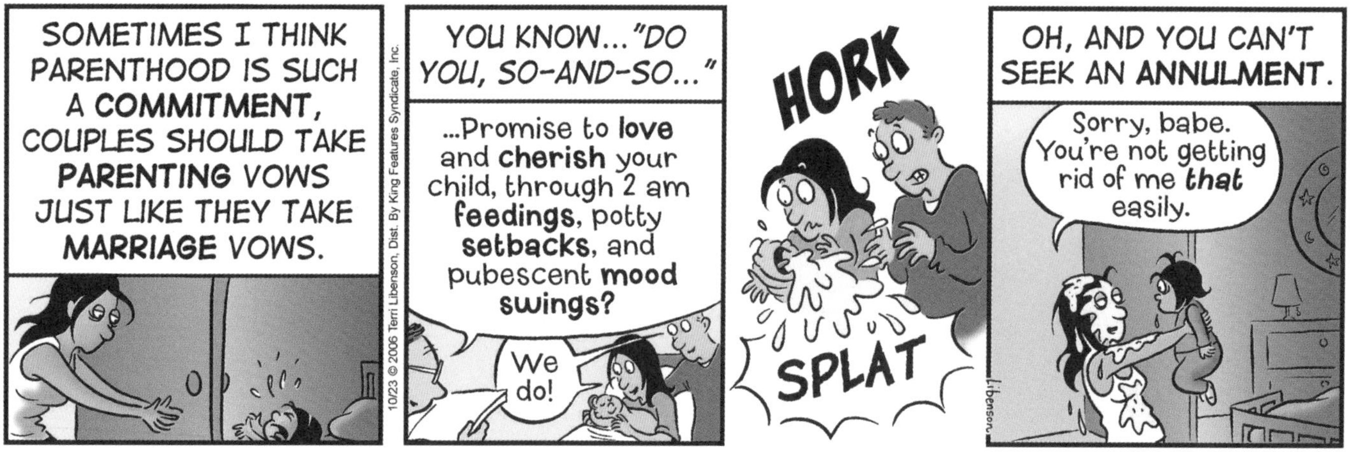
SOMETIMES I THINK PARENTHOOD IS SUCH A **COMMITMENT**, COUPLES SHOULD TAKE **PARENTING** VOWS JUST LIKE THEY TAKE **MARRIAGE** VOWS.
10/23 © 2006 Terri Libenson, Dist. By King Features Syndicate, Inc.
YOU KNOW... "DO YOU, SO-AND-SO..."
...Promise to **love** and **cherish** your child, through 2 am **feedings**, potty **setbacks**, and pubescent **mood swings**?
We do!
HORK
SPLAT
OH, AND YOU CAN'T SEEK AN **ANNULMENT**.
Sorry, babe. You're not getting rid of me ***that*** easily.
Libenson

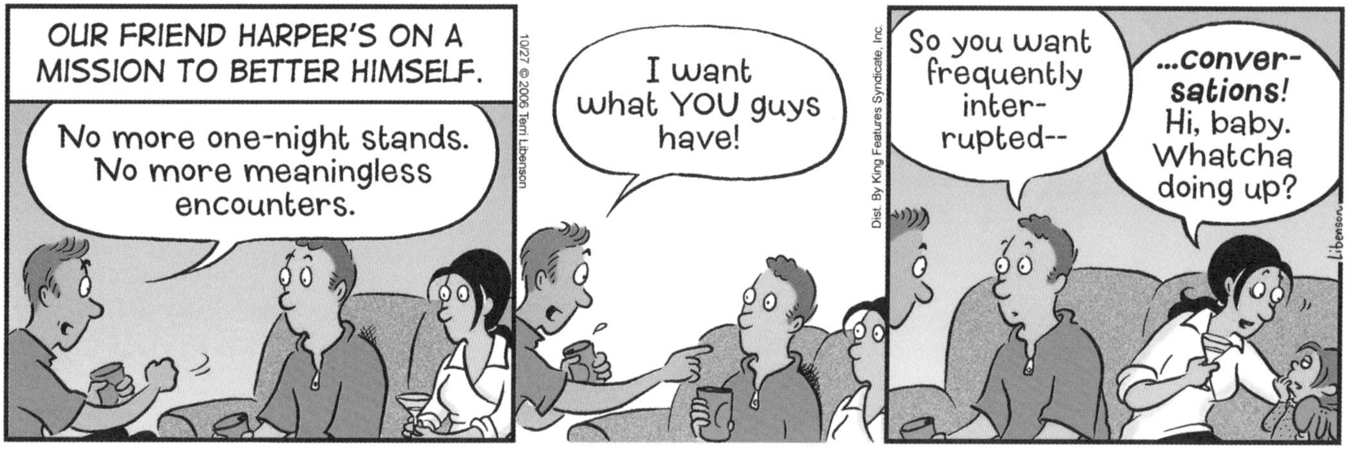
OUR FRIEND HARPER'S ON A MISSION TO BETTER HIMSELF.
No more one-night stands. No more meaningless encounters.
10/27 © 2006 Terri Libenson
I want what YOU guys have!
Dist. By King Features Syndicate, Inc.
So you want frequently inter-rupted--
...conver-sations! Hi, baby. Whatcha doing up?
Libenson

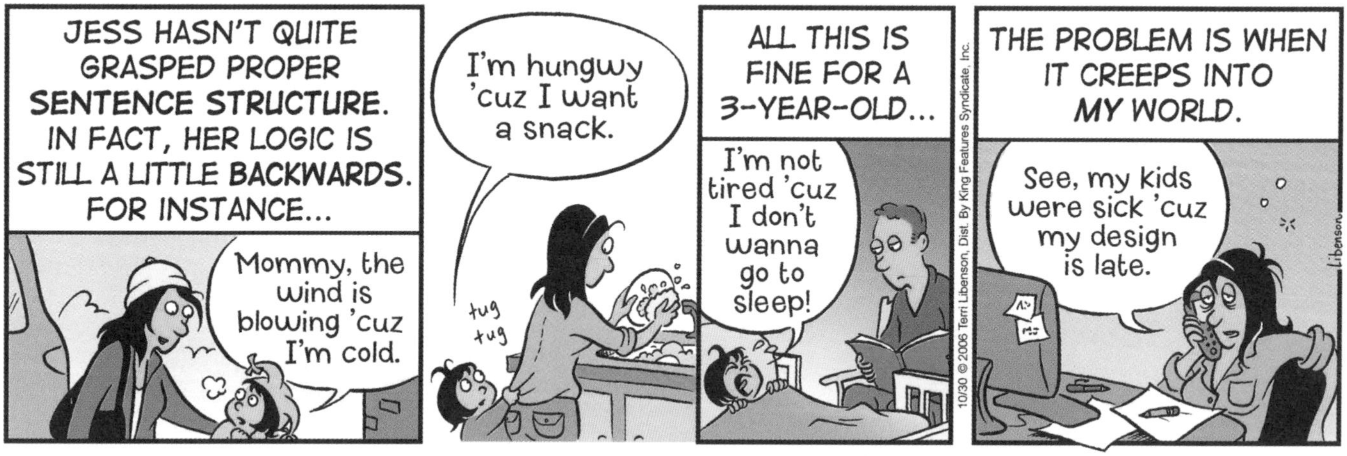
JESS HASN'T QUITE GRASPED PROPER **SENTENCE STRUCTURE**. IN FACT, HER LOGIC IS STILL A LITTLE **BACKWARDS**. FOR INSTANCE...
Mommy, the wind is blowing 'cuz I'm cold.
I'm hungwy 'cuz I want a snack.
tug tug
ALL THIS IS FINE FOR A 3-YEAR-OLD...
I'm not tired 'cuz I don't wanna go to sleep!
10/30 © 2006 Terri Libenson, Dist. By King Features Syndicate, Inc.
THE PROBLEM IS WHEN IT CREEPS INTO ***MY WORLD***.
See, my kids were sick 'cuz my design is late.
Libenson

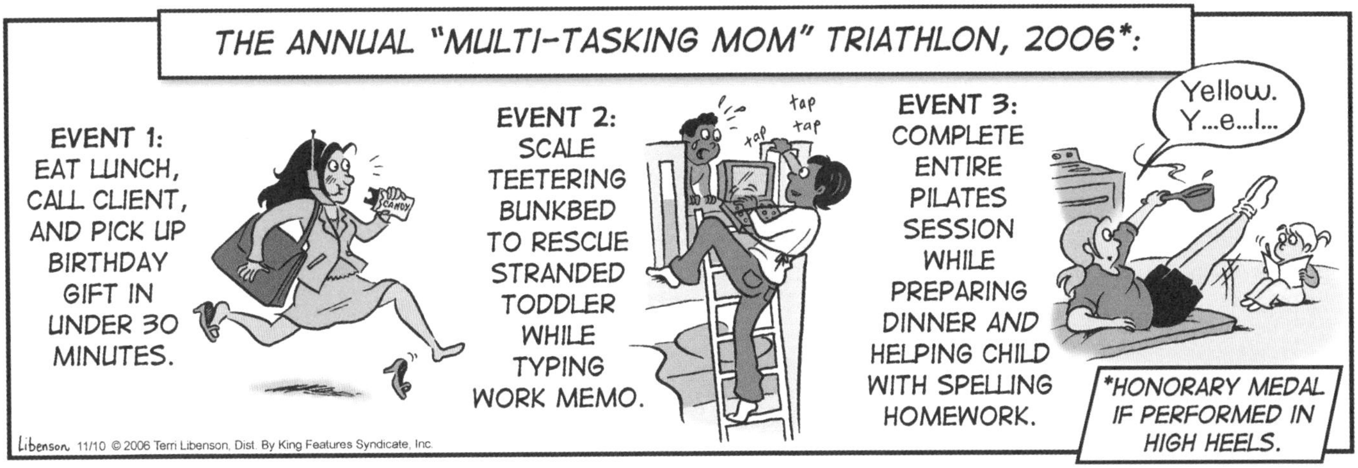
THE ANNUAL "MULTI-TASKING MOM" TRIATHLON, 2006*:
EVENT 1: EAT LUNCH, CALL CLIENT, AND PICK UP BIRTHDAY GIFT IN UNDER 30 MINUTES.
CANDY
EVENT 2: SCALE TEETERING BUNKBED TO RESCUE STRANDED TODDLER WHILE TYPING WORK MEMO.
tap tap tap
EVENT 3: COMPLETE ENTIRE PILATES SESSION WHILE PREPARING DINNER AND HELPING CHILD WITH SPELLING HOMEWORK.
Yellow. Y...e...l...
*HONORARY MEDAL IF PERFORMED IN HIGH HEELS.
Libenson 11/10 © 2006 Terri Libenson, Dist. By King Features Syndicate, Inc.

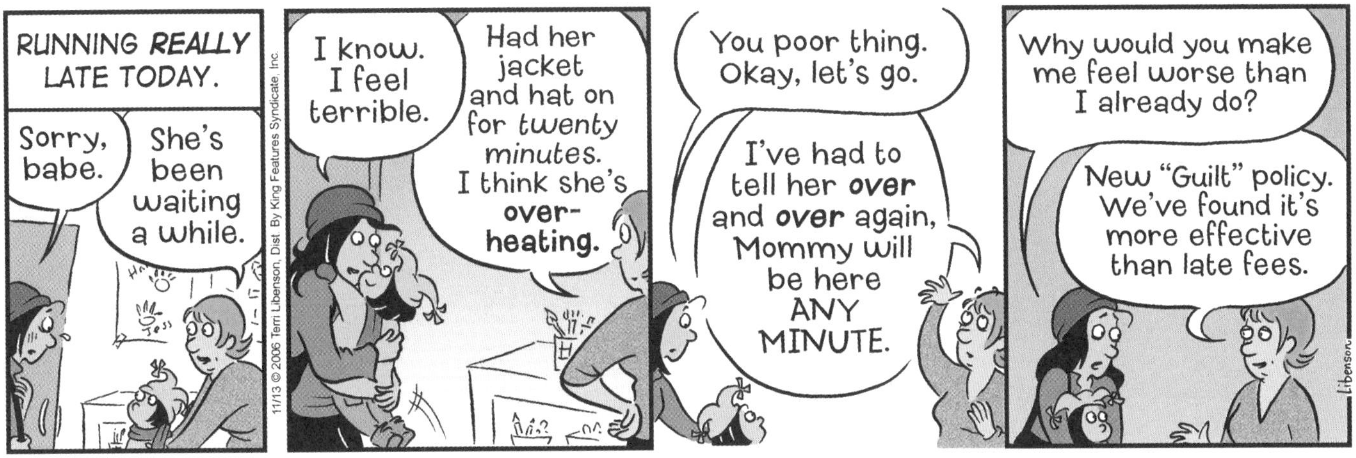
RUNNING REALLY LATE TODAY.
Sorry, babe.
She's been waiting a while.
11/13 © 2006 Terri Libenson, Dist. By King Features Syndicate, Inc.
I know. I feel terrible.
Had her jacket and hat on for twenty minutes. I think she's over-heating.
You poor thing. Okay, let's go.
I've had to tell her over and over again, Mommy will be here ANY MINUTE.
Why would you make me feel worse than I already do?
New "Guilt" policy. We've found it's more effective than late fees.
Libenson

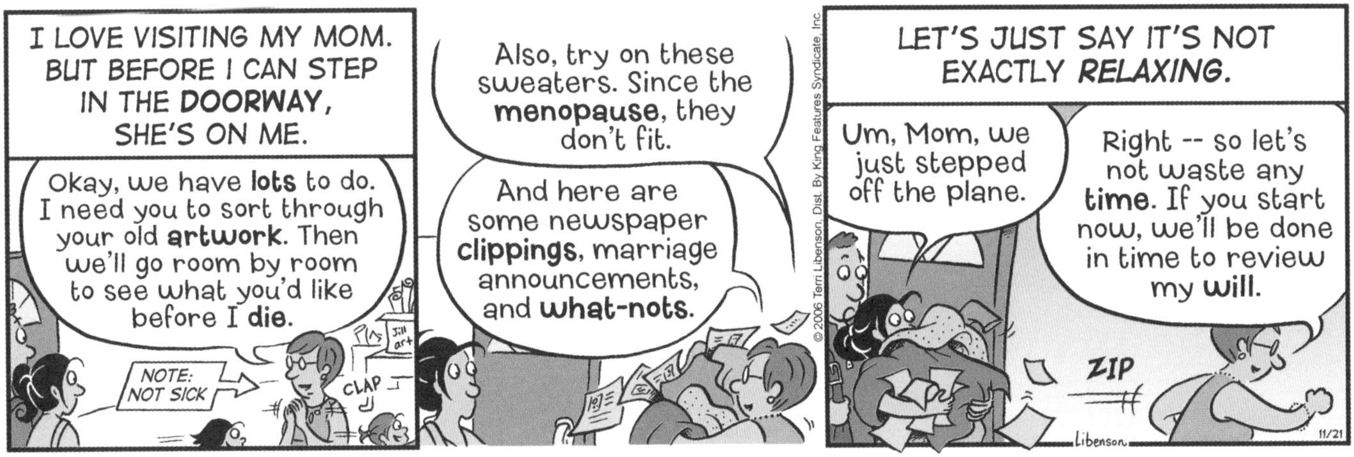
I LOVE VISITING MY MOM. BUT BEFORE I CAN STEP IN THE DOORWAY, SHE'S ON ME.
Okay, we have lots to do. I need you to sort through your old artwork. Then we'll go room by room to see what you'd like before I die.
NOTE: NOT SICK
CLAP
Jill art
Also, try on these sweaters. Since the menopause, they don't fit.
And here are some newspaper clippings, marriage announcements, and what-nots.
© 2006 Terri Libenson, Dist. By King Features Syndicate, Inc.
LET'S JUST SAY IT'S NOT EXACTLY RELAXING.
Um, Mom, we just stepped off the plane.
Right -- so let's not waste any time. If you start now, we'll be done in time to review my will.
ZIP
Libenson 11/21

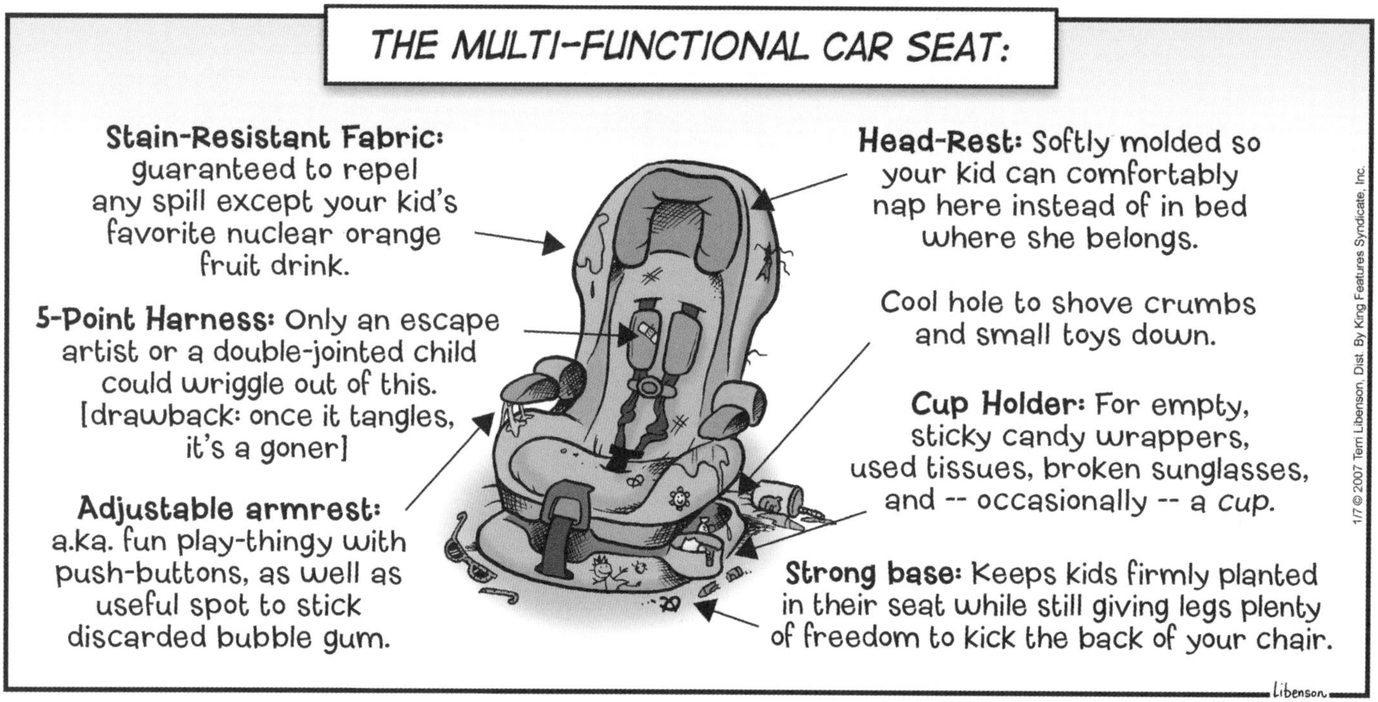
THE MULTI-FUNCTIONAL CAR SEAT:
Stain-Resistant Fabric: guaranteed to repel any spill except your kid's favorite nuclear orange fruit drink.
5-Point Harness: Only an escape artist or a double-jointed child could wriggle out of this. [drawback: once it tangles, it's a goner]
Adjustable armrest: a.ka. fun play-thingy with push-buttons, as well as useful spot to stick discarded bubble gum.
Head-Rest: Softly molded so your kid can comfortably nap here instead of in bed where she belongs.
Cool hole to shove crumbs and small toys down.
Cup Holder: For empty, sticky candy wrappers, used tissues, broken sunglasses, and -- occasionally -- a cup.
Strong base: Keeps kids firmly planted in their seat while still giving legs plenty of freedom to kick the back of your chair.
1/7 © 2007 Terri Libenson, Dist. By King Features Syndicate, Inc.
Libenson

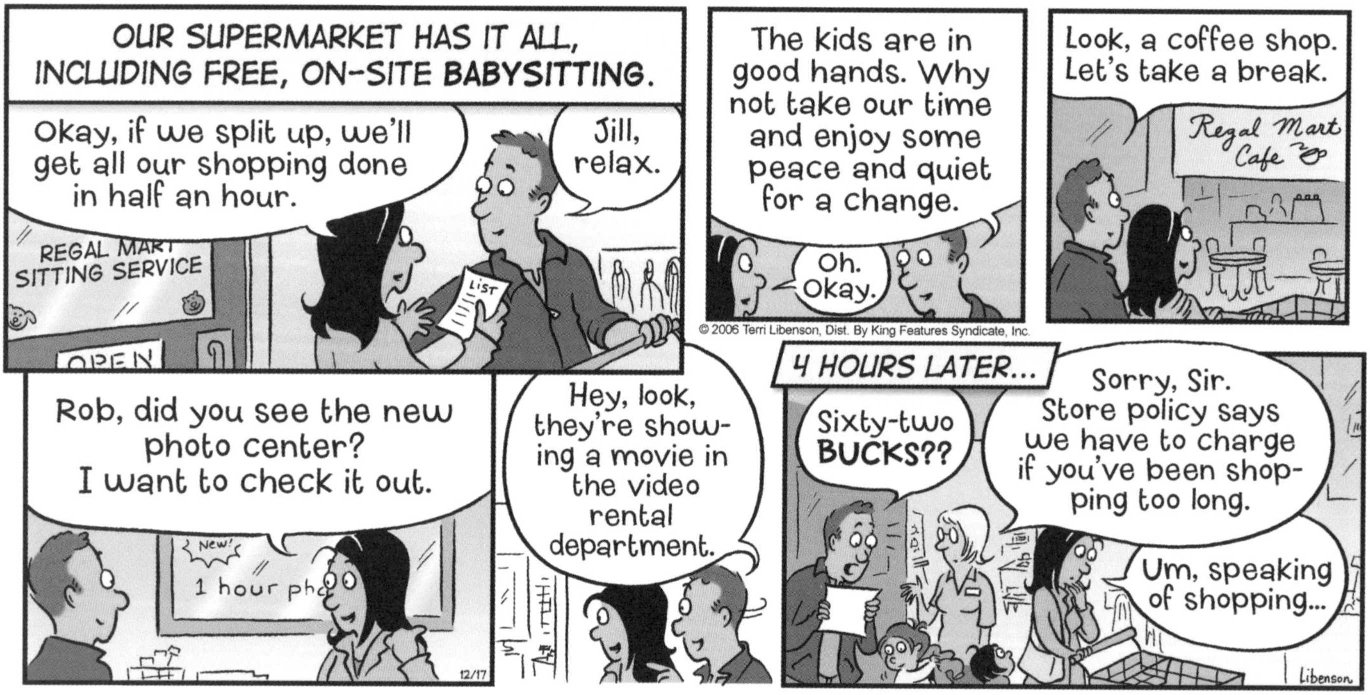
OUR SUPERMARKET HAS IT ALL, INCLUDING FREE, ON-SITE BABYSITTING.
Okay, if we split up, we'll get all our shopping done in half an hour.
Jill, relax.
REGAL MART SITTING SERVICE
LIST
OPEN
The kids are in good hands. Why not take our time and enjoy some peace and quiet for a change.
Oh. Okay.
© 2006 Terri Libenson, Dist. By King Features Syndicate, Inc.
Look, a coffee shop. Let's take a break.
Regal Mart Cafe
Rob, did you see the new photo center? I want to check it out.
New!
1 hour ph
12/17
Hey, look, they're showing a movie in the video rental department.
4 HOURS LATER...
Sixty-two BUCKS??
Sorry, Sir. Store policy says we have to charge if you've been shopping too long.
Um, speaking of shopping...
Libenson

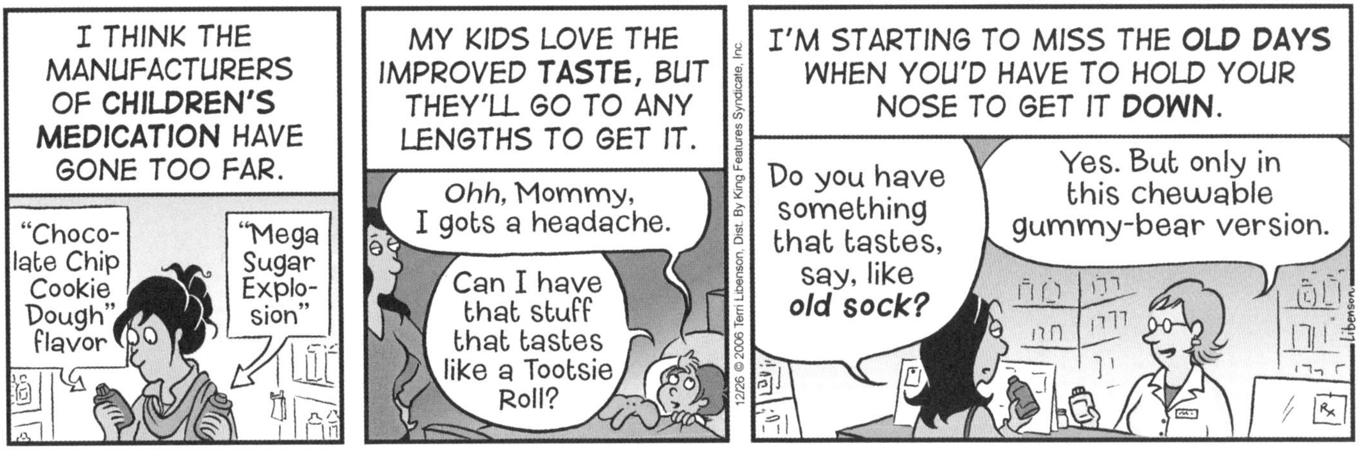
I THINK THE MANUFACTURERS OF **CHILDREN'S MEDICATION** HAVE GONE TOO FAR.
"Chocolate Chip Cookie Dough" flavor
"Mega Sugar Explosion"
MY KIDS LOVE THE IMPROVED **TASTE,** BUT THEY'LL GO TO ANY LENGTHS TO GET IT.
Ohh, Mommy, I gots a headache.
Can I have that stuff that tastes like a Tootsie Roll?
12/26 © 2006 Terri Libenson, Dist. By King Features Syndicate, Inc.
I'M STARTING TO MISS THE **OLD DAYS** WHEN YOU'D HAVE TO HOLD YOUR NOSE TO GET IT **DOWN**.
Do you have something that tastes, say, like ***old sock?***
Yes. But only in this chewable gummy-bear version.
Libenson

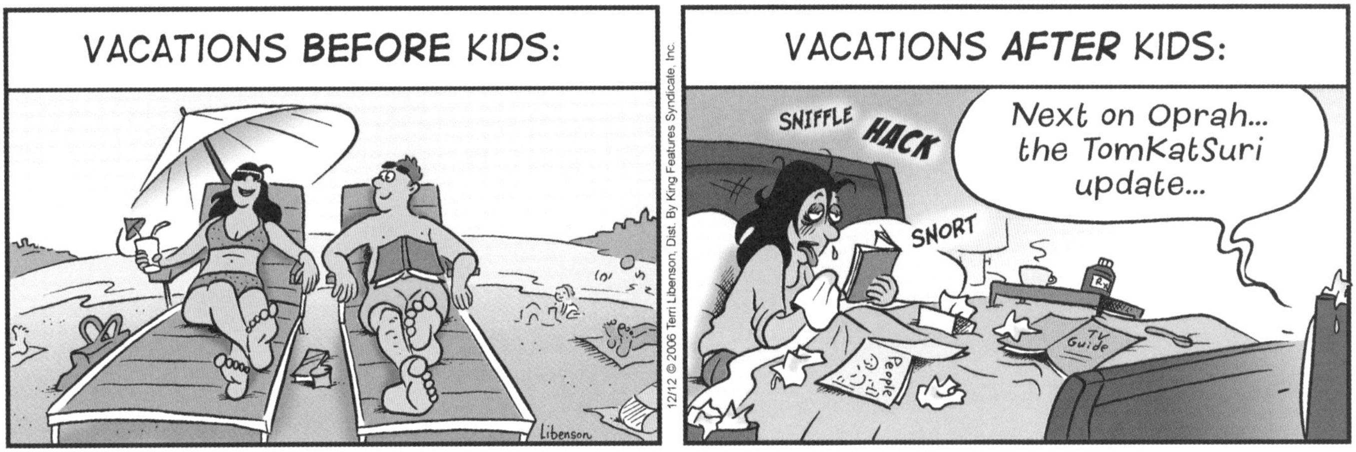
VACATIONS **BEFORE** KIDS:
Libenson
12/12 © 2006 Terri Libenson, Dist. By King Features Syndicate, Inc.
VACATIONS ***AFTER*** KIDS:
SNIFFLE
HACK
SNORT
Next on Oprah... the TomKatSuri update...
People
TV Guide

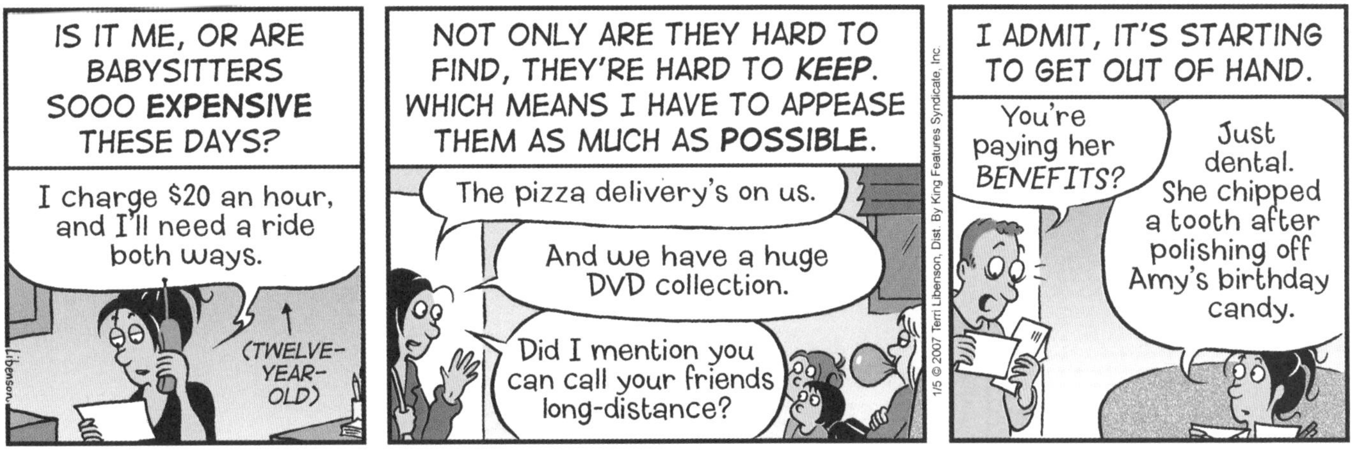
IS IT ME, OR ARE BABYSITTERS SOOO **EXPENSIVE** THESE DAYS?
I charge $20 an hour, and I'll need a ride both ways.
(TWELVE-YEAR-OLD)
Libenson
NOT ONLY ARE THEY HARD TO FIND, THEY'RE HARD TO ***KEEP***. WHICH MEANS I HAVE TO APPEASE THEM AS MUCH AS **POSSIBLE**.
The pizza delivery's on us.
And we have a huge DVD collection.
Did I mention you can call your friends long-distance?
1/5 © 2007 Terri Libenson, Dist. By King Features Syndicate, Inc.
I ADMIT, IT'S STARTING TO GET OUT OF HAND.
You're paying her *BENEFITS?*
Just dental. She chipped a tooth after polishing off Amy's birthday candy.

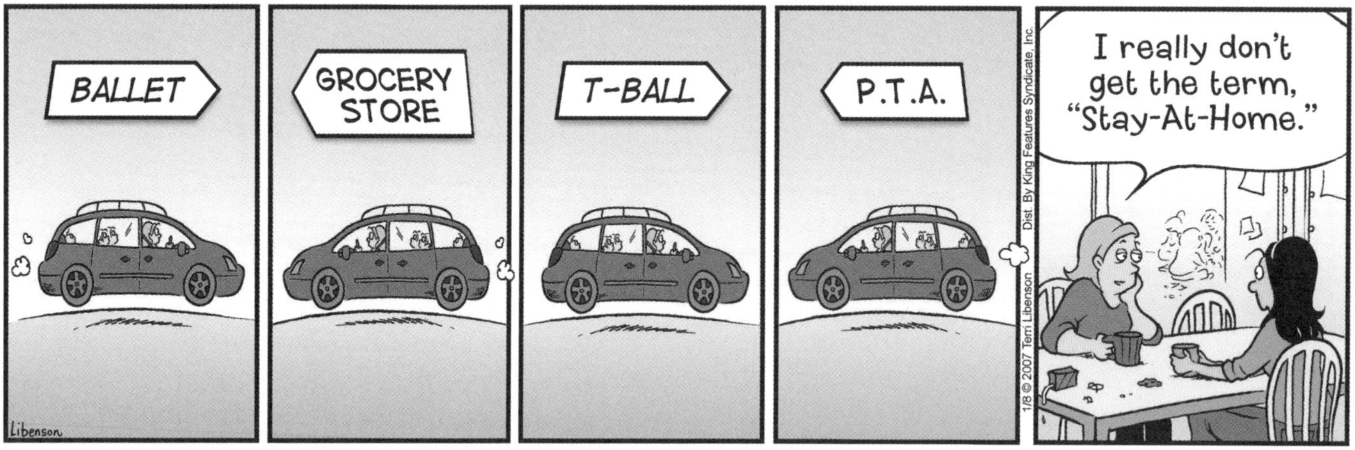
BALLET
GROCERY STORE
T-BALL
P.T.A.
I really don't get the term, "Stay-At-Home."
Libenson
1/8 © 2007 Terri Libenson Dist. By King Features Syndicate, Inc.

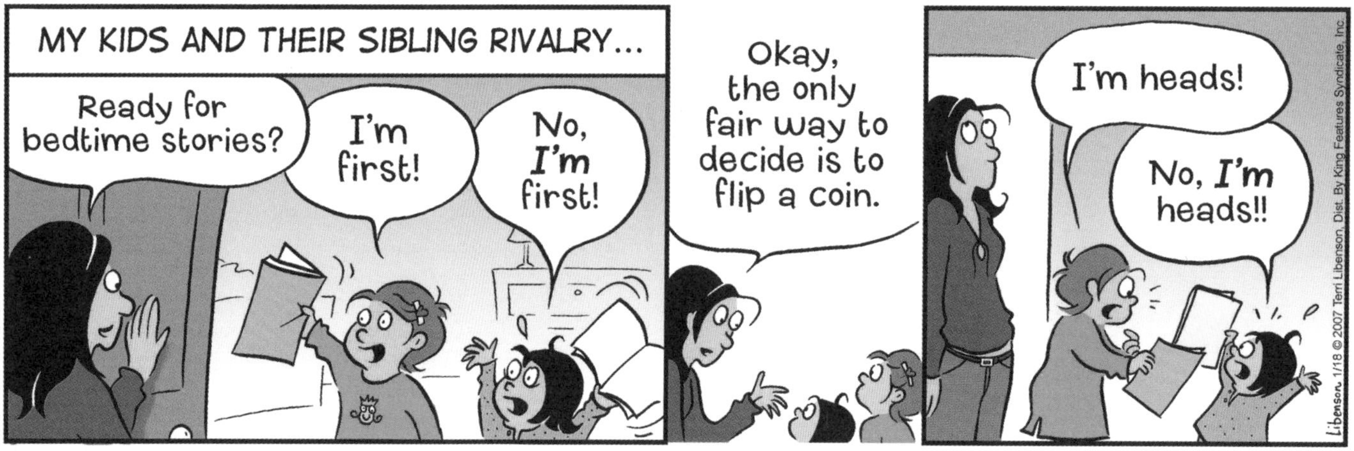
MY KIDS AND THEIR SIBLING RIVALRY...
Ready for bedtime stories?
I'm first!
No, ***I'm*** first!
Okay, the only fair way to decide is to flip a coin.
I'm heads!
No, ***I'm*** heads!!
Libenson 1/18 © 2007 Terri Libenson Dist. By King Features Syndicate, Inc.

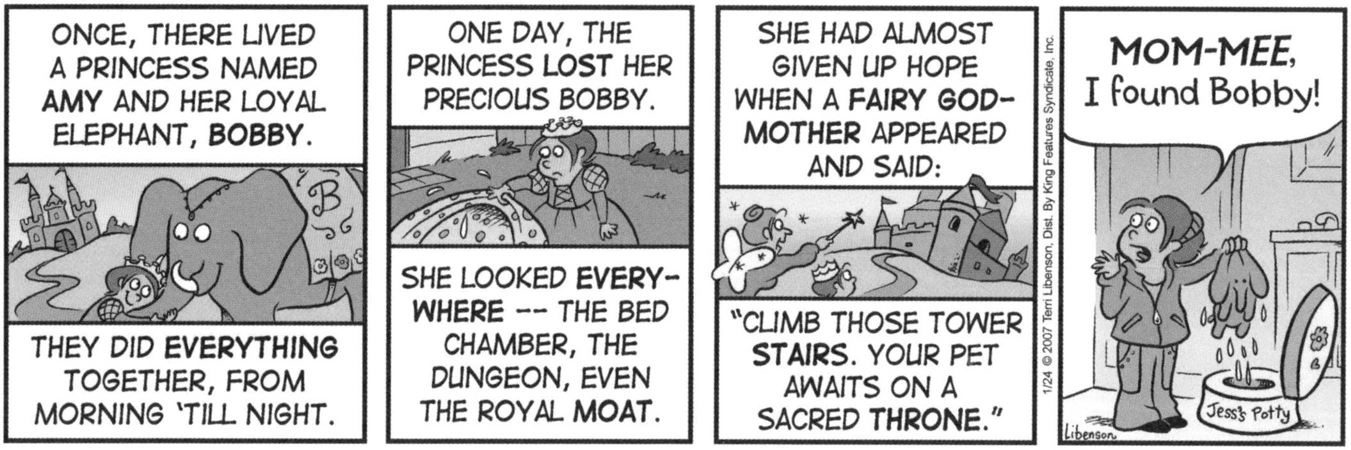
ONCE, THERE LIVED A PRINCESS NAMED **AMY** AND HER LOYAL ELEPHANT, **BOBBY**.
THEY DID **EVERYTHING** TOGETHER, FROM MORNING 'TILL NIGHT.
ONE DAY, THE PRINCESS **LOST** HER PRECIOUS BOBBY.
SHE LOOKED **EVERY-WHERE** -- THE BED CHAMBER, THE DUNGEON, EVEN THE ROYAL **MOAT**.
SHE HAD ALMOST GIVEN UP HOPE WHEN A **FAIRY GOD-MOTHER** APPEARED AND SAID:
"CLIMB THOSE TOWER **STAIRS**. YOUR PET AWAITS ON A SACRED **THRONE**."
MOM-MEE, I found Bobby!
Jess's Potty
Libenson
1/24 © 2007 Terri Libenson Dist. By King Features Syndicate, Inc.

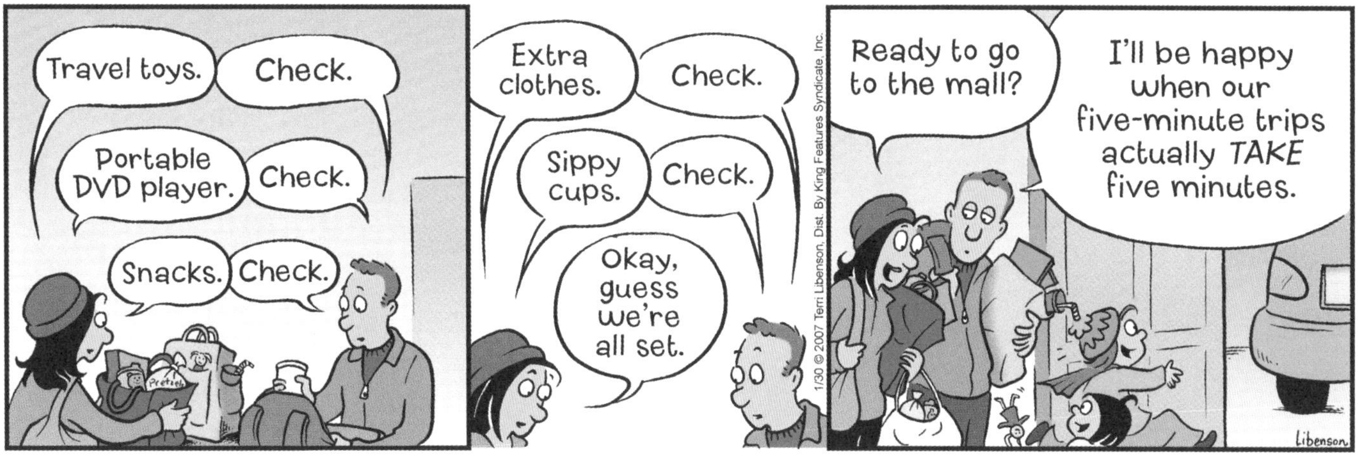
Travel toys.
Check.
Portable DVD player.
Check.
Snacks.
Check.
Pretzels
Extra clothes.
Check.
Sippy cups.
Check.
Okay, guess we're all set.
Ready to go to the mall?
I'll be happy when our five-minute trips actually *TAKE* five minutes.
Libenson

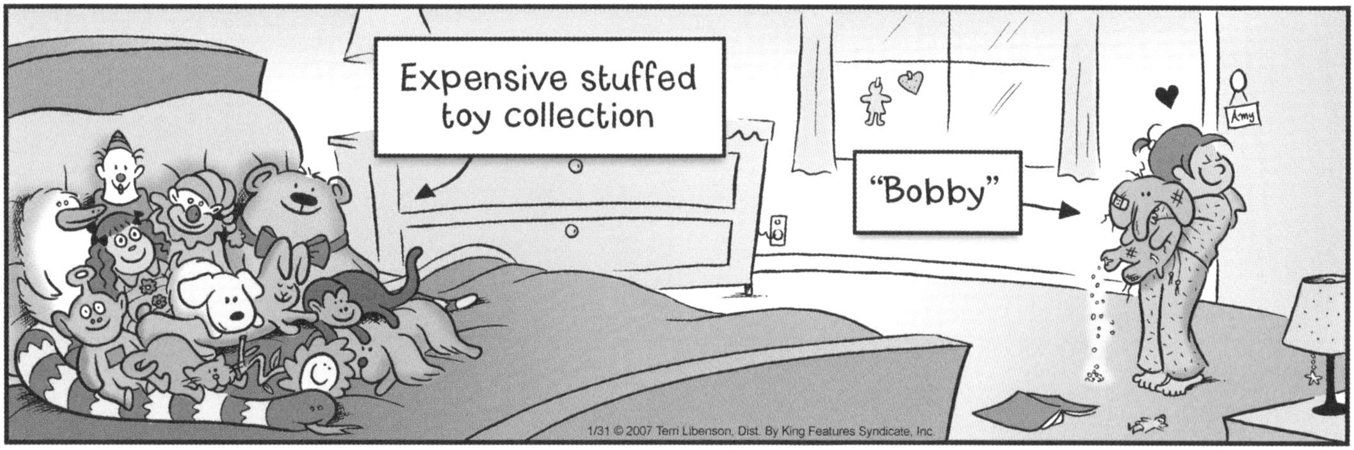
Expensive stuffed toy collection
"Bobby"
Amy

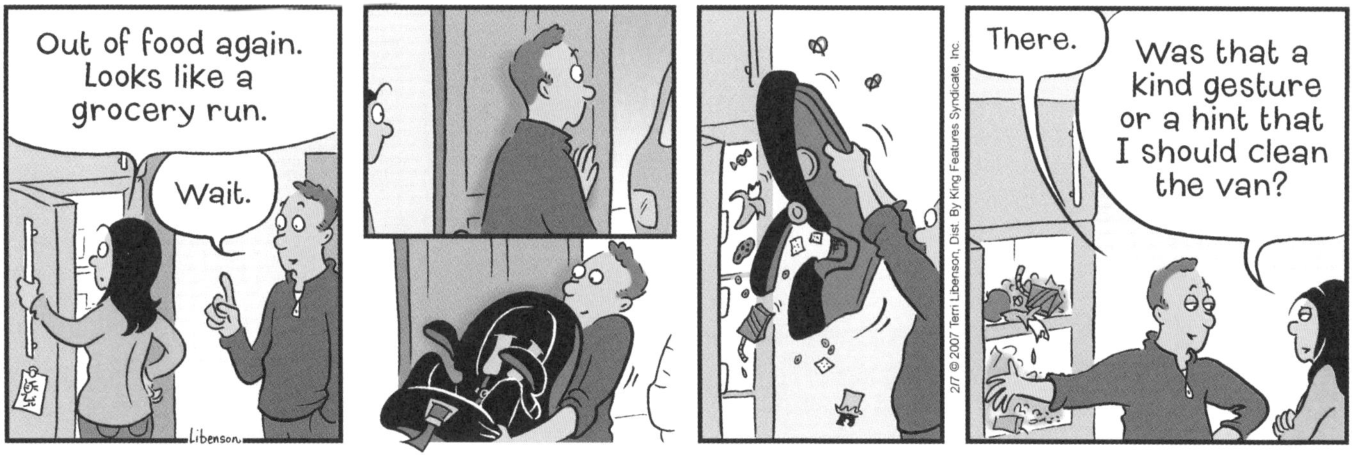
Out of food again. Looks like a grocery run.
Wait.
Libenson
There.
Was that a kind gesture or a hint that I should clean the van?

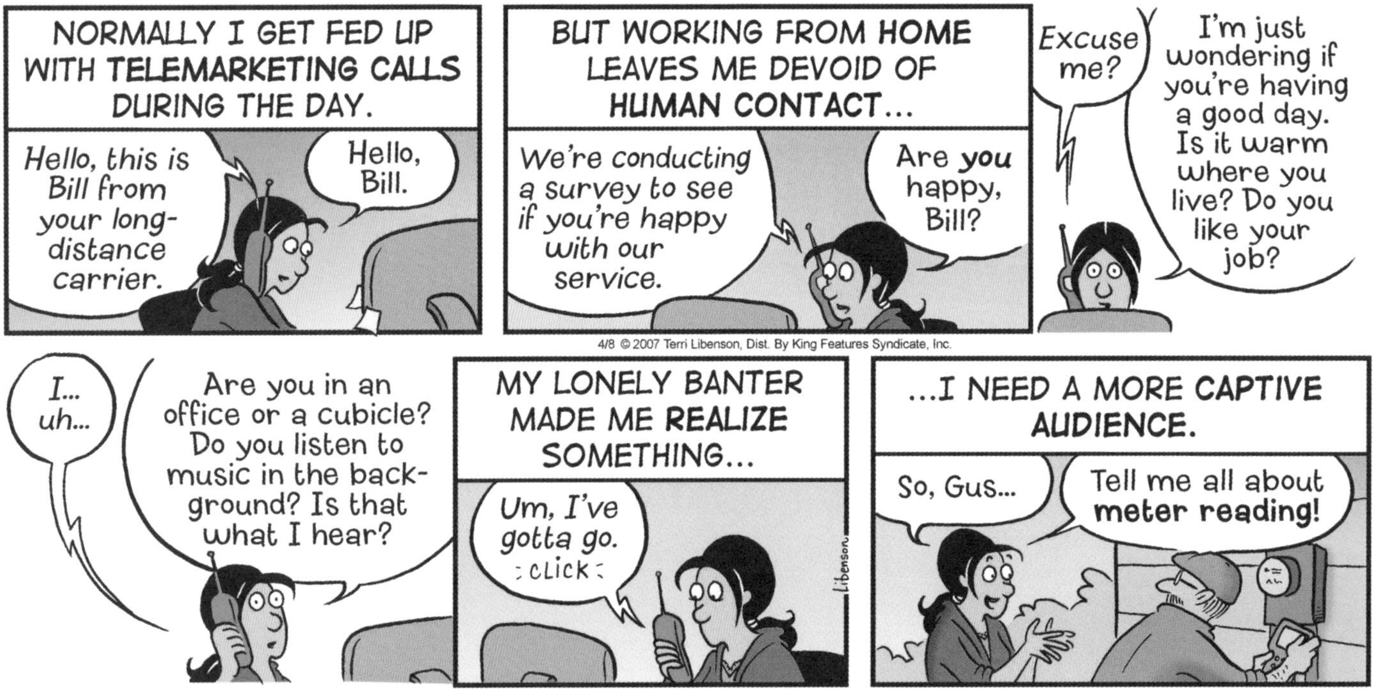
NORMALLY I GET FED UP WITH TELEMARKETING CALLS DURING THE DAY.
Hello, this is Bill from your long-distance carrier.
Hello, Bill.
BUT WORKING FROM HOME LEAVES ME DEVOID OF HUMAN CONTACT...
We're conducting a survey to see if you're happy with our service.
Are you happy, Bill?
Excuse me?
I'm just wondering if you're having a good day. Is it warm where you live? Do you like your job?
4/8 © 2007 Terri Libenson, Dist. By King Features Syndicate, Inc.
I... uh...
Are you in an office or a cubicle? Do you listen to music in the back-ground? Is that what I hear?
MY LONELY BANTER MADE ME REALIZE SOMETHING...
Um, I've gotta go.
CLICK
Libenson
...I NEED A MORE CAPTIVE AUDIENCE.
So, Gus...
Tell me all about meter reading!

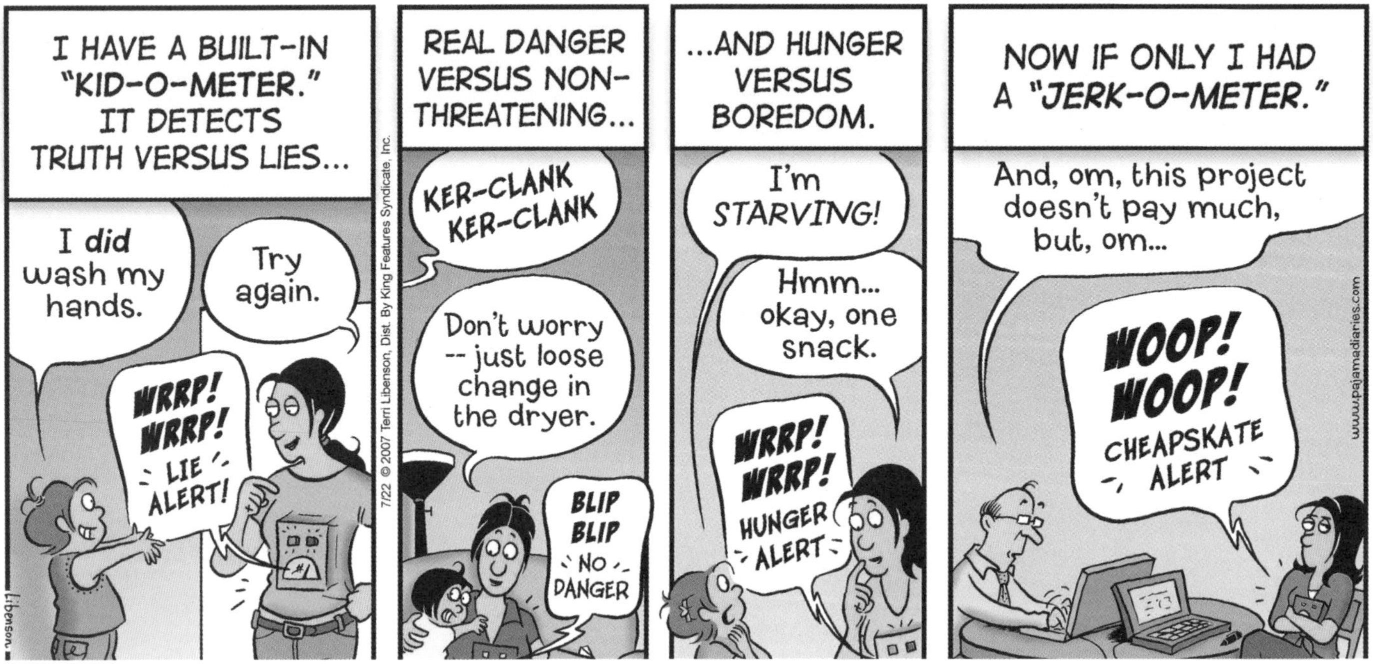
I HAVE A BUILT-IN "KID-O-METER." IT DETECTS TRUTH VERSUS LIES...
I did wash my hands.
Try again.
WRRP! WRRP! LIE ALERT!
Libenson
7/22 © 2007 Terri Libenson, Dist. By King Features Syndicate, Inc.
REAL DANGER VERSUS NON-THREATENING...
KER-CLANK KER-CLANK
Don't worry -- just loose change in the dryer.
BLIP BLIP NO DANGER
...AND HUNGER VERSUS BOREDOM.
I'm STARVING!
Hmm... okay, one snack.
WRRP! WRRP! HUNGER ALERT
NOW IF ONLY I HAD A "JERK-O-METER."
And, om, this project doesn't pay much, but, om...
WOOP! WOOP! CHEAPSKATE ALERT
www.pajamadiaries.com

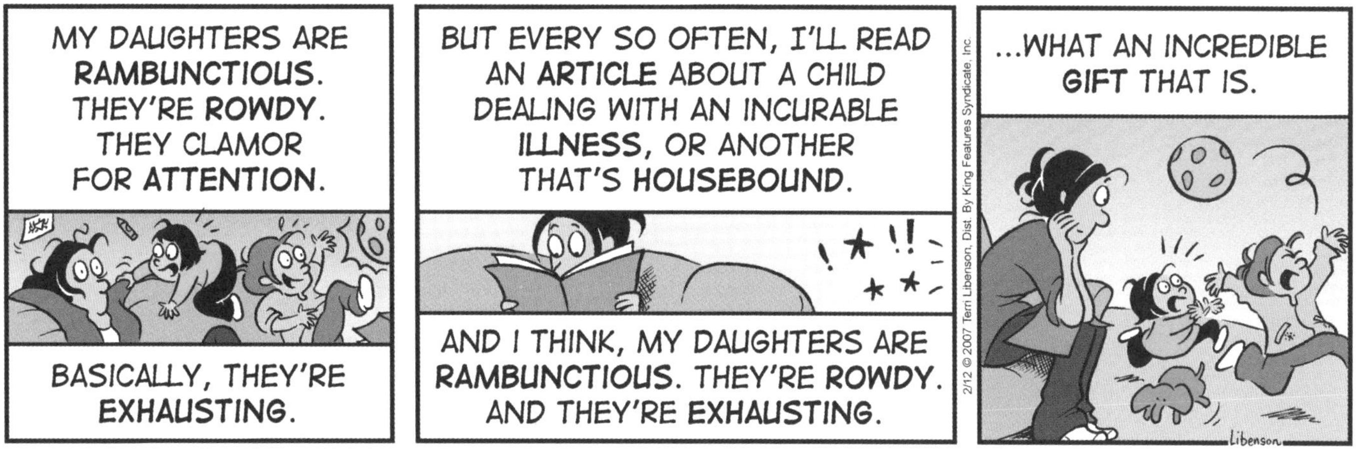
MY DAUGHTERS ARE RAMBUNCTIOUS. THEY'RE ROWDY. THEY CLAMOR FOR ATTENTION.
BASICALLY, THEY'RE EXHAUSTING.
BUT EVERY SO OFTEN, I'LL READ AN ARTICLE ABOUT A CHILD DEALING WITH AN INCURABLE ILLNESS, OR ANOTHER THAT'S HOUSEBOUND.
AND I THINK, MY DAUGHTERS ARE RAMBUNCTIOUS. THEY'RE ROWDY. AND THEY'RE EXHAUSTING.
2/12 © 2007 Terri Libenson, Dist. By King Features Syndicate, Inc.
...WHAT AN INCREDIBLE GIFT THAT IS.
Libenson

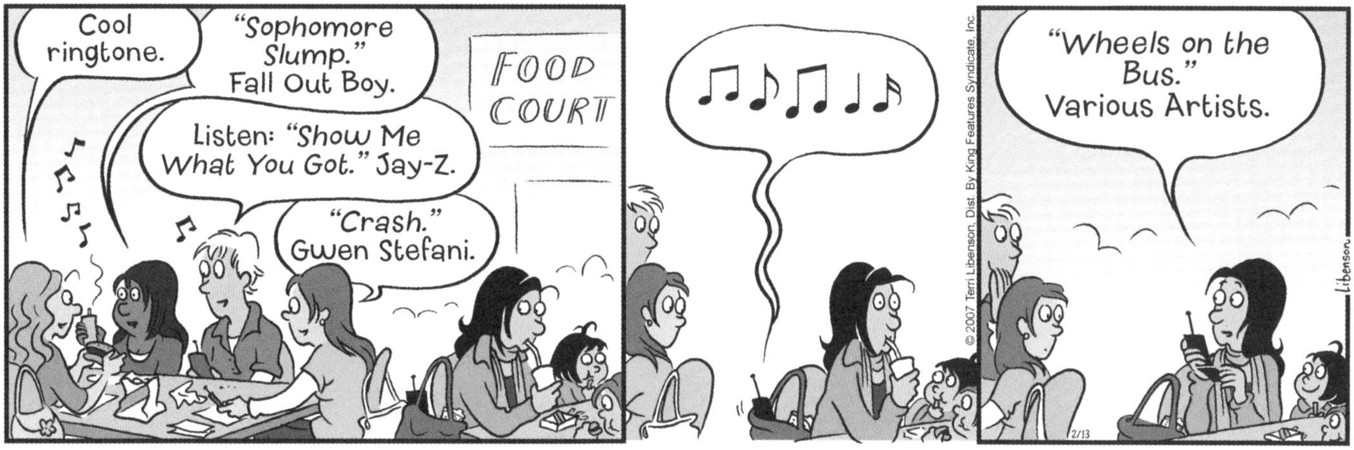
Cool ringtone.
"Sophomore Slump." Fall Out Boy.
Listen: "Show Me What You Got." Jay-Z.
"Crash." Gwen Stefani.
FOOD COURT
© 2007 Terri Libenson, Dist. By King Features Syndicate, Inc.
"Wheels on the Bus." Various Artists.
Libenson
2/13

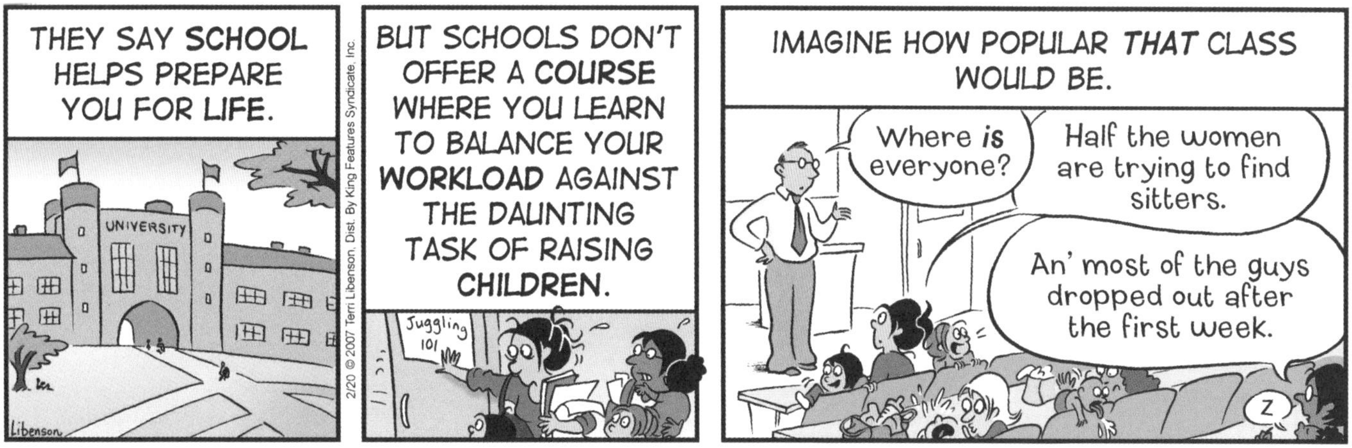
THEY SAY SCHOOL HELPS PREPARE YOU FOR LIFE.
UNIVERSITY
Libenson
2/20 © 2007 Terri Libenson, Dist. By King Features Syndicate, Inc.
BUT SCHOOLS DON'T OFFER A COURSE WHERE YOU LEARN TO BALANCE YOUR WORKLOAD AGAINST THE DAUNTING TASK OF RAISING CHILDREN.
Juggling 101
IMAGINE HOW POPULAR THAT CLASS WOULD BE.
Where is everyone?
Half the women are trying to find sitters.
An' most of the guys dropped out after the first week.
Z

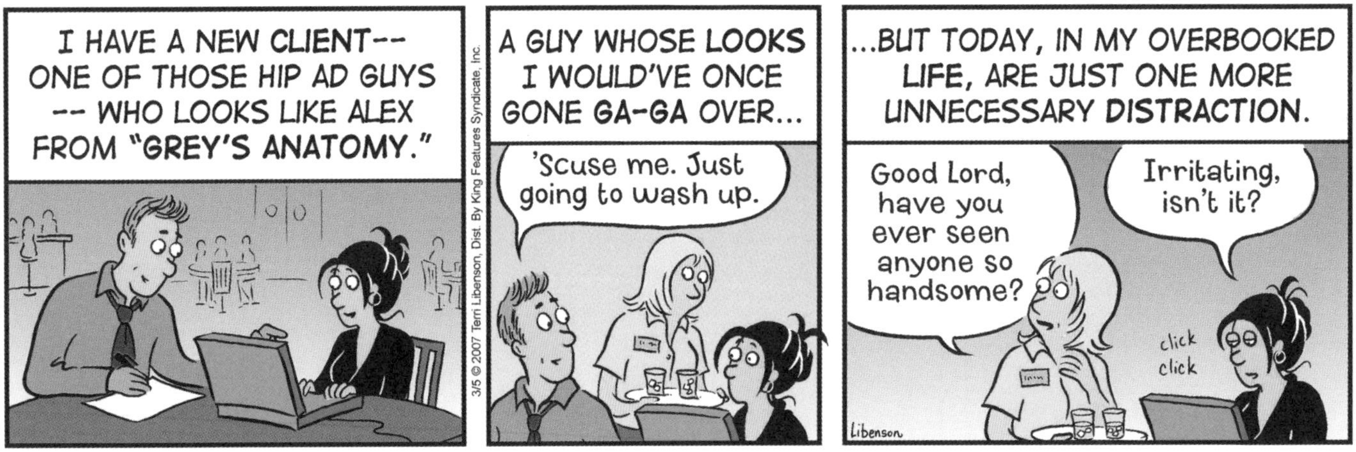
I HAVE A NEW CLIENT-- ONE OF THOSE HIP AD GUYS -- WHO LOOKS LIKE ALEX FROM "GREY'S ANATOMY."
3/5 © 2007 Terri Libenson, Dist. By King Features Syndicate, Inc.
A GUY WHOSE LOOKS I WOULD'VE ONCE GONE GA-GA OVER...
'Scuse me. Just going to wash up.
...BUT TODAY, IN MY OVERBOOKED LIFE, ARE JUST ONE MORE UNNECESSARY DISTRACTION.
Good Lord, have you ever seen anyone so handsome?
Irritating, isn't it?
click click
Libenson

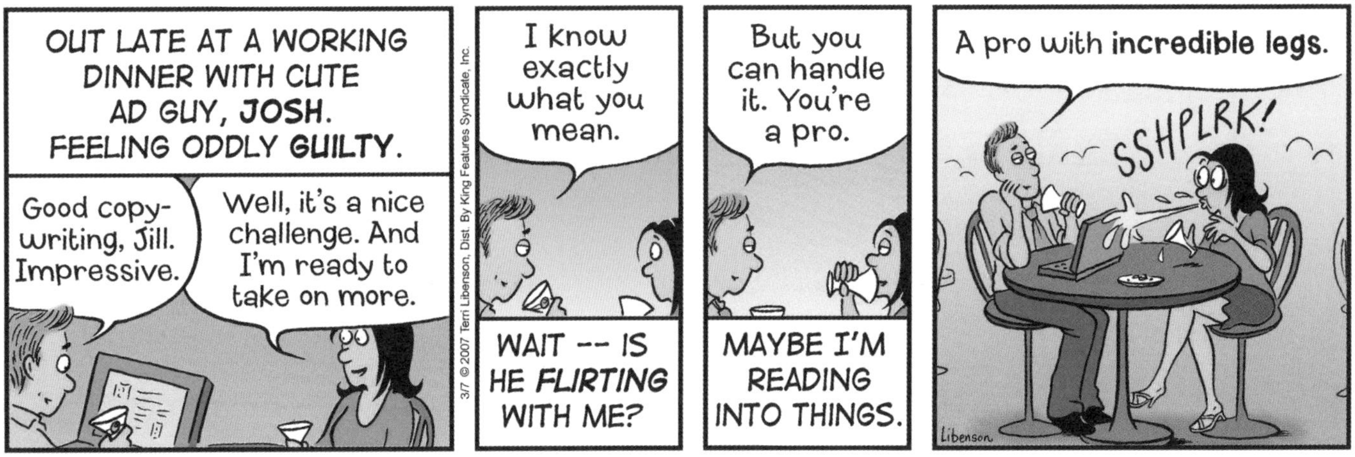
OUT LATE AT A WORKING DINNER WITH CUTE AD GUY, JOSH. FEELING ODDLY GUILTY.
Good copy-writing, Jill. Impressive.
Well, it's a nice challenge. And I'm ready to take on more.
3/7 © 2007 Terri Libenson, Dist. By King Features Syndicate, Inc.
I know exactly what you mean.
WAIT -- IS HE FLIRTING WITH ME?
But you can handle it. You're a pro.
MAYBE I'M READING INTO THINGS.
A pro with incredible legs.
SSHPLRK!
Libenson

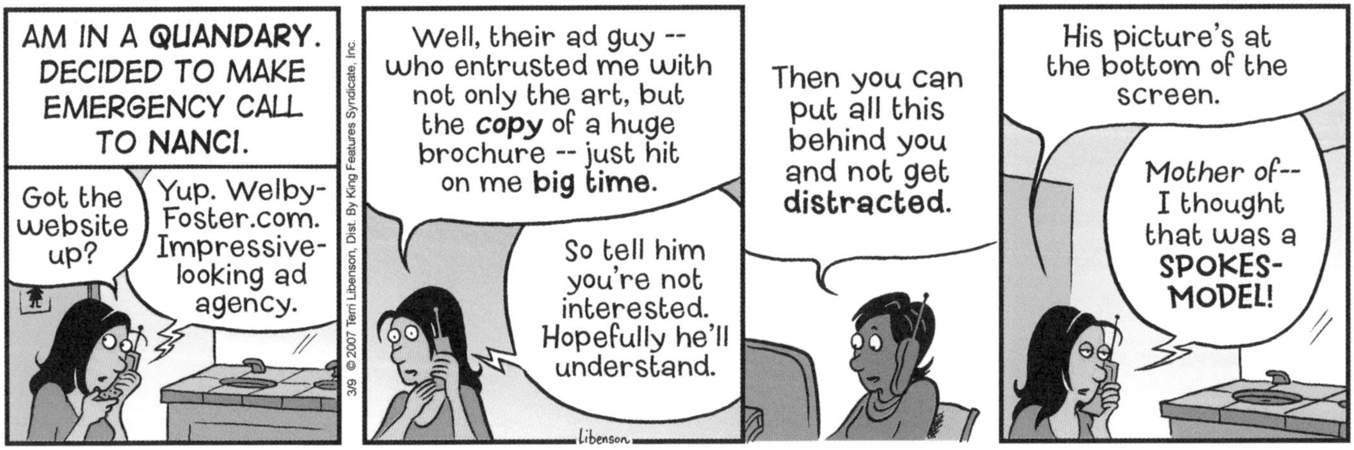
AM IN A QUANDARY. DECIDED TO MAKE EMERGENCY CALL TO NANCI.
Got the website up?
Yup. Welby-Foster.com. Impressive-looking ad agency.
3/9 © 2007 Terri Libenson, Dist. By King Features Syndicate, Inc.
Well, their ad guy -- who entrusted me with not only the art, but the copy of a huge brochure -- just hit on me big time.
So tell him you're not interested. Hopefully he'll understand.
Then you can put all this behind you and not get distracted.
Libenson
His picture's at the bottom of the screen.
Mother of-- I thought that was a SPOKES-MODEL!

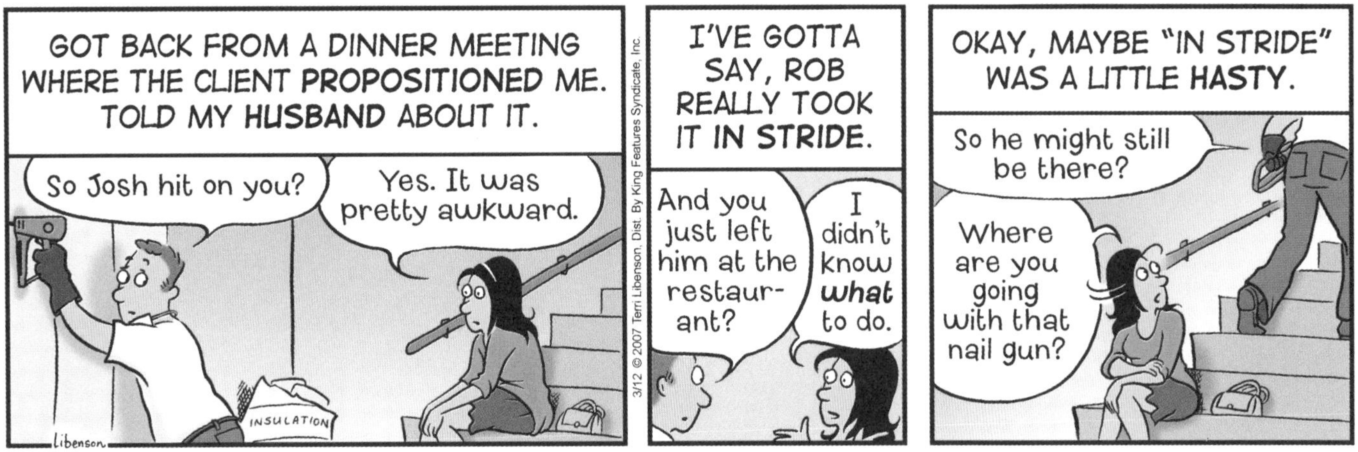
GOT BACK FROM A DINNER MEETING WHERE THE CLIENT **PROPOSITIONED** ME. TOLD MY **HUSBAND** ABOUT IT.
So Josh hit on you?
Yes. It was pretty awkward.
INSULATION
Libenson
3/12 © 2007 Terri Libenson. Dist. By King Features Syndicate, Inc.
I'VE GOTTA SAY, ROB REALLY TOOK IT **IN STRIDE**.
And you just left him at the restaur-ant?
I didn't know ***what*** to do.
OKAY, MAYBE "IN STRIDE" WAS A LITTLE **HASTY**.
So he might still be there?
Where are you going with that nail gun?

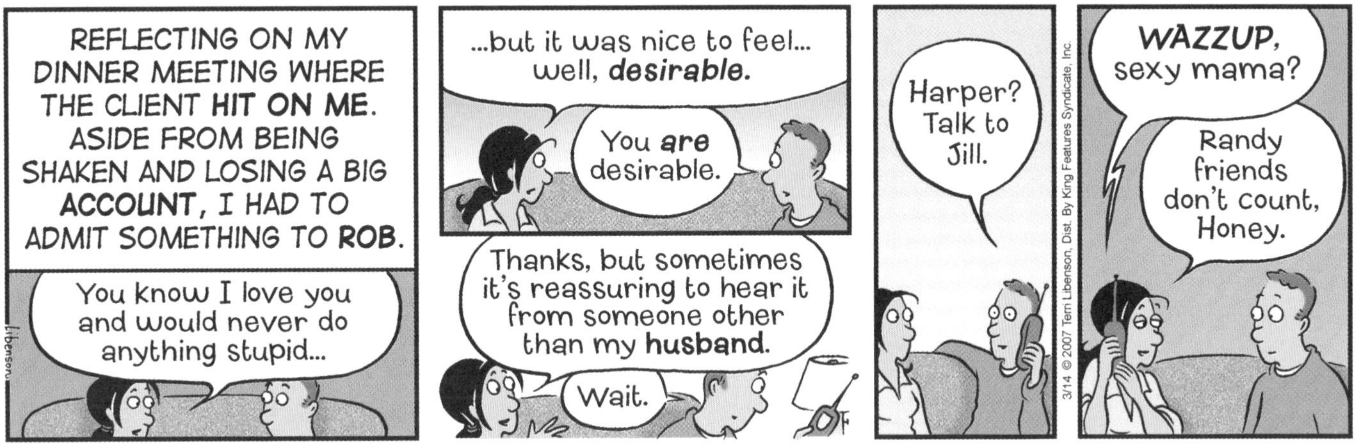
REFLECTING ON MY DINNER MEETING WHERE THE CLIENT **HIT ON ME**. ASIDE FROM BEING SHAKEN AND LOSING A BIG **ACCOUNT**, I HAD TO ADMIT SOMETHING TO **ROB**.
You know I love you and would never do anything stupid...
Libenson
...but it was nice to feel... well, ***desirable.***
You **are** desirable.
Thanks, but sometimes it's reassuring to hear it from someone other than my **husband**.
Wait.
Harper? Talk to Jill.
3/14 © 2007 Terri Libenson, Dist. By King Features Syndicate, Inc.
WAZZUP, sexy mama?
Randy friends don't count, Honey.

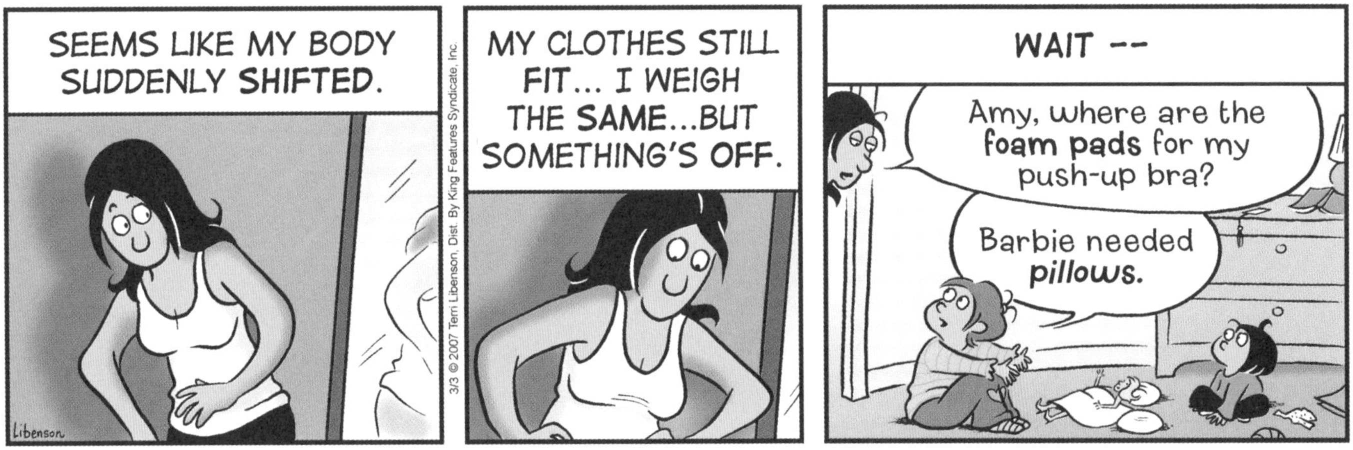
SEEMS LIKE MY BODY SUDDENLY **SHIFTED**.
Libenson
3/3 © 2007 Terri Libenson, Dist. By King Features Syndicate, Inc.
MY CLOTHES STILL **FIT**... I WEIGH THE **SAME**...BUT **SOMETHING'S OFF**.
WAIT --
Amy, where are the **foam pads** for my push-up bra?
Barbie needed ***pillows.***

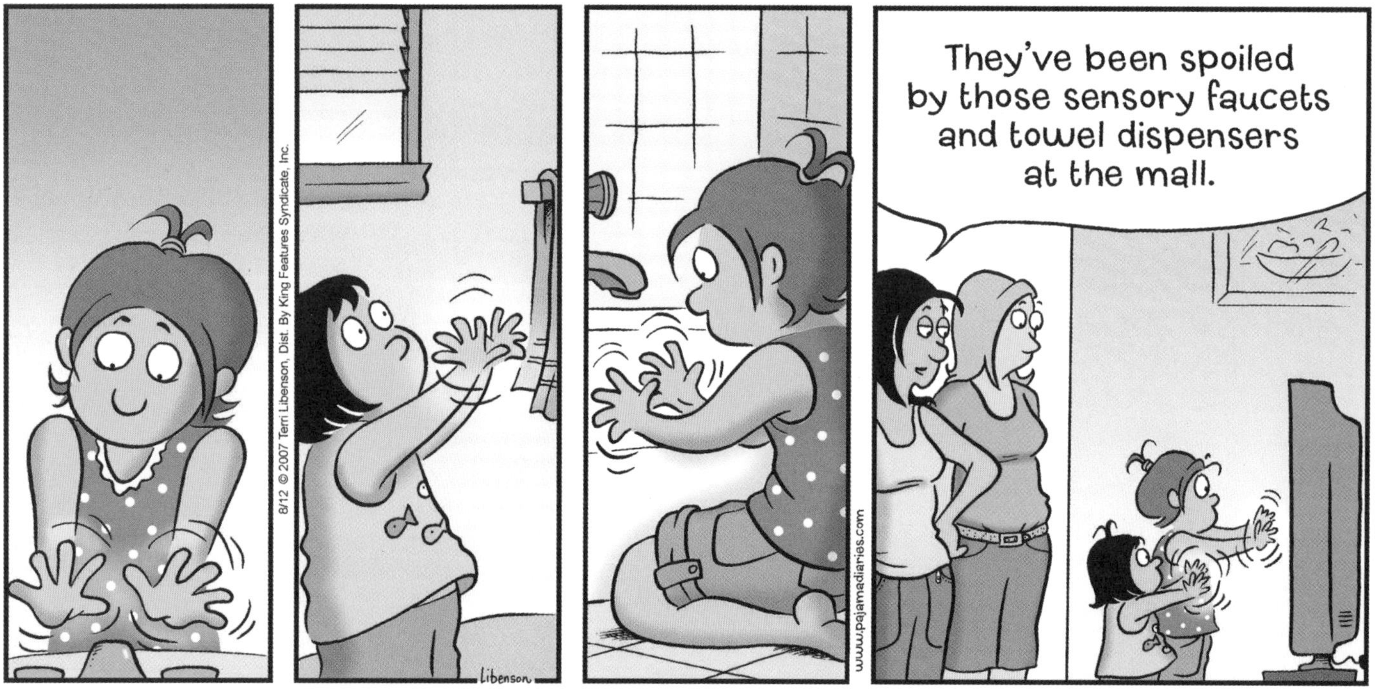
8/12 © 2007 Terri Libenson, Dist. By King Features Syndicate, Inc.
Libenson
www.pajamadiaries.com
They've been spoiled by those sensory faucets and towel dispensers at the mall.

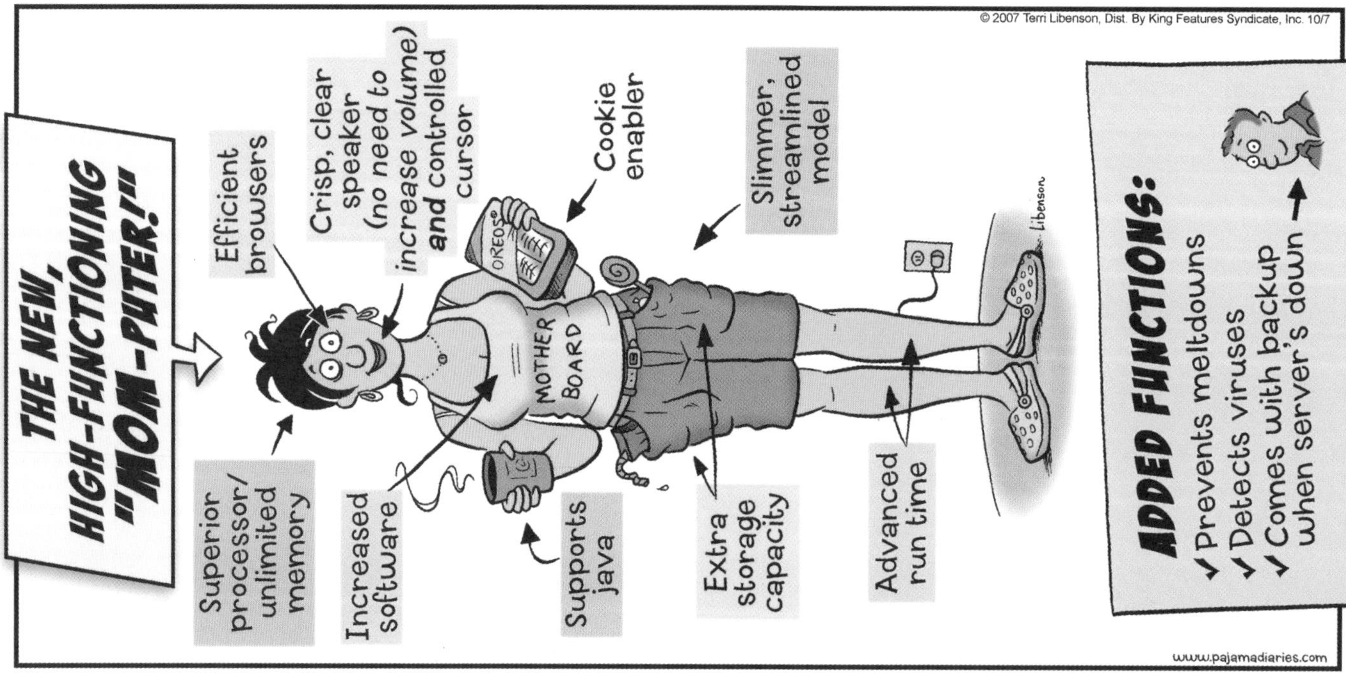
© 2007 Terri Libenson, Dist. By King Features Syndicate, Inc. 10/7
THE NEW, HIGH-FUNCTIONING "MOM-PUTER!"
Superior processor/ unlimited memory
Efficient browsers
Crisp, clear speaker (no need to increase volume) and controlled cursor
Increased software
Supports java
Cookie enabler
OREOS
MOTHER BOARD
Slimmer, streamlined model
Extra storage capacity
Advanced run time
Libenson
ADDED FUNCTIONS:
✓ Prevents meltdowns
✓ Detects viruses
✓ Comes with backup when server's down
www.pajamadiaries.com

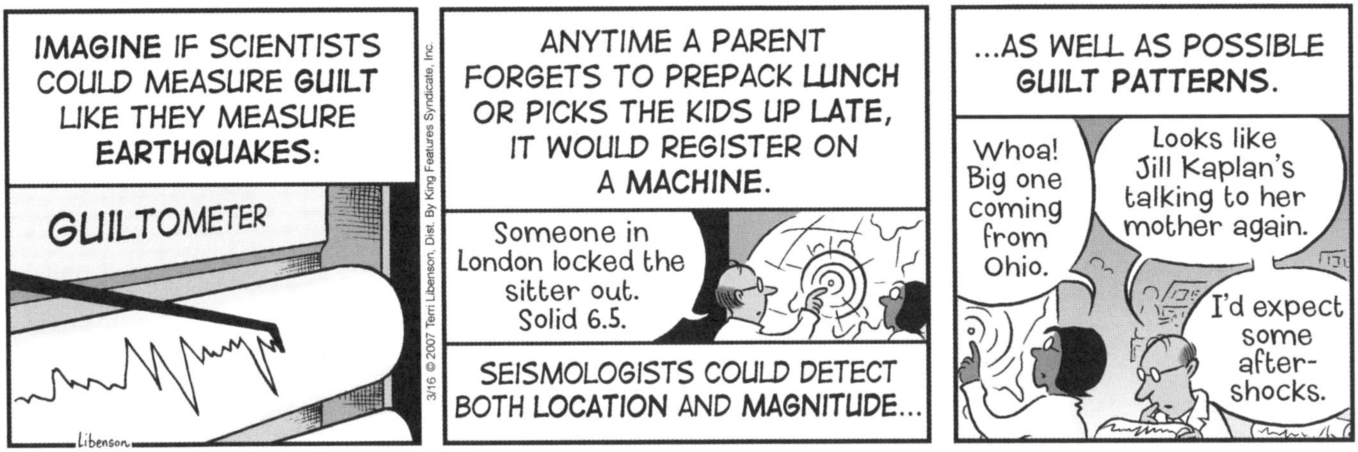
IMAGINE IF SCIENTISTS COULD MEASURE GUILT LIKE THEY MEASURE EARTHQUAKES:
GUILTOMETER
Libenson
3/16 © 2007 Terri Libenson, Dist. By King Features Syndicate, Inc.
ANYTIME A PARENT FORGETS TO PREPACK LUNCH OR PICKS THE KIDS UP LATE, IT WOULD REGISTER ON A MACHINE.
Someone in London locked the sitter out. Solid 6.5.
SEISMOLOGISTS COULD DETECT BOTH LOCATION AND MAGNITUDE...
...AS WELL AS POSSIBLE GUILT PATTERNS.
Whoa! Big one coming from Ohio.
Looks like Jill Kaplan's talking to her mother again.
I'd expect some after-shocks.

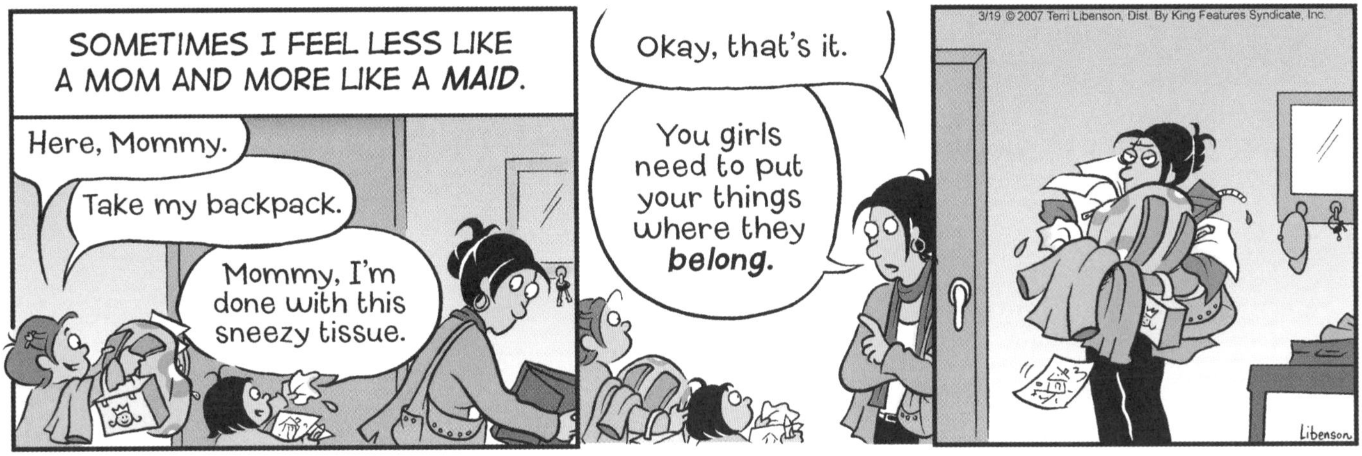
SOMETIMES I FEEL LESS LIKE A MOM AND MORE LIKE A *MAID*.
Here, Mommy.
Take my backpack.
Mommy, I'm done with this sneezy tissue.
Okay, that's it.
You girls need to put your things where they ***belong.***
3/19 © 2007 Terri Libenson, Dist. By King Features Syndicate, Inc.
Libenson

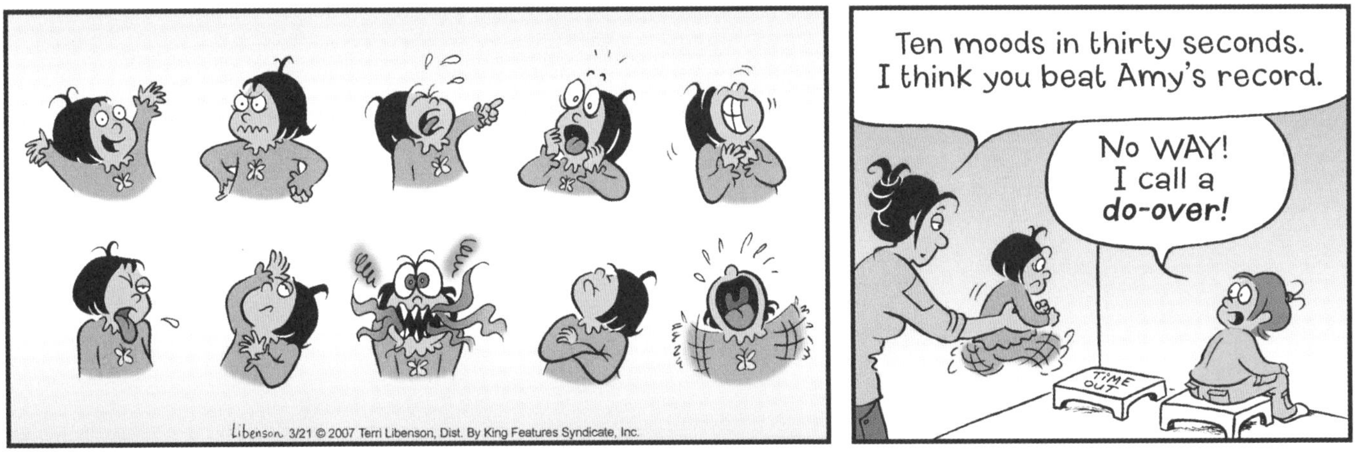
Libenson 3/21 © 2007 Terri Libenson, Dist. By King Features Syndicate, Inc.
Ten moods in thirty seconds. I think you beat Amy's record.
No WAY! I call a ***do-over!***
TIME OUT

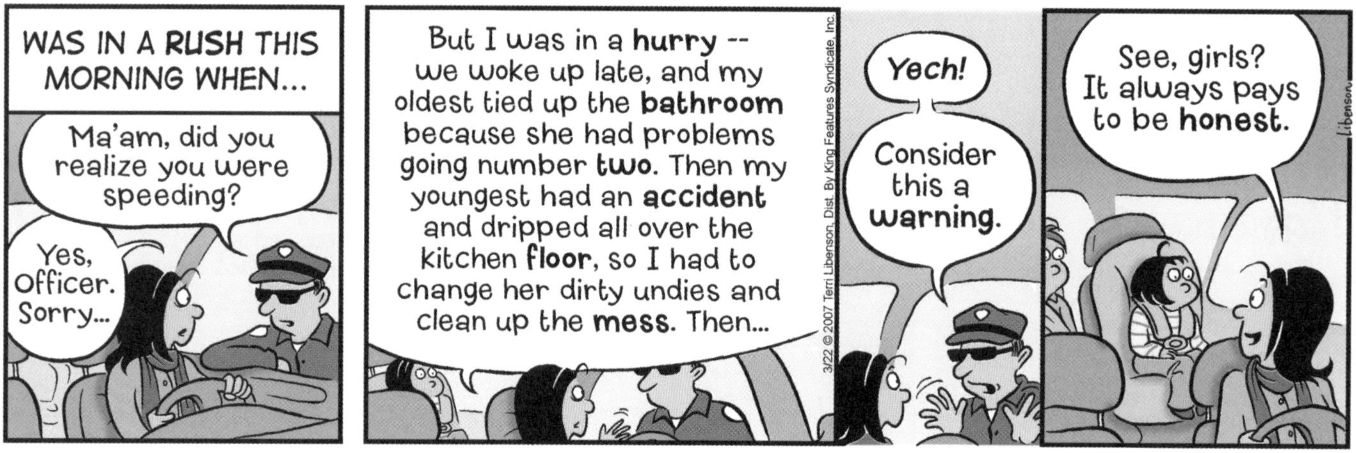
WAS IN A RUSH THIS MORNING WHEN...
Ma'am, did you realize you were speeding?
Yes, Officer. Sorry...
But I was in a hurry -- we woke up late, and my oldest tied up the bathroom because she had problems going number two. Then my youngest had an accident and dripped all over the kitchen floor, so I had to change her dirty undies and clean up the mess. Then...
3/22 © 2007 Terri Libenson, Dist. By King Features Syndicate, Inc.
Yech!
Consider this a warning.
See, girls? It always pays to be honest.
Libenson

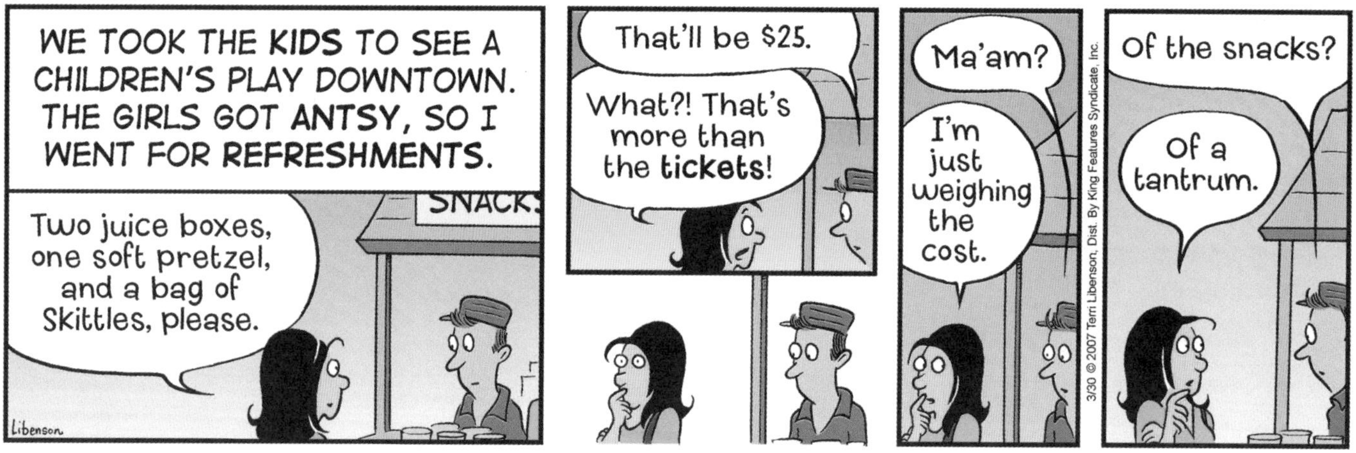
WE TOOK THE KIDS TO SEE A CHILDREN'S PLAY DOWNTOWN. THE GIRLS GOT ANTSY, SO I WENT FOR REFRESHMENTS.
SNACKS
Two juice boxes, one soft pretzel, and a bag of Skittles, please.
Libenson
That'll be $25.
What?! That's more than the tickets!
Ma'am?
I'm just weighing the cost.
3/30 © 2007 Terri Libenson, Dist. By King Features Syndicate, Inc.
Of the snacks?
Of a tantrum.

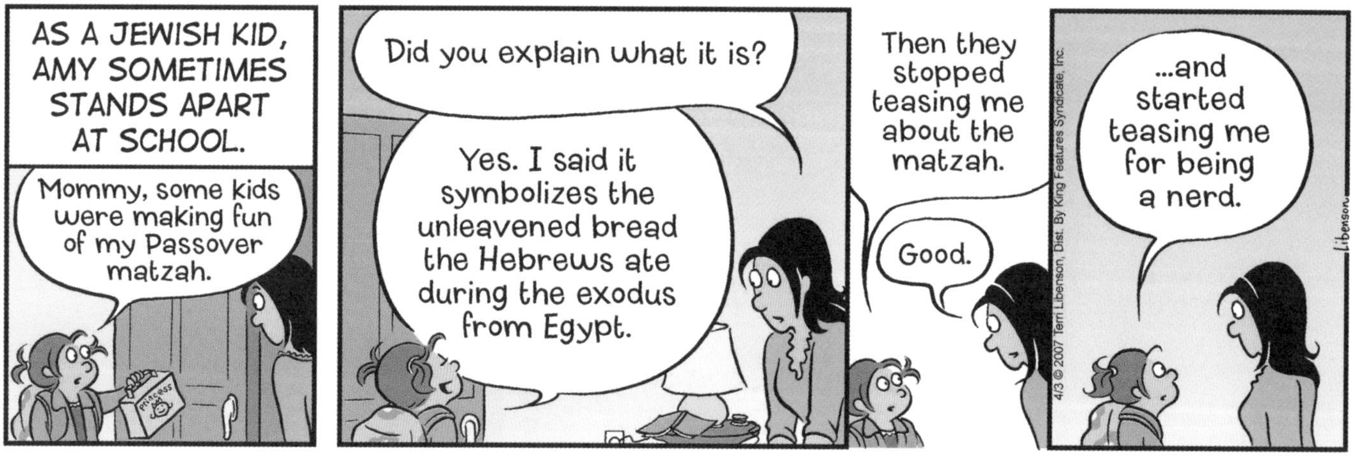
AS A JEWISH KID, AMY SOMETIMES STANDS APART AT SCHOOL.
Mommy, some kids were making fun of my Passover matzah.
Princess
Did you explain what it is?
Yes. I said it symbolizes the unleavened bread the Hebrews ate during the exodus from Egypt.
Then they stopped teasing me about the matzah.
Good.
4/3 © 2007 Terri Libenson, Dist. By King Features Syndicate, Inc.
...and started teasing me for being a nerd.
Libenson

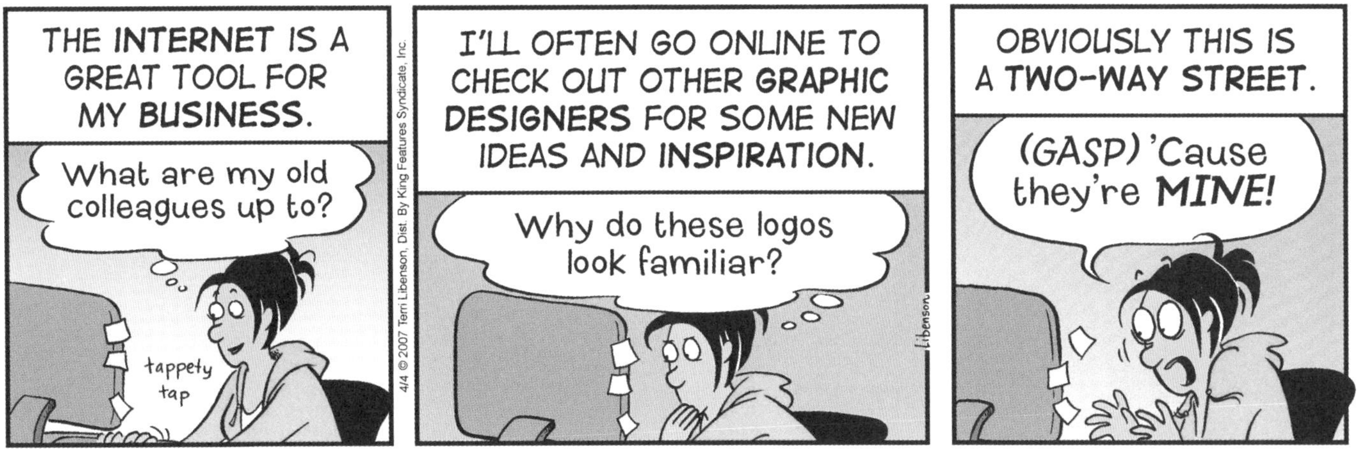

THE **INTERNET** IS A GREAT TOOL FOR MY **BUSINESS**.
What are my old colleagues up to?
tappety tap
4/4 © 2007 Terri Libenson. Dist. By King Features Syndicate, Inc.
I'LL OFTEN GO ONLINE TO CHECK OUT OTHER **GRAPHIC DESIGNERS** FOR SOME NEW IDEAS AND **INSPIRATION**.
Why do these logos look familiar?
Libenson
OBVIOUSLY THIS IS A **TWO-WAY STREET**.
(GASP) 'Cause they're **MINE!**

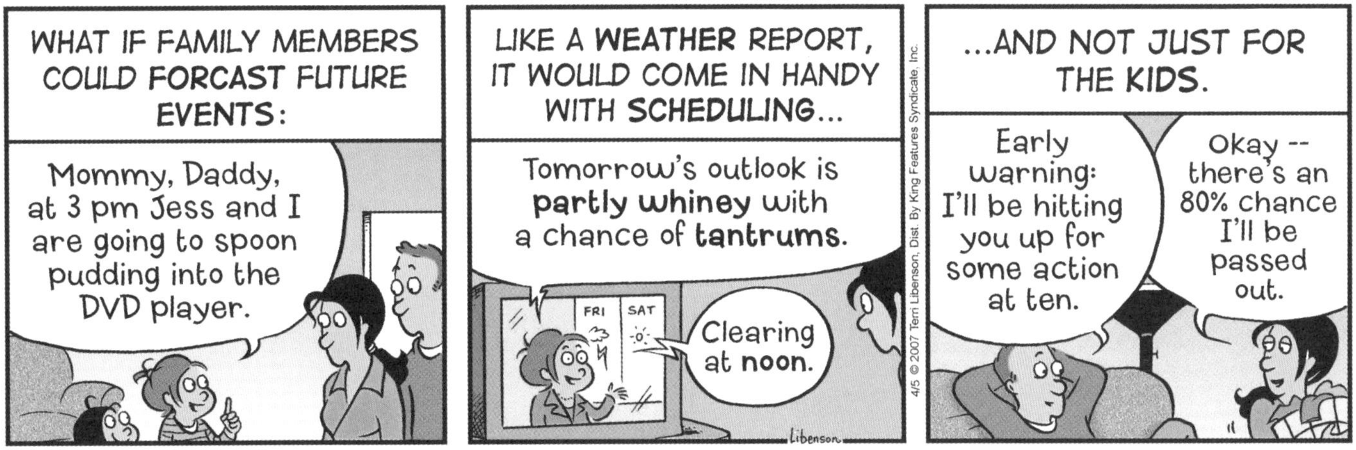

WHAT IF FAMILY MEMBERS COULD **FORCAST** FUTURE **EVENTS**:
Mommy, Daddy, at 3 pm Jess and I are going to spoon pudding into the DVD player.
LIKE A **WEATHER** REPORT, IT WOULD COME IN HANDY WITH **SCHEDULING**...
Tomorrow's outlook is **partly whiney** with a chance of **tantrums**.
FRI
SAT
Clearing at **noon**.
Libenson
4/5 © 2007 Terri Libenson. Dist. By King Features Syndicate, Inc.
...AND NOT JUST FOR THE **KIDS**.
Early warning: I'll be hitting you up for some action at ten.
Okay -- there's an 80% chance I'll be passed out.

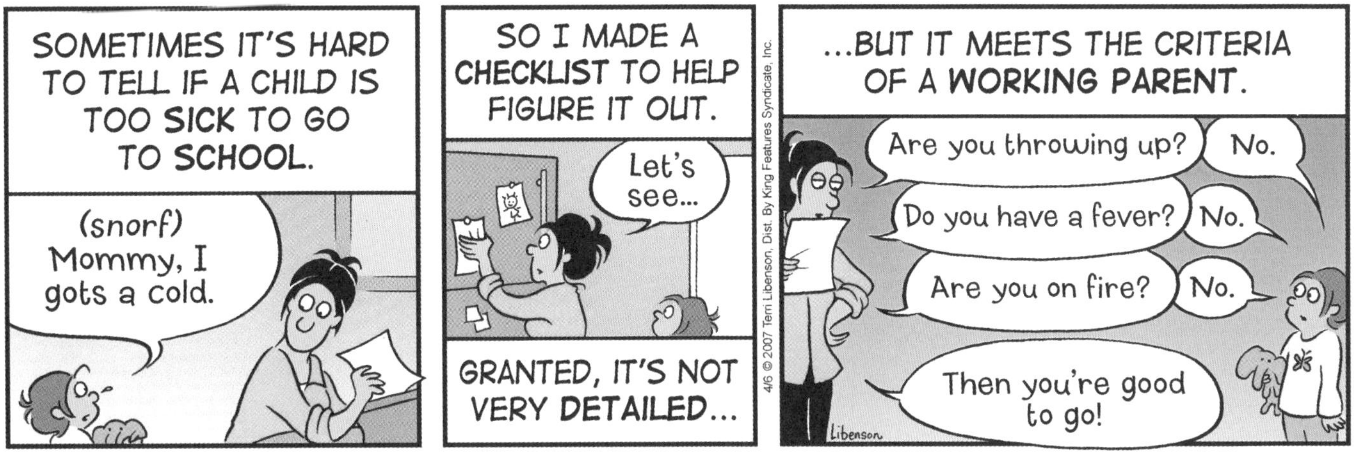

SOMETIMES IT'S HARD TO TELL IF A CHILD IS TOO **SICK** TO GO TO **SCHOOL**.
(snorf) Mommy, I gots a cold.
SO I MADE A **CHECKLIST** TO HELP FIGURE IT OUT.
Let's see...
GRANTED, IT'S NOT VERY **DETAILED**...
4/6 © 2007 Terri Libenson. Dist. By King Features Syndicate, Inc.
...BUT IT MEETS THE CRITERIA OF A **WORKING PARENT**.
Are you throwing up?
No.
Do you have a fever?
No.
Are you on fire?
No.
Then you're good to go!
Libenson

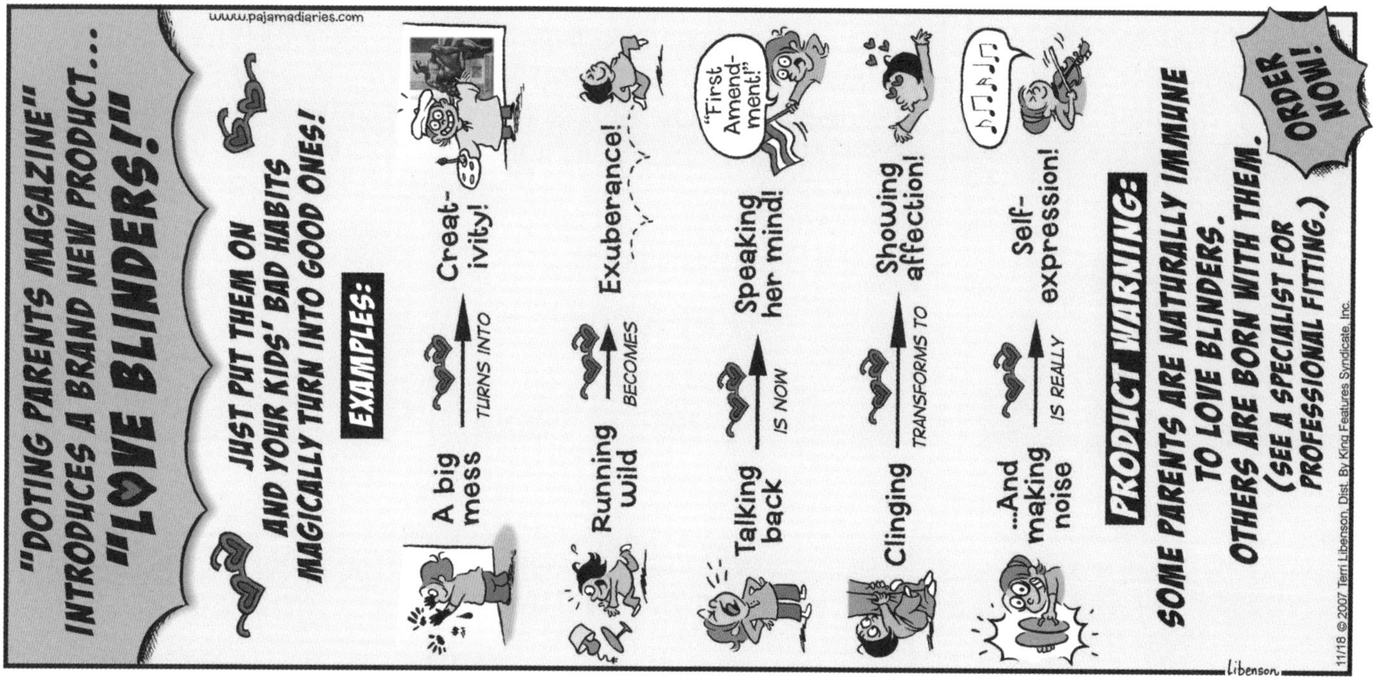
www.pajamadiaries.com
"DOTING PARENTS MAGAZINE" INTRODUCES A BRAND NEW PRODUCT...
"LOVE BLINDERS!"
JUST PUT THEM ON AND YOUR KIDS' BAD HABITS MAGICALLY TURN INTO GOOD ONES!
EXAMPLES:
A big mess
TURNS INTO
Creat-ivity!
Running wild
BECOMES
Exuberance!
Talking back
IS NOW
Speaking her mind!
"First Amend-ment!"
Clinging
TRANSFORMS TO
Showing affection!
...And making noise
IS REALLY
Self-expression!
PRODUCT WARNING:
SOME PARENTS ARE NATURALLY IMMUNE TO LOVE BLINDERS.
OTHERS ARE BORN WITH THEM.
(SEE A SPECIALIST FOR PROFESSIONAL FITTING.)
ORDER NOW!
11/18 © 2007 Terri Libenson, Dist. By King Features Syndicate, Inc.
Libenson

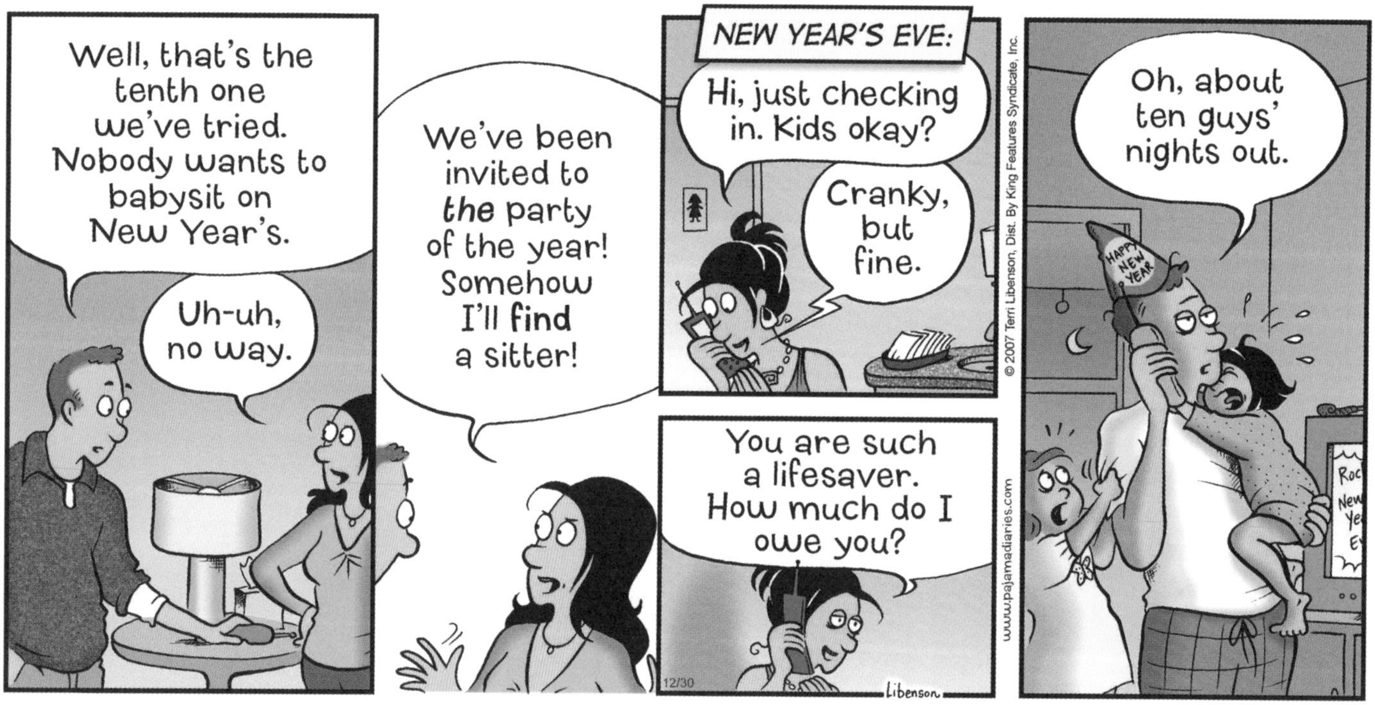
Well, that's the tenth one we've tried. Nobody wants to babysit on New Year's.
Uh-uh, no way.
We've been invited to *the* party of the year! Somehow I'll **find** a sitter!
NEW YEAR'S EVE:
Hi, just checking in. Kids okay?
Cranky, but fine.
You are such a lifesaver. How much do I owe you?
12/30
Libenson
© 2007 Terri Libenson, Dist. By King Features Syndicate, Inc.
www.pajamadiaries.com
Oh, about ten guys' nights out.
HAPPY NEW YEAR

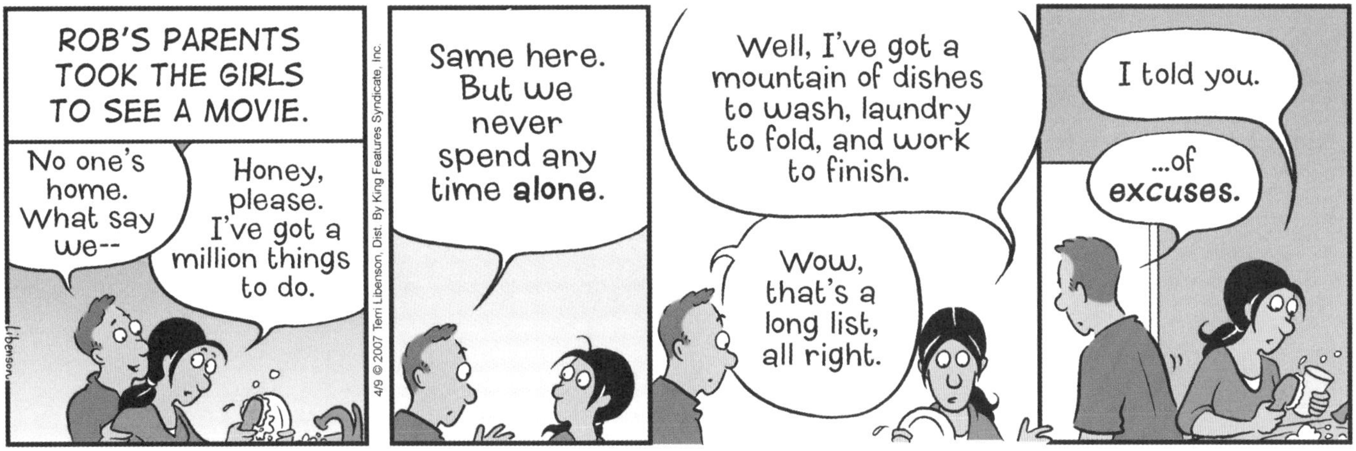
ROB'S PARENTS TOOK THE GIRLS TO SEE A MOVIE.
No one's home. What say we--
Honey, please. I've got a million things to do.
Libenson
4/9 © 2007 Terri Libenson, Dist. By King Features Syndicate, Inc.
Same here. But we never spend any time **alone**.
Well, I've got a mountain of dishes to wash, laundry to fold, and work to finish.
Wow, that's a long list, all right.
I told you.
...of **excuses**.

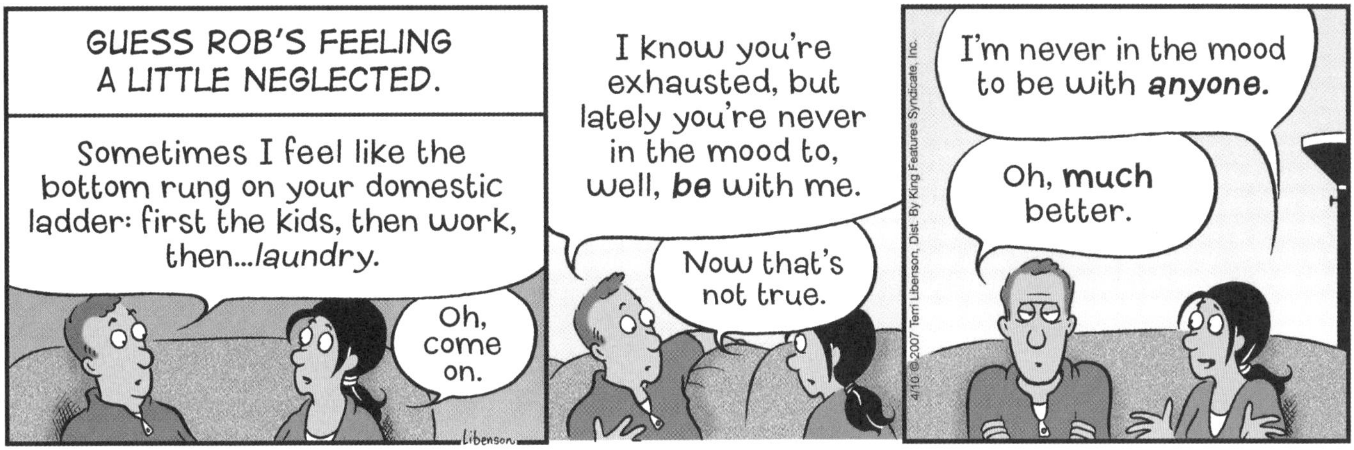
GUESS ROB'S FEELING A LITTLE NEGLECTED.
Sometimes I feel like the bottom rung on your domestic ladder: first the kids, then work, then...*laundry*.
Oh, come on.
Libenson
I know you're exhausted, but lately you're never in the mood to, well, **be** with me.
Now that's not true.
4/10 © 2007 Terri Libenson, Dist. By King Features Syndicate, Inc.
I'm never in the mood to be with **anyone**.
Oh, **much** better.

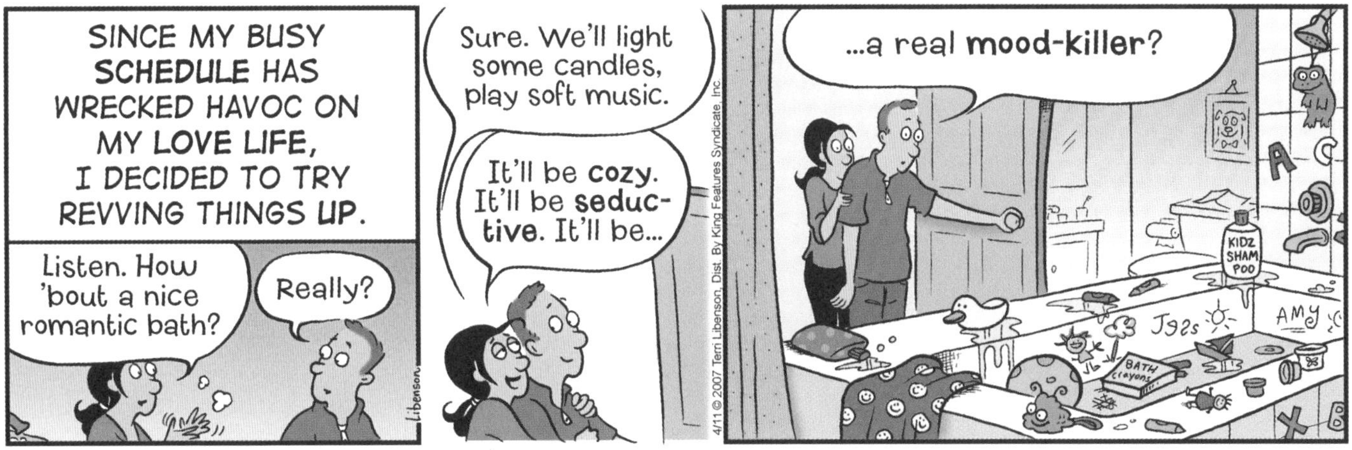
SINCE MY BUSY **SCHEDULE** HAS WRECKED HAVOC ON MY **LOVE LIFE**, I DECIDED TO TRY REVVING THINGS **UP**.
Listen. How 'bout a nice romantic bath?
Really?
Libenson
Sure. We'll light some candles, play soft music.
It'll be **cozy**. It'll be **seductive**. It'll be...
4/11 © 2007 Terri Libenson, Dist. By King Features Syndicate, Inc.
...a real **mood-killer**?
KIDZ SHAMPOO
BATH crayons
AMY

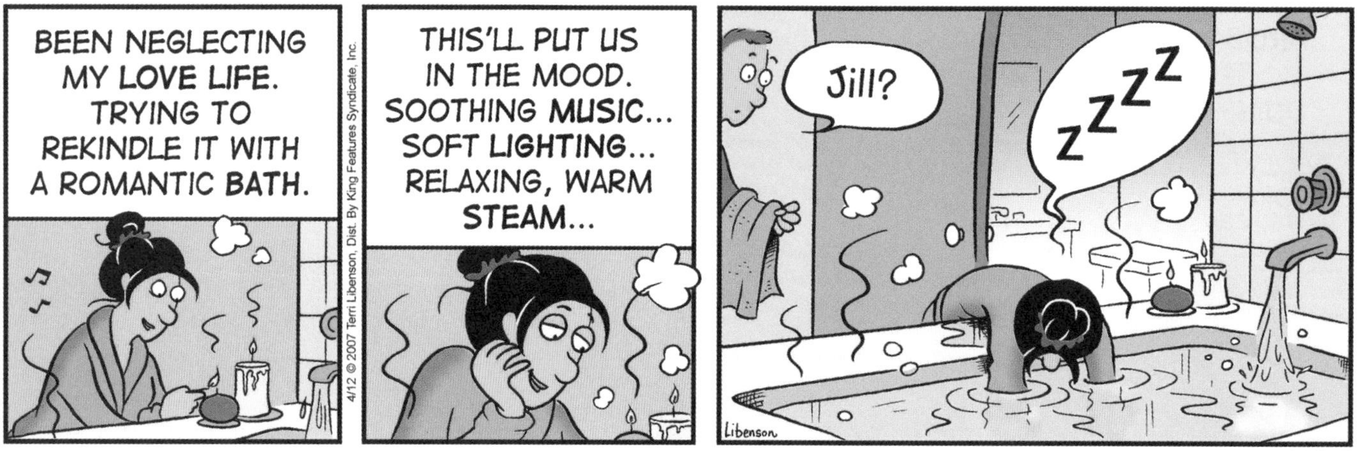
BEEN NEGLECTING MY LOVE LIFE. TRYING TO REKINDLE IT WITH A ROMANTIC BATH.
4/12 © 2007 Terri Libenson, Dist. By King Features Syndicate, Inc.
THIS'LL PUT US IN THE MOOD. SOOTHING MUSIC... SOFT LIGHTING... RELAXING, WARM STEAM...
Jill?
ZZZZ
Libenson

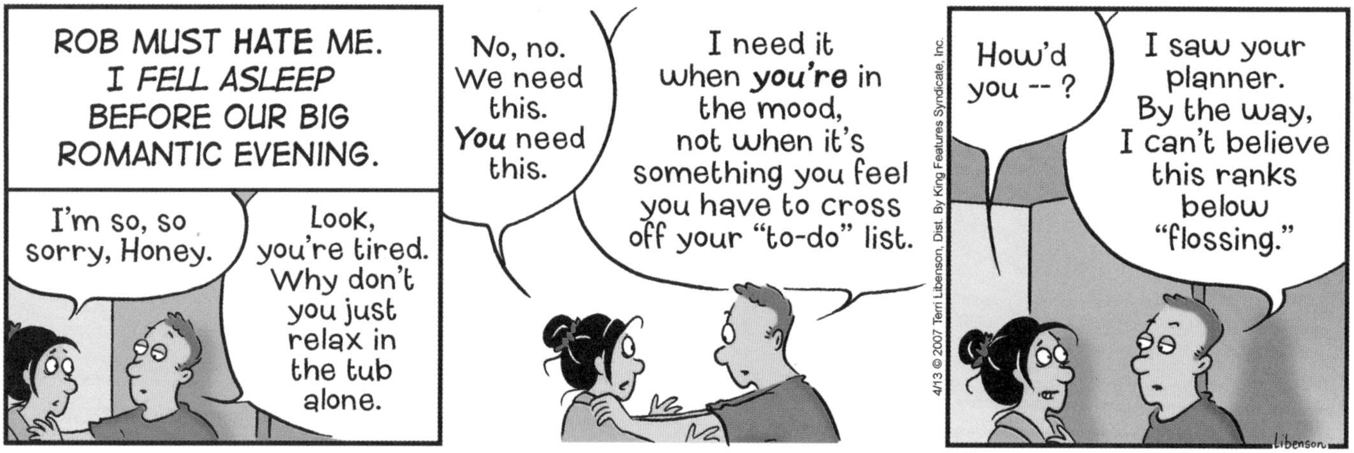
ROB MUST HATE ME. I *FELL ASLEEP* BEFORE OUR BIG ROMANTIC EVENING.
I'm so, so sorry, Honey.
Look, you're tired. Why don't you just relax in the tub alone.
No, no. We need this. *You* need this.
I need it when *you're* in the mood, not when it's something you feel you have to cross off your "to-do" list.
4/13 © 2007 Terri Libenson, Dist. By King Features Syndicate, Inc.
How'd you -- ?
I saw your planner. By the way, I can't believe this ranks below "flossing."
Libenson

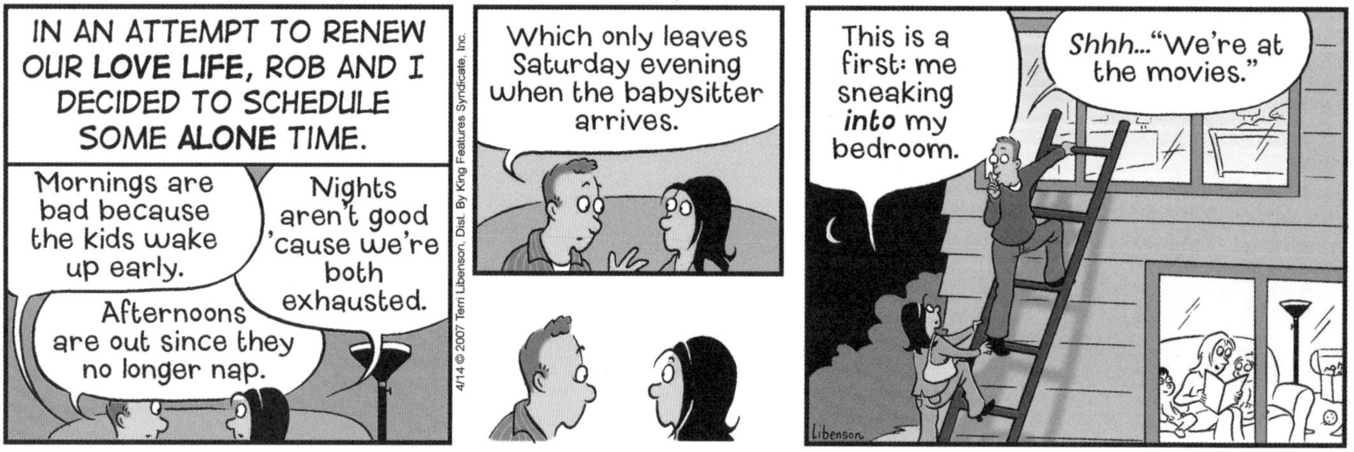
IN AN ATTEMPT TO RENEW OUR LOVE LIFE, ROB AND I DECIDED TO SCHEDULE SOME ALONE TIME.
Mornings are bad because the kids wake up early.
Nights aren't good 'cause we're both exhausted.
Afternoons are out since they no longer nap.
4/14 © 2007 Terri Libenson, Dist. By King Features Syndicate, Inc.
Which only leaves Saturday evening when the babysitter arrives.
This is a first: me sneaking *into* my bedroom.
Shhh..."We're at the movies."
Libenson

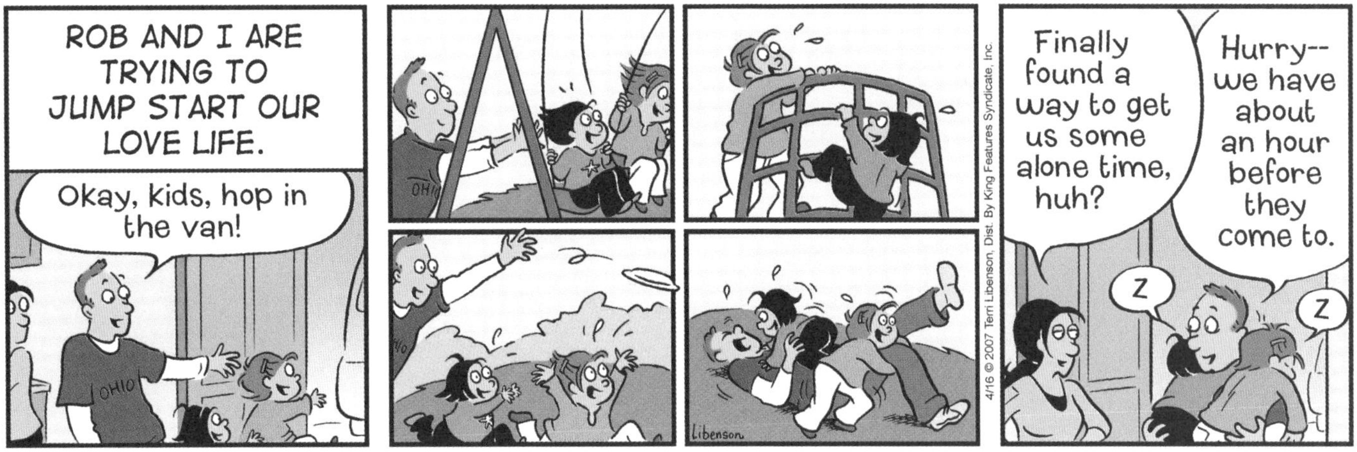
ROB AND I ARE TRYING TO JUMP START OUR LOVE LIFE.
Okay, kids, hop in the van!
OHIO
Finally found a way to get us some alone time, huh?
Hurry-- we have about an hour before they come to.
Z
Z
Libenson
4/16 © 2007 Terri Libenson, Dist. By King Features Syndicate, Inc.

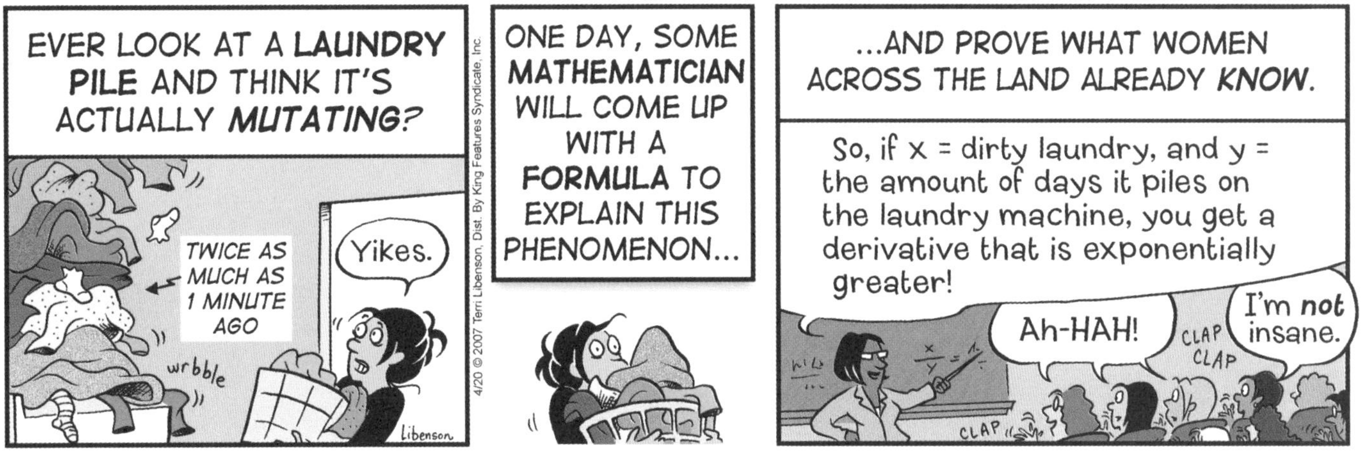
EVER LOOK AT A **LAUNDRY PILE** AND THINK IT'S ACTUALLY ***MUTATING***?
TWICE AS MUCH AS 1 MINUTE AGO
wrbble
Yikes.
Libenson
4/20 © 2007 Terri Libenson, Dist. By King Features Syndicate, Inc.
ONE DAY, SOME **MATHEMATICIAN** WILL COME UP WITH A **FORMULA** TO EXPLAIN THIS PHENOMENON...
...AND PROVE WHAT WOMEN ACROSS THE LAND ALREADY ***KNOW***.
So, if x = dirty laundry, and y = the amount of days it piles on the laundry machine, you get a derivative that is exponentially greater!
Ah-HAH!
CLAP CLAP
I'm **not** insane.
CLAP

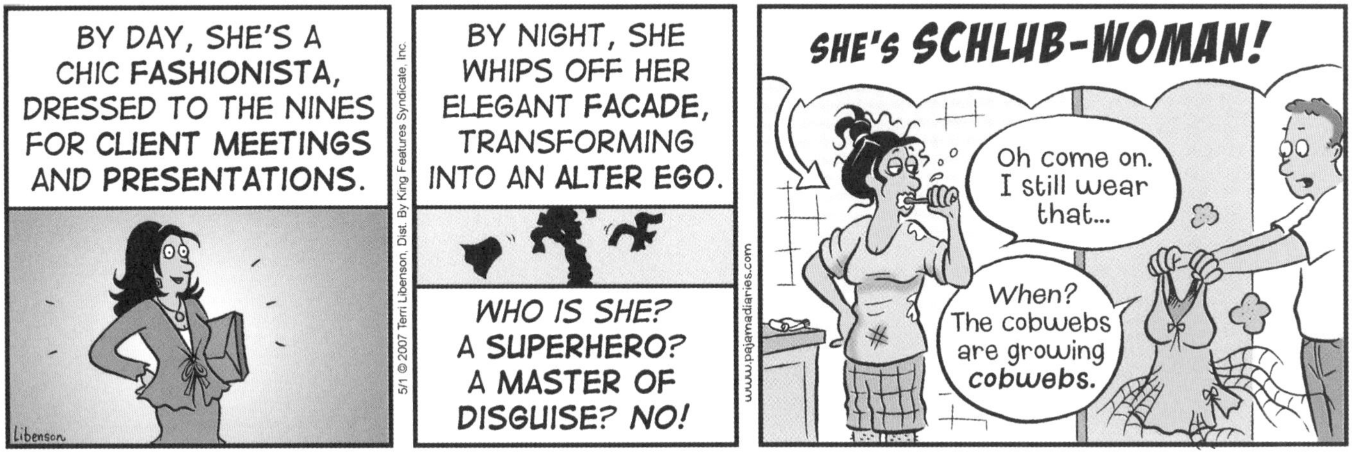
BY DAY, SHE'S A CHIC **FASHIONISTA**, DRESSED TO THE NINES FOR **CLIENT MEETINGS** AND **PRESENTATIONS**.
Libenson
5/1 © 2007 Terri Libenson, Dist. By King Features Syndicate, Inc.
BY NIGHT, SHE WHIPS OFF HER ELEGANT **FACADE**, TRANSFORMING INTO AN **ALTER EGO**.
WHO IS SHE? A **SUPERHERO?** A **MASTER OF DISGUISE?** ***NO!***
www.pajamadiaries.com
SHE'S SCHLUB-WOMAN!
Oh come on. I still wear that...
When? The cobwebs are growing **cobwebs.**

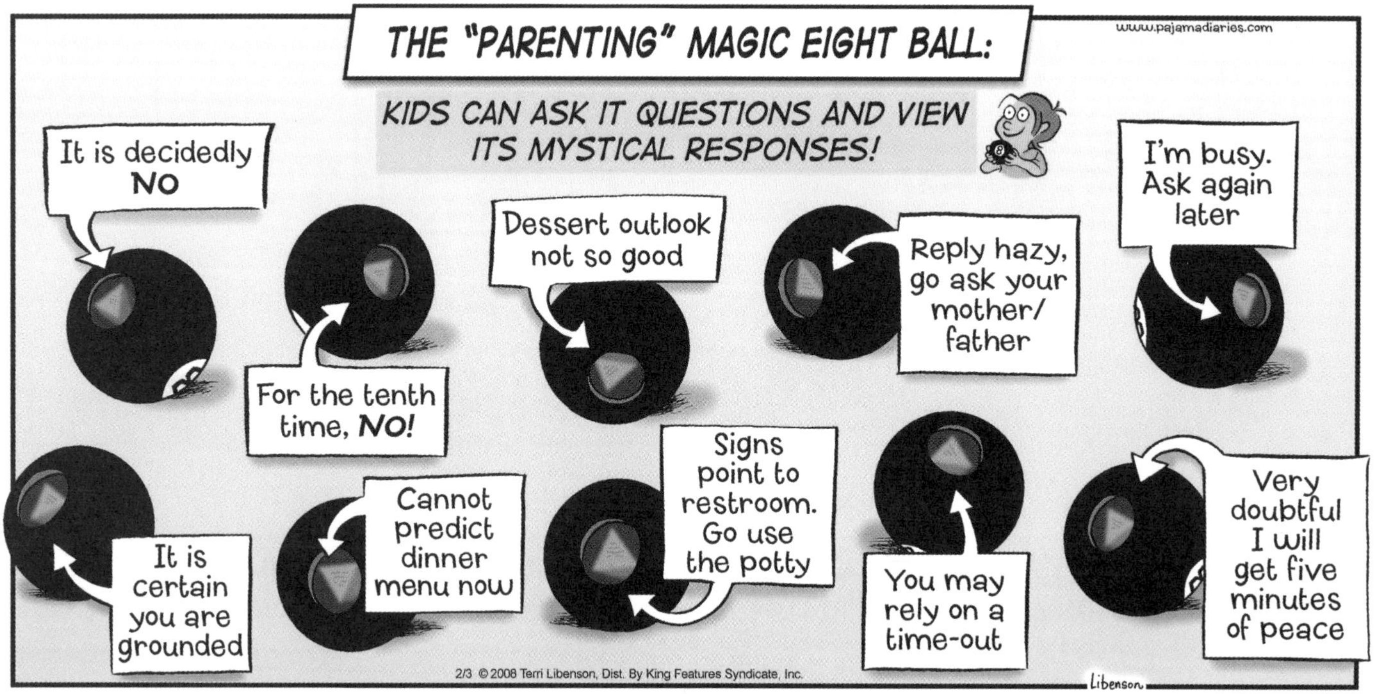

THE "PARENTING" MAGIC EIGHT BALL:
www.pajamadiaries.com
KIDS CAN ASK IT QUESTIONS AND VIEW ITS MYSTICAL RESPONSES!
It is decidedly NO
For the tenth time, NO!
Dessert outlook not so good
Reply hazy, go ask your mother/ father
I'm busy. Ask again later
It is certain you are grounded
Cannot predict dinner menu now
Signs point to restroom. Go use the potty
You may rely on a time-out
Very doubtful I will get five minutes of peace
2/3 © 2008 Terri Libenson, Dist. By King Features Syndicate, Inc.
Libenson

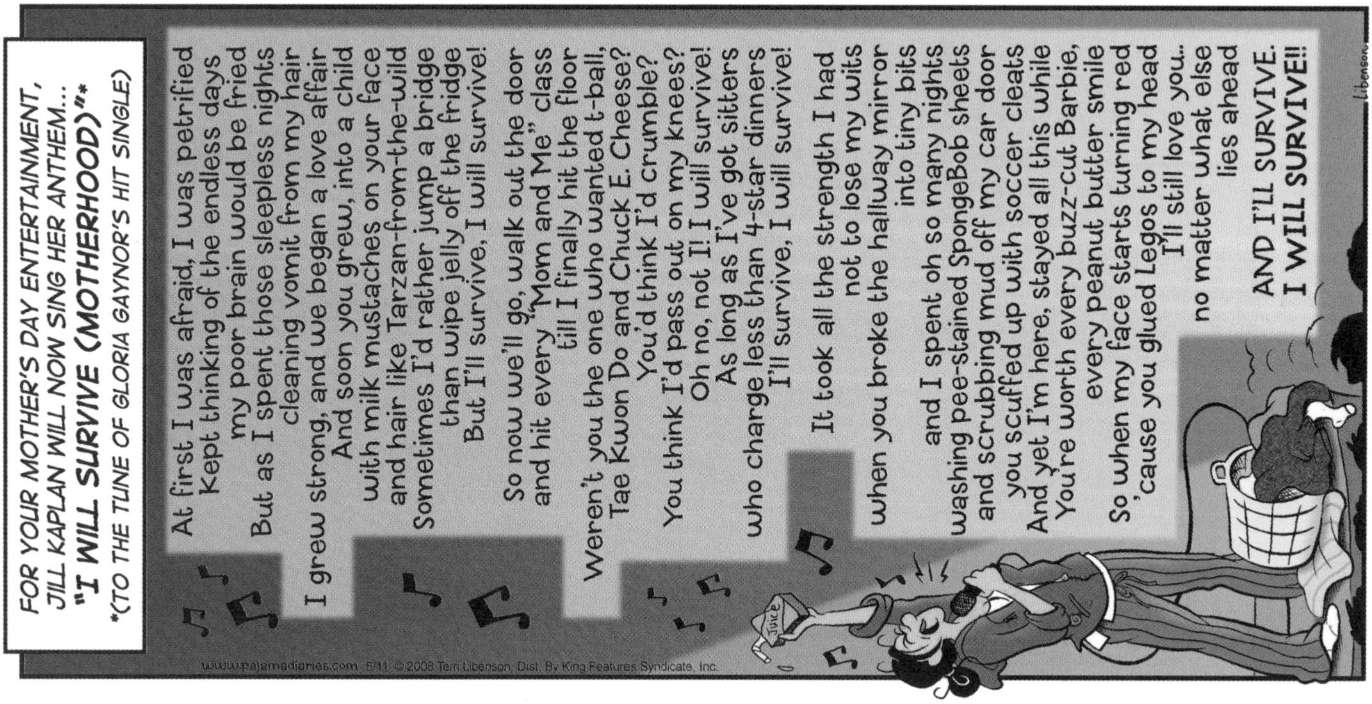

FOR YOUR MOTHER'S DAY ENTERTAINMENT, JILL KAPLAN WILL NOW SING HER ANTHEM...
"I WILL SURVIVE (MOTHERHOOD)"*
*(TO THE TUNE OF GLORIA GAYNOR'S HIT SINGLE)
At first I was afraid, I was petrified
Kept thinking of the endless days
my poor brain would be fried
But as I spent those sleepless nights
cleaning vomit from my hair
I grew strong, and we began a love affair
And soon you grew, into a child
with milk mustaches on your face
and hair like Tarzan-from-the-wild
Sometimes I'd rather jump a bridge
than wipe jelly off the fridge
But I'll survive, I will survive!
So now we'll go, walk out the door
and hit every "Mom and Me" class
till I finally hit the floor
Weren't you the one who wanted t-ball,
Tae Kwon Do and Chuck E. Cheese?
You'd think I'd crumble?
You think I'd pass out on my knees?
Oh no, not I! I will survive!
As long as I've got sitters
who charge less than 4-star dinners
I'll survive, I will survive!
It took all the strength I had
not to lose my wits
when you broke the hallway mirror
into tiny bits
and I spent oh so many nights
washing pee-stained SpongeBob sheets
and scrubbing mud off my car door
you scuffed up with soccer cleats
And yet I'm here, stayed all this while
You're worth every buzz-cut Barbie,
every peanut butter smile
So when my face starts turning red
'cause you glued Legos to my head
I'll still love you..
no matter what else
lies ahead
AND I'LL SURVIVE.
I WILL SURVIVE!!
JUICE
www.pajamadiaries.com 5/11 © 2008 Terri Libenson, Dist. By King Features Syndicate, Inc.
Libenson

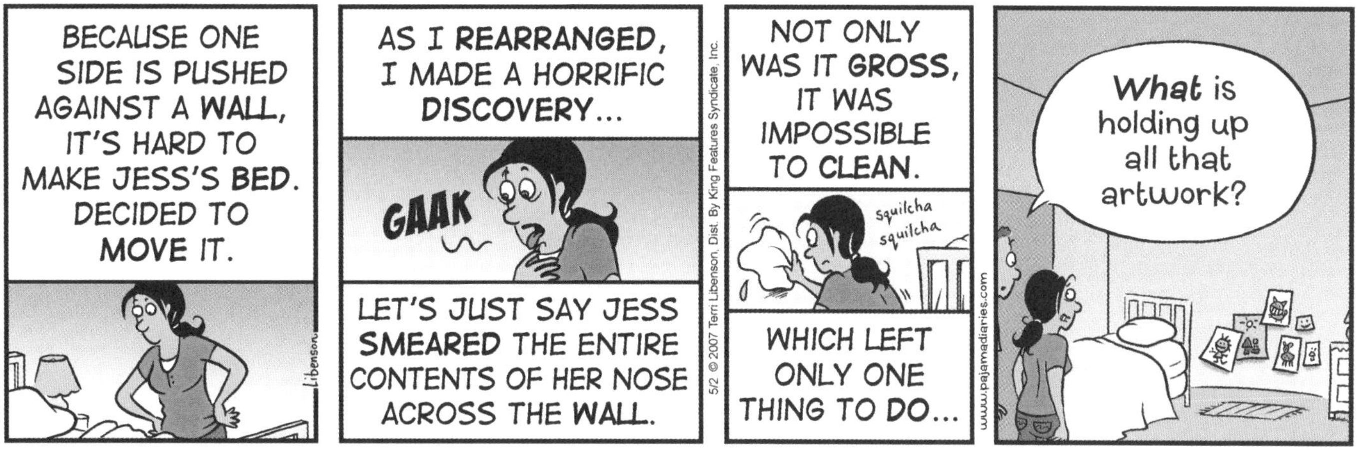
BECAUSE ONE SIDE IS PUSHED AGAINST A **WALL**, IT'S HARD TO MAKE JESS'S **BED**. DECIDED TO **MOVE** IT.
Libenson
AS I **REARRANGED**, I MADE A HORRIFIC **DISCOVERY**...
GAAK
LET'S JUST SAY JESS **SMEARED** THE ENTIRE CONTENTS OF HER NOSE ACROSS THE **WALL**.
5/2 © 2007 Terri Libenson, Dist. By King Features Syndicate, Inc.
NOT ONLY WAS IT **GROSS**, IT WAS IMPOSSIBLE TO **CLEAN**.
squilcha squilcha
WHICH LEFT ONLY ONE THING TO **DO**...
www.pajamadiaries.com
What is holding up all that artwork?

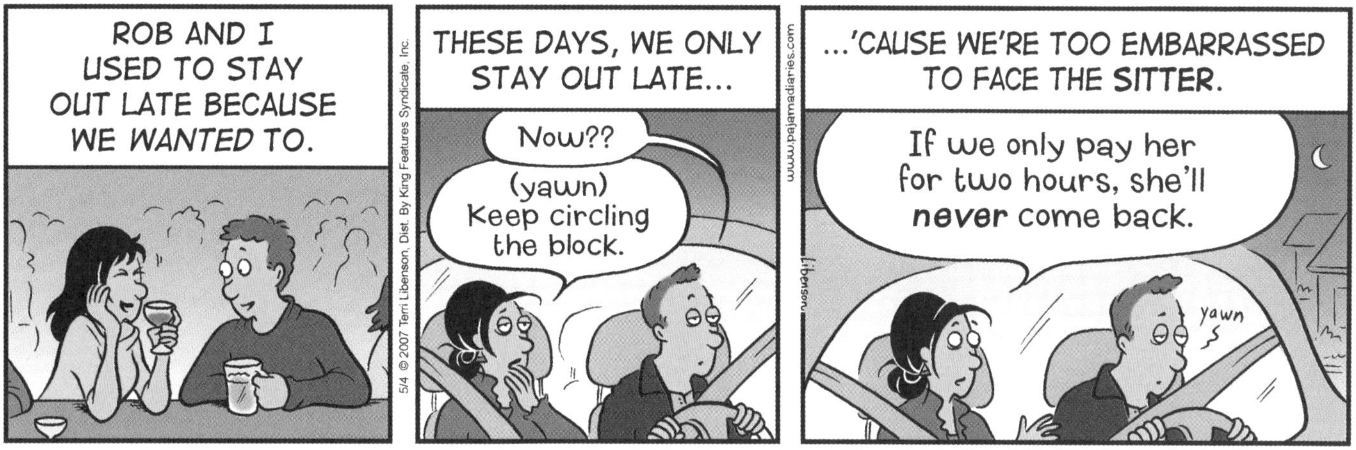
ROB AND I USED TO STAY OUT LATE BECAUSE WE *WANTED* TO.
5/4 © 2007 Terri Libenson, Dist. By King Features Syndicate, Inc.
THESE DAYS, WE ONLY STAY OUT LATE...
Now??
(yawn) Keep circling the block.
www.pajamadiaries.com
Libenson
...'CAUSE WE'RE TOO EMBARRASSED TO FACE THE **SITTER**.
If we only pay her for two hours, she'll **never** come back.
yawn

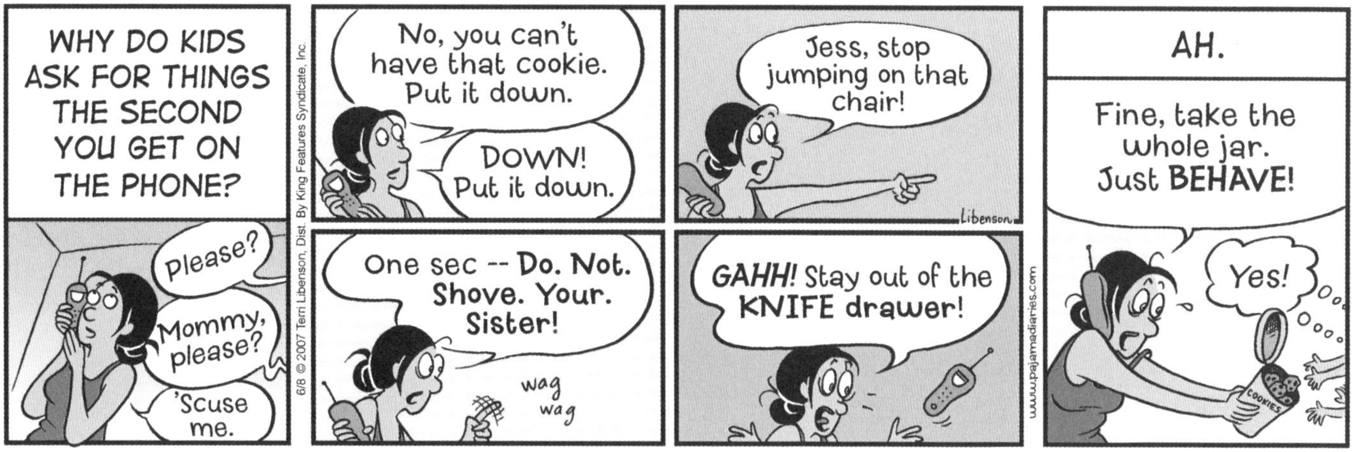
WHY DO KIDS ASK FOR THINGS THE SECOND YOU GET ON THE PHONE?
Please?
Mommy, please?
'Scuse me.
6/8 © 2007 Terri Libenson, Dist. By King Features Syndicate, Inc.
No, you can't have that cookie. Put it down.
DOWN! Put it down.
One sec -- **Do. Not. Shove. Your. Sister!**
wag wag
Jess, stop jumping on that chair!
Libenson
GAHH! Stay out of the **KNIFE drawer**!
www.pajamadiaries.com
AH.
Fine, take the whole jar. Just **BEHAVE**!
Yes!
COOKIES

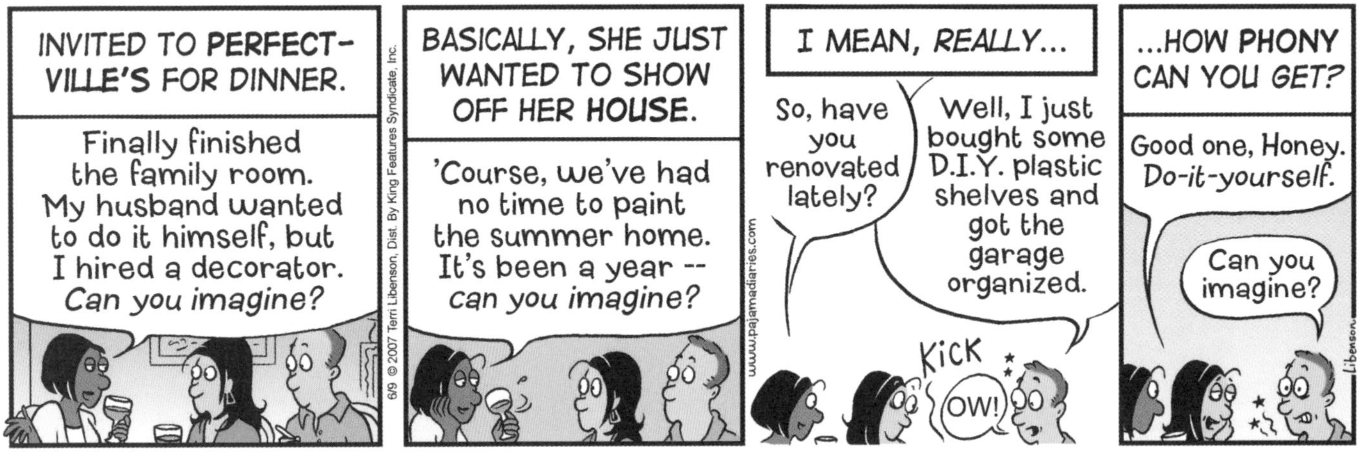
INVITED TO **PERFECTVILLE'S** FOR DINNER.
Finally finished the family room. My husband wanted to do it himself, but I hired a decorator. *Can you imagine?*
6/9 © 2007 Terri Libenson, Dist. By King Features Syndicate, Inc.
BASICALLY, SHE JUST WANTED TO SHOW OFF HER **HOUSE**.
'Course, we've had no time to paint the summer home. It's been a year -- *can you imagine?*
www.pajamadiaries.com
I MEAN, *REALLY*...
So, have you renovated lately?
Well, I just bought some D.I.Y. plastic shelves and got the garage organized.
KICK
OW!
...HOW **PHONY** CAN YOU *GET?*
Good one, Honey. *Do-it-yourself.*
Can you imagine?
Libenson

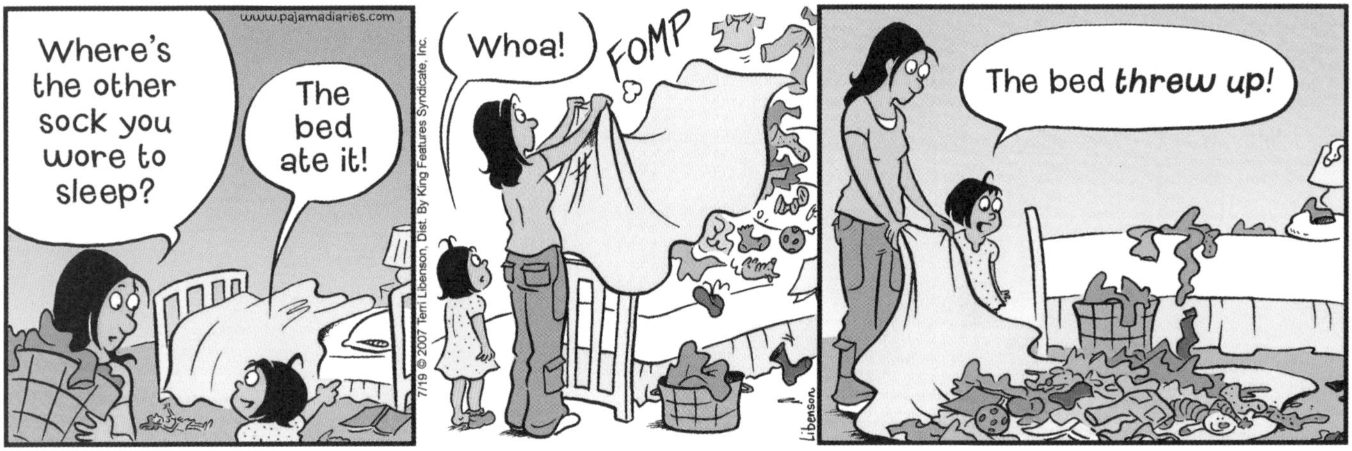
www.pajamadiaries.com
Where's the other sock you wore to sleep?
The bed ate it!
7/19 © 2007 Terri Libenson, Dist. By King Features Syndicate, Inc.
Whoa!
FOMP
The bed **threw up**!
Libenson

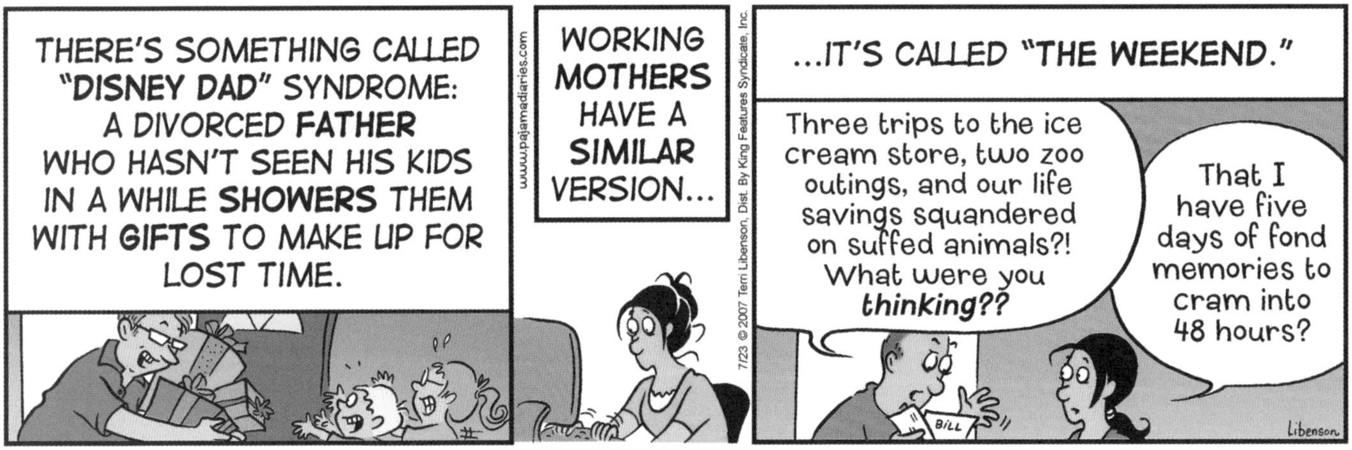
THERE'S SOMETHING CALLED **"DISNEY DAD"** SYNDROME: A DIVORCED **FATHER** WHO HASN'T SEEN HIS KIDS IN A WHILE **SHOWERS** THEM WITH **GIFTS** TO MAKE UP FOR LOST TIME.
www.pajamadiaries.com
WORKING **MOTHERS** HAVE A **SIMILAR** VERSION...
7/23 © 2007 Terri Libenson, Dist. By King Features Syndicate, Inc.
...IT'S CALLED **"THE WEEKEND."**
Three trips to the ice cream store, two zoo outings, and our life savings squandered on suffed animals?! What were you **thinking??**
That I have five days of fond memories to cram into 48 hours?
BILL
Libenson

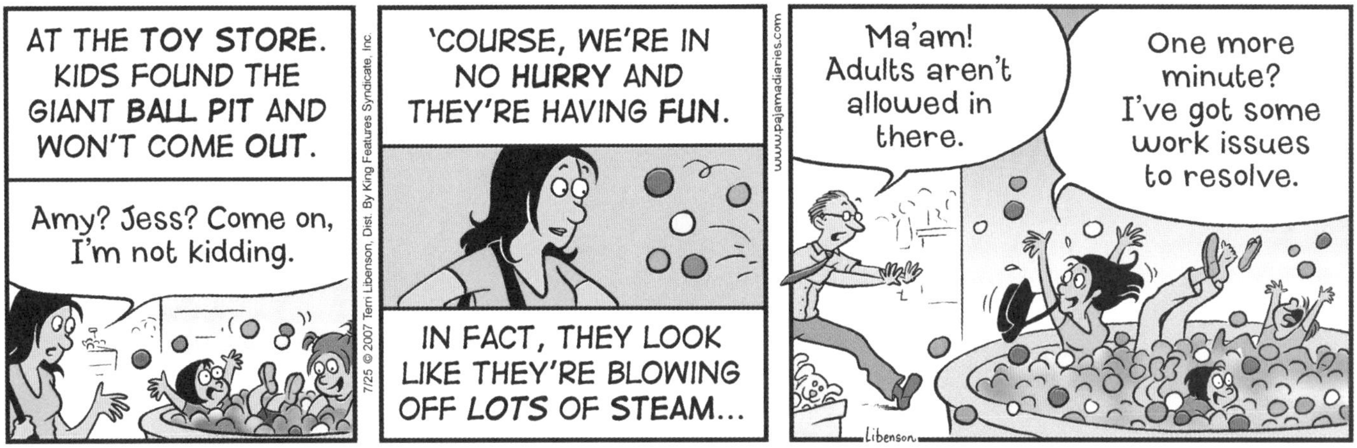
AT THE **TOY STORE**. KIDS FOUND THE GIANT **BALL PIT** AND WON'T COME **OUT**.
Amy? Jess? Come on, I'm not kidding.
7/25 © 2007 Terri Libenson, Dist. By King Features Syndicate, Inc.
'COURSE, WE'RE IN NO **HURRY** AND THEY'RE HAVING **FUN**.
IN FACT, THEY LOOK LIKE THEY'RE BLOWING OFF ***LOTS*** OF **STEAM**...
www.pajamadiaries.com
Ma'am! Adults aren't allowed in there.
One more minute? I've got some work issues to resolve.
Libenson

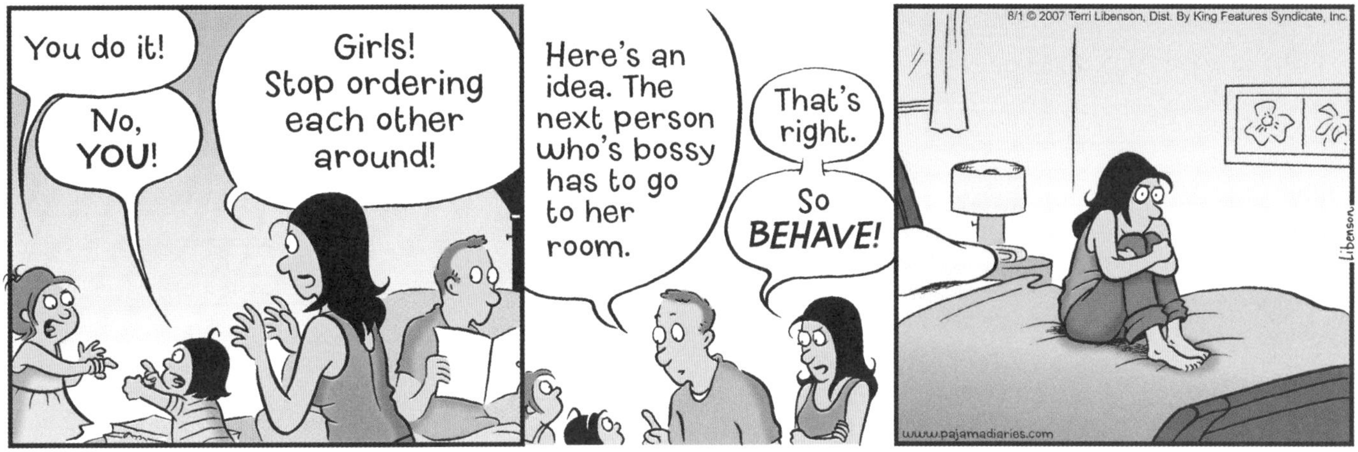
You do it!
No, **YOU**!
Girls! Stop ordering each other around!
Here's an idea. The next person who's bossy has to go to her room.
That's right.
So ***BEHAVE!***
8/1 © 2007 Terri Libenson, Dist. By King Features Syndicate, Inc.
Libenson
www.pajamadiaries.com

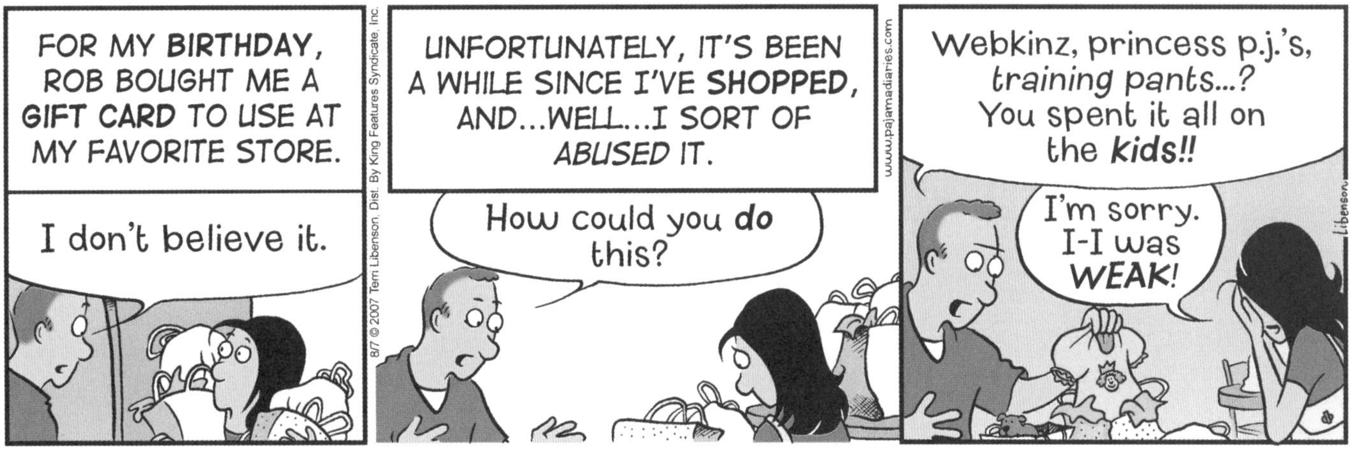
FOR MY **BIRTHDAY**, ROB BOUGHT ME A **GIFT CARD** TO USE AT MY FAVORITE STORE.
I don't believe it.
8/7 © 2007 Terri Libenson, Dist. By King Features Syndicate, Inc.
UNFORTUNATELY, IT'S BEEN A WHILE SINCE I'VE **SHOPPED**, AND...WELL...I SORT OF *ABUSED* IT.
How could you **do** this?
www.pajamadiaries.com
Webkinz, princess p.j.'s, *training pants...?* You spent it all on the ***kids!!***
I'm sorry. I-I was ***WEAK!***
Libenson

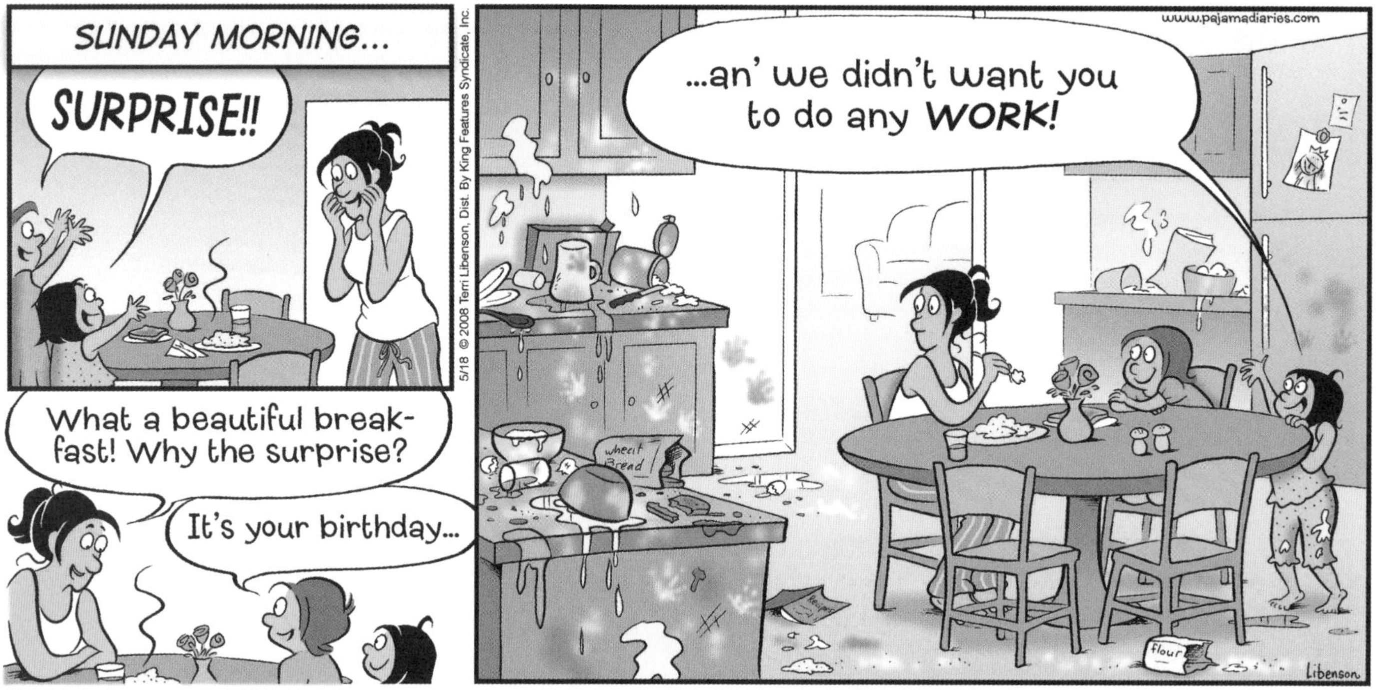
SUNDAY MORNING...
SURPRISE!!
What a beautiful break-fast! Why the surprise?
It's your birthday...
...an' we didn't want you to do any **WORK!**
wheat Bread
flour
5/18 © 2008 Terri Libenson, Dist. By King Features Syndicate, Inc.
www.pajamadiaries.com
Libenson

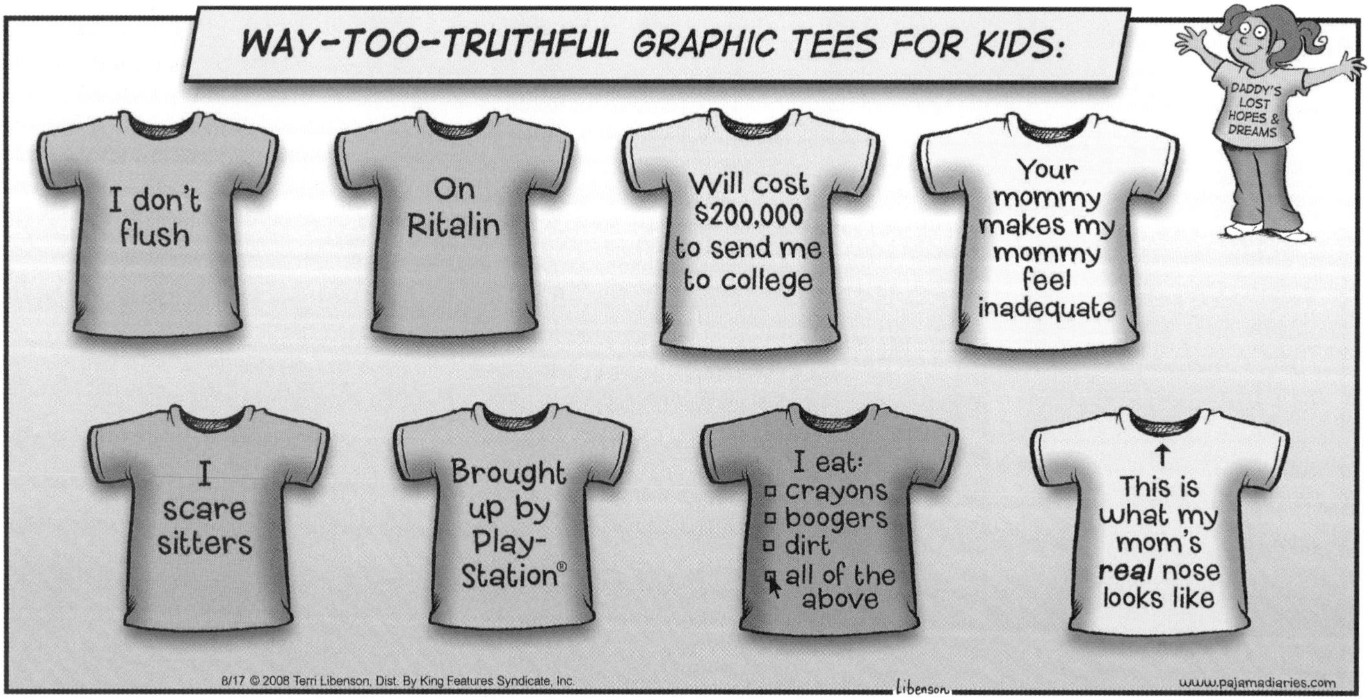
WAY-TOO-TRUTHFUL GRAPHIC TEES FOR KIDS:
DADDY'S LOST HOPES & DREAMS
I don't flush
On Ritalin
Will cost $200,000 to send me to college
Your mommy makes my mommy feel inadequate
I scare sitters
Brought up by Play-Station®
I eat:
crayons
boogers
dirt
all of the above
This is what my mom's *real* nose looks like
8/17 © 2008 Terri Libenson, Dist. By King Features Syndicate, Inc.
Libenson
www.pajamadiaries.com

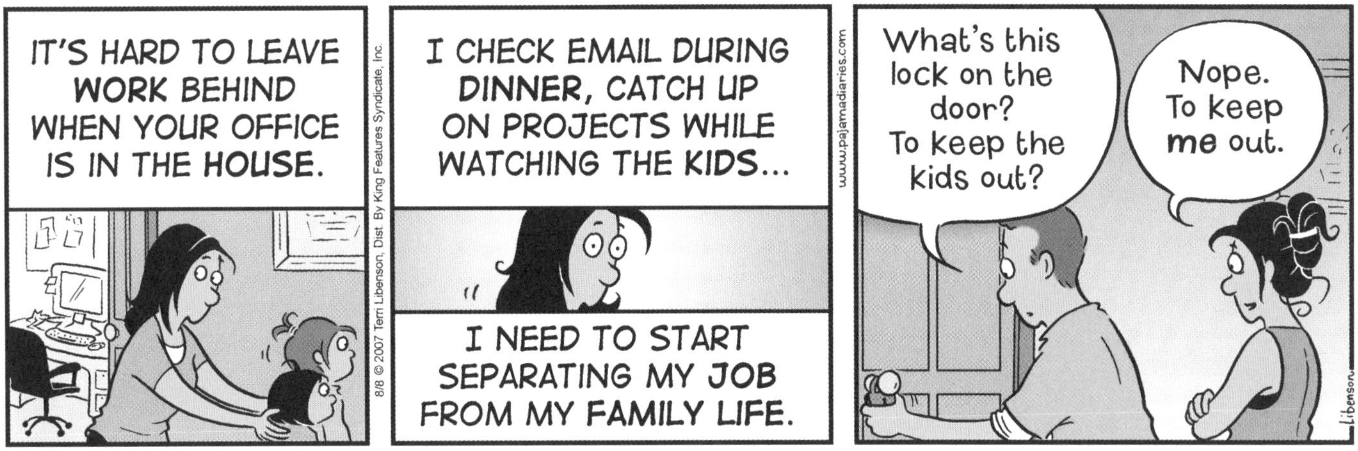
IT'S HARD TO LEAVE **WORK** BEHIND WHEN YOUR OFFICE IS IN THE **HOUSE**.
8/8 © 2007 Terri Libenson, Dist. By King Features Syndicate, Inc.
I CHECK EMAIL DURING **DINNER**, CATCH UP ON PROJECTS WHILE WATCHING THE **KIDS**...
I NEED TO START SEPARATING MY **JOB** FROM MY **FAMILY LIFE**.
www.pajamadiaries.com
What's this lock on the door? To keep the kids out?
Nope. To keep **me** out.
Libenson

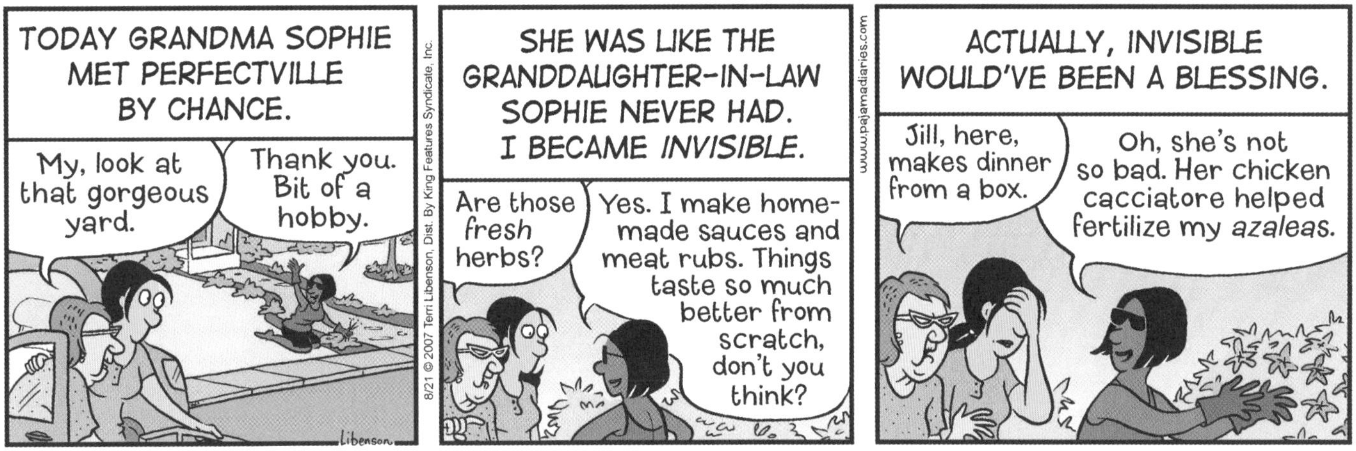
TODAY GRANDMA SOPHIE MET PERFECTVILLE BY CHANCE.
My, look at that gorgeous yard.
Thank you. Bit of a hobby.
Libenson
8/21 © 2007 Terri Libenson, Dist. By King Features Syndicate, Inc.
SHE WAS LIKE THE GRANDDAUGHTER-IN-LAW SOPHIE NEVER HAD. I BECAME *INVISIBLE*.
Are those *fresh* herbs?
Yes. I make home-made sauces and meat rubs. Things taste so much better from scratch, don't you think?
www.pajamadiaries.com
ACTUALLY, INVISIBLE WOULD'VE BEEN A BLESSING.
Jill, here, makes dinner from a box.
Oh, she's not so bad. Her chicken cacciatore helped fertilize my *azaleas*.

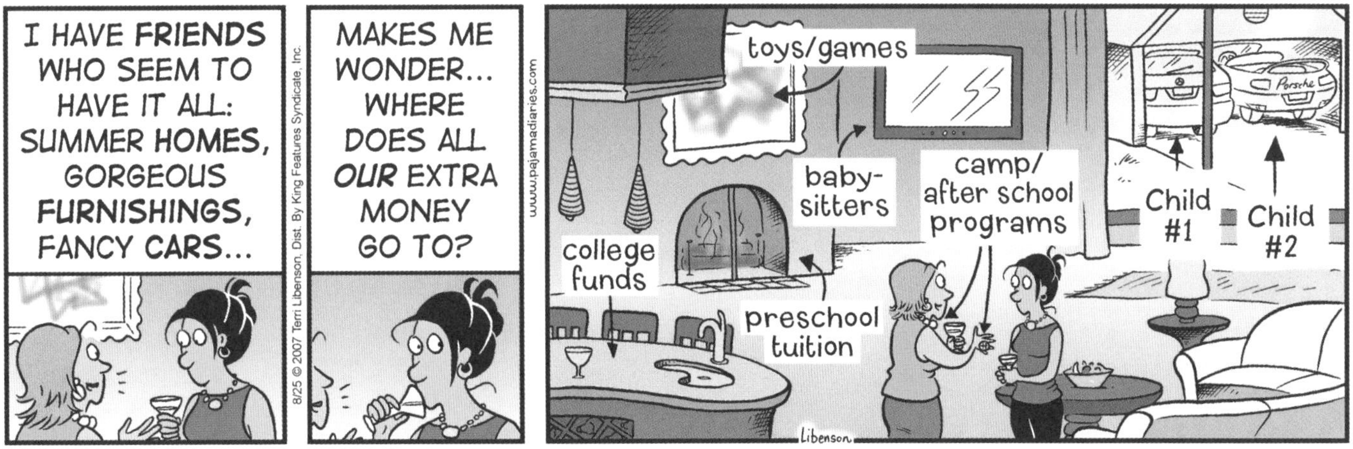
I HAVE **FRIENDS** WHO SEEM TO HAVE IT ALL: SUMMER **HOMES**, GORGEOUS **FURNISHINGS**, FANCY **CARS**...
8/25 © 2007 Terri Libenson, Dist. By King Features Syndicate, Inc.
MAKES ME WONDER... WHERE DOES ALL ***OUR*** EXTRA MONEY GO TO?
www.pajamadiaries.com
toys/games
baby-sitters
camp/ after school programs
Child #1
Child #2
Porsche
college funds
preschool tuition
Libenson

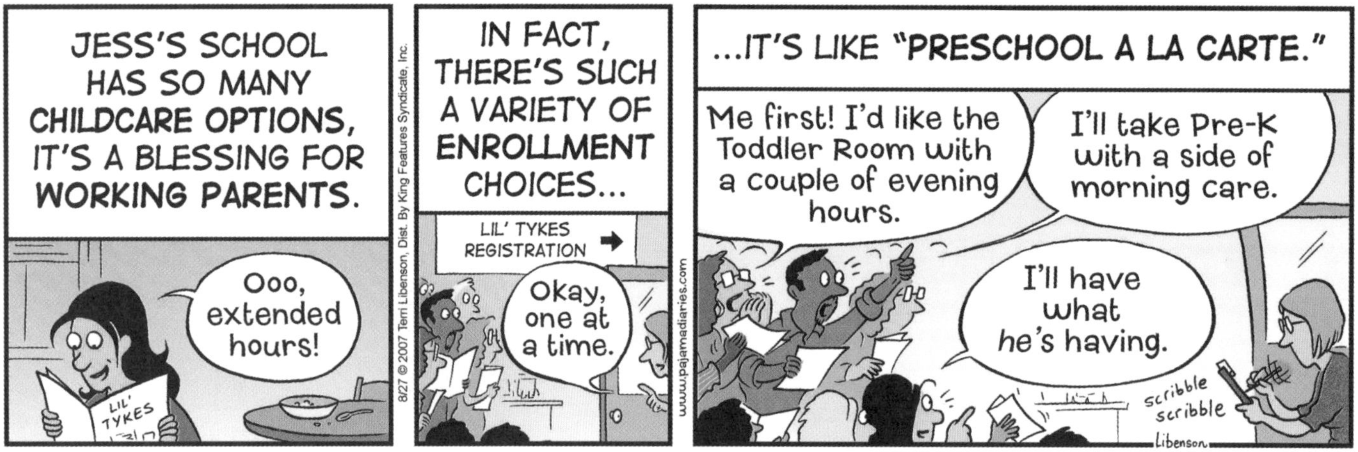
JESS'S SCHOOL HAS SO MANY CHILDCARE OPTIONS, IT'S A BLESSING FOR WORKING PARENTS.
Ooo, extended hours!
LIL' TYKES
8/27 © 2007 Terri Libenson, Dist. By King Features Syndicate, Inc.
IN FACT, THERE'S SUCH A VARIETY OF ENROLLMENT CHOICES...
LIL' TYKES REGISTRATION
Okay, one at a time.
www.pajamadiaries.com
...IT'S LIKE "PRESCHOOL A LA CARTE."
Me first! I'd like the Toddler Room with a couple of evening hours.
I'll take Pre-K with a side of morning care.
I'll have what he's having.
scribble scribble
Libenson

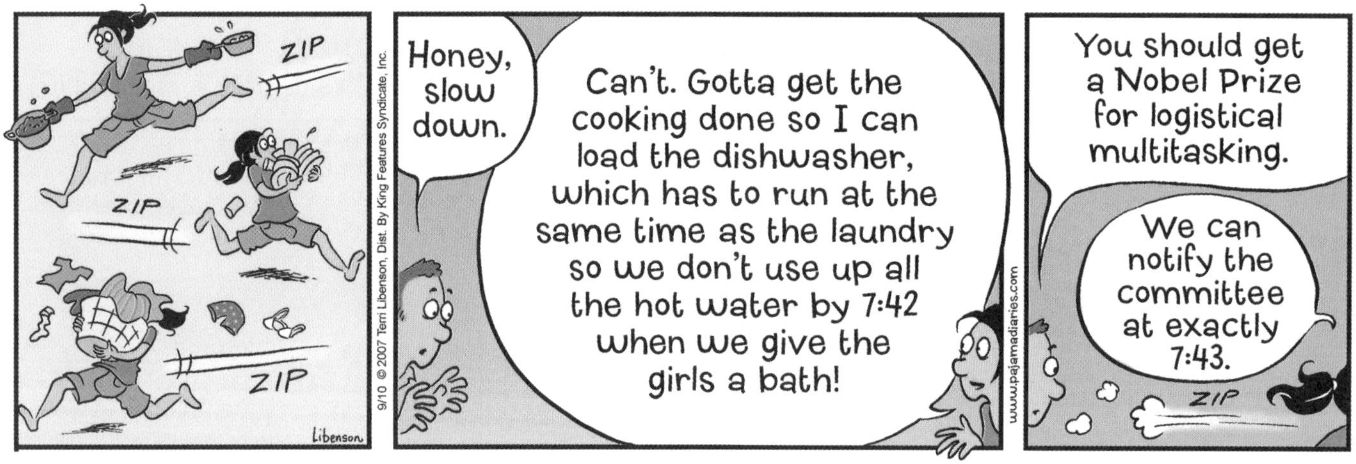
ZIP
ZIP
ZIP
Libenson
9/10 © 2007 Terri Libenson, Dist. By King Features Syndicate, Inc.
Honey, slow down.
Can't. Gotta get the cooking done so I can load the dishwasher, which has to run at the same time as the laundry so we don't use up all the hot water by 7:42 when we give the girls a bath!
www.pajamadiaries.com
You should get a Nobel Prize for logistical multitasking.
We can notify the committee at exactly 7:43.
ZIP

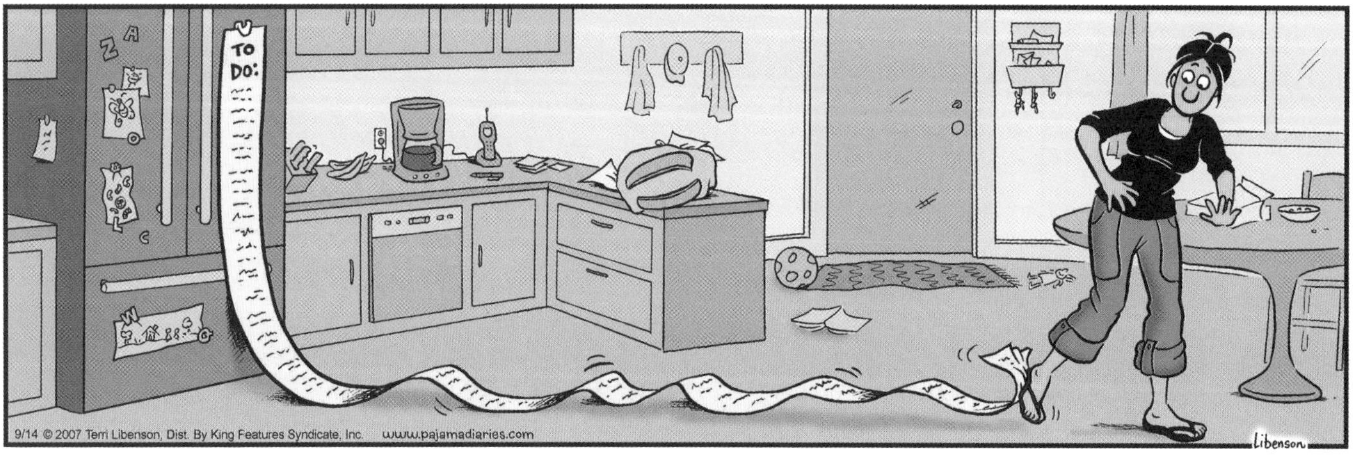
TO DO:
9/14 © 2007 Terri Libenson, Dist. By King Features Syndicate, Inc. www.pajamadiaries.com
Libenson

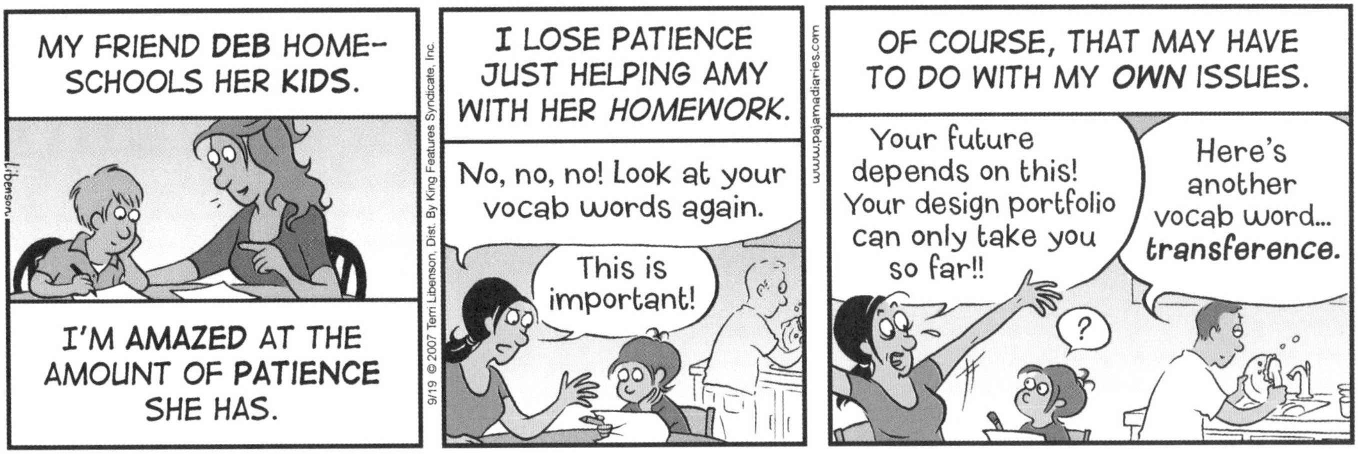
MY FRIEND DEB HOME-SCHOOLS HER KIDS.
Libenson
I'M AMAZED AT THE AMOUNT OF PATIENCE SHE HAS.
9/19 © 2007 Terri Libenson, Dist. By King Features Syndicate, Inc.
I LOSE PATIENCE JUST HELPING AMY WITH HER HOMEWORK.
No, no, no! Look at your vocab words again.
This is important!
www.pajamadiaries.com
OF COURSE, THAT MAY HAVE TO DO WITH MY OWN ISSUES.
Your future depends on this! Your design portfolio can only take you so far!!
Here's another vocab word... transference.
?

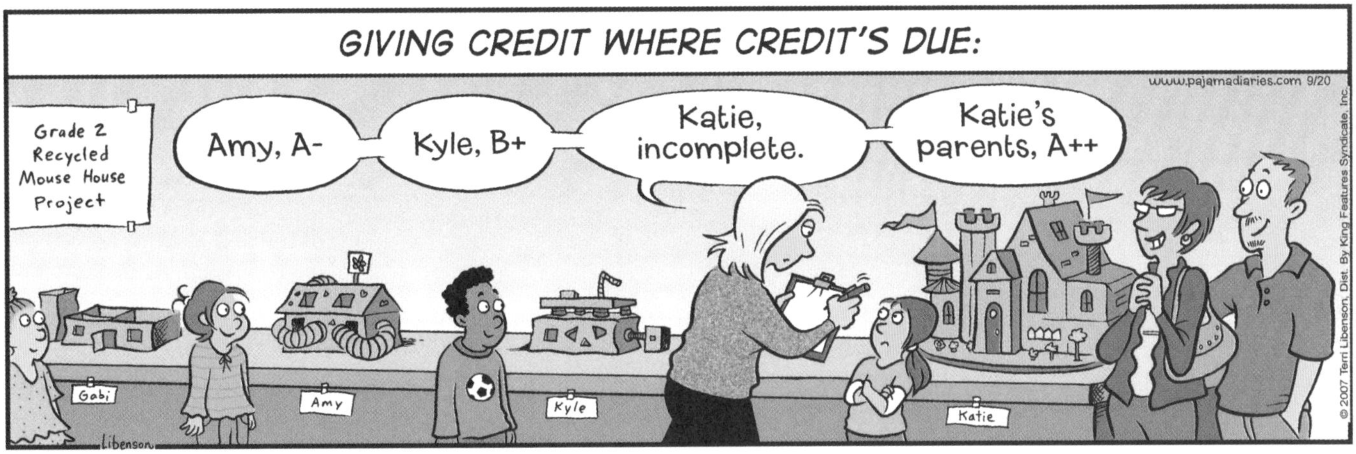
GIVING CREDIT WHERE CREDIT'S DUE:
www.pajamadiaries.com 9/20
Grade 2 Recycled Mouse House Project
Amy, A-
Kyle, B+
Katie, incomplete.
Katie's parents, A++
Gabi
Amy
Kyle
Katie
Libenson
© 2007 Terri Libenson, Dist. By King Features Syndicate, Inc.

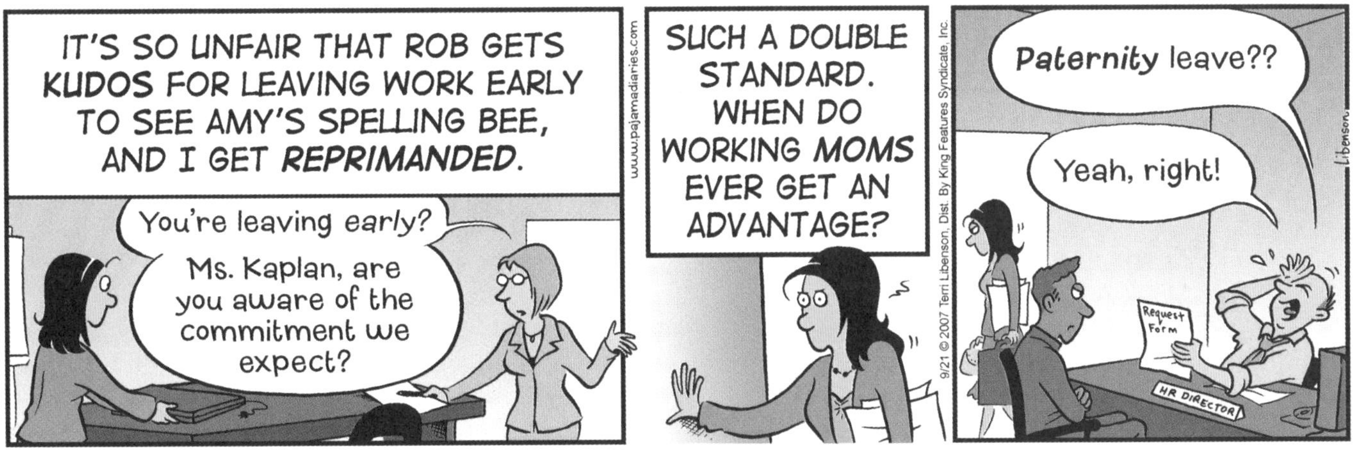
IT'S SO UNFAIR THAT ROB GETS KUDOS FOR LEAVING WORK EARLY TO SEE AMY'S SPELLING BEE, AND I GET REPRIMANDED.
You're leaving early?
Ms. Kaplan, are you aware of the commitment we expect?
www.pajamadiaries.com
SUCH A DOUBLE STANDARD. WHEN DO WORKING MOMS EVER GET AN ADVANTAGE?
9/21 © 2007 Terri Libenson, Dist. By King Features Syndicate, Inc.
Paternity leave??
Yeah, right!
Request Form
HR DIRECTOR
Libenson

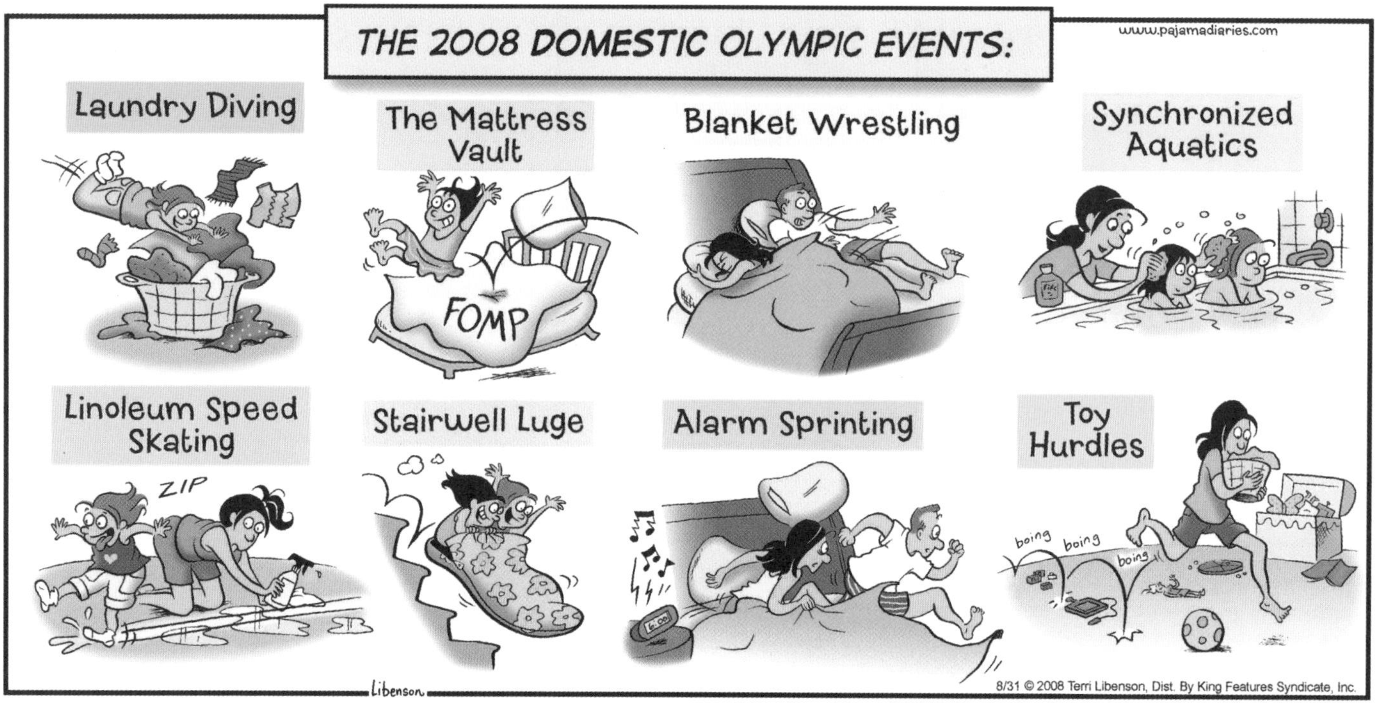
THE 2008 DOMESTIC OLYMPIC EVENTS:
www.pajamadiaries.com
Laundry Diving
The Mattress Vault
FOMP
Blanket Wrestling
Synchronized Aquatics
Linoleum Speed Skating
ZIP
Stairwell Luge
Alarm Sprinting
Toy Hurdles
boing
boing
boing
Libenson
8/31 © 2008 Terri Libenson, Dist. By King Features Syndicate, Inc.

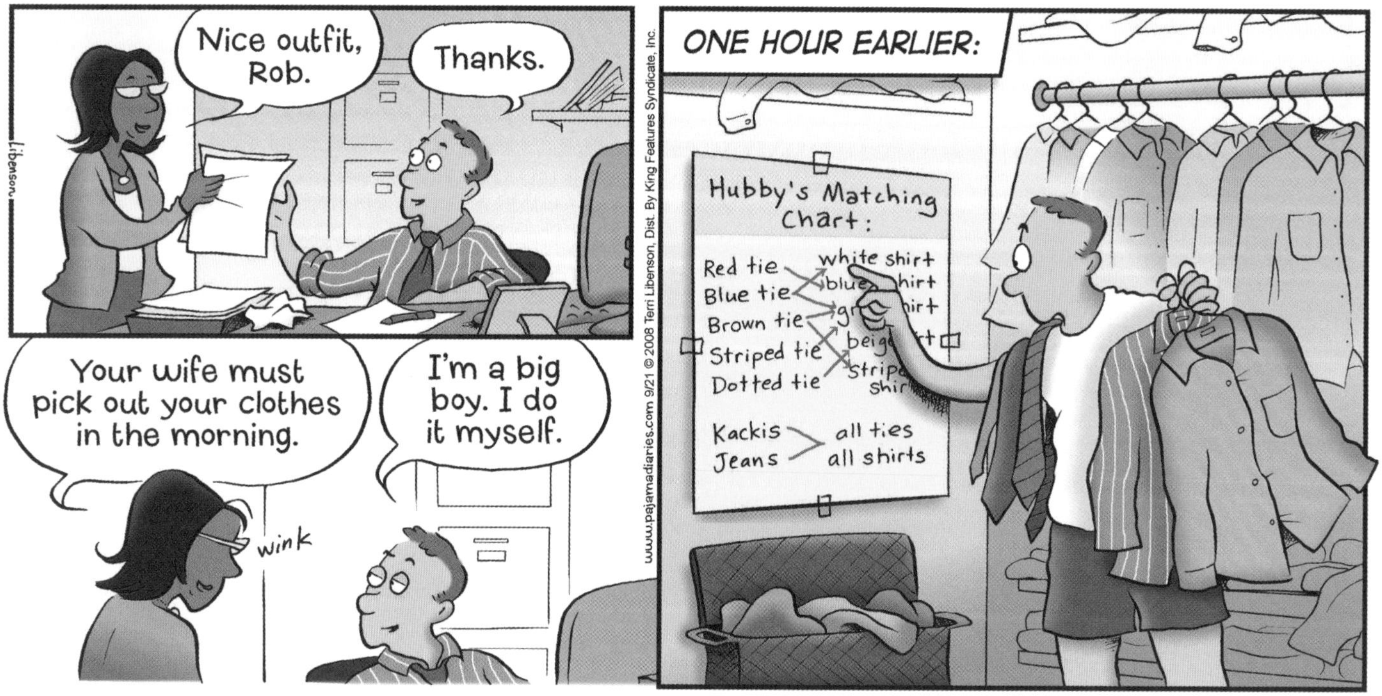
Nice outfit, Rob.
Thanks.
Libenson
Your wife must pick out your clothes in the morning.
I'm a big boy. I do it myself.
wink
www.pajamadiaries.com 9/21 © 2008 Terri Libenson, Dist. By King Features Syndicate, Inc.
ONE HOUR EARLIER:
Hubby's Matching Chart:
Red tie
Blue tie
Brown tie
Striped tie
Dotted tie
white shirt
Kackis
Jeans
all ties
all shirts

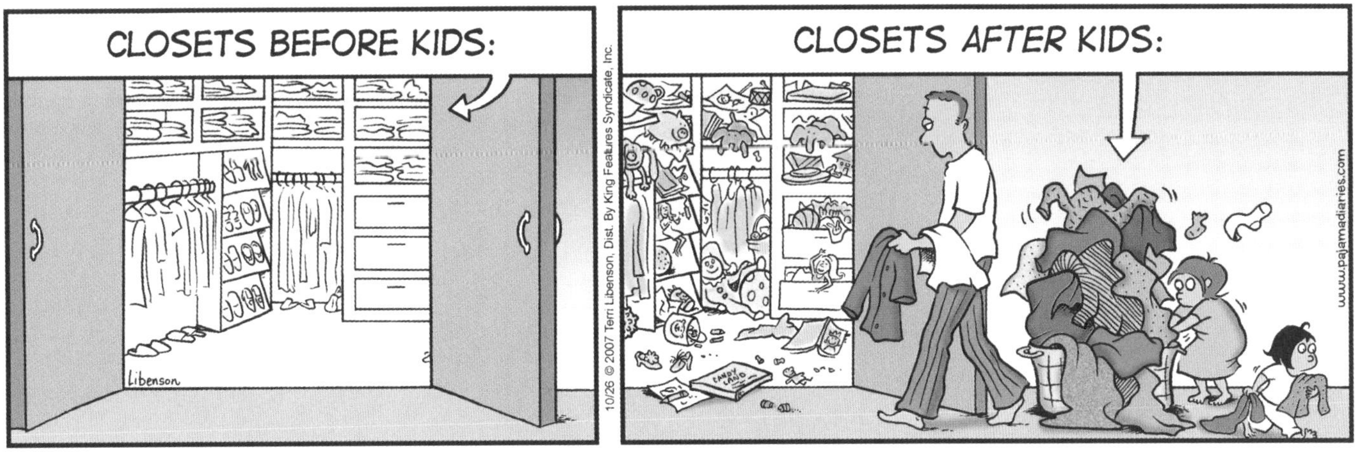
CLOSETS BEFORE KIDS:
CLOSETS AFTER KIDS:
Libenson
10/26 © 2007 Terri Libenson, Dist. By King Features Syndicate, Inc.
www.pajamadiaries.com

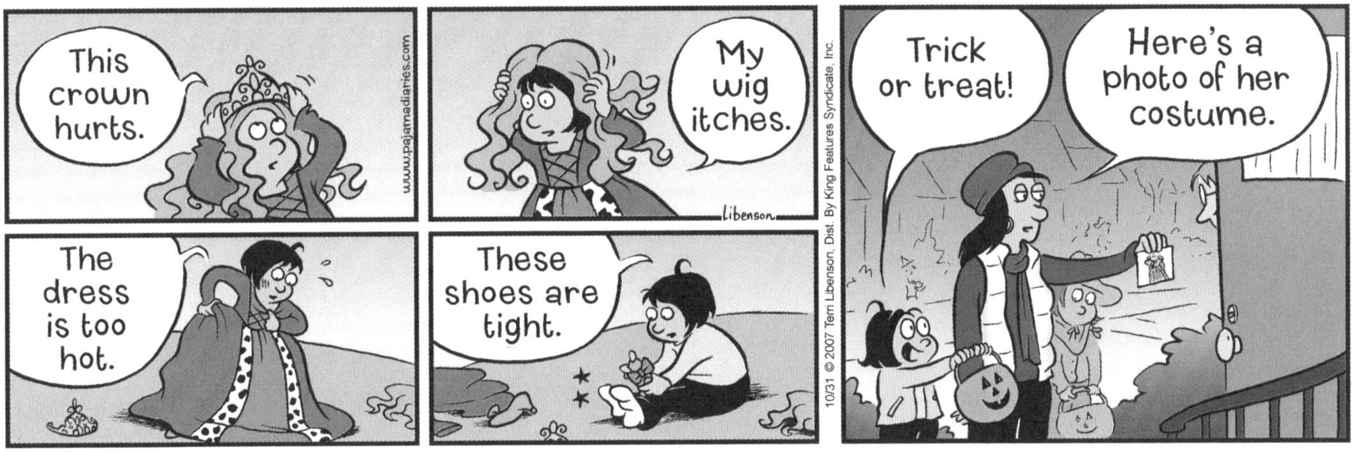
This crown hurts.
My wig itches.
The dress is too hot.
These shoes are tight.
Trick or treat!
Here's a photo of her costume.
www.pajamadiaries.com
Libenson
10/31 © 2007 Terri Libenson, Dist. By King Features Syndicate, Inc.

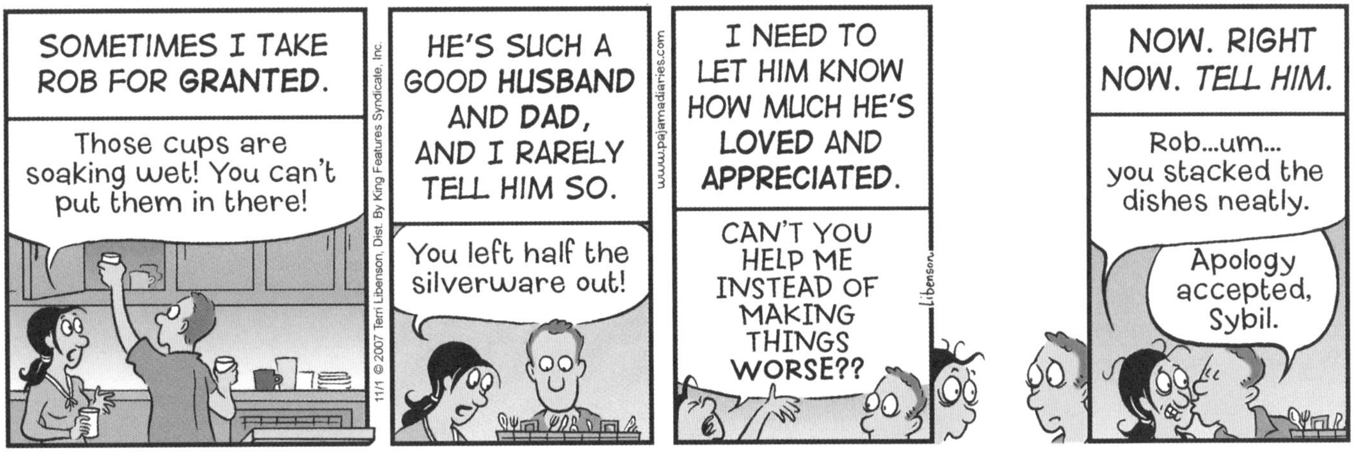
SOMETIMES I TAKE ROB FOR GRANTED.
Those cups are soaking wet! You can't put them in there!
HE'S SUCH A GOOD HUSBAND AND DAD, AND I RARELY TELL HIM SO.
You left half the silverware out!
I NEED TO LET HIM KNOW HOW MUCH HE'S LOVED AND APPRECIATED.
CAN'T YOU HELP ME INSTEAD OF MAKING THINGS WORSE??
NOW. RIGHT NOW. TELL HIM.
Rob...um... you stacked the dishes neatly.
Apology accepted, Sybil.
11/1 © 2007 Terri Libenson, Dist. By King Features Syndicate, Inc.
www.pajamadiaries.com
Libenson

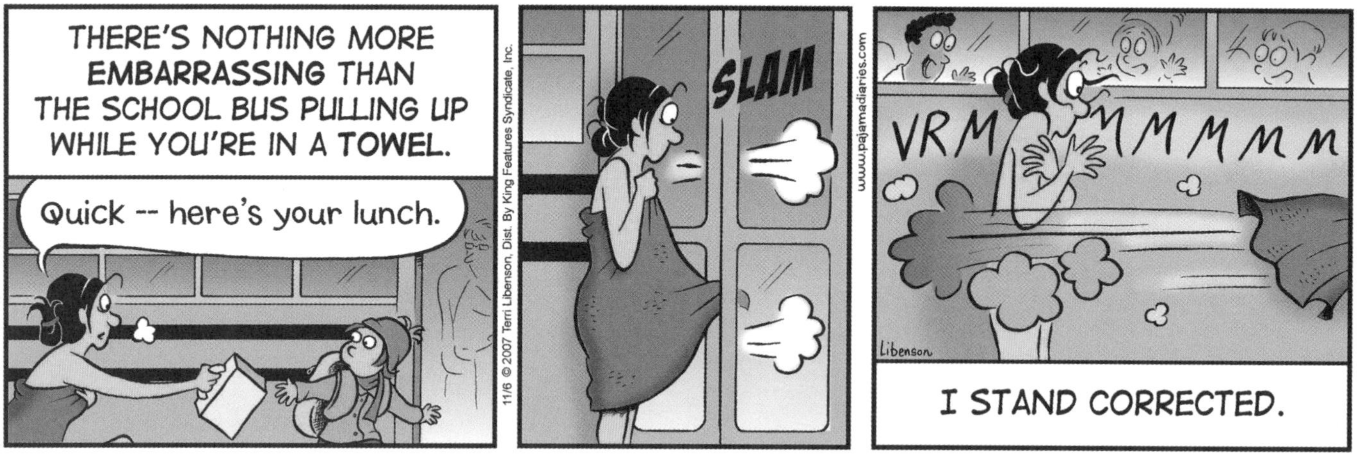
THERE'S NOTHING MORE EMBARRASSING THAN THE SCHOOL BUS PULLING UP WHILE YOU'RE IN A TOWEL.
Quick -- here's your lunch.
11/6 © 2007 Terri Libenson, Dist. By King Features Syndicate, Inc.
SLAM
www.pajamadiaries.com
VRMMMMMMM
Libenson
I STAND CORRECTED.

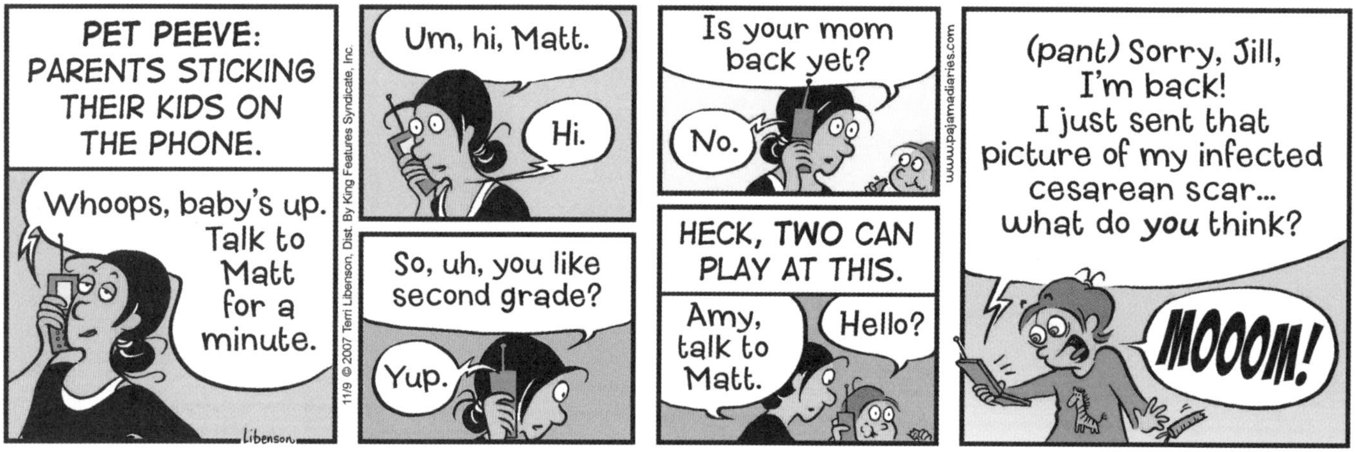
PET PEEVE: PARENTS STICKING THEIR KIDS ON THE PHONE.
Whoops, baby's up. Talk to Matt for a minute.
Libenson
11/9 © 2007 Terri Libenson, Dist. By King Features Syndicate, Inc.
Um, hi, Matt.
Hi.
So, uh, you like second grade?
Yup.
Is your mom back yet?
No.
HECK, TWO CAN PLAY AT THIS.
Amy, talk to Matt.
Hello?
www.pajamadiaries.com
(pant) Sorry, Jill, I'm back! I just sent that picture of my infected cesarean scar... what do you think?
MOOOM!

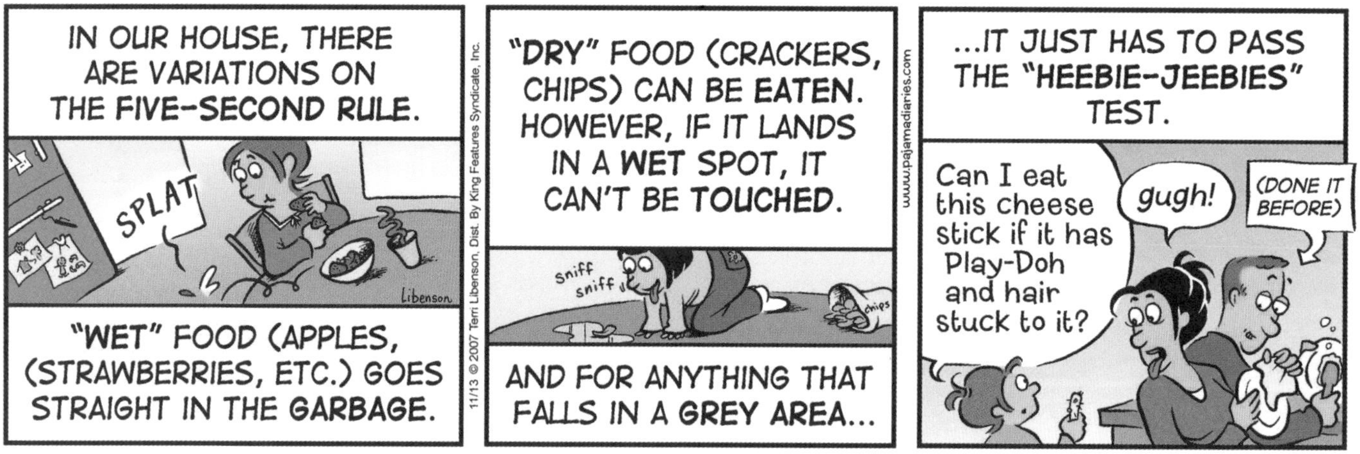
IN OUR HOUSE, THERE ARE VARIATIONS ON THE FIVE-SECOND RULE.
SPLAT
Libenson
"WET" FOOD (APPLES, (STRAWBERRIES, ETC.) GOES STRAIGHT IN THE GARBAGE.
11/13 © 2007 Terri Libenson, Dist. By King Features Syndicate, Inc.
"DRY" FOOD (CRACKERS, CHIPS) CAN BE EATEN. HOWEVER, IF IT LANDS IN A WET SPOT, IT CAN'T BE TOUCHED.
sniff sniff
chips
AND FOR ANYTHING THAT FALLS IN A GREY AREA...
www.pajamadiaries.com
...IT JUST HAS TO PASS THE "HEEBIE-JEEBIES" TEST.
Can I eat this cheese stick if it has Play-Doh and hair stuck to it?
gugh!
(DONE IT BEFORE)

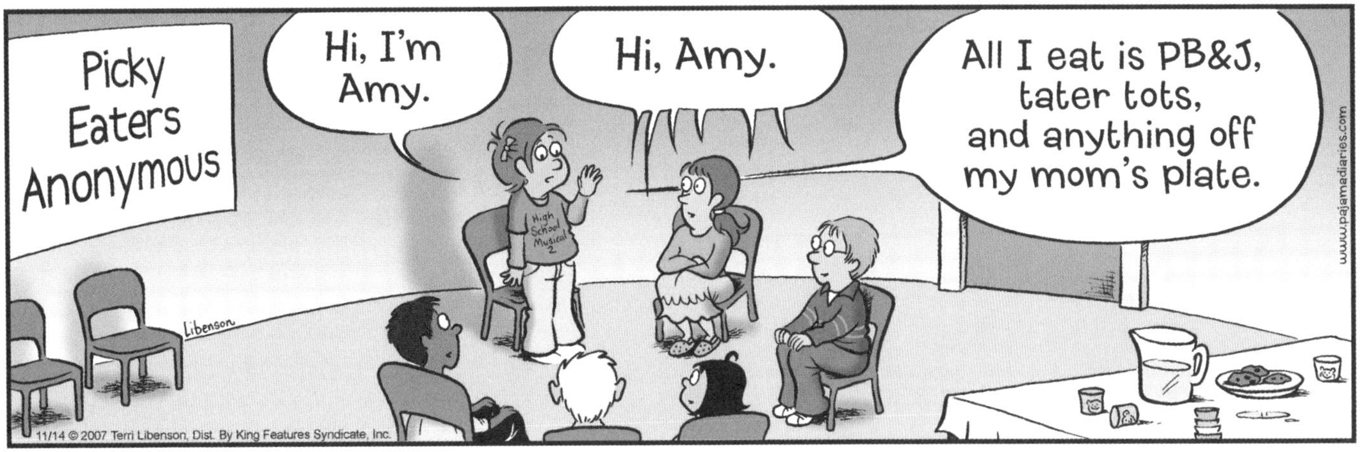
Picky Eaters Anonymous
Hi, I'm Amy.
Hi, Amy.
All I eat is PB&J, tater tots, and anything off my mom's plate.
High School Musical 2
Libenson
www.pajamadiaries.com
11/14 © 2007 Terri Libenson, Dist. By King Features Syndicate, Inc.

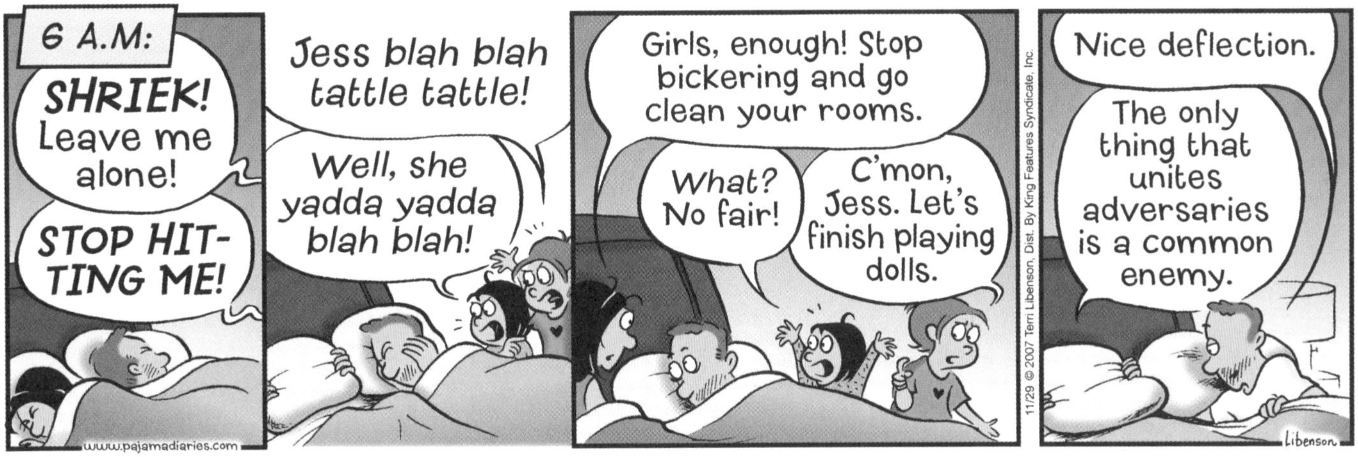
6 A.M:
SHRIEK! Leave me alone!
STOP HIT-TING ME!
www.pajamadiaries.com
Jess blah blah tattle tattle!
Well, she yadda yadda blah blah!
Girls, enough! Stop bickering and go clean your rooms.
What? No fair!
C'mon, Jess. Let's finish playing dolls.
11/29 © 2007 Terri Libenson, Dist. By King Features Syndicate, Inc.
Nice deflection.
The only thing that unites adversaries is a common enemy.
Libenson

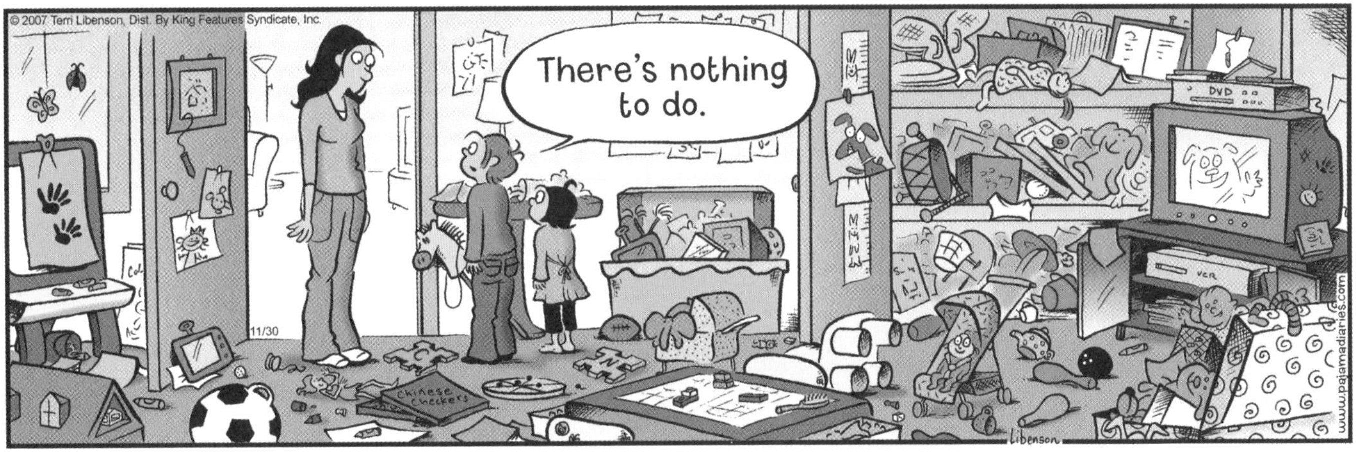
© 2007 Terri Libenson, Dist. By King Features Syndicate, Inc.
There's nothing to do.
11/30
Chinese Checkers
DVD
VCR
Libenson
www.pajamadiaries.com

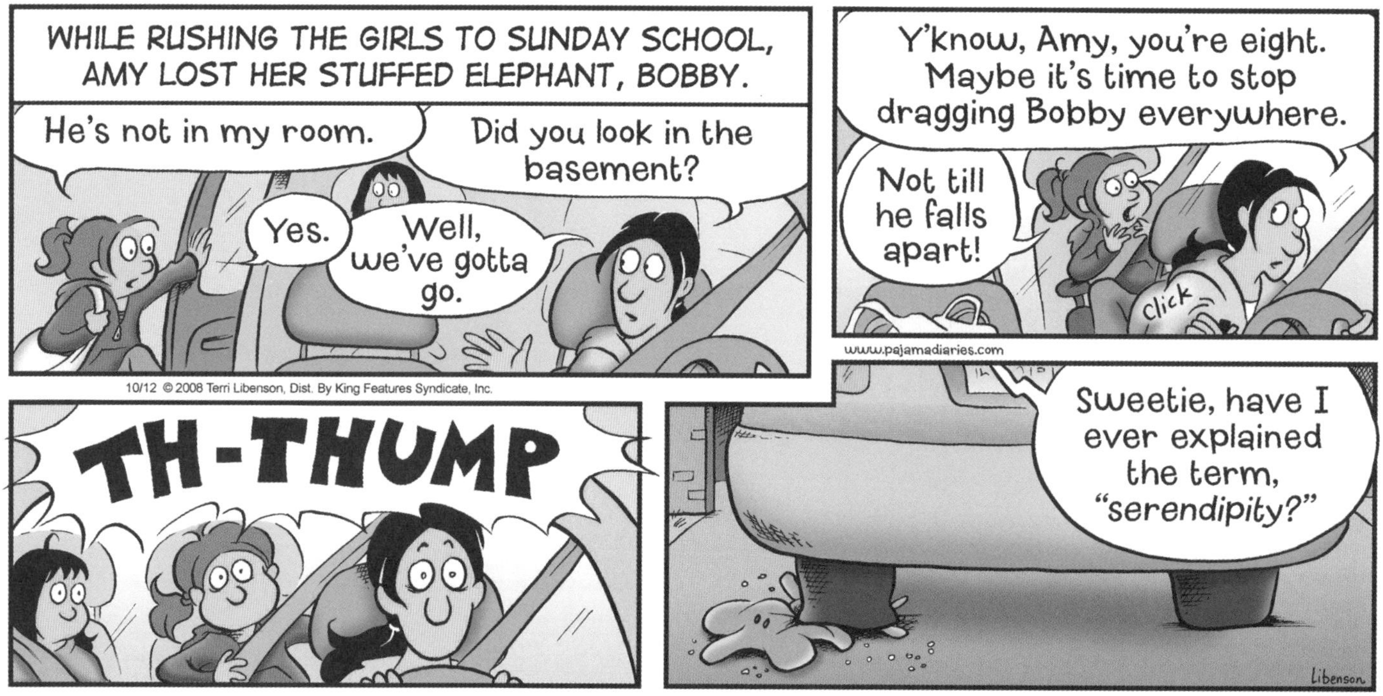
WHILE RUSHING THE GIRLS TO SUNDAY SCHOOL, AMY LOST HER STUFFED ELEPHANT, BOBBY.
He's not in my room.
Did you look in the basement?
Yes.
Well, we've gotta go.
10/12 © 2008 Terri Libenson, Dist. By King Features Syndicate, Inc.
Y'know, Amy, you're eight. Maybe it's time to stop dragging Bobby everywhere.
Not till he falls apart!
Click
www.pajamadiaries.com
TH-THUMP
Sweetie, have I ever explained the term, "serendipity?"
Libenson

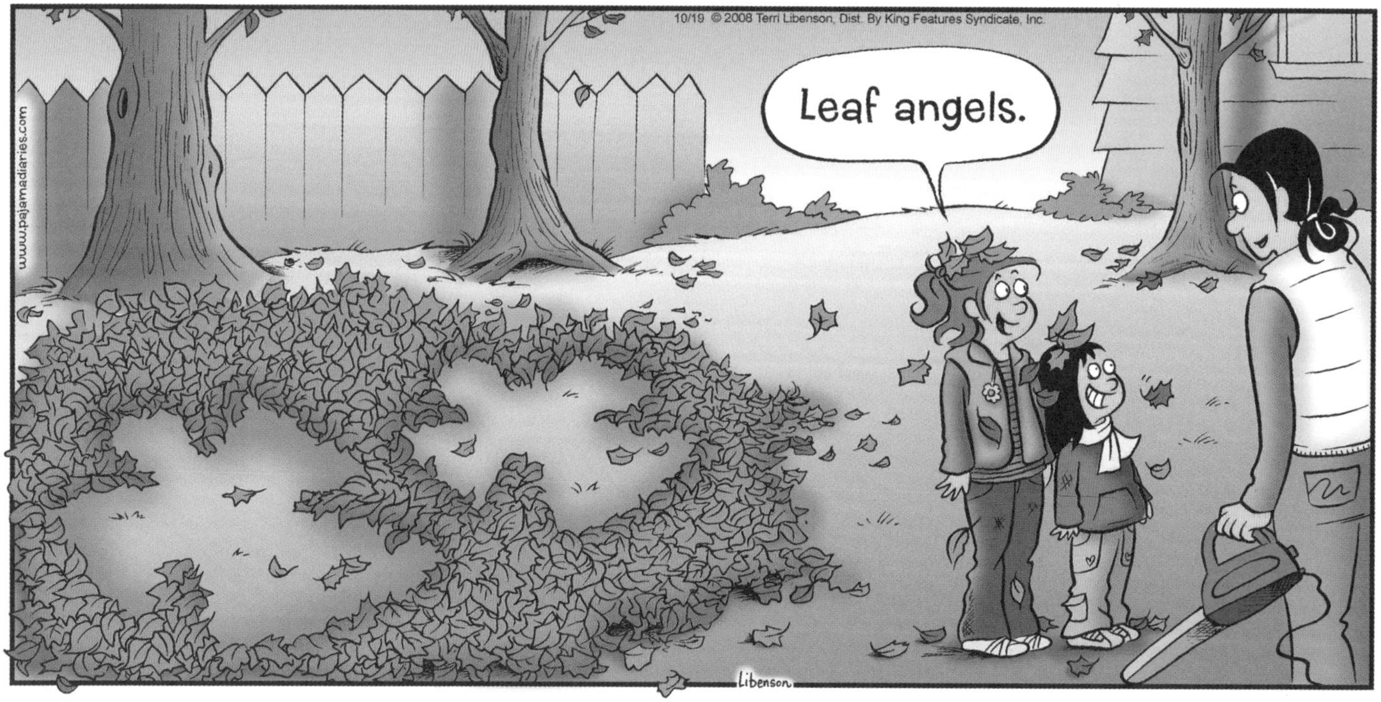
10/19 © 2008 Terri Libenson, Dist. By King Features Syndicate, Inc.
www.pajamadiaries.com
Leaf angels.
Libenson

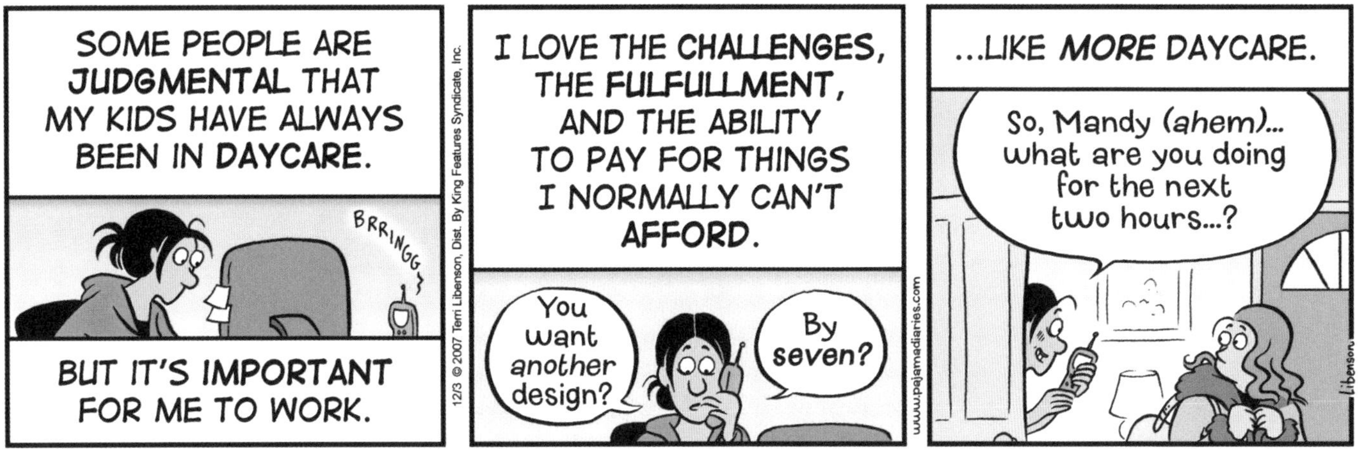
SOME PEOPLE ARE JUDGMENTAL THAT MY KIDS HAVE ALWAYS BEEN IN DAYCARE.
BRRINGG
BUT IT'S IMPORTANT FOR ME TO WORK.
12/3 © 2007 Terri Libenson, Dist. By King Features Syndicate, Inc.
I LOVE THE CHALLENGES, THE FULFULLMENT, AND THE ABILITY TO PAY FOR THINGS I NORMALLY CAN'T AFFORD.
You want another design?
By seven?
www.pajamadiaries.com
...LIKE MORE DAYCARE.
So, Mandy (ahem)... what are you doing for the next two hours...?
Libenson

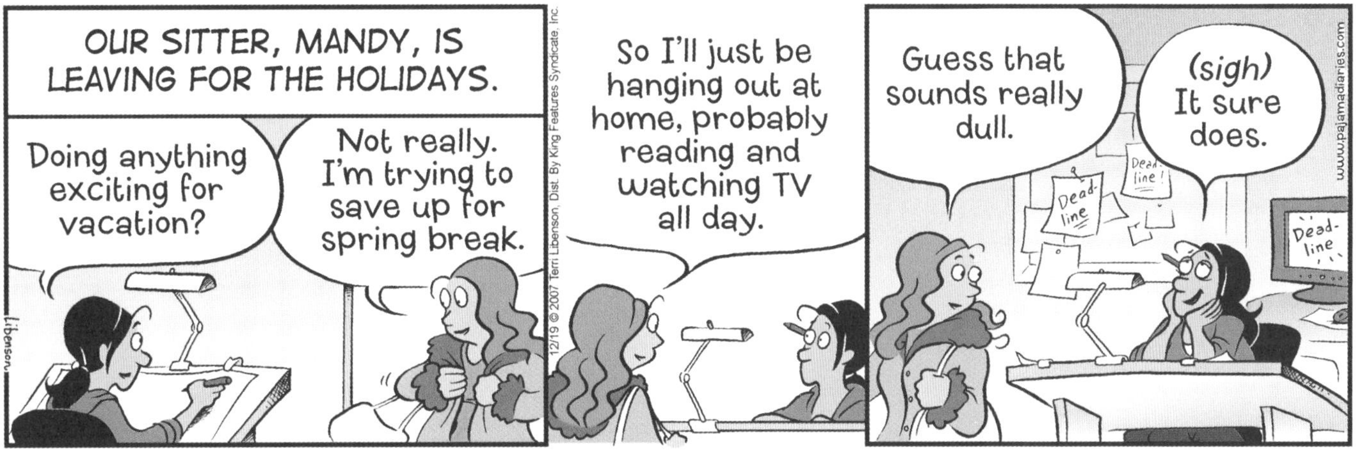
OUR SITTER, MANDY, IS LEAVING FOR THE HOLIDAYS.
Doing anything exciting for vacation?
Not really. I'm trying to save up for spring break.
Libenson
12/19 © 2007 Terri Libenson, Dist. By King Features Syndicate, Inc.
So I'll just be hanging out at home, probably reading and watching TV all day.
Guess that sounds really dull.
(sigh) It sure does.
Deadline
Deadline!
Deadline
www.pajamadiaries.com

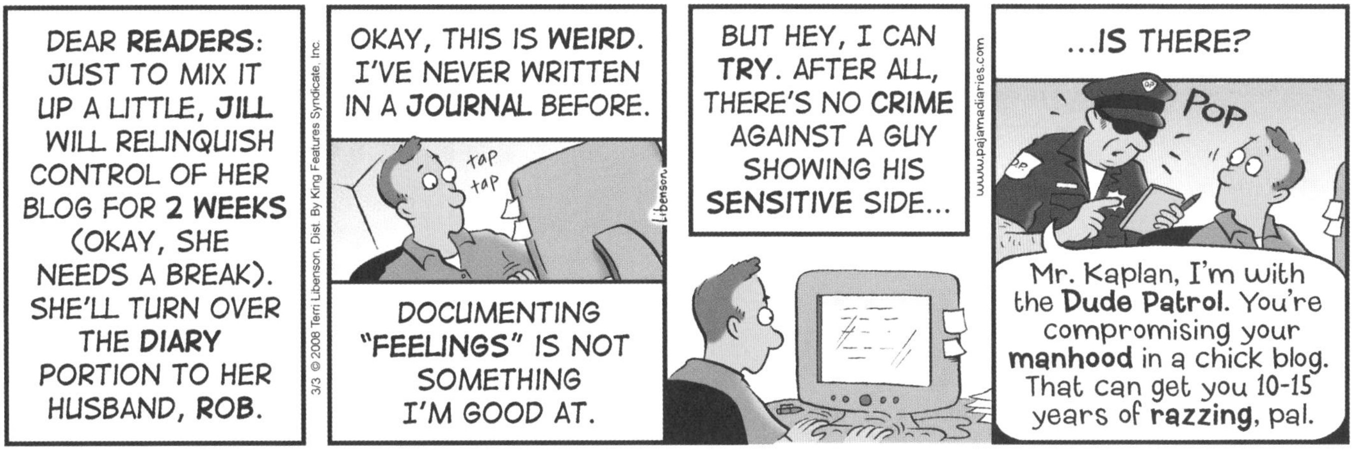
DEAR READERS: JUST TO MIX IT UP A LITTLE, JILL WILL RELINQUISH CONTROL OF HER BLOG FOR 2 WEEKS (OKAY, SHE NEEDS A BREAK). SHE'LL TURN OVER THE DIARY PORTION TO HER HUSBAND, ROB.
3/3 © 2008 Terri Libenson, Dist. By King Features Syndicate, Inc.
OKAY, THIS IS WEIRD. I'VE NEVER WRITTEN IN A JOURNAL BEFORE.
tap tap
Libenson
DOCUMENTING "FEELINGS" IS NOT SOMETHING I'M GOOD AT.
BUT HEY, I CAN TRY. AFTER ALL, THERE'S NO CRIME AGAINST A GUY SHOWING HIS SENSITIVE SIDE...
www.pajamadiaries.com
...IS THERE?
POP
Mr. Kaplan, I'm with the Dude Patrol. You're compromising your manhood in a chick blog. That can get you 10-15 years of razzing, pal.

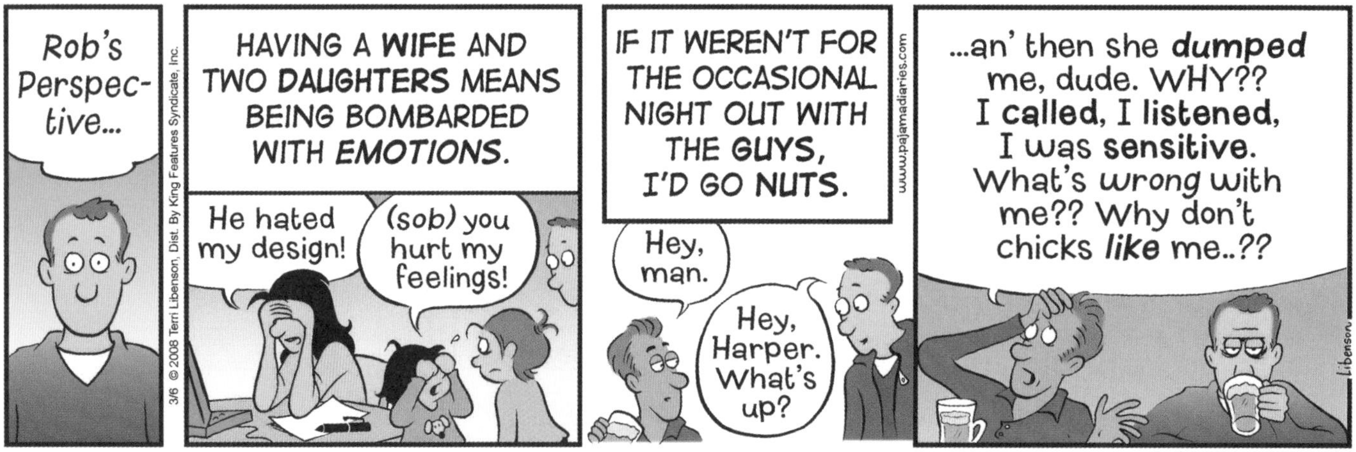
Rob's Perspective...
3/6 © 2008 Terri Libenson, Dist. By King Features Syndicate, Inc.
HAVING A **WIFE** AND TWO **DAUGHTERS** MEANS BEING BOMBARDED WITH ***EMOTIONS***.
He hated my design!
(sob) you hurt my feelings!
IF IT WEREN'T FOR THE OCCASIONAL NIGHT OUT WITH THE **GUYS**, I'D GO **NUTS**.
Hey, man.
Hey, Harper. What's up?
www.pajamadiaries.com
...an' then she **dumped** me, dude. WHY?? I **called**, I **listened**, I was **sensitive**. What's *wrong* with me?? Why don't chicks ***like*** me..??
Libenson

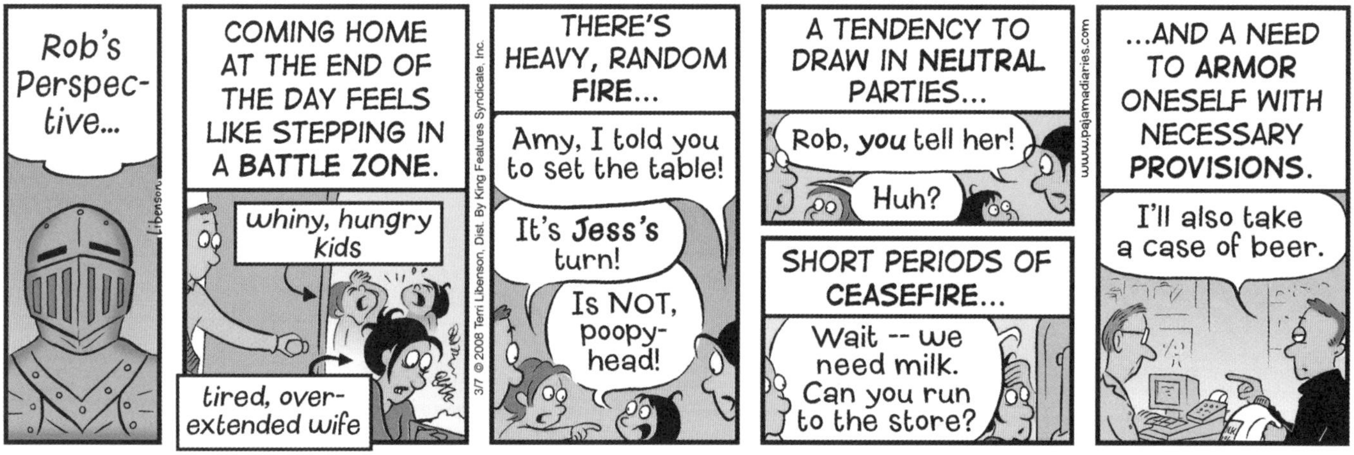
Rob's Perspective...
Libenson
COMING HOME AT THE END OF THE DAY FEELS LIKE STEPPING IN A **BATTLE ZONE**.
whiny, hungry kids
tired, over-extended wife
3/7 © 2008 Terri Libenson, Dist. By King Features Syndicate, Inc.
THERE'S HEAVY, RANDOM **FIRE**...
Amy, I told you to set the table!
It's **Jess's** turn!
Is NOT, poopy-head!
A TENDENCY TO DRAW IN **NEUTRAL** PARTIES...
Rob, ***you*** tell her!
Huh?
SHORT PERIODS OF **CEASEFIRE**...
Wait -- we need milk. Can you run to the store?
www.pajamadiaries.com
...AND A NEED TO **ARMOR** ONESELF WITH NECESSARY **PROVISIONS**.
I'll also take a case of beer.

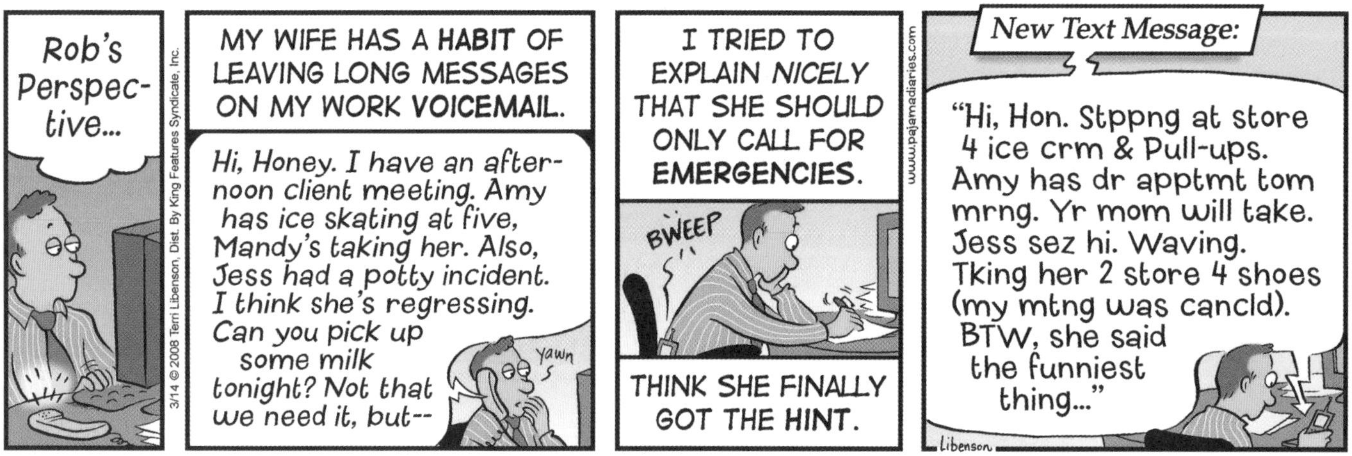
Rob's Perspective...
3/14 © 2008 Terri Libenson, Dist. By King Features Syndicate, Inc.
MY WIFE HAS A **HABIT** OF LEAVING LONG MESSAGES ON MY WORK **VOICEMAIL**.
Hi, Honey. I have an afternoon client meeting. Amy has ice skating at five, Mandy's taking her. Also, Jess had a potty incident. I think she's regressing. Can you pick up some milk tonight? Not that we need it, but--
yawn
I TRIED TO EXPLAIN *NICELY* THAT SHE SHOULD ONLY CALL FOR **EMERGENCIES**.
BWEEP
THINK SHE FINALLY GOT THE **HINT**.
www.pajamadiaries.com
New Text Message:
"Hi, Hon. Stppng at store 4 ice crm & Pull-ups. Amy has dr apptmt tom mrng. Yr mom will take. Jess sez hi. Waving. Tking her 2 store 4 shoes (my mtng was cancld). BTW, she said the funniest thing..."
Libenson

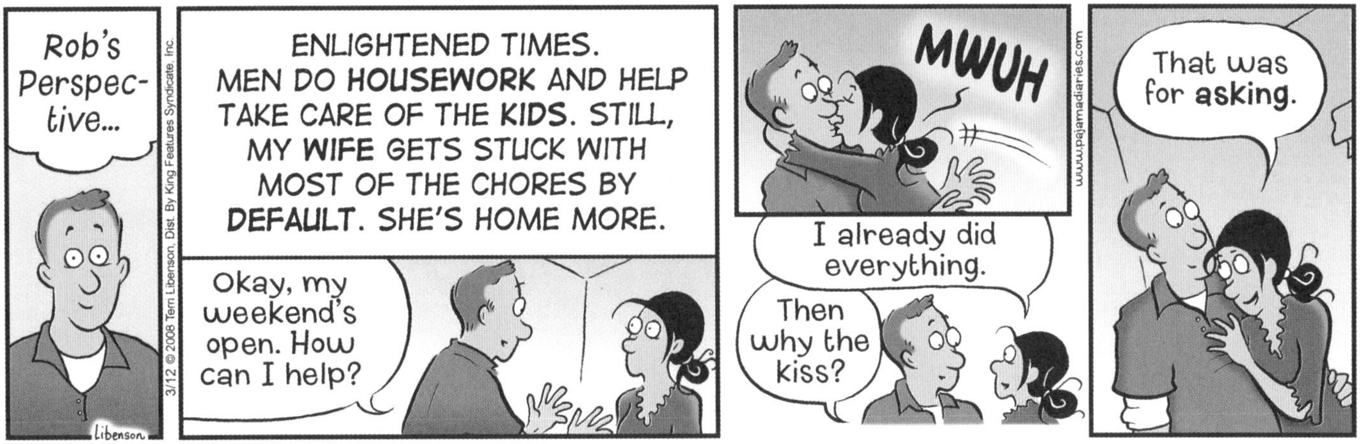
Rob's Perspective...
3/12 © 2008 Terri Libenson, Dist. By King Features Syndicate, Inc.
Libenson
ENLIGHTENED TIMES. MEN DO **HOUSEWORK** AND HELP TAKE CARE OF THE **KIDS**. STILL, MY **WIFE** GETS STUCK WITH MOST OF THE CHORES BY **DEFAULT**. SHE'S HOME MORE.
Okay, my weekend's open. How can I help?
MWUH
I already did everything.
Then why the kiss?
www.pajamadiaries.com
That was for **asking**.

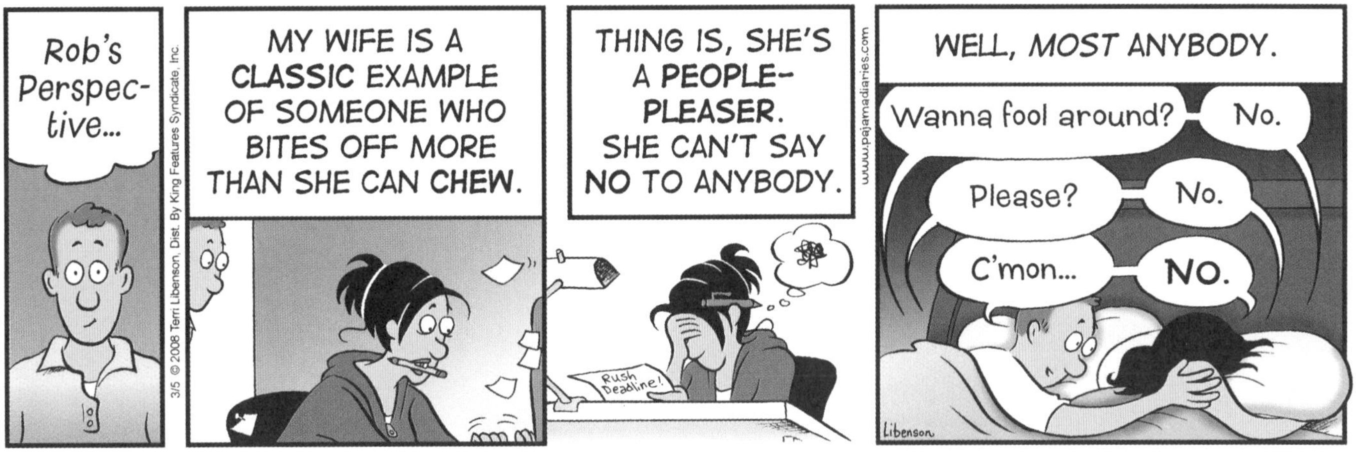
Rob's Perspective...
3/5 © 2008 Terri Libenson, Dist. By King Features Syndicate, Inc.
MY WIFE IS A **CLASSIC** EXAMPLE OF SOMEONE WHO BITES OFF MORE THAN SHE CAN **CHEW**.
THING IS, SHE'S A **PEOPLE-PLEASER**. SHE CAN'T SAY **NO** TO ANYBODY.
Rush Deadline!
www.pajamadiaries.com
WELL, *MOST* ANYBODY.
Wanna fool around?
No.
Please?
No.
C'mon...
NO.
Libenson

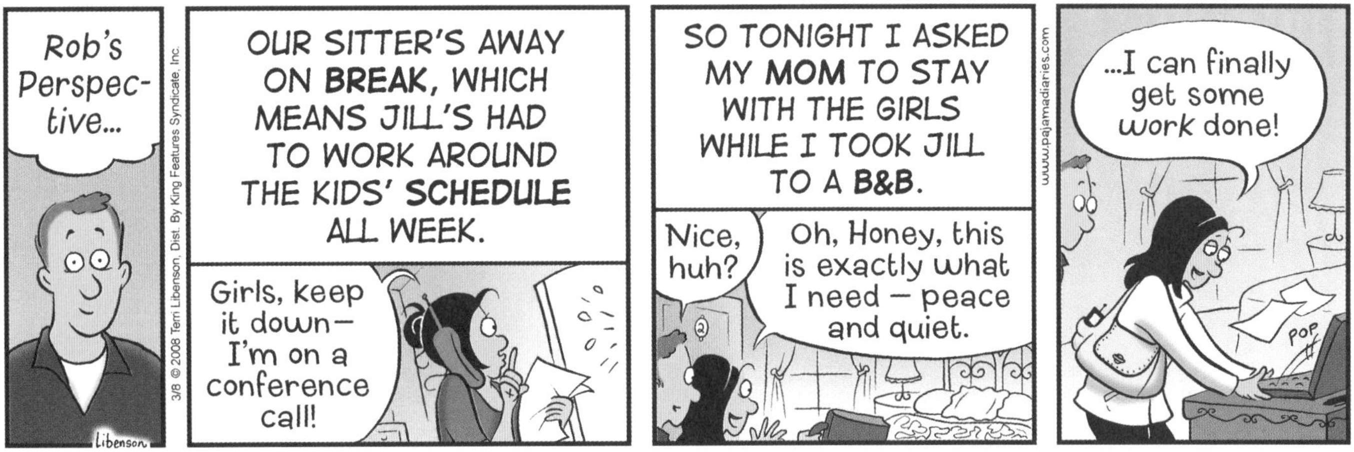
Rob's Perspective...
3/8 © 2008 Terri Libenson, Dist. By King Features Syndicate, Inc.
Libenson
OUR SITTER'S AWAY ON **BREAK**, WHICH MEANS JILL'S HAD TO WORK AROUND THE KIDS' **SCHEDULE** ALL WEEK.
Girls, keep it down— I'm on a conference call!
SO TONIGHT I ASKED MY **MOM** TO STAY WITH THE GIRLS WHILE I TOOK JILL TO A **B&B**.
Nice, huh?
Oh, Honey, this is exactly what I need — peace and quiet.
www.pajamadiaries.com
...I can finally get some *work* done!
POP

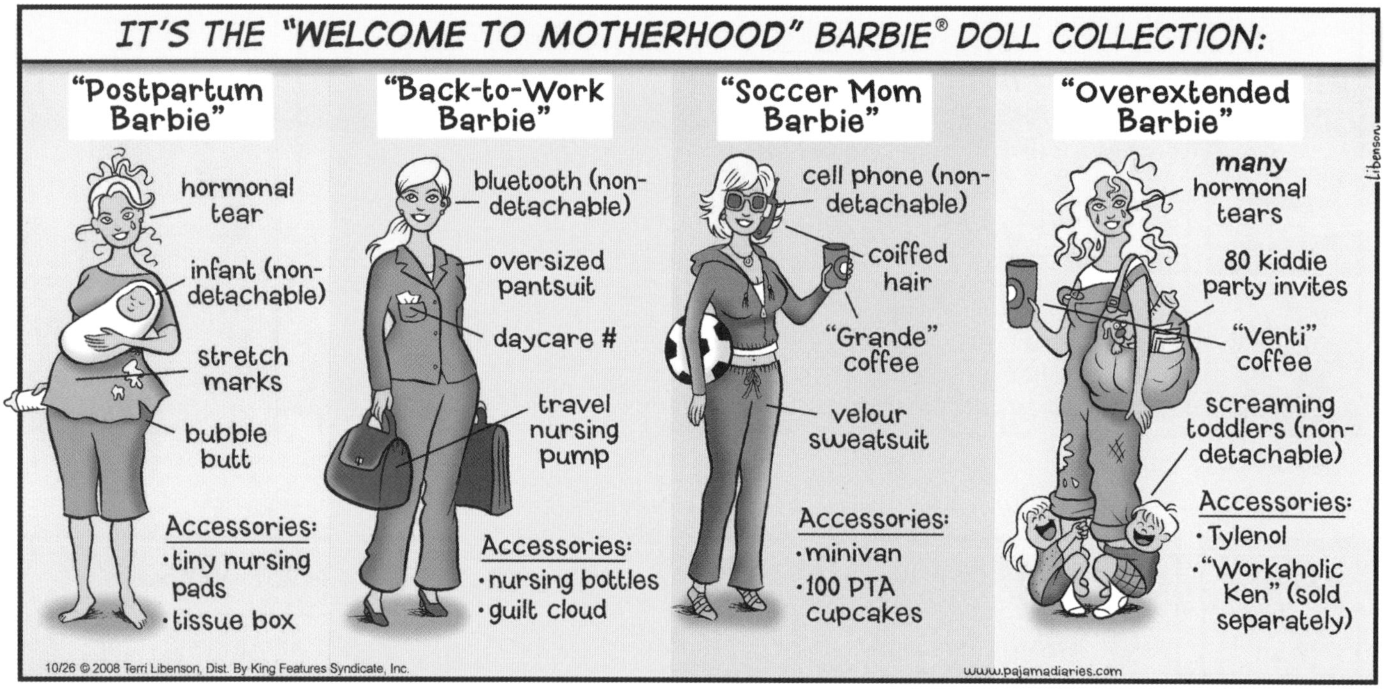
IT'S THE "WELCOME TO MOTHERHOOD" BARBIE® DOLL COLLECTION:
"Postpartum Barbie"
hormonal tear
infant (non-detachable)
stretch marks
bubble butt
Accessories:
·tiny nursing pads
·tissue box
"Back-to-Work Barbie"
bluetooth (non-detachable)
oversized pantsuit
daycare #
travel nursing pump
Accessories:
·nursing bottles
·guilt cloud
"Soccer Mom Barbie"
cell phone (non-detachable)
coiffed hair
"Grande" coffee
velour sweatsuit
Accessories:
·minivan
·100 PTA cupcakes
"Overextended Barbie"
many hormonal tears
80 kiddie party invites
"Venti" coffee
screaming toddlers (non-detachable)
Accessories:
·Tylenol
·"Workaholic Ken" (sold separately)
Libenson
10/26 © 2008 Terri Libenson, Dist. By King Features Syndicate, Inc.
www.pajamadiaries.com

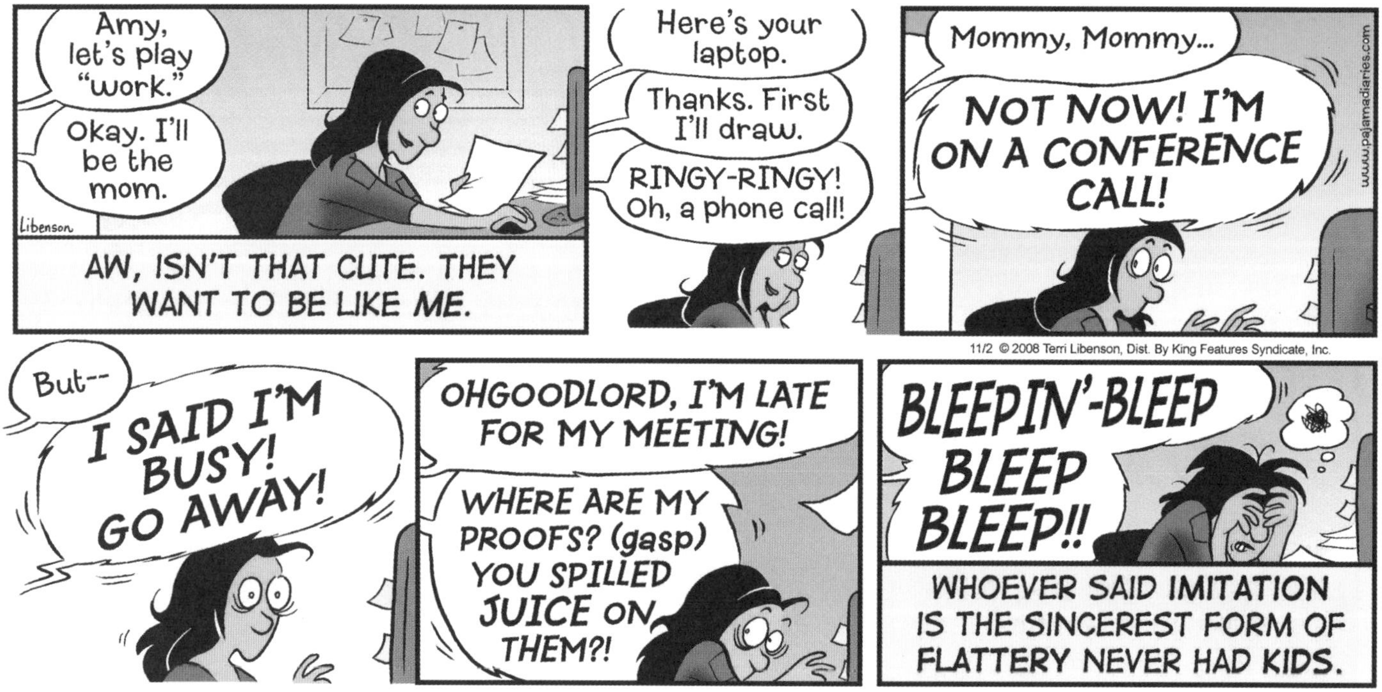
Amy, let's play "work."
Okay. I'll be the mom.
Libenson
AW, ISN'T THAT CUTE. THEY WANT TO BE LIKE ME.
Here's your laptop.
Thanks. First I'll draw.
RINGY-RINGY! Oh, a phone call!
Mommy, Mommy...
NOT NOW! I'M ON A CONFERENCE CALL!
www.pajamadiaries.com
11/2 © 2008 Terri Libenson, Dist. By King Features Syndicate, Inc.
But--
I SAID I'M BUSY! GO AWAY!
OHGOODLORD, I'M LATE FOR MY MEETING!
WHERE ARE MY PROOFS? (gasp) YOU SPILLED JUICE ON THEM?!
BLEEPIN'-BLEEP BLEEP BLEEP!!
WHOEVER SAID IMITATION IS THE SINCEREST FORM OF FLATTERY NEVER HAD KIDS.

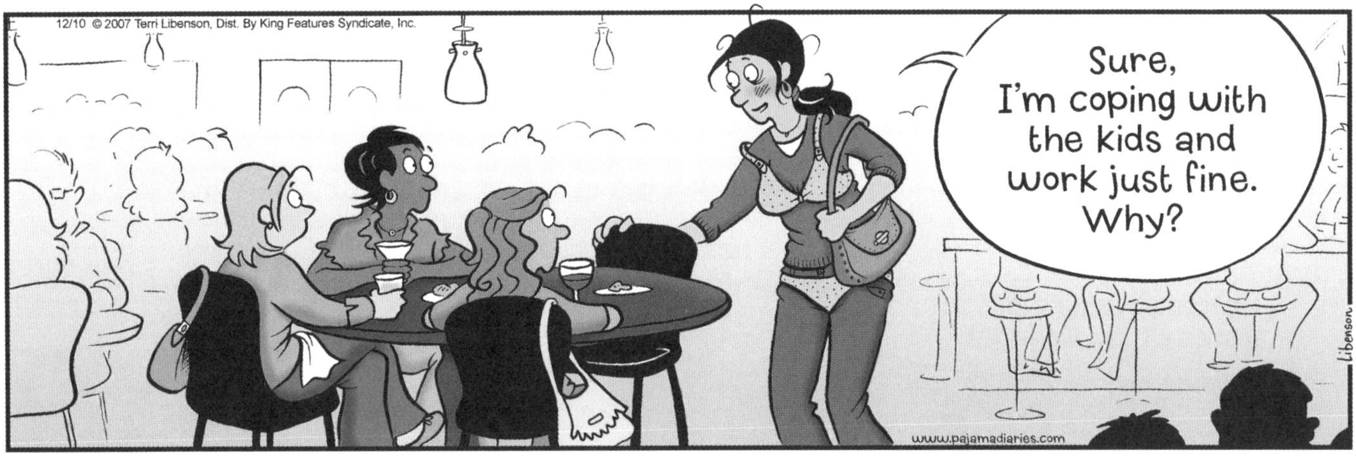
12/10 © 2007 Terri Libenson, Dist. By King Features Syndicate, Inc.
Sure, I'm coping with the kids and work just fine. Why?
Libenson
www.pajamadiaries.com

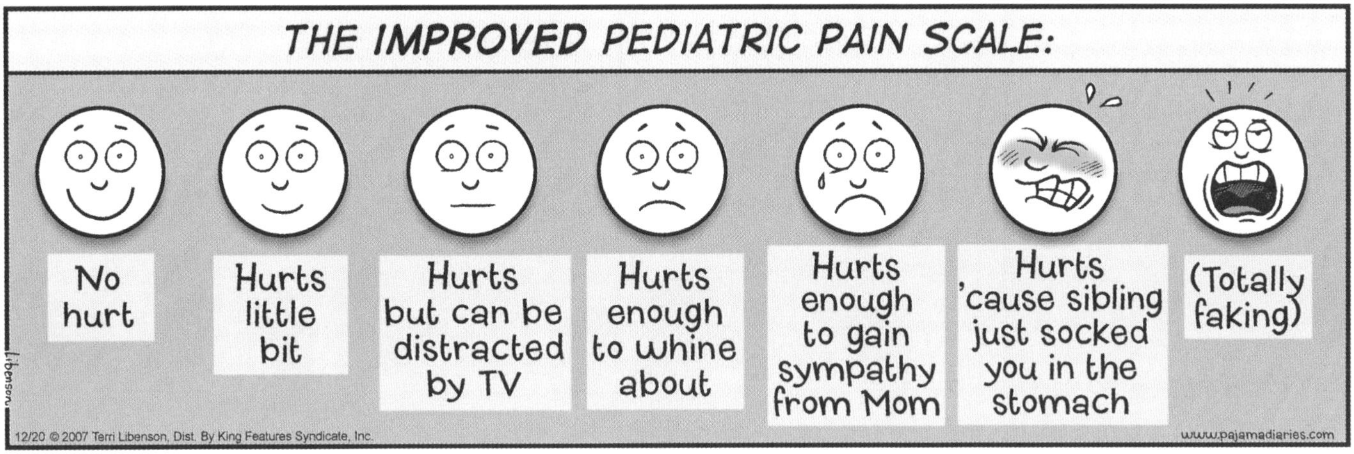
THE IMPROVED PEDIATRIC PAIN SCALE:
No hurt
Hurts little bit
Hurts but can be distracted by TV
Hurts enough to whine about
Hurts enough to gain sympathy from Mom
Hurts 'cause sibling just socked you in the stomach
(Totally faking)
Libenson
12/20 © 2007 Terri Libenson, Dist. By King Features Syndicate, Inc.
www.pajamadiaries.com

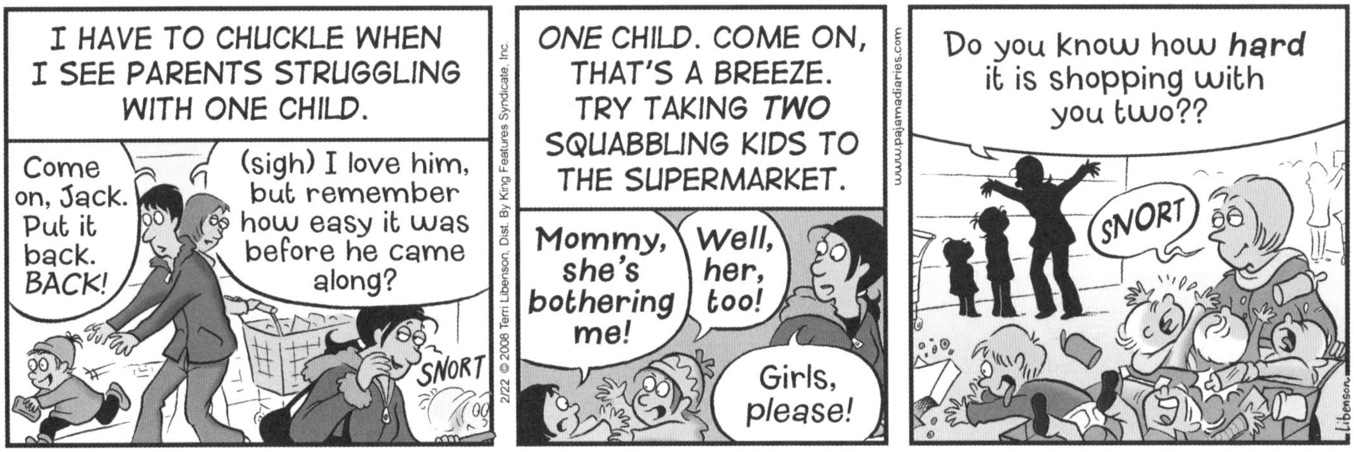
I HAVE TO CHUCKLE WHEN I SEE PARENTS STRUGGLING WITH ONE CHILD.
Come on, Jack. Put it back. BACK!
(sigh) I love him, but remember how easy it was before he came along?
SNORT
2/22 © 2008 Terri Libenson, Dist. By King Features Syndicate, Inc.
ONE CHILD. COME ON, THAT'S A BREEZE. TRY TAKING *TWO* SQUABBLING KIDS TO THE SUPERMARKET.
Mommy, she's bothering me!
Well, her, too!
Girls, please!
www.pajamadiaries.com
Do you know how **hard** it is shopping with you two??
SNORT
Libenson

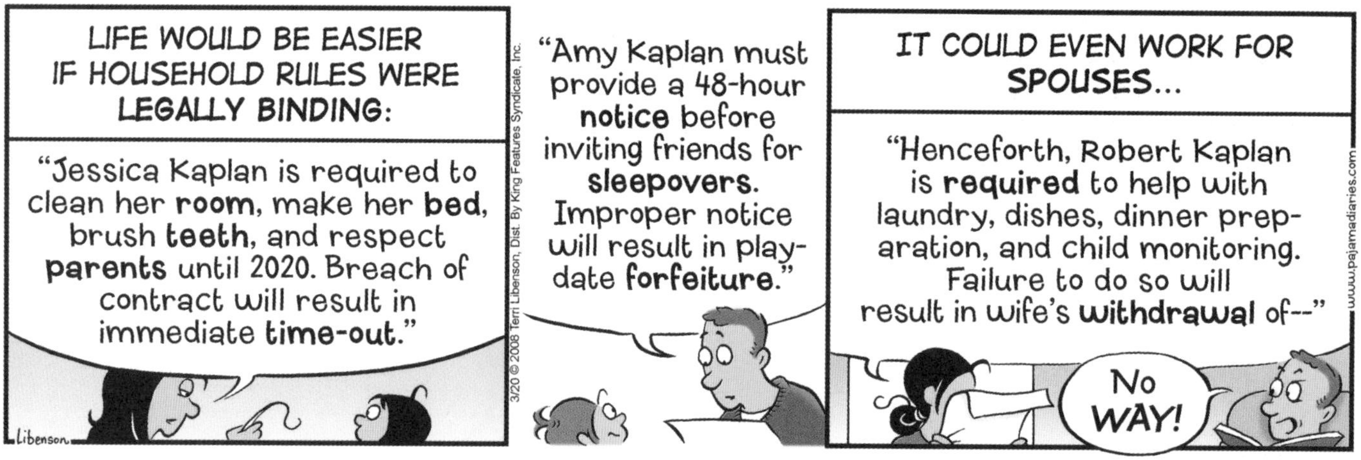
LIFE WOULD BE EASIER IF HOUSEHOLD RULES WERE **LEGALLY BINDING**:
"Jessica Kaplan is required to clean her **room**, make her **bed**, brush **teeth**, and respect **parents** until 2020. Breach of contract will result in immediate **time-out**."
Libenson
3/20 © 2008 Terri Libenson, Dist. By King Features Syndicate, Inc.
"Amy Kaplan must provide a 48-hour **notice** before inviting friends for **sleepovers**. Improper notice will result in play-date **forfeiture**."
IT COULD EVEN WORK FOR **SPOUSES**...
"Henceforth, Robert Kaplan is **required** to help with laundry, dishes, dinner preparation, and child monitoring. Failure to do so will result in wife's **withdrawal** of--"
No WAY!
www.pajamadiaries.com

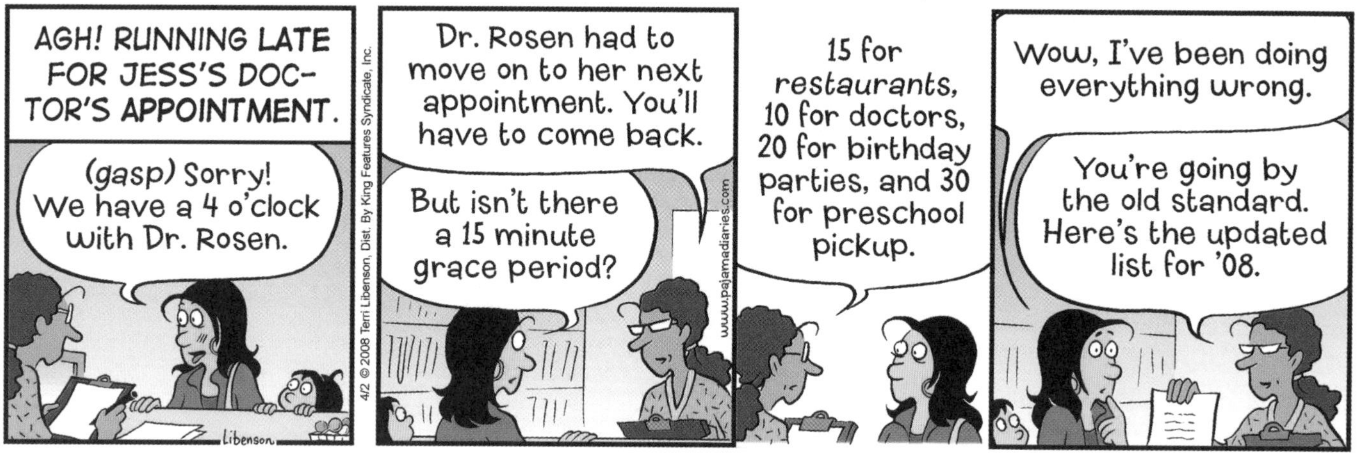
AGH! RUNNING LATE FOR JESS'S DOCTOR'S APPOINTMENT.
(gasp) Sorry! We have a 4 o'clock with Dr. Rosen.
Libenson
4/2 © 2008 Terri Libenson, Dist. By King Features Syndicate, Inc.
Dr. Rosen had to move on to her next appointment. You'll have to come back.
But isn't there a 15 minute grace period?
www.pajamadiaries.com
15 for *restaurants*, 10 for doctors, 20 for birthday parties, and 30 for preschool pickup.
Wow, I've been doing everything wrong.
You're going by the old standard. Here's the updated list for '08.

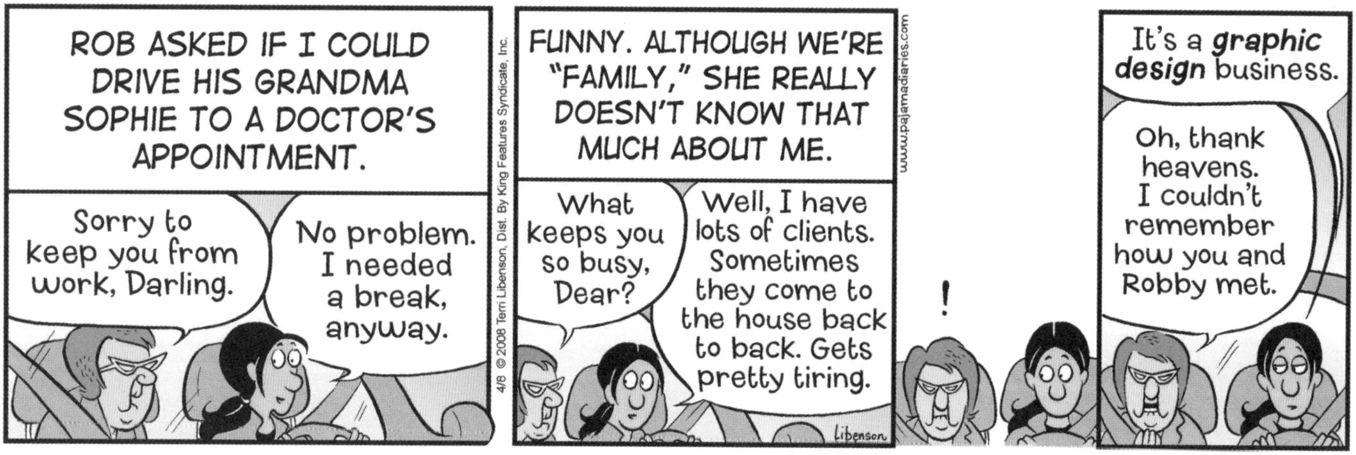
ROB ASKED IF I COULD DRIVE HIS GRANDMA SOPHIE TO A DOCTOR'S APPOINTMENT.
Sorry to keep you from work, Darling.
No problem. I needed a break, anyway.
4/8 © 2008 Terri Libenson, Dist. By King Features Syndicate, Inc.
FUNNY. ALTHOUGH WE'RE "FAMILY," SHE REALLY DOESN'T KNOW THAT MUCH ABOUT ME.
What keeps you so busy, Dear?
Well, I have lots of clients. Sometimes they come to the house back to back. Gets pretty tiring.
Libenson
www.pajamadiaries.com
!
It's a ***graphic design*** business.
Oh, thank heavens. I couldn't remember how you and Robby met.

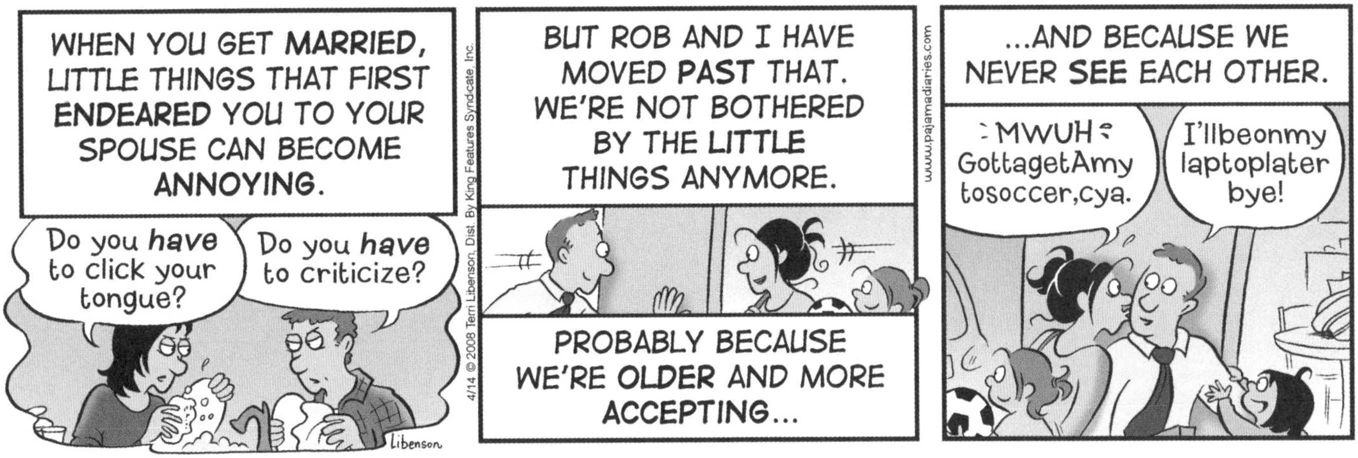
WHEN YOU GET MARRIED, LITTLE THINGS THAT FIRST ENDEARED YOU TO YOUR SPOUSE CAN BECOME ANNOYING.
Do you have to click your tongue?
Do you have to criticize?
Libenson
4/14 © 2008 Terri Libenson, Dist. By King Features Syndicate, Inc.
BUT ROB AND I HAVE MOVED PAST THAT. WE'RE NOT BOTHERED BY THE LITTLE THINGS ANYMORE.
PROBABLY BECAUSE WE'RE OLDER AND MORE ACCEPTING...
www.pajamadiaries.com
...AND BECAUSE WE NEVER SEE EACH OTHER.
MWUH GottagetAmy tosoccer,cya.
I'llbeonmy laptoplater bye!

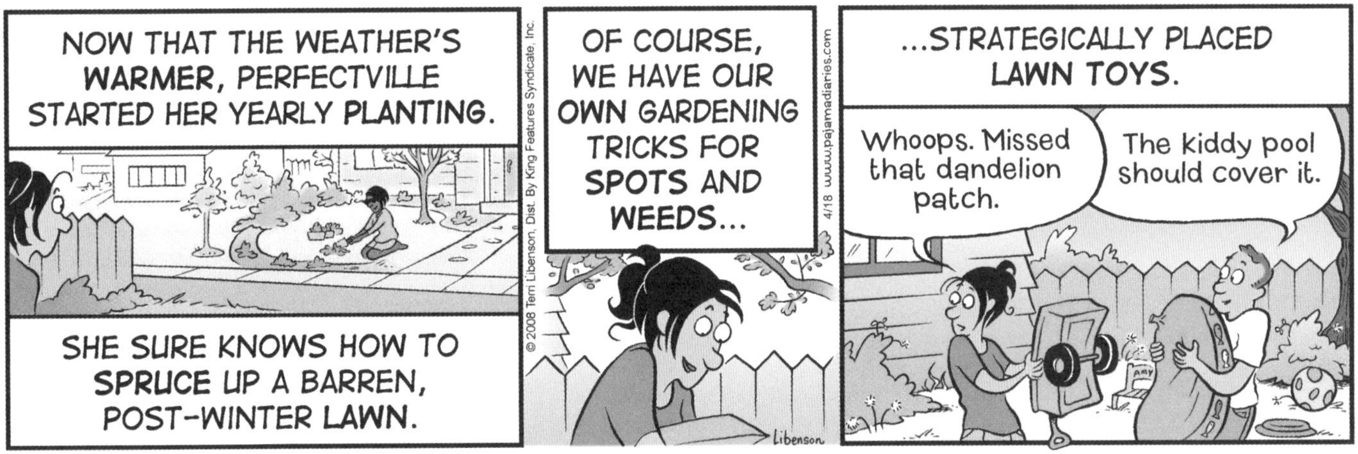
NOW THAT THE WEATHER'S WARMER, PERFECTVILLE STARTED HER YEARLY PLANTING.
SHE SURE KNOWS HOW TO SPRUCE UP A BARREN, POST-WINTER LAWN.
© 2008 Terri Libenson, Dist. By King Features Syndicate, Inc.
OF COURSE, WE HAVE OUR OWN GARDENING TRICKS FOR SPOTS AND WEEDS...
Libenson
4/18 www.pajamadiaries.com
...STRATEGICALLY PLACED LAWN TOYS.
Whoops. Missed that dandelion patch.
The kiddy pool should cover it.

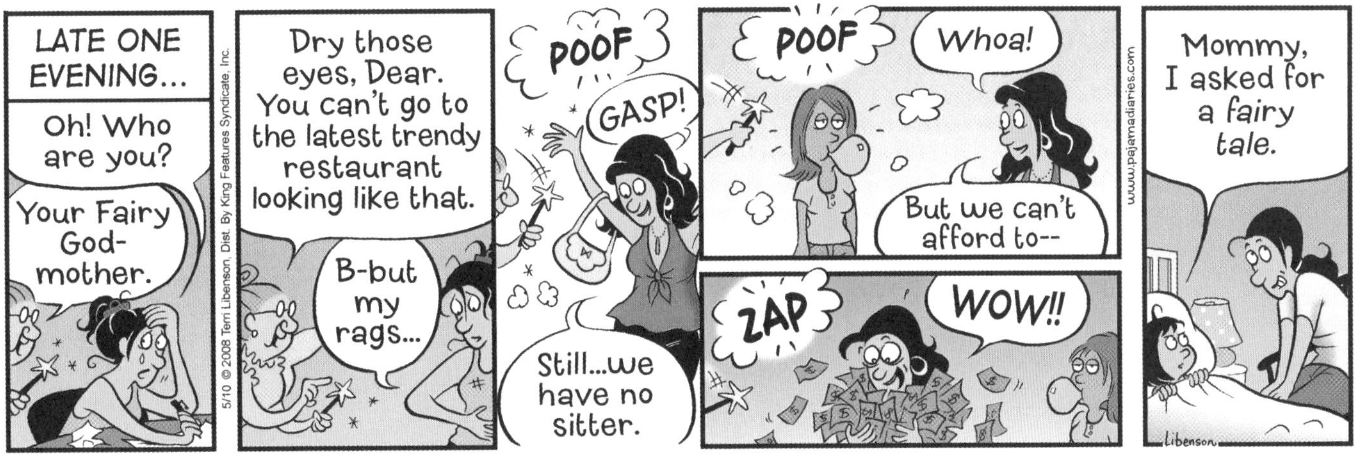
LATE ONE EVENING...
Oh! Who are you?
Your Fairy God-mother.
5/10 © 2008 Terri Libenson, Dist. By King Features Syndicate, Inc.
Dry those eyes, Dear. You can't go to the latest trendy restaurant looking like that.
B-but my rags...
POOF
GASP!
Still...we have no sitter.
POOF
Whoa!
But we can't afford to--
ZAP
WOW!!
www.pajamadiaries.com
Mommy, I asked for a fairy tale.
Libenson

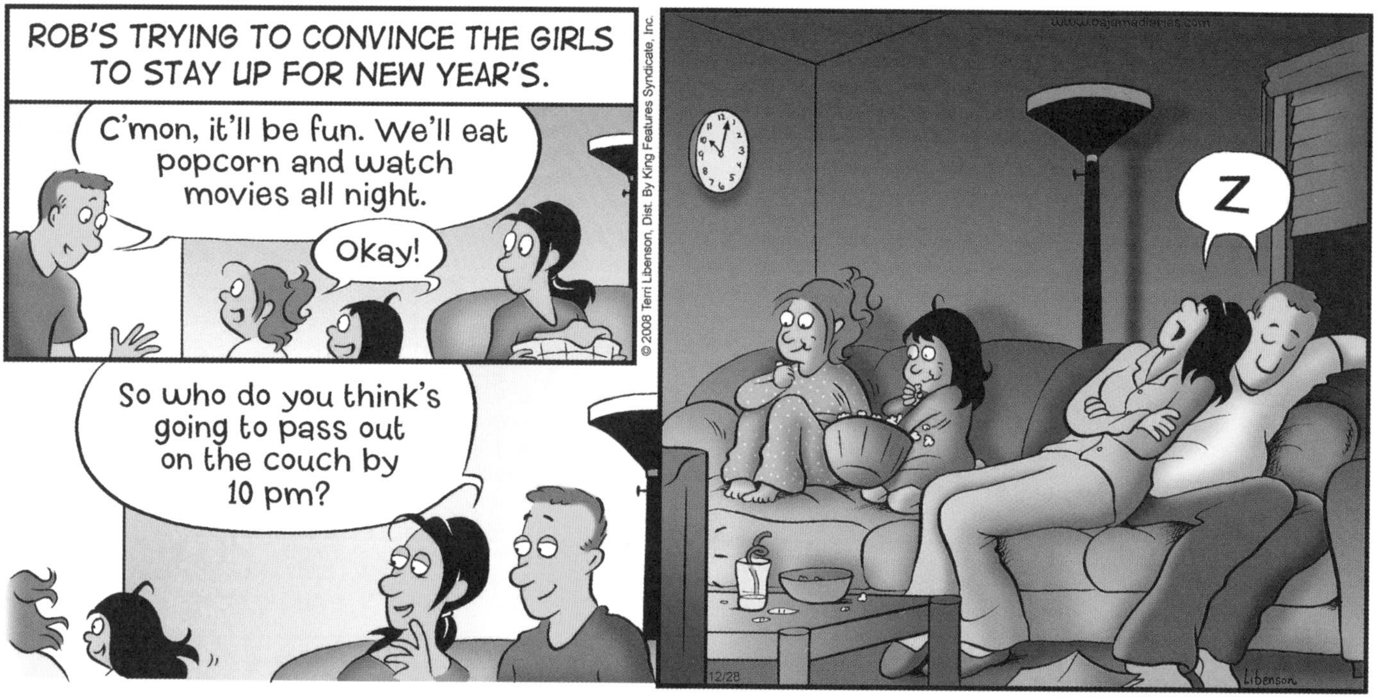
ROB'S TRYING TO CONVINCE THE GIRLS TO STAY UP FOR NEW YEAR'S.
C'mon, it'll be fun. We'll eat popcorn and watch movies all night.
Okay!
So who do you think's going to pass out on the couch by 10 pm?
Z
© 2008 Terri Libenson, Dist. By King Features Syndicate, Inc.
www.pajamadiaries.com
12/28
Libenson

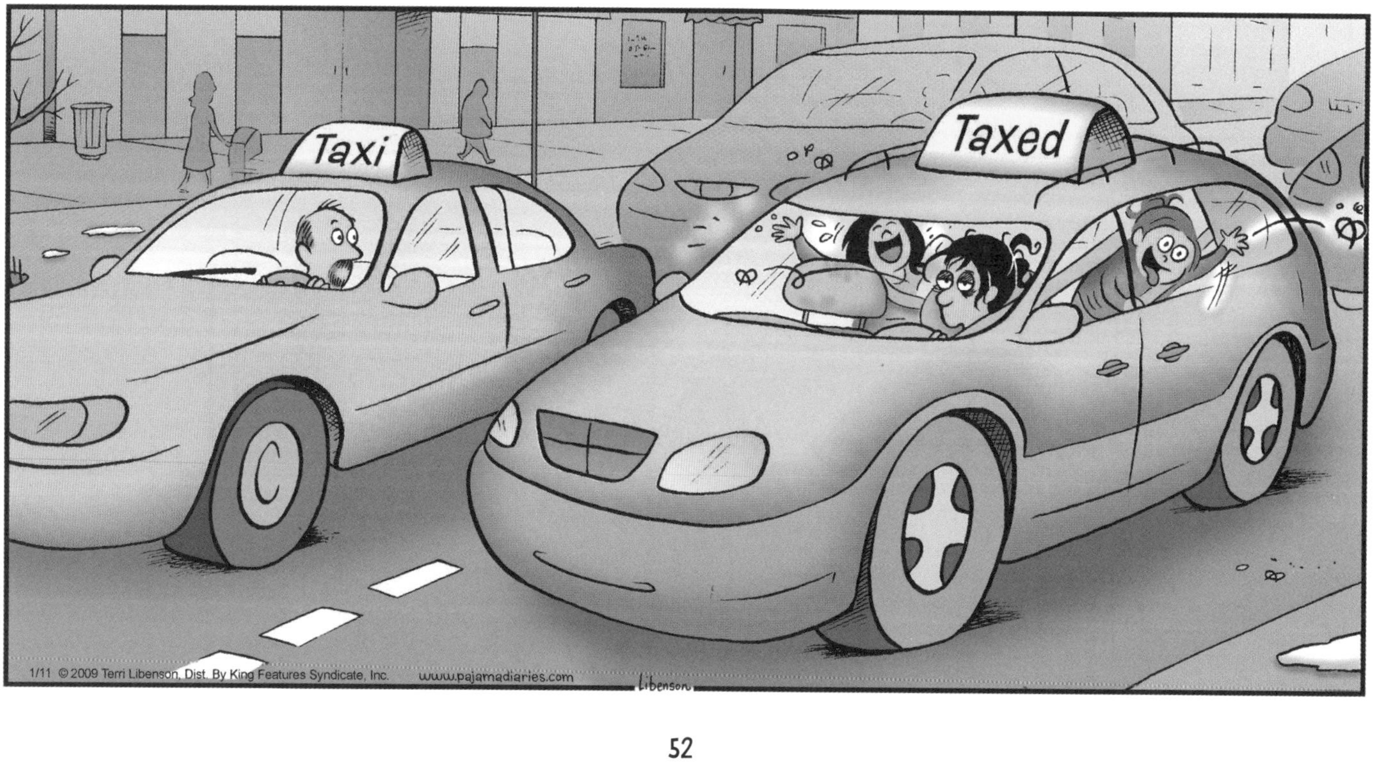
Taxi
Taxed
1/11 © 2009 Terri Libenson, Dist. By King Features Syndicate, Inc.
www.pajamadiaries.com
Libenson

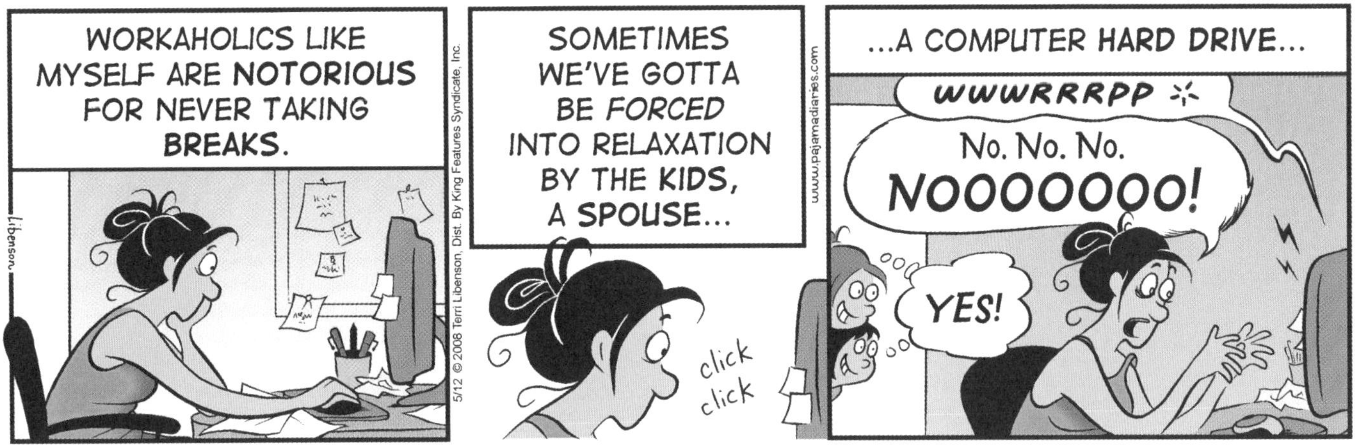
WORKAHOLICS LIKE MYSELF ARE **NOTORIOUS** FOR NEVER TAKING **BREAKS**.
5/12 © 2008 Terri Libenson, Dist. By King Features Syndicate, Inc.
SOMETIMES WE'VE GOTTA BE *FORCED* INTO RELAXATION BY THE **KIDS**, A **SPOUSE**...
click click
www.pajamadiaries.com
...A COMPUTER **HARD DRIVE**...
WWWRRRPP
No. No. No.
NOOOOOOO!
YES!
Libenson

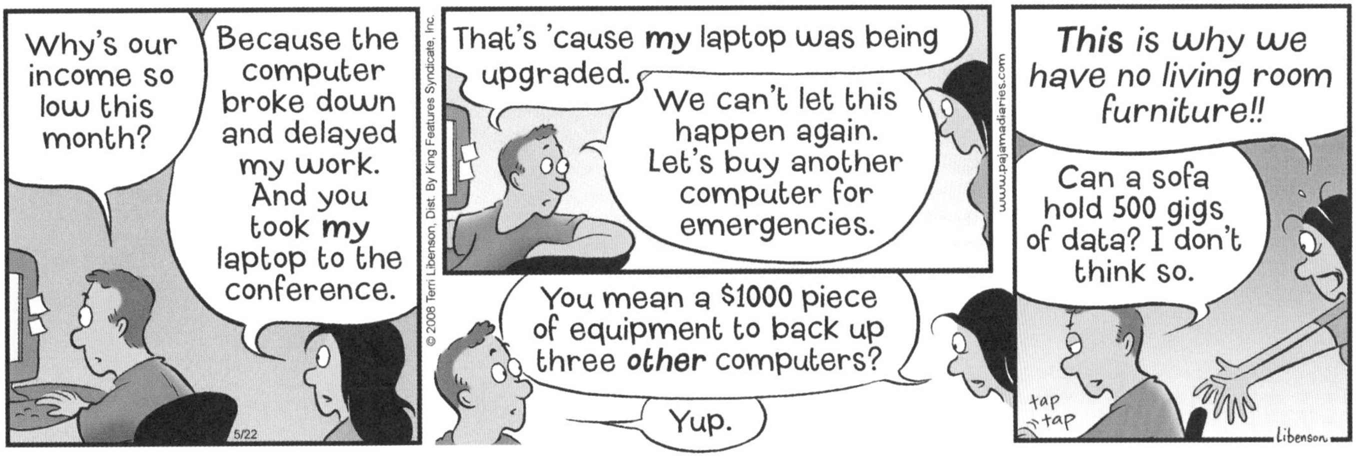
Why's our income so low this month?
Because the computer broke down and delayed my work. And you took **my** laptop to the conference.
5/22
© 2008 Terri Libenson, Dist. By King Features Syndicate, Inc.
That's 'cause **my** laptop was being upgraded.
We can't let this happen again. Let's buy another computer for emergencies.
You mean a $1000 piece of equipment to back up three *other* computers?
Yup.
www.pajamadiaries.com
This is why we have no living room furniture!!
Can a sofa hold 500 gigs of data? I don't think so.
tap tap
Libenson

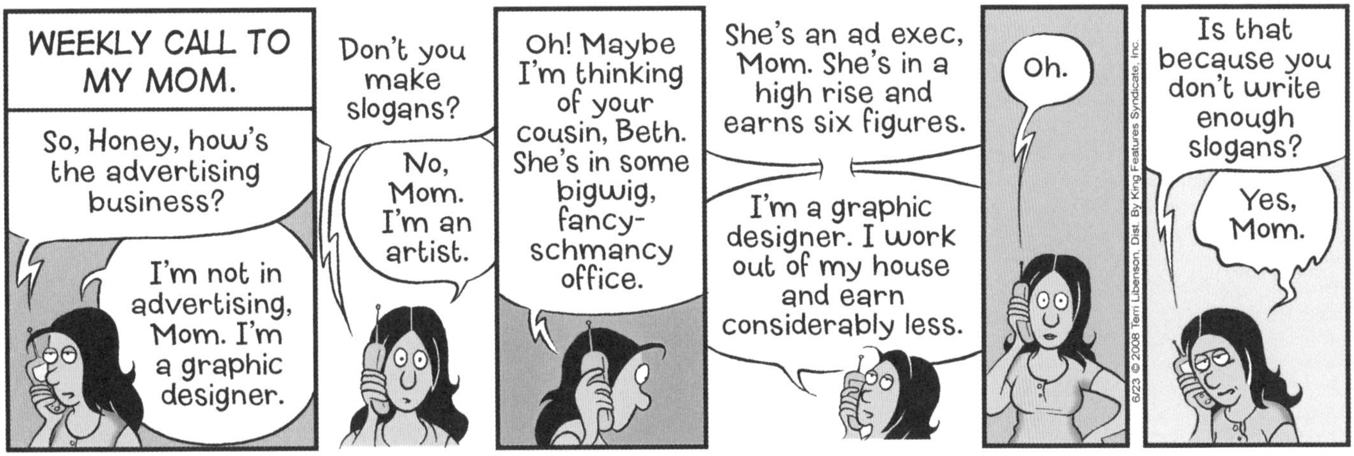
WEEKLY CALL TO MY MOM.
So, Honey, how's the advertising business?
I'm not in advertising, Mom. I'm a graphic designer.
Don't you make slogans?
No, Mom. I'm an artist.
Oh! Maybe I'm thinking of your cousin, Beth. She's in some bigwig, fancy-schmancy office.
She's an ad exec, Mom. She's in a high rise and earns six figures.
I'm a graphic designer. I work out of my house and earn considerably less.
Oh.
6/23 © 2008 Terri Libenson, Dist. By King Features Syndicate, Inc.
Is that because you don't write enough slogans?
Yes, Mom.

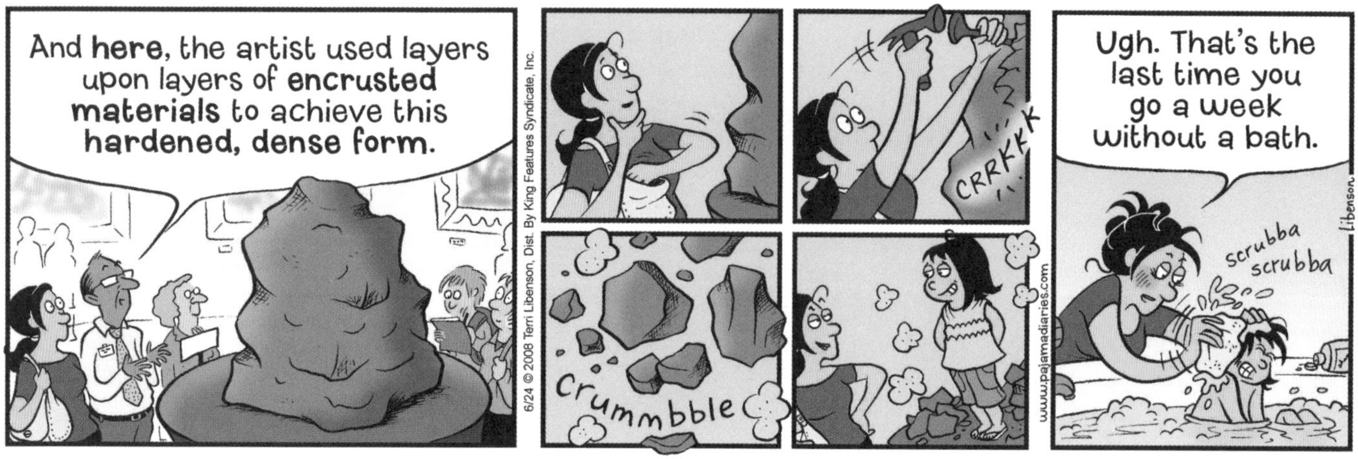
And here, the artist used layers upon layers of encrusted materials to achieve this hardened, dense form.
6/24 © 2008 Terri Libenson, Dist. By King Features Syndicate, Inc.
CRRKKK
Crummbble
www.pajamadiaries.com
Ugh. That's the last time you go a week without a bath.
scrubba scrubba
Libenson

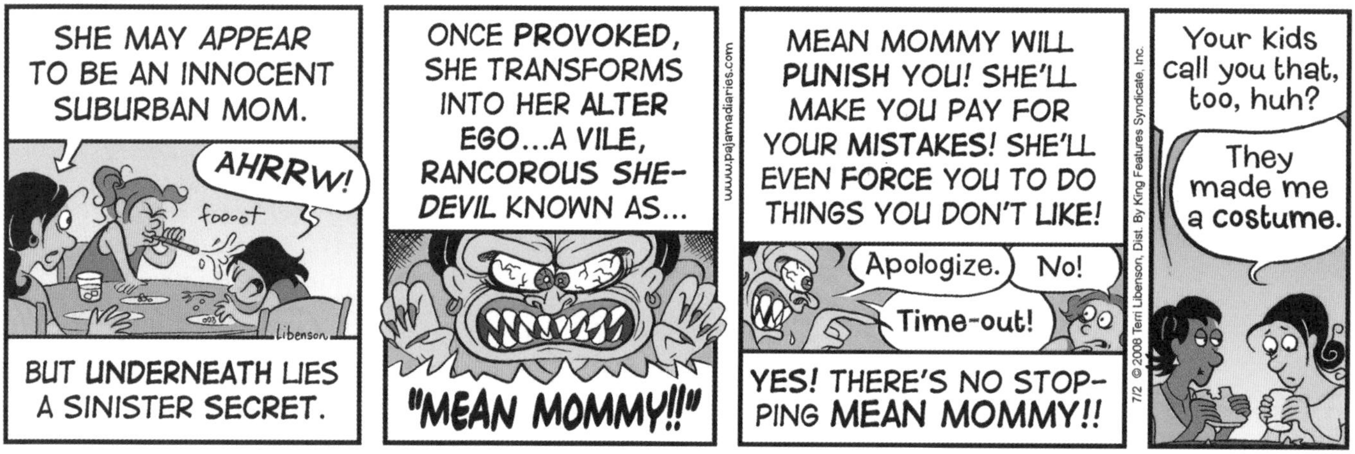
SHE MAY APPEAR TO BE AN INNOCENT SUBURBAN MOM.
AHRRW!
foooot
Libenson
BUT UNDERNEATH LIES A SINISTER SECRET.
ONCE PROVOKED, SHE TRANSFORMS INTO HER ALTER EGO...A VILE, RANCOROUS SHE-DEVIL KNOWN AS...
"MEAN MOMMY!!"
www.pajamadiaries.com
MEAN MOMMY WILL PUNISH YOU! SHE'LL MAKE YOU PAY FOR YOUR MISTAKES! SHE'LL EVEN FORCE YOU TO DO THINGS YOU DON'T LIKE!
Apologize.
No!
Time-out!
YES! THERE'S NO STOPPING MEAN MOMMY!!
7/2 © 2008 Terri Libenson, Dist. By King Features Syndicate, Inc.
Your kids call you that, too, huh?
They made me a costume.

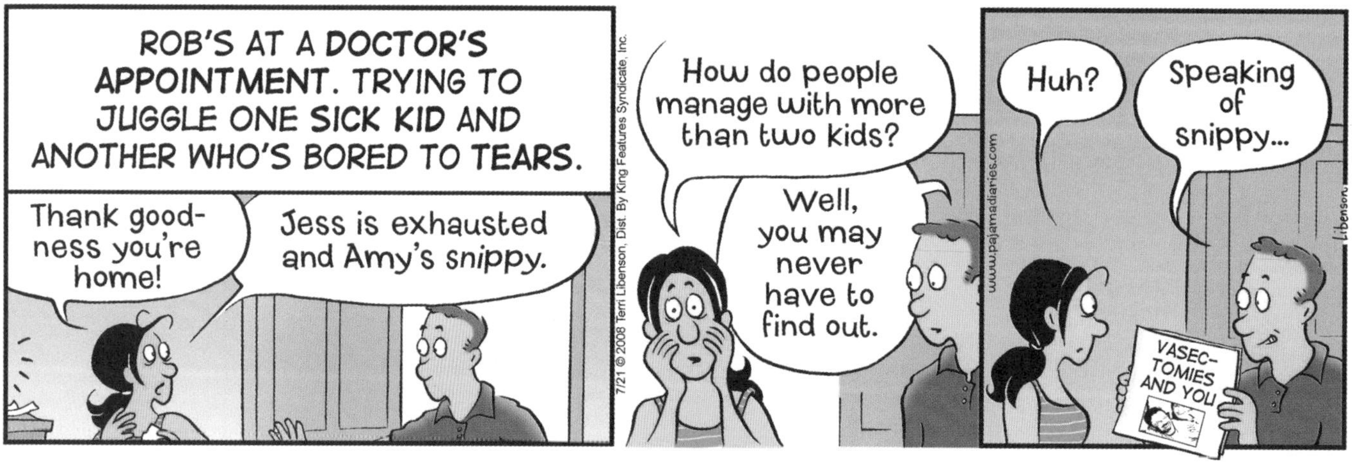
ROB'S AT A DOCTOR'S APPOINTMENT. TRYING TO JUGGLE ONE SICK KID AND ANOTHER WHO'S BORED TO TEARS.
Thank goodness you're home!
Jess is exhausted and Amy's snippy.
7/21 © 2008 Terri Libenson, Dist. By King Features Syndicate, Inc.
How do people manage with more than two kids?
Well, you may never have to find out.
www.pajamadiaries.com
Huh?
Speaking of snippy...
VASECTOMIES AND YOU
Libenson

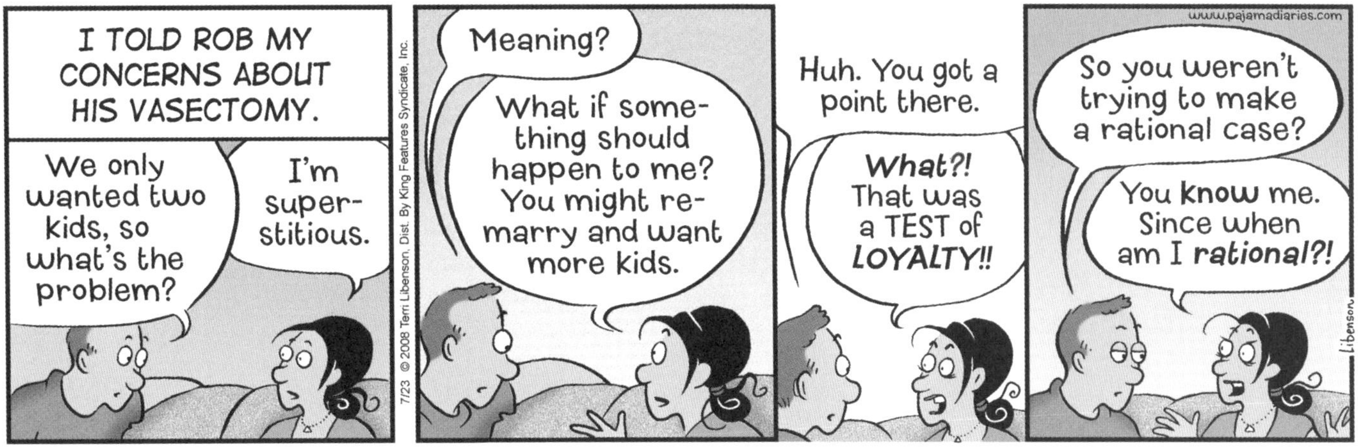
I TOLD ROB MY CONCERNS ABOUT HIS VASECTOMY.
We only wanted two kids, so what's the problem?
I'm super-stitious.
7/23 © 2008 Terri Libenson. Dist. By King Features Syndicate, Inc.
Meaning?
What if some-thing should happen to me? You might re-marry and want more kids.
Huh. You got a point there.
What?! That was a TEST of **LOYALTY!!**
www.pajamadiaries.com
So you weren't trying to make a rational case?
You **know** me. Since when am I ***rational?!***
Libenson

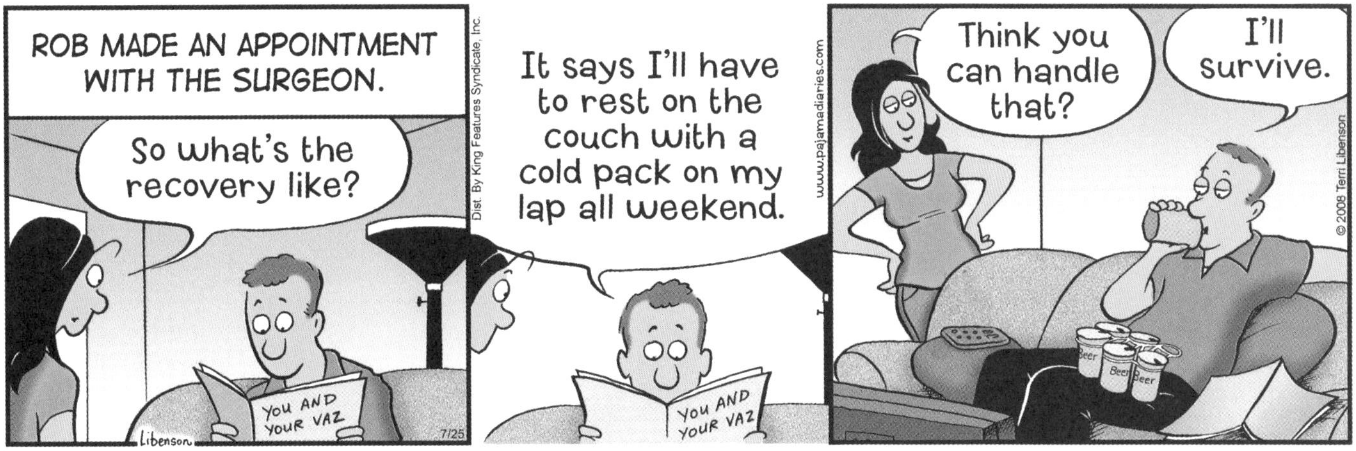
ROB MADE AN APPOINTMENT WITH THE SURGEON.
So what's the recovery like?
YOU AND YOUR VAZ
Libenson
7/25
Dist. By King Features Syndicate, Inc.
It says I'll have to rest on the couch with a cold pack on my lap all weekend.
YOU AND YOUR VAZ
www.pajamadiaries.com
Think you can handle that?
I'll survive.
Beer
Beer
Beer
© 2008 Terri Libenson

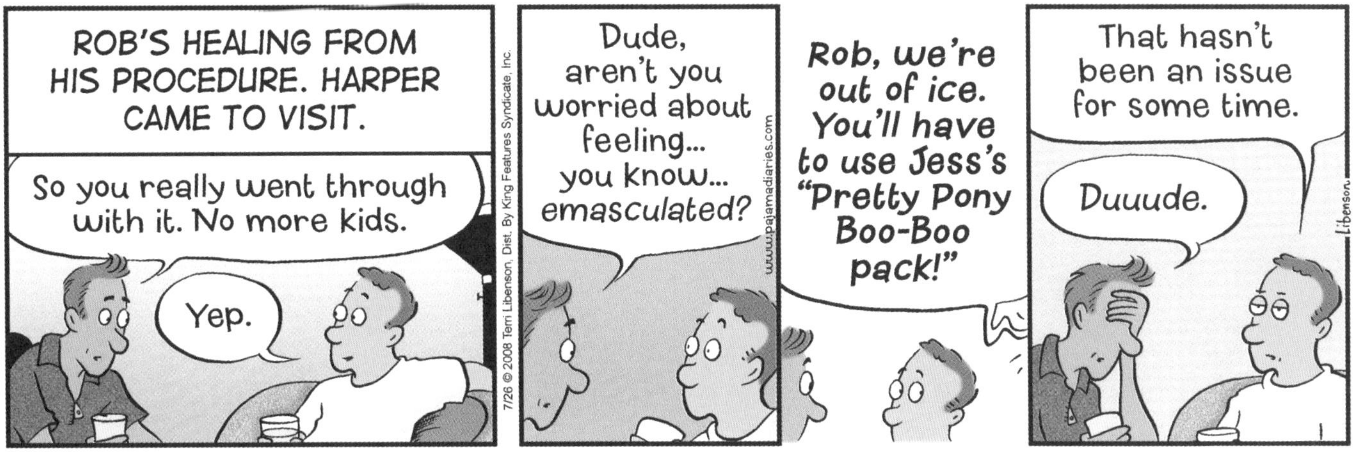
ROB'S HEALING FROM HIS PROCEDURE. HARPER CAME TO VISIT.
So you really went through with it. No more kids.
Yep.
7/26 © 2008 Terri Libenson. Dist. By King Features Syndicate, Inc.
Dude, aren't you worried about feeling... you know... *emasculated?*
www.pajamadiaries.com
Rob, we're out of ice. You'll have to use Jess's "Pretty Pony Boo-Boo pack!"
That hasn't been an issue for some time.
Duuude.
Libenson

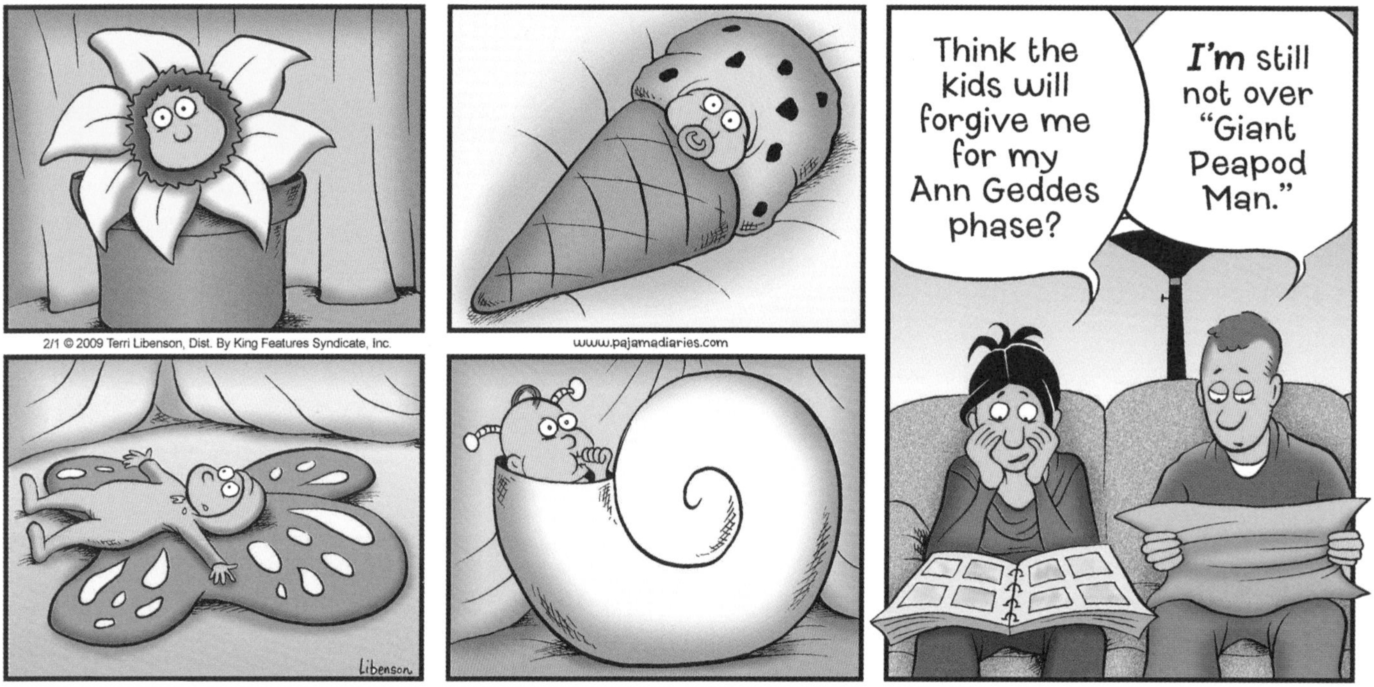
2/1 © 2009 Terri Libenson, Dist. By King Features Syndicate, Inc.
www.pajamadiaries.com
Libenson
Think the kids will forgive me for my Ann Geddes phase?
I'm still not over "Giant Peapod Man."

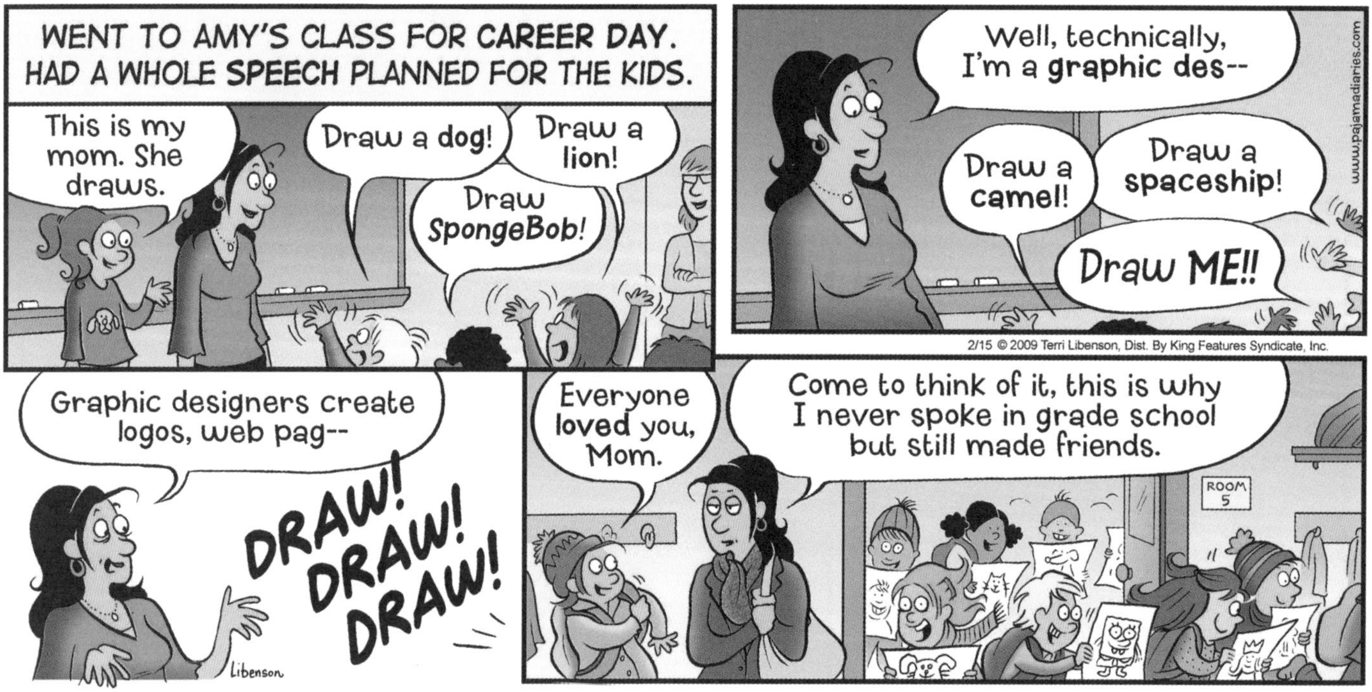
WENT TO AMY'S CLASS FOR **CAREER DAY**. HAD A WHOLE **SPEECH** PLANNED FOR THE KIDS.
This is my mom. She draws.
Draw a **dog**!
Draw a lion!
Draw *SpongeBob*!
Well, technically, I'm a **graphic des**--
Draw a **camel**!
Draw a **spaceship**!
Draw **ME**!!
www.pajamadiaries.com
2/15 © 2009 Terri Libenson, Dist. By King Features Syndicate, Inc.
Graphic designers create logos, web pag--
DRAW! DRAW! DRAW!
Libenson
Everyone **loved** you, Mom.
Come to think of it, this is why I never spoke in grade school but still made friends.
ROOM 5

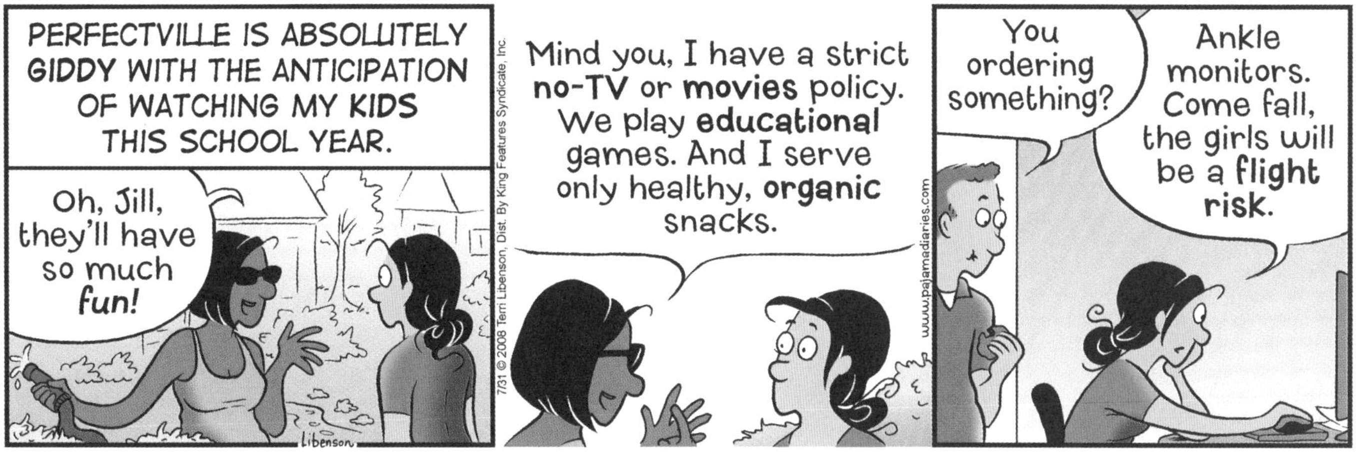
PERFECTVILLE IS ABSOLUTELY **GIDDY** WITH THE ANTICIPATION OF WATCHING MY **KIDS** THIS SCHOOL YEAR.
Oh, Jill, they'll have so much **fun!**
Libenson
7/31 © 2008 Terri Libenson, Dist. By King Features Syndicate, Inc.
Mind you, I have a strict **no-TV** or **movies** policy. We play **educational** games. And I serve only healthy, **organic** snacks.
www.pajamadiaries.com
You ordering something?
Ankle monitors. Come fall, the girls will be a **flight risk.**

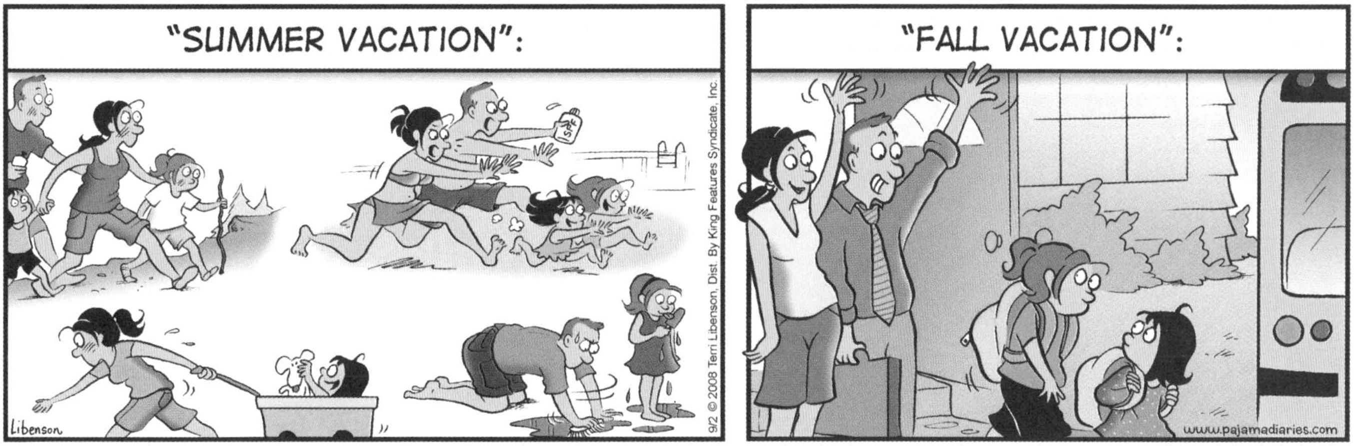
"SUMMER VACATION":
Libenson
9/2 © 2008 Terri Libenson, Dist. By King Features Syndicate, Inc.
"FALL VACATION":
www.pajamadiaries.com

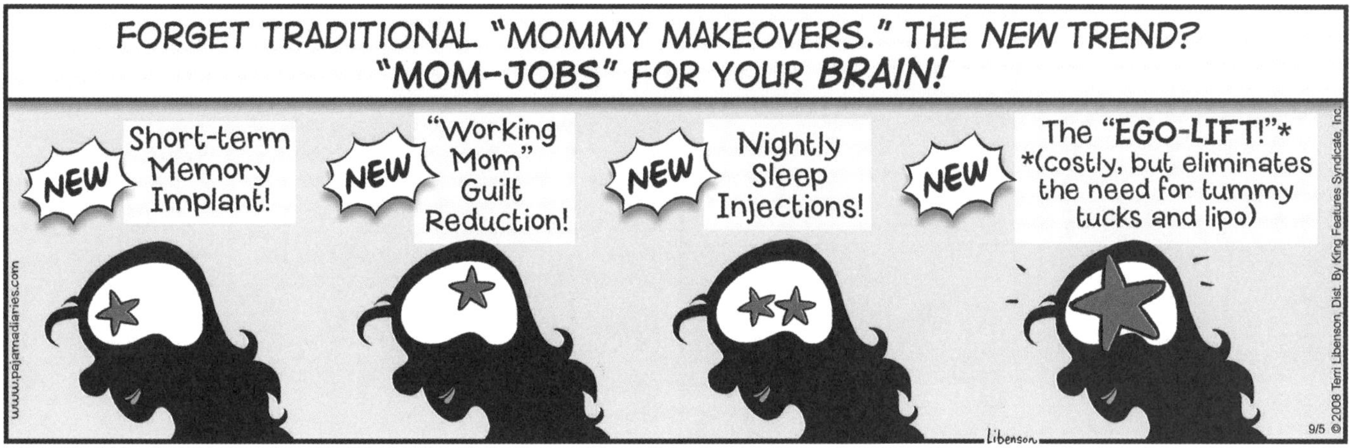
FORGET TRADITIONAL "MOMMY MAKEOVERS." THE *NEW* TREND? "MOM-JOBS" FOR YOUR ***BRAIN!***
NEW
Short-term Memory Implant!
NEW
"Working Mom" Guilt Reduction!
NEW
Nightly Sleep Injections!
NEW
The "**EGO-LIFT!**"*
*(costly, but eliminates the need for tummy tucks and lipo)
www.pajamadiaries.com
Libenson
9/5 © 2008 Terri Libenson, Dist. By King Features Syndicate, Inc.

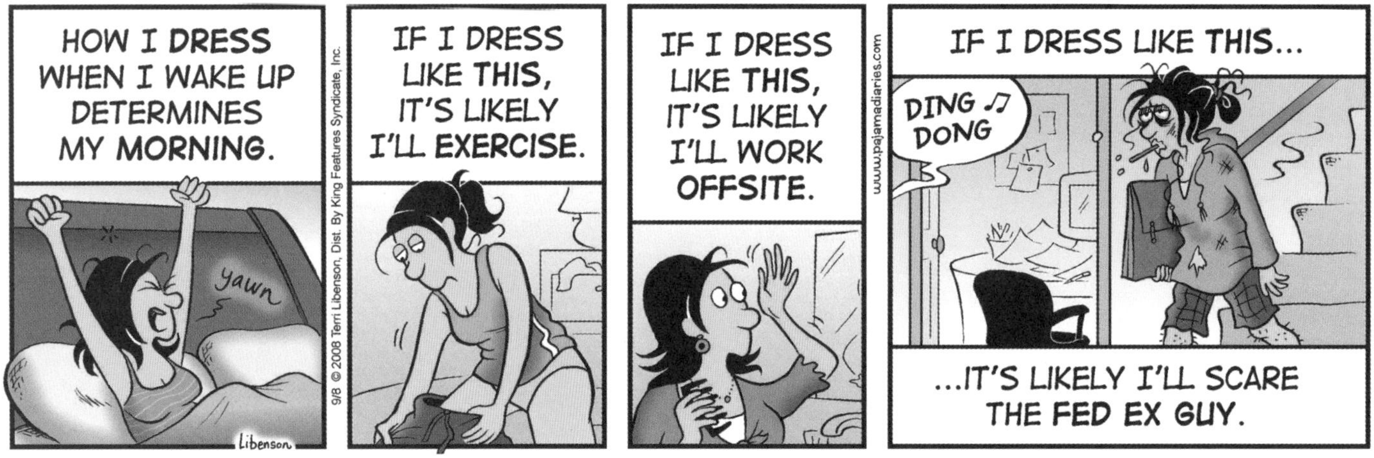
HOW I DRESS WHEN I WAKE UP DETERMINES MY MORNING.
yawn
Libenson
9/8 © 2008 Terri Libenson, Dist. By King Features Syndicate, Inc.
IF I DRESS LIKE THIS, IT'S LIKELY I'LL EXERCISE.
IF I DRESS LIKE THIS, IT'S LIKELY I'LL WORK OFFSITE.
www.pajamadiaries.com
IF I DRESS LIKE THIS...
DING ♫ DONG
...IT'S LIKELY I'LL SCARE THE FED EX GUY.

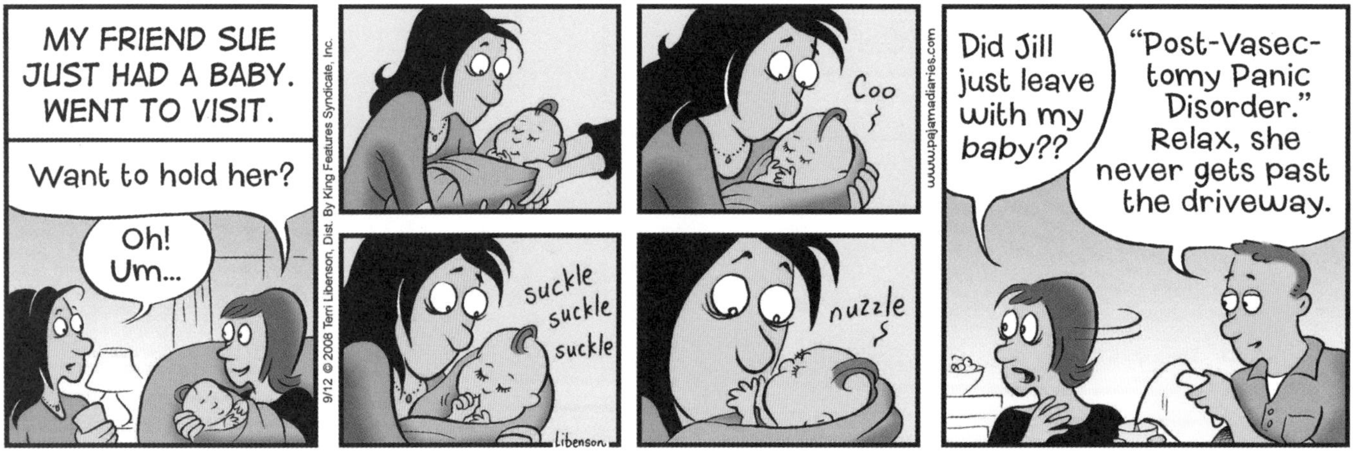
MY FRIEND SUE JUST HAD A BABY. WENT TO VISIT.
Want to hold her?
Oh! Um...
9/12 © 2008 Terri Libenson, Dist. By King Features Syndicate, Inc.
Coo
suckle suckle suckle
Libenson
nuzzle
www.pajamadiaries.com
Did Jill just leave with my baby??
"Post-Vasec-tomy Panic Disorder." Relax, she never gets past the driveway.

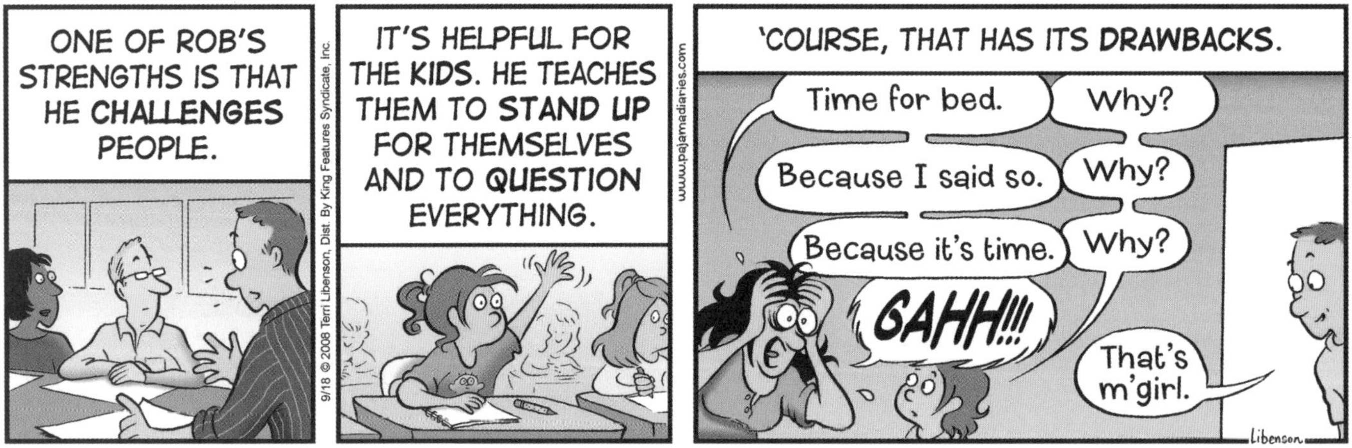
ONE OF ROB'S STRENGTHS IS THAT HE CHALLENGES PEOPLE.
9/18 © 2008 Terri Libenson, Dist. By King Features Syndicate, Inc.
IT'S HELPFUL FOR THE KIDS. HE TEACHES THEM TO STAND UP FOR THEMSELVES AND TO QUESTION EVERYTHING.
www.pajamadiaries.com
'COURSE, THAT HAS ITS DRAWBACKS.
Time for bed.
Why?
Because I said so.
Why?
Because it's time.
Why?
GAHH!!!
That's m'girl.
Libenson

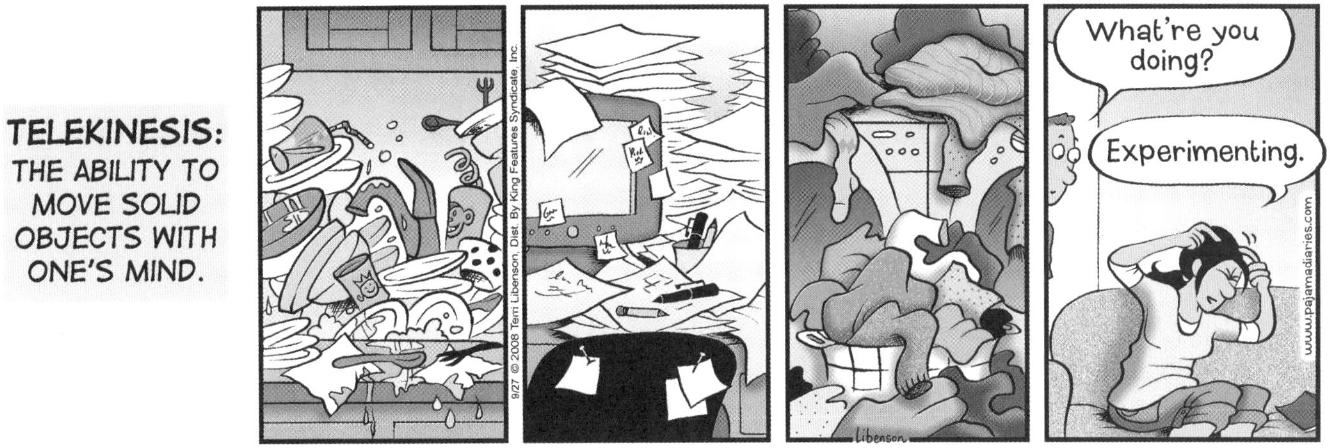
TELEKINESIS:
THE ABILITY TO MOVE SOLID OBJECTS WITH ONE'S MIND.
9/27 © 2008 Terri Libenson, Dist. By King Features Syndicate, Inc.
Libenson
What're you doing?
Experimenting.
www.pajamadiaries.com

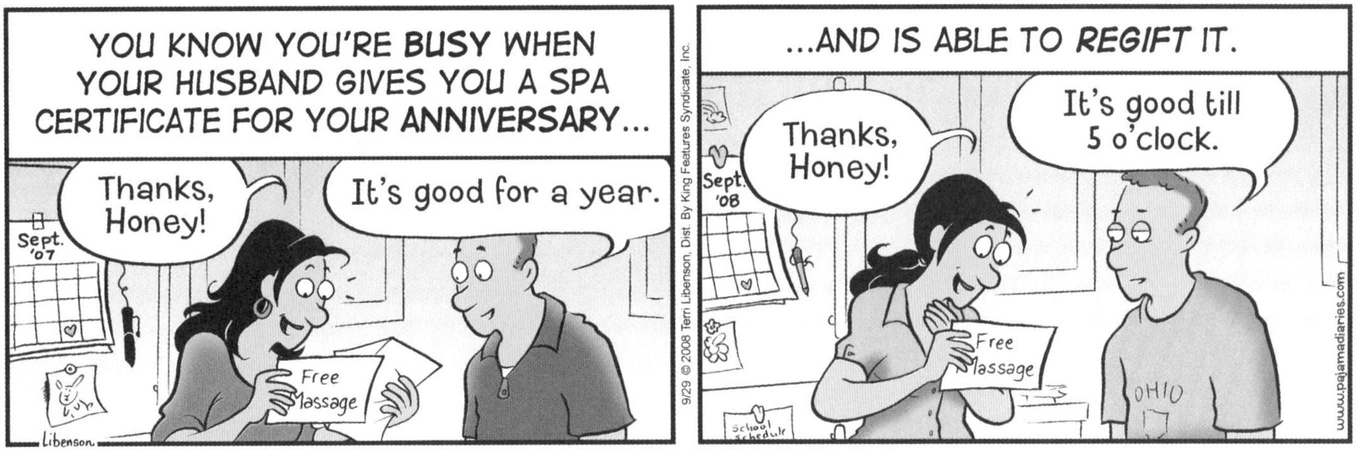
YOU KNOW YOU'RE BUSY WHEN YOUR HUSBAND GIVES YOU A SPA CERTIFICATE FOR YOUR ANNIVERSARY...
Sept. '07
Thanks, Honey!
It's good for a year.
Free Massage
Libenson
9/29 © 2008 Terri Libenson, Dist. By King Features Syndicate, Inc.
...AND IS ABLE TO REGIFT IT.
Sept. '08
Thanks, Honey!
It's good till 5 o'clock.
Free Massage
OHIO
School Schedule
www.pajamadiaries.com

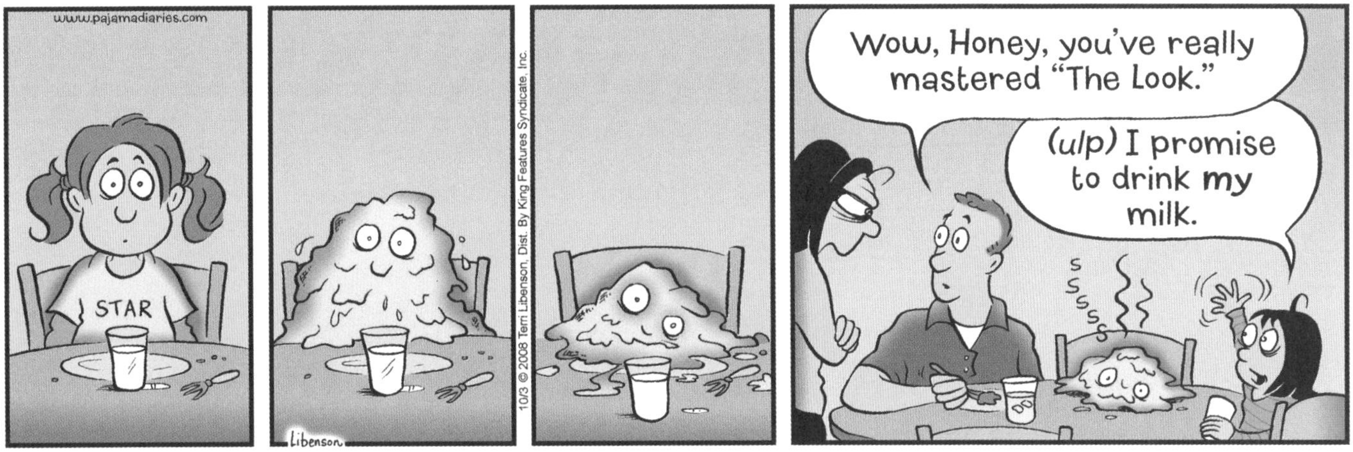
www.pajamadiaries.com
STAR
Libenson
10/3 © 2008 Terri Libenson, Dist. By King Features Syndicate, Inc.
Wow, Honey, you've really mastered "The Look."
(ulp) I promise to drink my milk.
SSSS

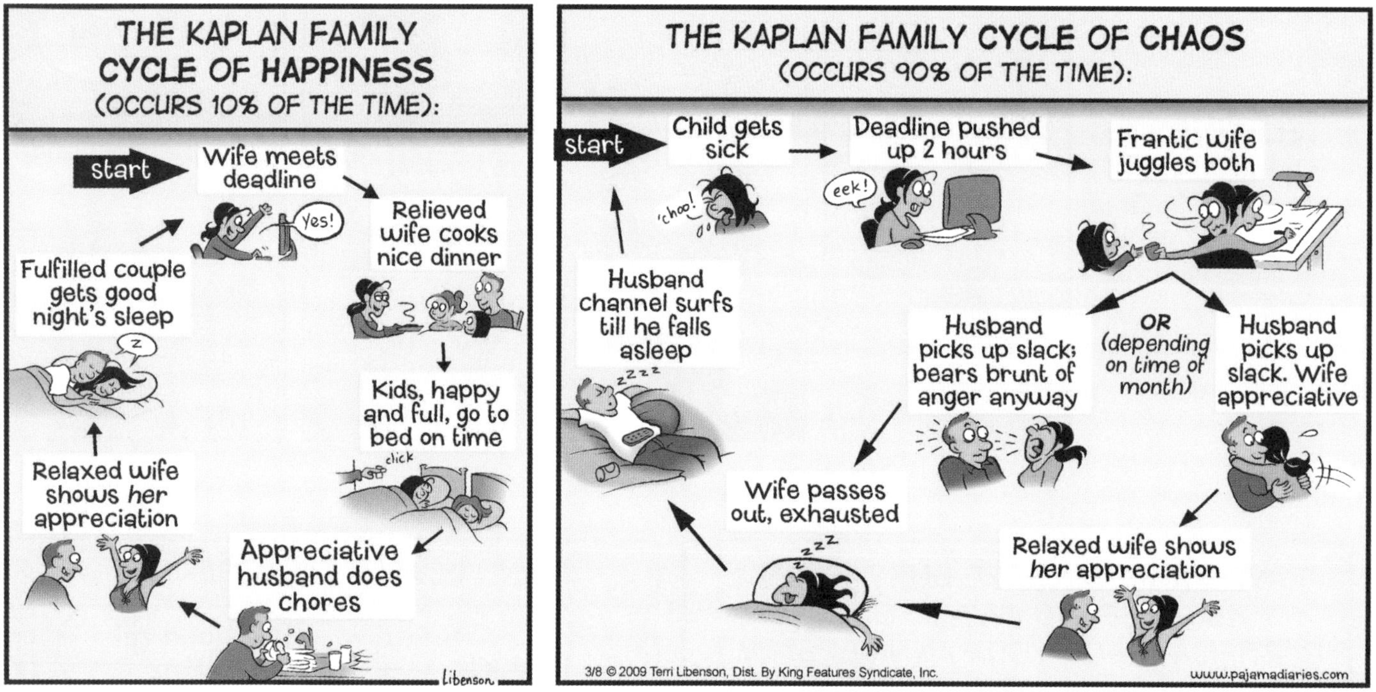
THE KAPLAN FAMILY CYCLE OF HAPPINESS
(OCCURS 10% OF THE TIME):
start
Wife meets deadline
Yes!
Relieved wife cooks nice dinner
Kids, happy and full, go to bed on time
click
Appreciative husband does chores
Relaxed wife shows *her* appreciation
Fulfilled couple gets good night's sleep
z
Libenson
THE KAPLAN FAMILY CYCLE OF CHAOS
(OCCURS 90% OF THE TIME):
start
Child gets sick
'choo!
Deadline pushed up 2 hours
eek!
Frantic wife juggles both
Husband picks up slack; bears brunt of anger anyway
OR (depending on time of month)
Husband picks up slack. Wife appreciative
Relaxed wife shows her appreciation
Wife passes out, exhausted
zzz
Husband channel surfs till he falls asleep
zzzz
3/8 © 2009 Terri Libenson, Dist. By King Features Syndicate, Inc.
www.pajamadiaries.com

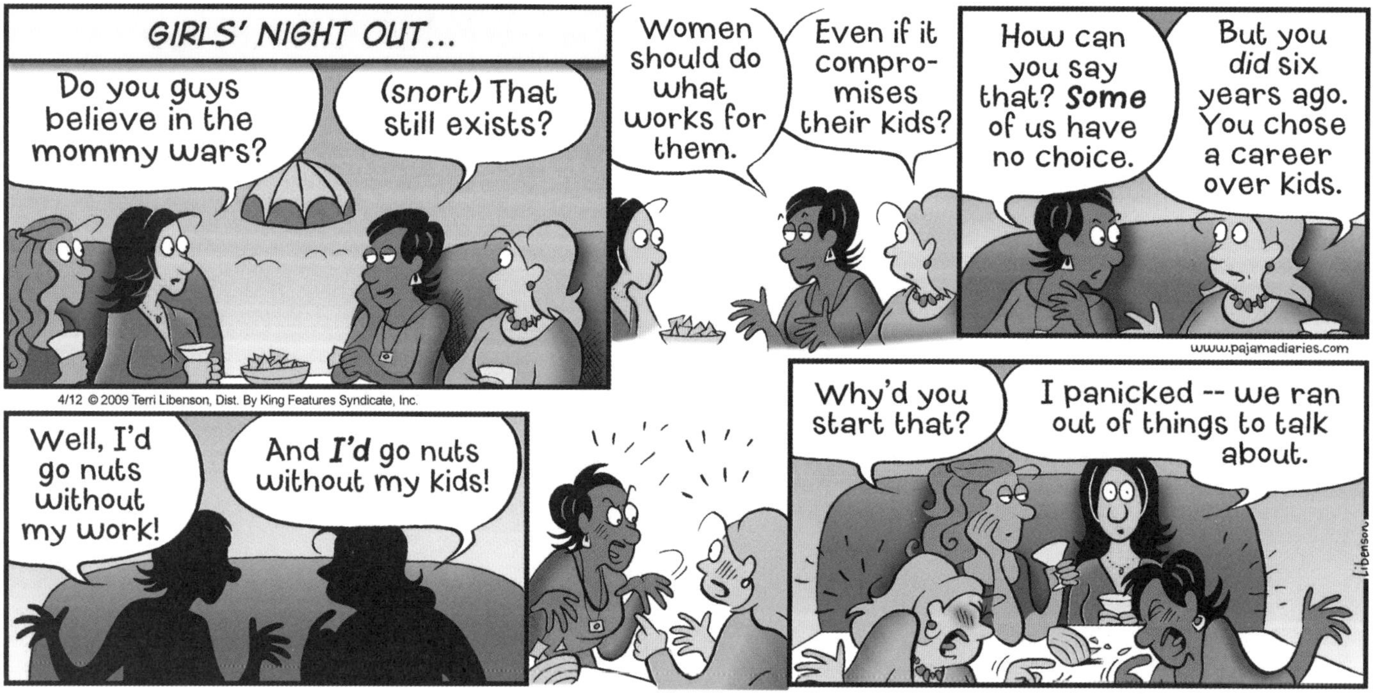
GIRLS' NIGHT OUT...
Do you guys believe in the mommy wars?
(snort) That still exists?
Women should do what works for them.
Even if it compromises their kids?
How can you say that? **Some** of us have no choice.
But you *did* six years ago. You chose a career over kids.
www.pajamadiaries.com
4/12 © 2009 Terri Libenson, Dist. By King Features Syndicate, Inc.
Well, I'd go nuts without my work!
And ***I'd*** go nuts without my kids!
Why'd you start that?
I panicked -- we ran out of things to talk about.
Libenson

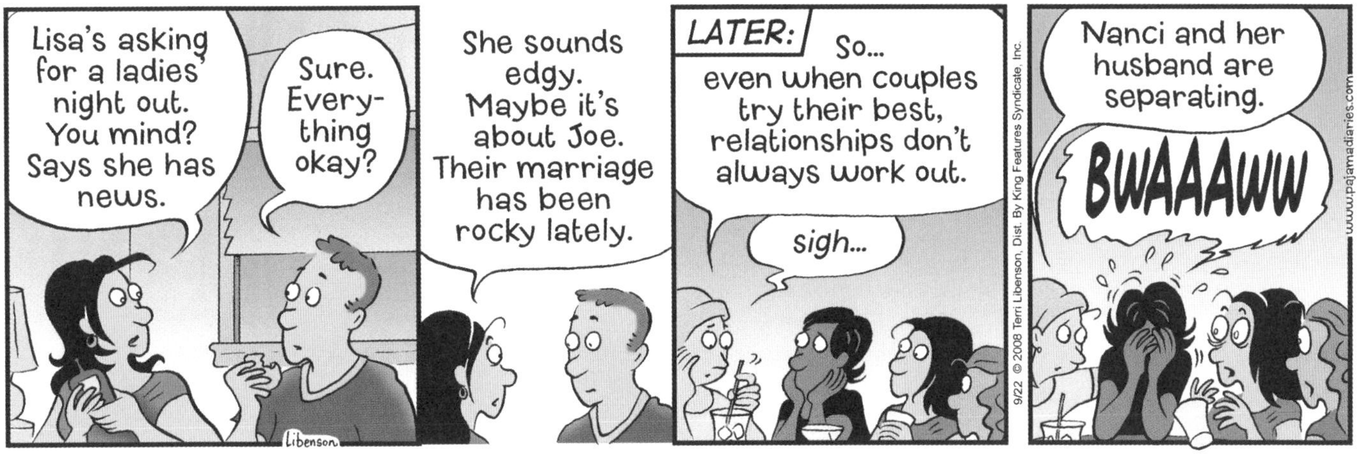
Lisa's asking for a ladies' night out. You mind? Says she has news.
Sure. Every-thing okay?
Libenson
She sounds edgy. Maybe it's about Joe. Their marriage has been rocky lately.
LATER:
So... even when couples try their best, relationships don't always work out.
sigh...
9/22 © 2008 Terri Libenson, Dist. By King Features Syndicate, Inc.
Nanci and her husband are separating.
BWAAAWW
www.pajamadiaries.com

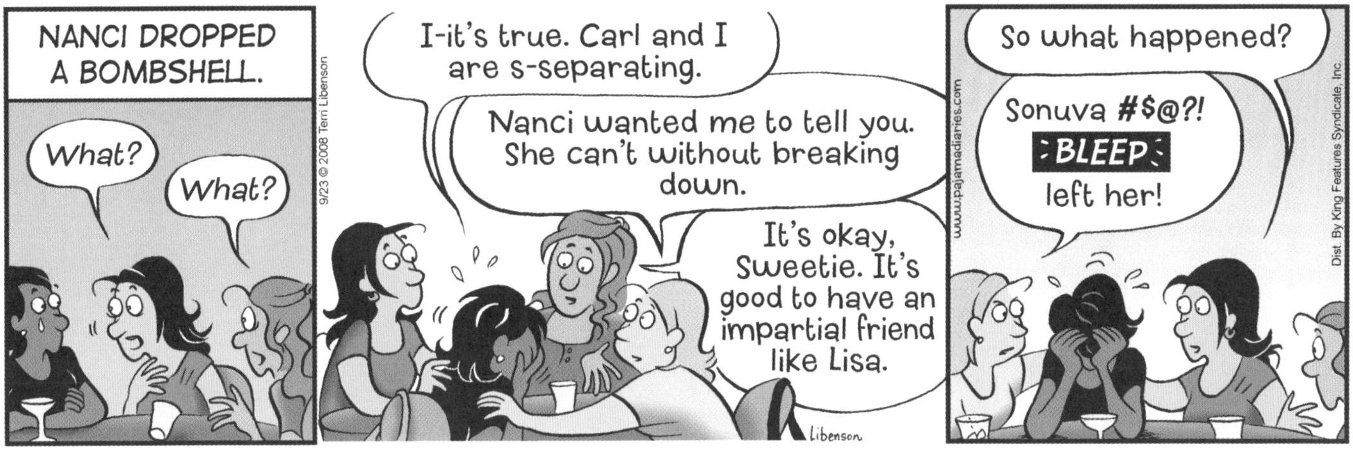
NANCI DROPPED A BOMBSHELL.
What?
What?
9/23 © 2008 Terri Libenson
I-it's true. Carl and I are s-separating.
Nanci wanted me to tell you. She can't without breaking down.
It's okay, Sweetie. It's good to have an impartial friend like Lisa.
Libenson
So what happened?
Sonuva #$@?! BLEEP left her!
www.pajamadiaries.com
Dist. By King Features Syndicate, Inc.

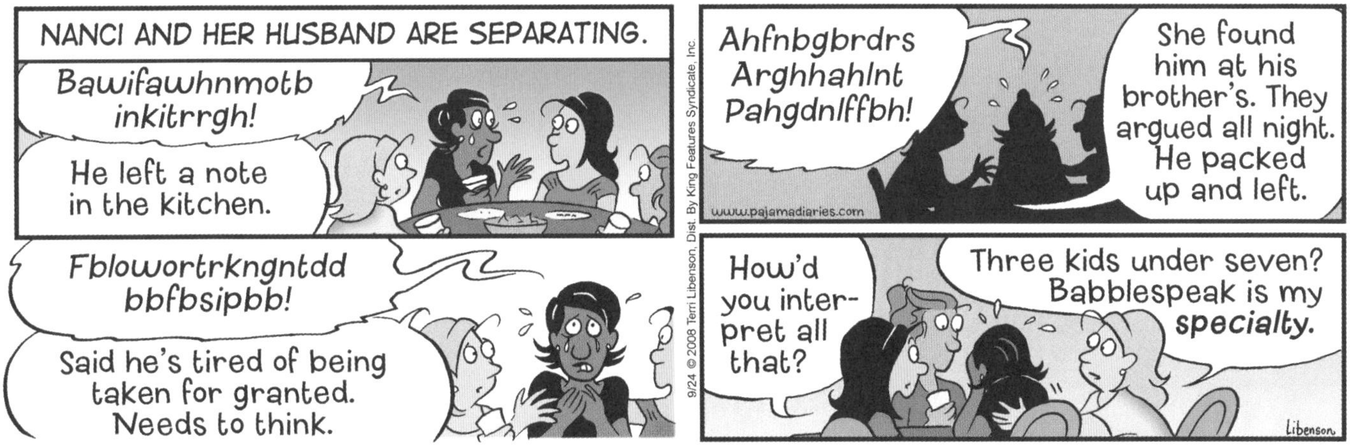
NANCI AND HER HUSBAND ARE SEPARATING.
Bawifawhnmotb inkitrrgh!
He left a note in the kitchen.
Fblowortrkngntdd bbfbsipbb!
Said he's tired of being taken for granted. Needs to think.
9/24 © 2008 Terri Libenson, Dist. By King Features Syndicate, Inc.
Ahfnbgbrdrs Arghhahlnt Pahgdnlffbh!
She found him at his brother's. They argued all night. He packed up and left.
www.pajamadiaries.com
How'd you inter-pret all that?
Three kids under seven? Babblespeak is my specialty.
Libenson

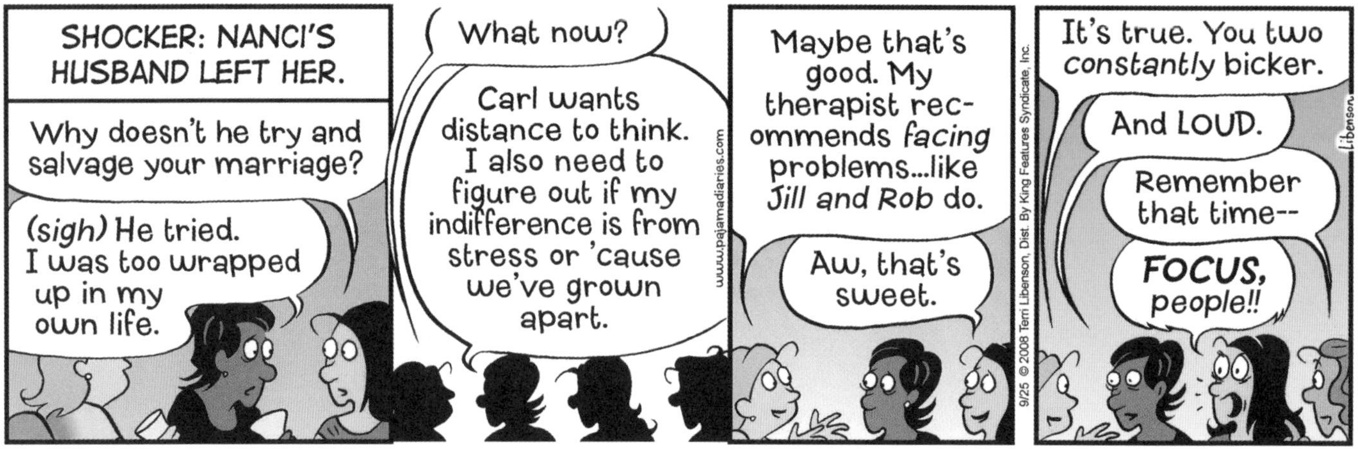
SHOCKER: NANCI'S HUSBAND LEFT HER.
Why doesn't he try and salvage your marriage?
(sigh) He tried. I was too wrapped up in my own life.
What now?
Carl wants distance to think. I also need to figure out if my indifference is from stress or 'cause we've grown apart.
www.pajamadiaries.com
Maybe that's good. My therapist recommends *facing* problems...like *Jill and Rob* do.
Aw, that's sweet.
9/25 © 2008 Terri Libenson, Dist. By King Features Syndicate, Inc.
It's true. You two *constantly* bicker.
And LOUD.
Remember that time--
FOCUS, *people!!*
Libenson

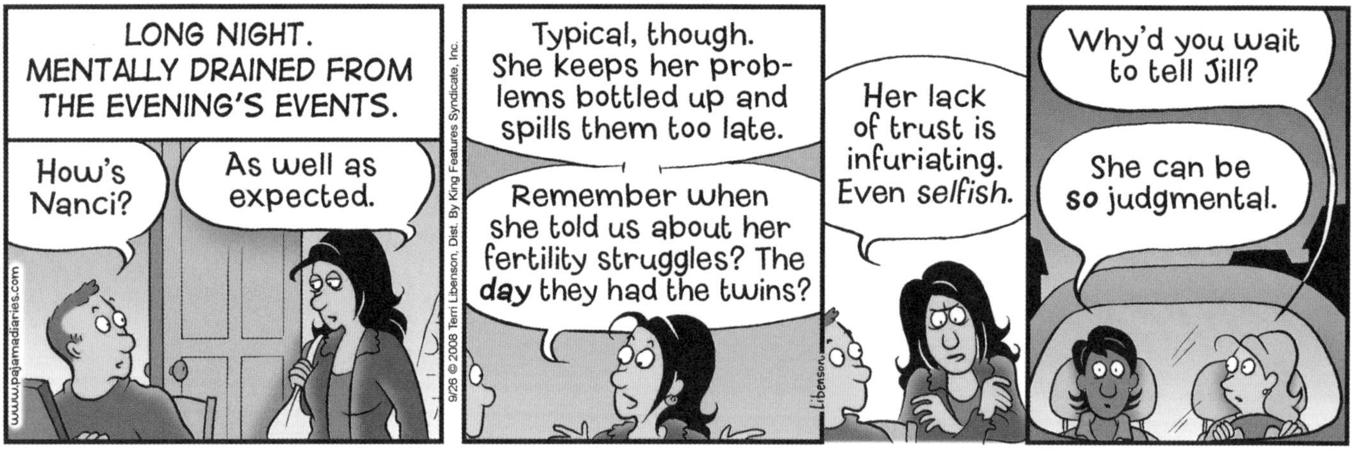
LONG NIGHT. MENTALLY DRAINED FROM THE EVENING'S EVENTS.
How's Nanci?
As well as expected.
www.pajamadiaries.com
9/26 © 2008 Terri Libenson, Dist. By King Features Syndicate, Inc.
Typical, though. She keeps her problems bottled up and spills them too late.
Remember when she told us about her fertility struggles? The **day** they had the twins?
Her lack of trust is infuriating. Even *selfish*.
Libenson
Why'd you wait to tell Jill?
She can be **so** judgmental.

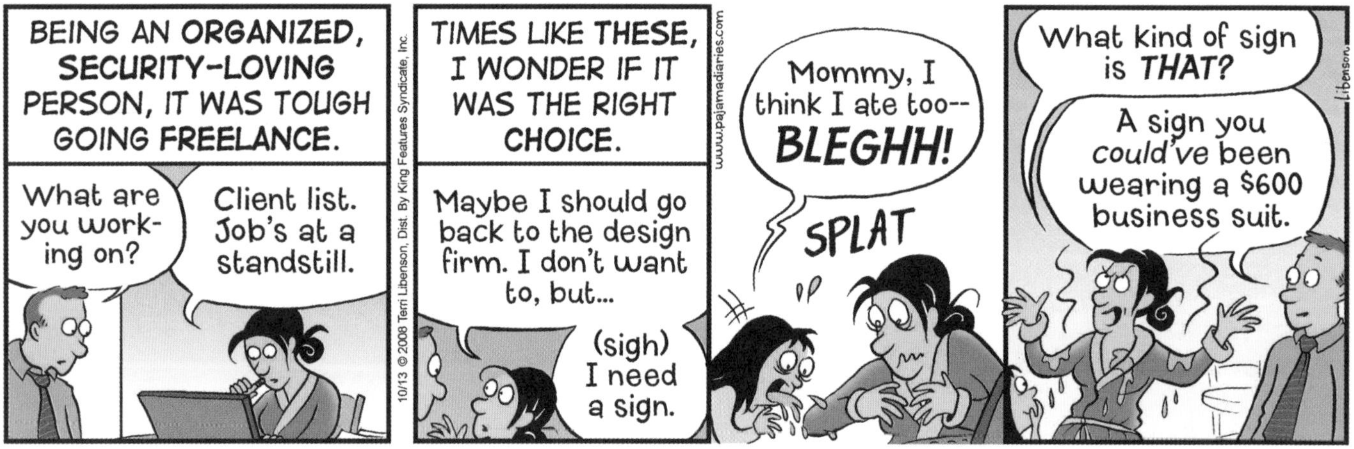
BEING AN **ORGANIZED, SECURITY-LOVING** PERSON, IT WAS TOUGH GOING **FREELANCE**.
What are you working on?
Client list. Job's at a standstill.
10/13 © 2008 Terri Libenson, Dist. By King Features Syndicate, Inc.
TIMES LIKE **THESE**, I WONDER IF IT WAS THE RIGHT **CHOICE**.
Maybe I should go back to the design firm. I don't want to, but...
(sigh) I need a sign.
www.pajamadiaries.com
Mommy, I think I ate too-- ***BLEGHH!***
SPLAT
What kind of sign is ***THAT?***
A sign you *could've* been wearing a $600 business suit.
Libenson

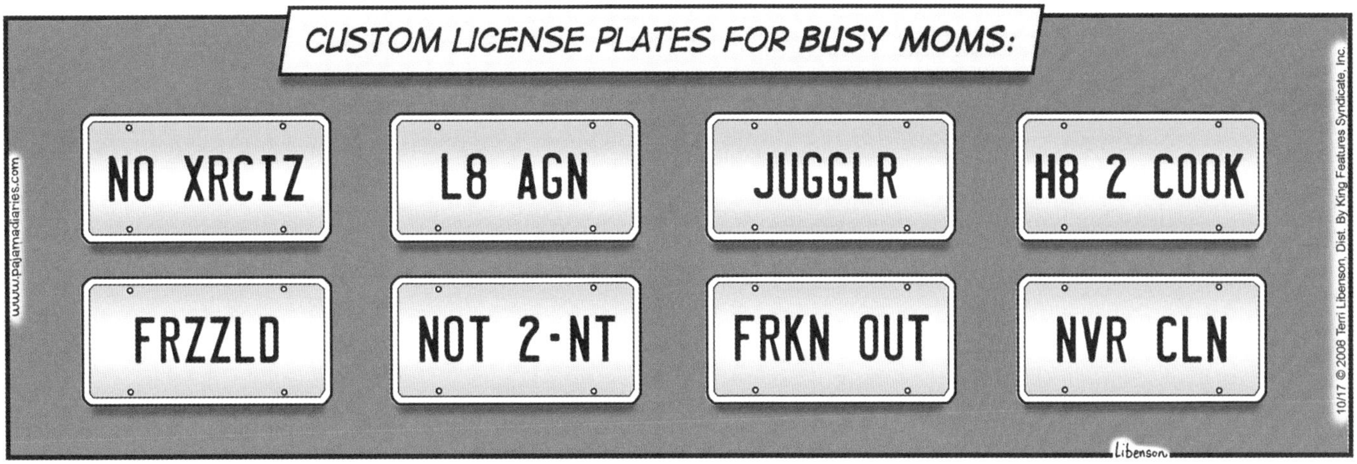
CUSTOM LICENSE PLATES FOR BUSY MOMS:
NO XRCIZ
L8 AGN
JUGGLR
H8 2 COOK
FRZZLD
NOT 2-NT
FRKN OUT
NVR CLN
www.pajamadiaries.com
10/17 © 2008 Terri Libenson. Dist. By King Features Syndicate, Inc.
Libenson

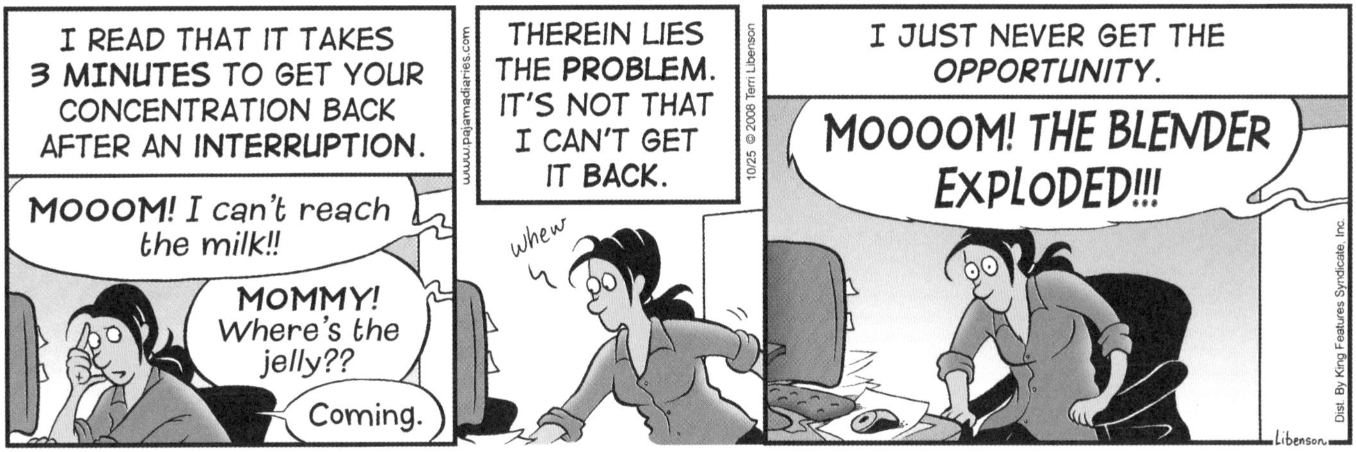
I READ THAT IT TAKES 3 MINUTES TO GET YOUR CONCENTRATION BACK AFTER AN INTERRUPTION.
MOOOM! I can't reach the milk!!
MOMMY! Where's the jelly??
Coming.
www.pajamadiaries.com
THEREIN LIES THE PROBLEM. IT'S NOT THAT I CAN'T GET IT BACK.
whew
10/25 © 2008 Terri Libenson
I JUST NEVER GET THE OPPORTUNITY.
MOOOOM! THE BLENDER EXPLODED!!!
Dist. By King Features Syndicate, Inc.
Libenson

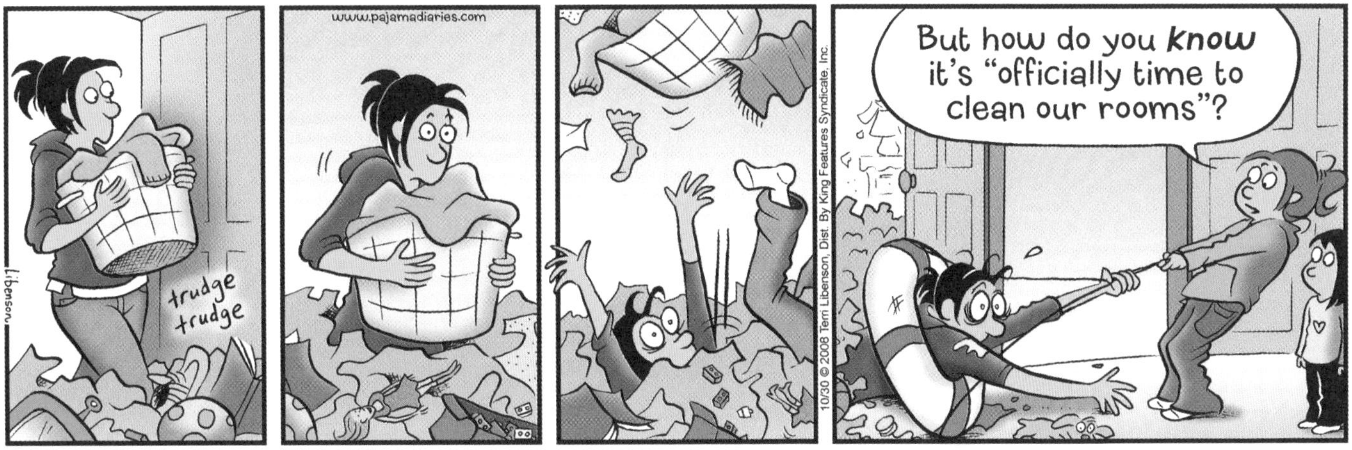
Libenson
trudge trudge
www.pajamadiaries.com
10/30 © 2008 Terri Libenson, Dist. By King Features Syndicate, Inc.
But how do you know it's "officially time to clean our rooms"?

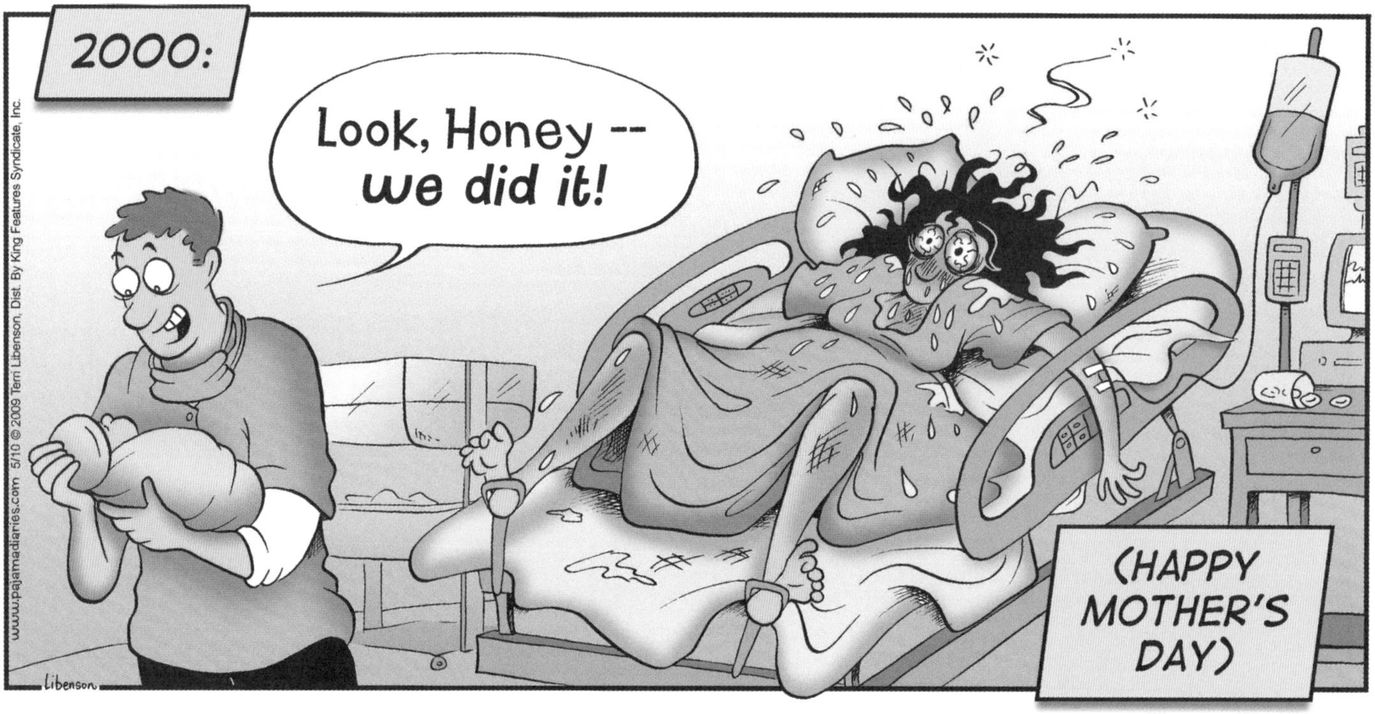
2000:
Look, Honey -- we did it!
(HAPPY MOTHER'S DAY)
www.pajamadiaries.com 5/10 © 2009 Terri Libenson, Dist. By King Features Syndicate, Inc.
Libenson

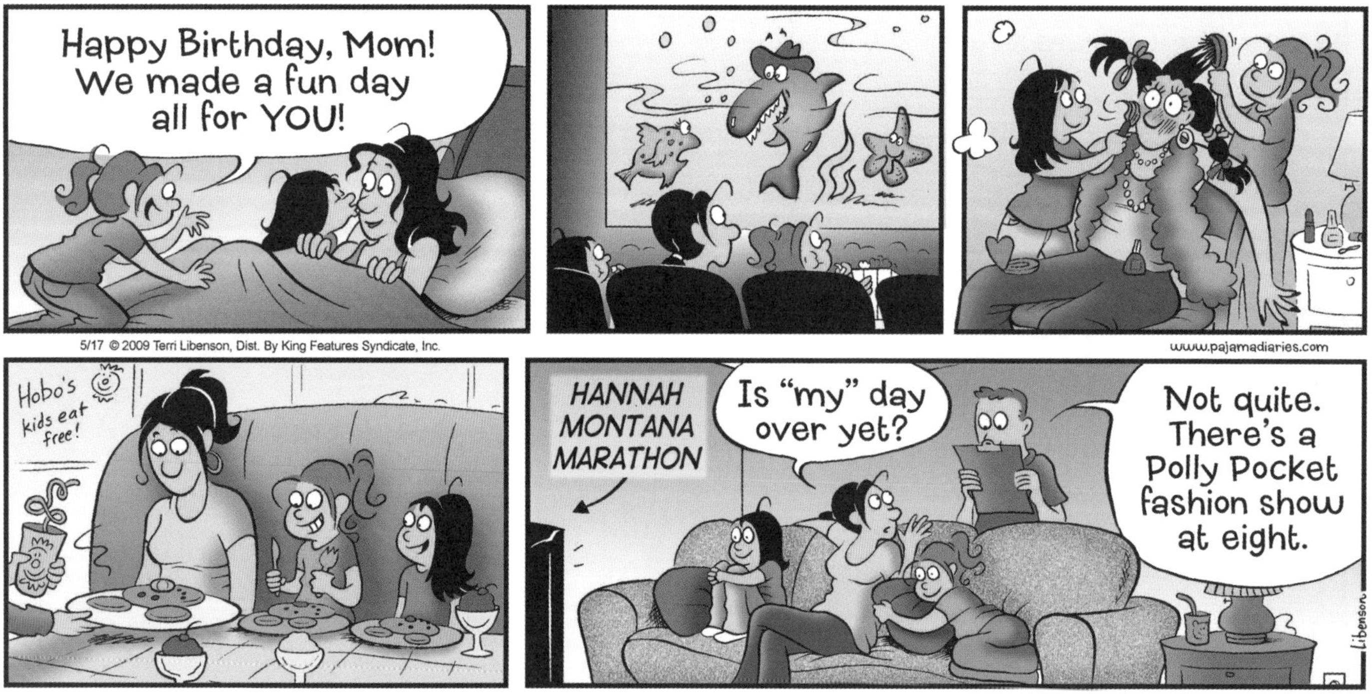
Happy Birthday, Mom! We made a fun day all for YOU!
5/17 © 2009 Terri Libenson, Dist. By King Features Syndicate, Inc.
www.pajamadiaries.com
Hobo's kids eat free!
HANNAH MONTANA MARATHON
Is "my" day over yet?
Not quite. There's a Polly Pocket fashion show at eight.
Libenson

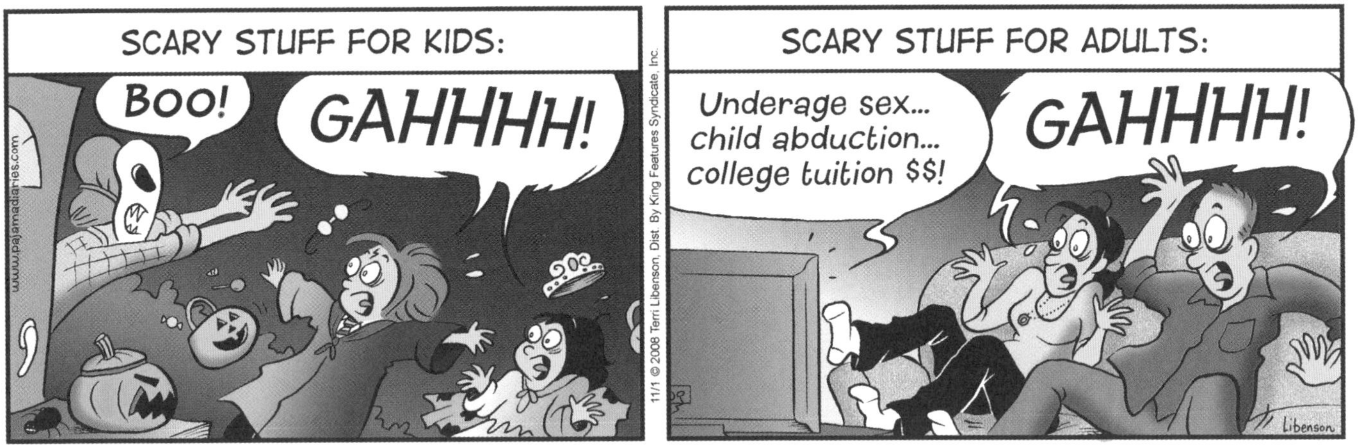
SCARY STUFF FOR KIDS:
BOO!
GAHHHH!
www.pajamadiaries.com
11/1 © 2008 Terri Libenson, Dist. By King Features Syndicate, Inc.
SCARY STUFF FOR ADULTS:
Underage sex... child abduction... college tuition $$!
GAHHHH!
Libenson

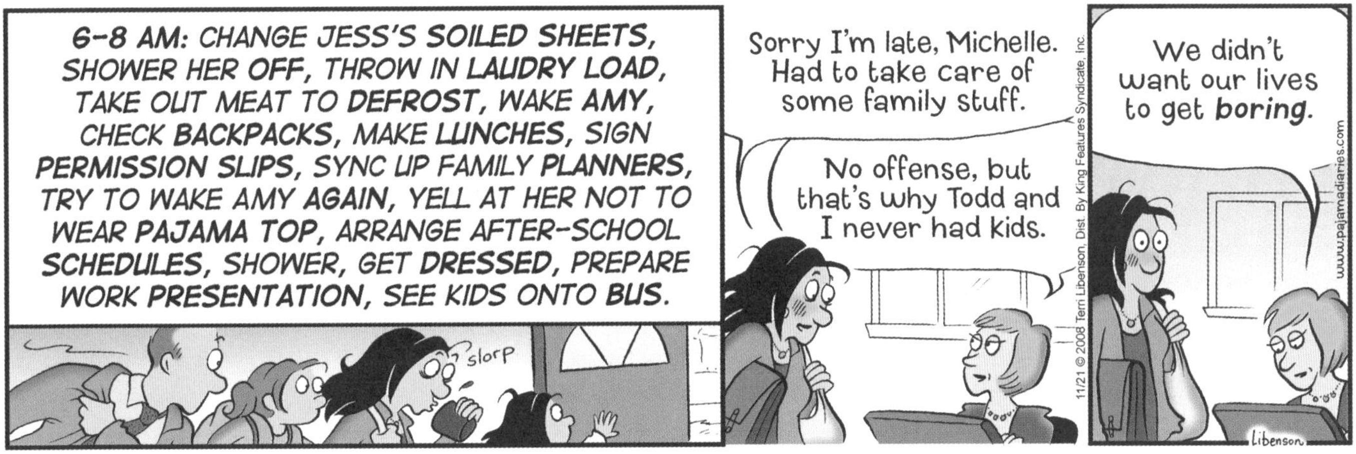
6-8 AM: CHANGE JESS'S SOILED SHEETS, SHOWER HER OFF, THROW IN LAUDRY LOAD, TAKE OUT MEAT TO DEFROST, WAKE AMY, CHECK BACKPACKS, MAKE LUNCHES, SIGN PERMISSION SLIPS, SYNC UP FAMILY PLANNERS, TRY TO WAKE AMY AGAIN, YELL AT HER NOT TO WEAR PAJAMA TOP, ARRANGE AFTER-SCHOOL SCHEDULES, SHOWER, GET DRESSED, PREPARE WORK PRESENTATION, SEE KIDS ONTO BUS.
slorp
Sorry I'm late, Michelle. Had to take care of some family stuff.
No offense, but that's why Todd and I never had kids.
11/21 © 2008 Terri Libenson, Dist. By King Features Syndicate, Inc.
We didn't want our lives to get boring.
www.pajamadiaries.com
Libenson

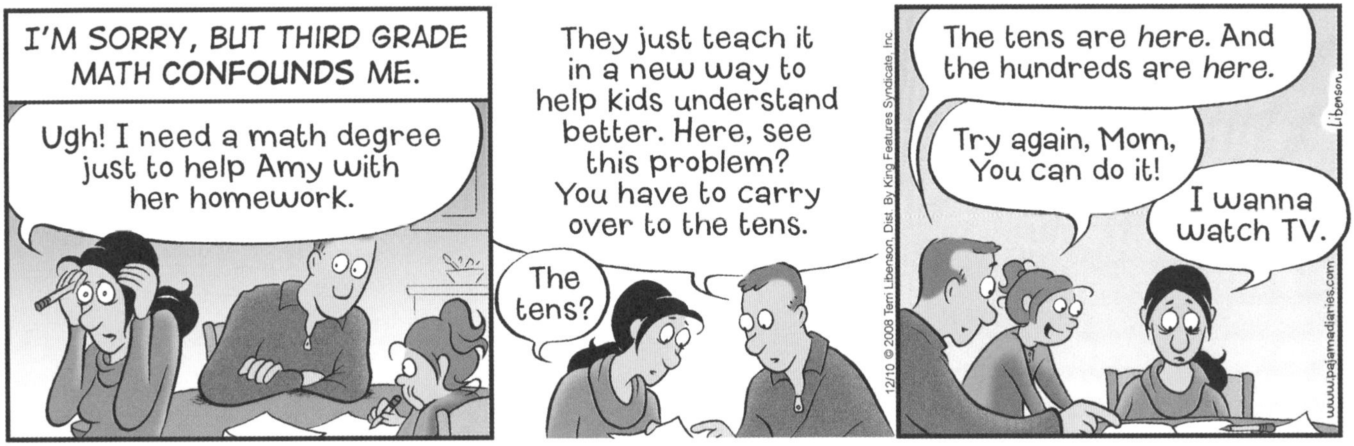
I'M SORRY, BUT THIRD GRADE MATH CONFOUNDS ME.
Ugh! I need a math degree just to help Amy with her homework.
They just teach it in a new way to help kids understand better. Here, see this problem? You have to carry over to the tens.
The tens?
12/10 © 2008 Terri Libenson, Dist. By King Features Syndicate, Inc.
The tens are here. And the hundreds are here.
Try again, Mom, You can do it!
I wanna watch TV.
Libenson
www.pajamadiaries.com

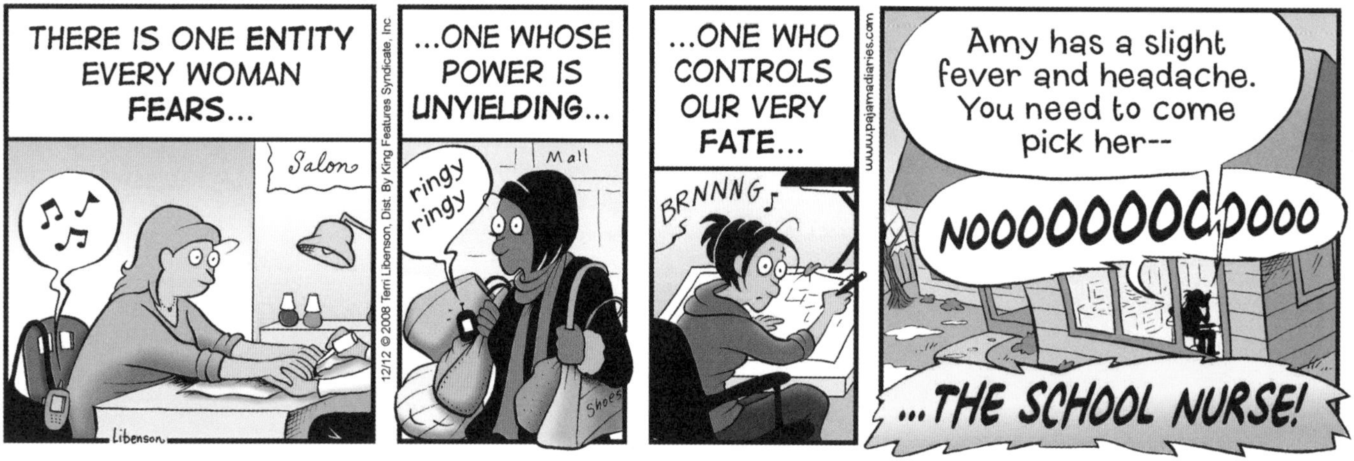
THERE IS ONE ENTITY EVERY WOMAN FEARS...
Salon
Libenson
12/12 © 2008 Terri Libenson, Dist. By King Features Syndicate, Inc.
...ONE WHOSE POWER IS UNYIELDING...
Mall
ringy ringy
Shoes
...ONE WHO CONTROLS OUR VERY FATE...
BRNNNG
www.pajamadiaries.com
Amy has a slight fever and headache. You need to come pick her--
NOOOOOOOOOOOO
...THE SCHOOL NURSE!

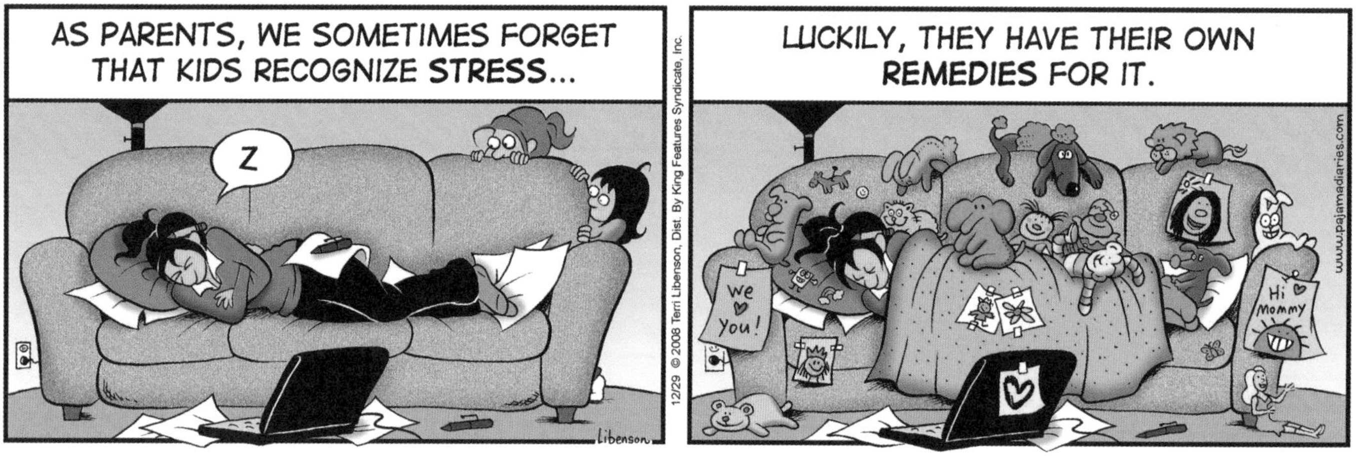
AS PARENTS, WE SOMETIMES FORGET THAT KIDS RECOGNIZE STRESS...
Z
Libenson
12/29 © 2008 Terri Libenson, Dist. By King Features Syndicate, Inc.
LUCKILY, THEY HAVE THEIR OWN REMEDIES FOR IT.
We ♥ you!
Hi ♥ Mommy
www.pajamadiaries.com

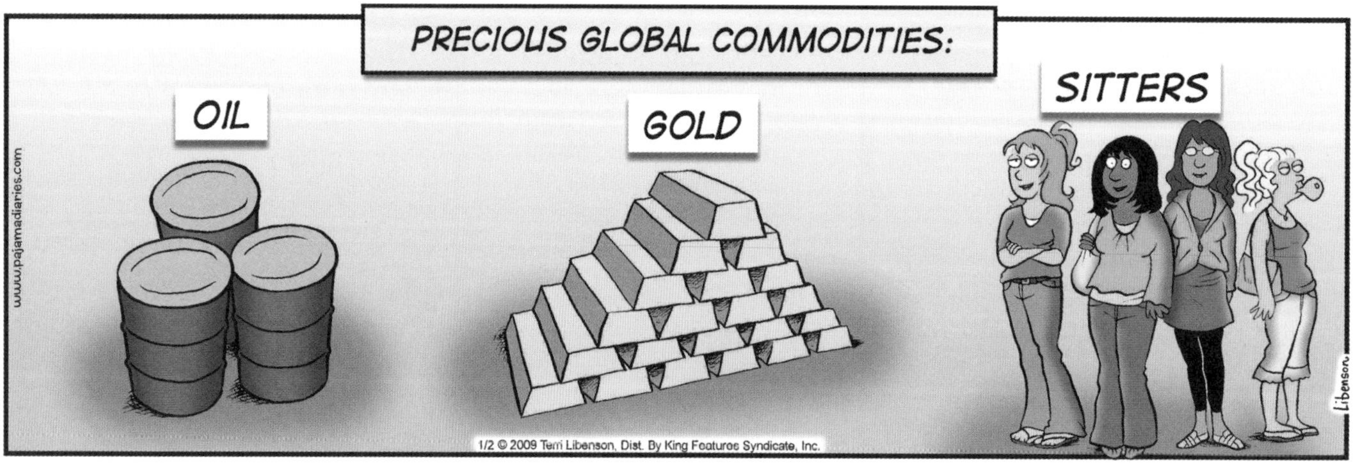
PRECIOUS GLOBAL COMMODITIES:
OIL
GOLD
SITTERS
www.pajamadiaries.com
Libenson
1/2 © 2009 Terri Libenson, Dist. By King Features Syndicate, Inc.

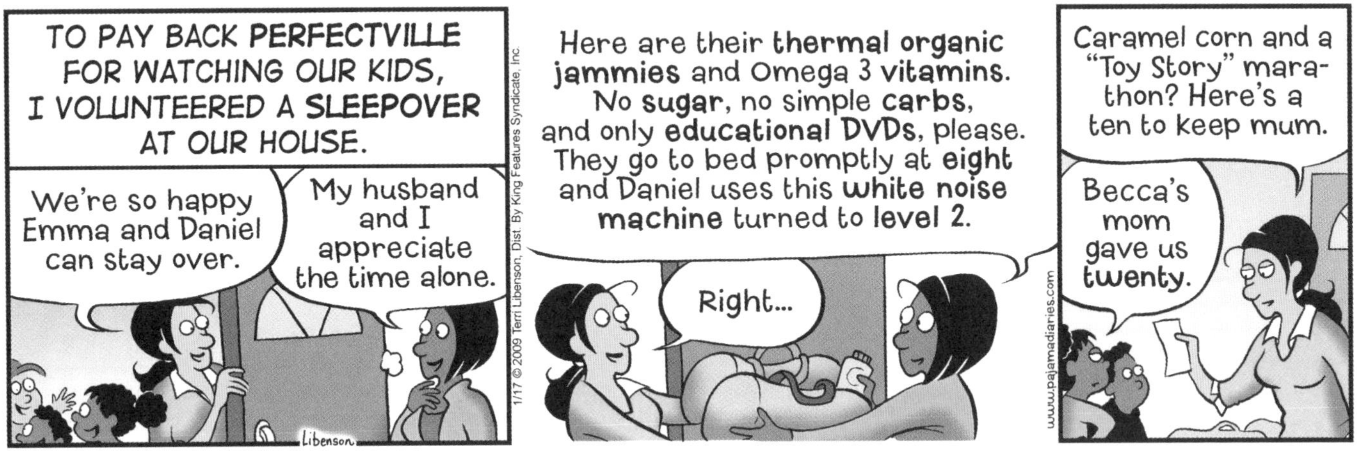
TO PAY BACK PERFECTVILLE FOR WATCHING OUR KIDS, I VOLUNTEERED A SLEEPOVER AT OUR HOUSE.
We're so happy Emma and Daniel can stay over.
My husband and I appreciate the time alone.
Libenson
1/17 © 2009 Terri Libenson, Dist. By King Features Syndicate, Inc.
Here are their thermal organic jammies and Omega 3 vitamins. No sugar, no simple carbs, and only educational DVDs, please. They go to bed promptly at eight and Daniel uses this white noise machine turned to level 2.
Right...
www.pajamadiaries.com
Caramel corn and a "Toy Story" marathon? Here's a ten to keep mum.
Becca's mom gave us twenty.

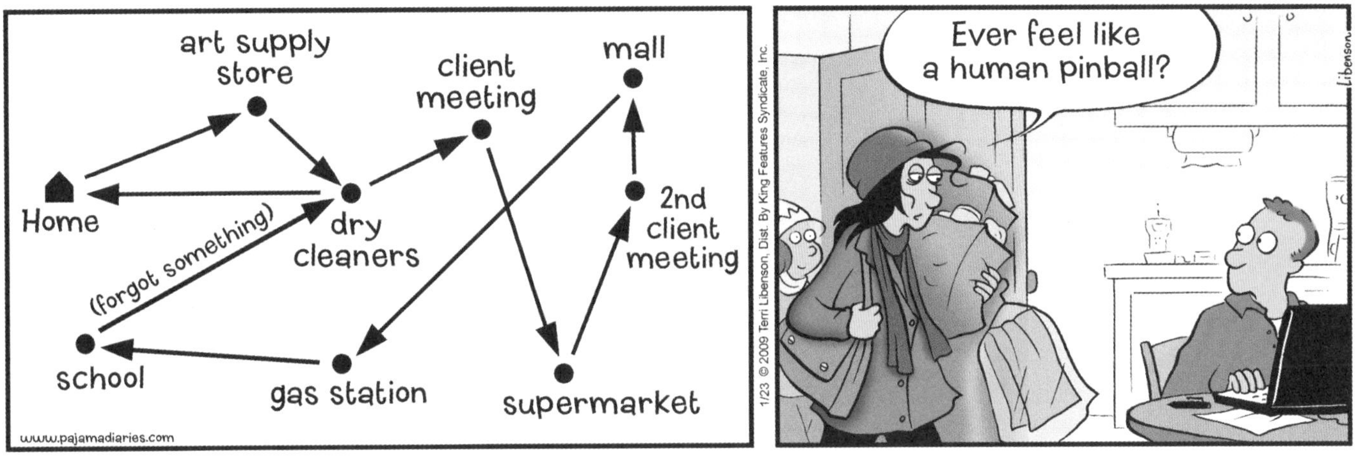
art supply store
client meeting
mall
Home
dry cleaners
2nd client meeting
(forgot something)
school
gas station
supermarket
www.pajamadiaries.com
1/23 © 2009 Terri Libenson, Dist. By King Features Syndicate, Inc.
Ever feel like a human pinball?
Libenson

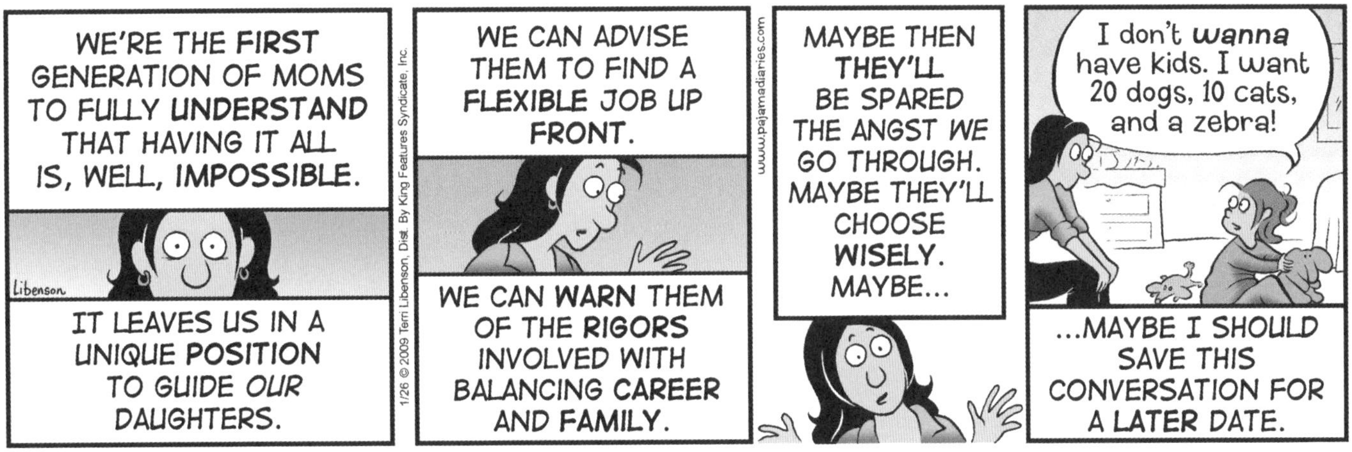
WE'RE THE FIRST GENERATION OF MOMS TO FULLY UNDERSTAND THAT HAVING IT ALL IS, WELL, IMPOSSIBLE.
Libenson
IT LEAVES US IN A UNIQUE POSITION TO GUIDE OUR DAUGHTERS.
1/26 © 2009 Terri Libenson, Dist. By King Features Syndicate, Inc.
WE CAN ADVISE THEM TO FIND A FLEXIBLE JOB UP FRONT.
WE CAN WARN THEM OF THE RIGORS INVOLVED WITH BALANCING CAREER AND FAMILY.
www.pajamadiaries.com
MAYBE THEN THEY'LL BE SPARED THE ANGST WE GO THROUGH. MAYBE THEY'LL CHOOSE WISELY. MAYBE...
I don't wanna have kids. I want 20 dogs, 10 cats, and a zebra!
...MAYBE I SHOULD SAVE THIS CONVERSATION FOR A LATER DATE.

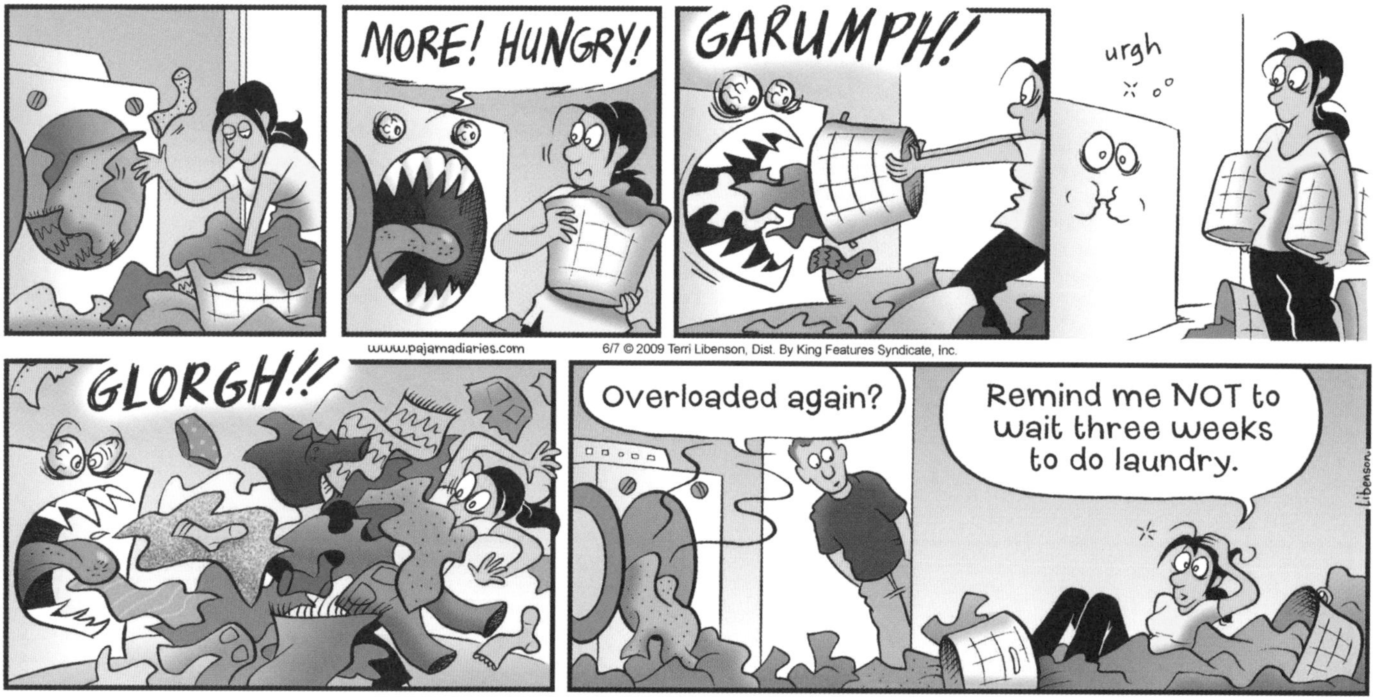
MORE! HUNGRY!
GARUMPH!
urgh
www.pajamadiaries.com
6/7 © 2009 Terri Libenson, Dist. By King Features Syndicate, Inc.
GLORGH!!
Overloaded again?
Remind me NOT to wait three weeks to do laundry.
Libenson

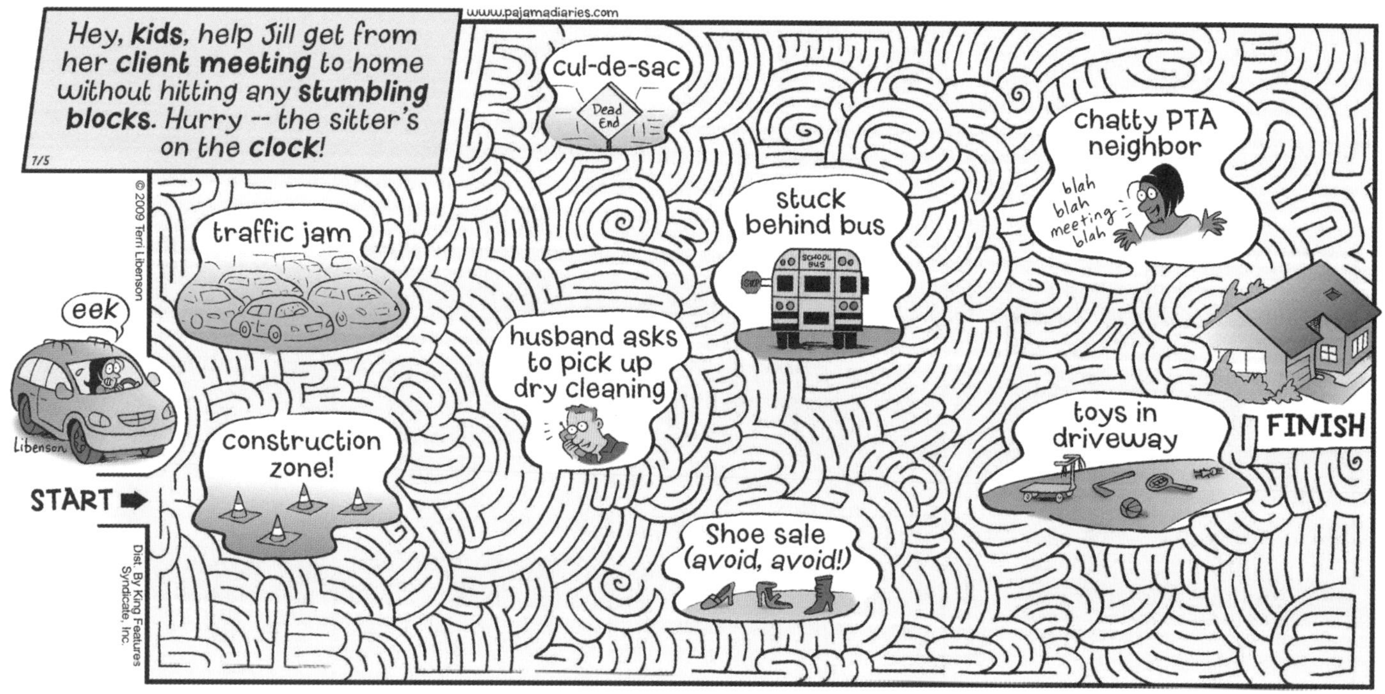
www.pajamadiaries.com
Hey, kids, help Jill get from her client meeting to home without hitting any stumbling blocks. Hurry -- the sitter's on the clock!
7/5
© 2009 Terri Libenson
Dist. By King Features Syndicate, Inc.
cul-de-sac
Dead End
chatty PTA neighbor
blah blah meeting blah
stuck behind bus
SCHOOL BUS
traffic jam
eek
Libenson
husband asks to pick up dry cleaning
toys in driveway
FINISH
construction zone!
START
Shoe sale (avoid, avoid!)

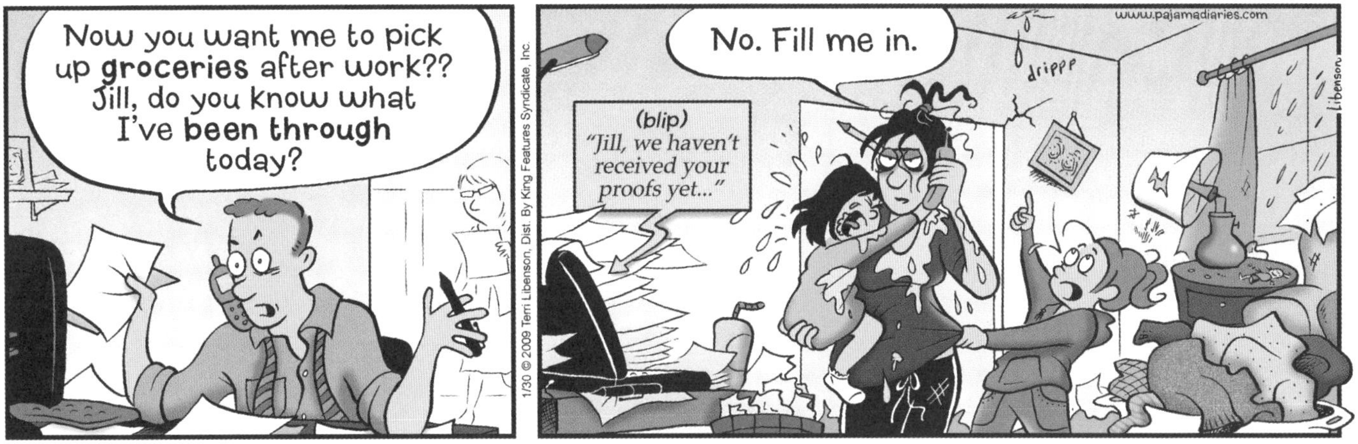
Now you want me to pick up **groceries** after work?? Jill, do you know what I've **been through** today?
1/30 © 2009 Terri Libenson, Dist. By King Features Syndicate, Inc.
www.pajamadiaries.com
Libenson
No. Fill me in.
(blip) "Jill, we haven't received your proofs yet..."
drippp

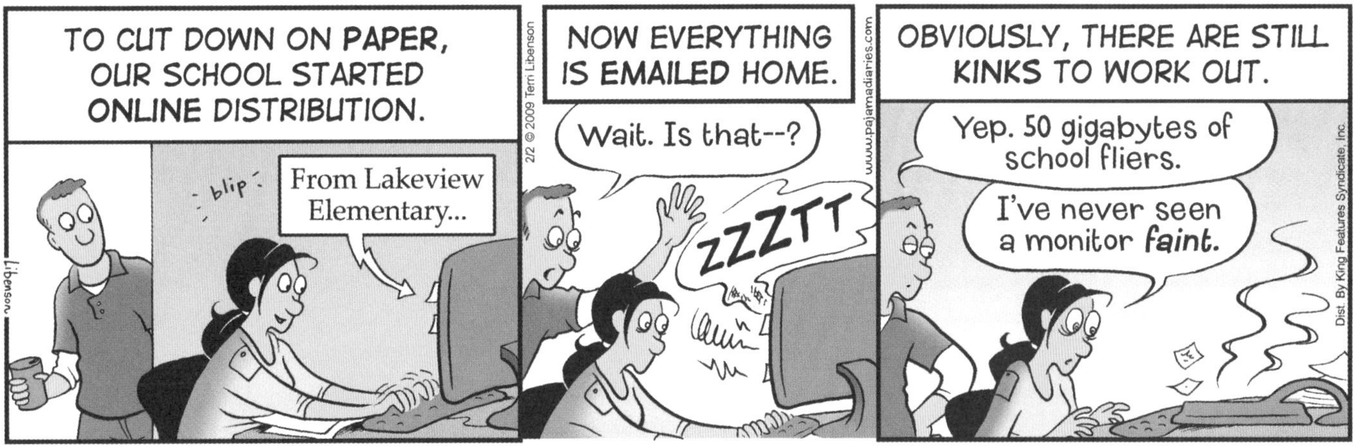
TO CUT DOWN ON **PAPER,** OUR SCHOOL STARTED **ONLINE** DISTRIBUTION.
blip
From Lakeview Elementary...
Libenson
2/2 © 2009 Terri Libenson
NOW EVERYTHING IS **EMAILED** HOME.
Wait. Is that--?
ZZZTT
www.pajamadiaries.com
OBVIOUSLY, THERE ARE STILL **KINKS** TO WORK OUT.
Yep. 50 gigabytes of school fliers.
I've never seen a monitor **faint.**
Dist. By King Features Syndicate, Inc.

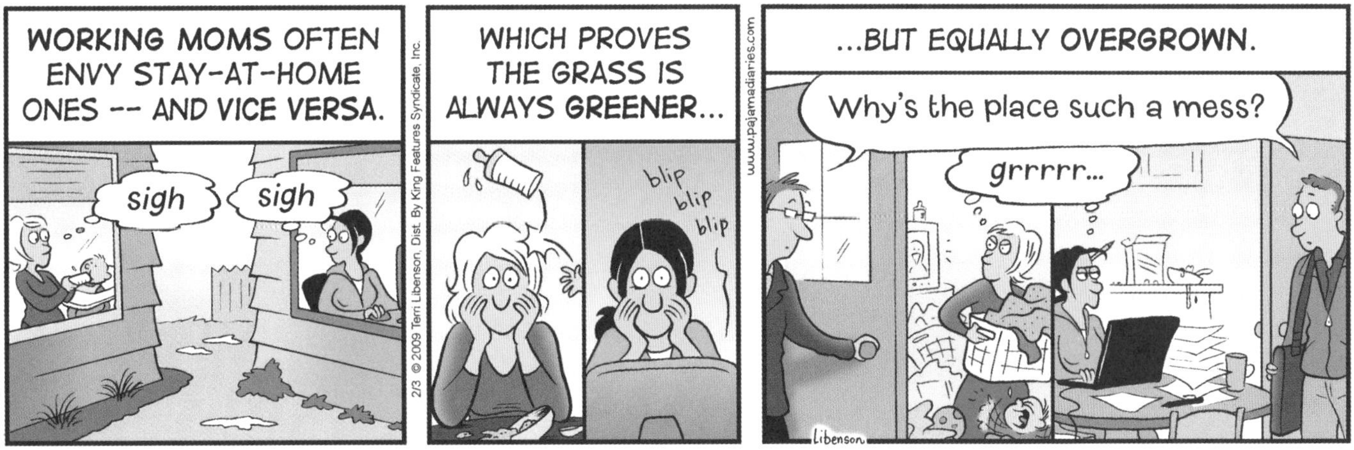
WORKING MOMS OFTEN ENVY STAY-AT-HOME ONES -- AND **VICE VERSA.**
sigh
sigh
2/3 © 2009 Terri Libenson, Dist. By King Features Syndicate, Inc.
WHICH PROVES THE GRASS IS ALWAYS **GREENER...**
blip
blip
blip
www.pajamadiaries.com
...BUT EQUALLY **OVERGROWN.**
Why's the place such a mess?
grrrrr...
Libenson

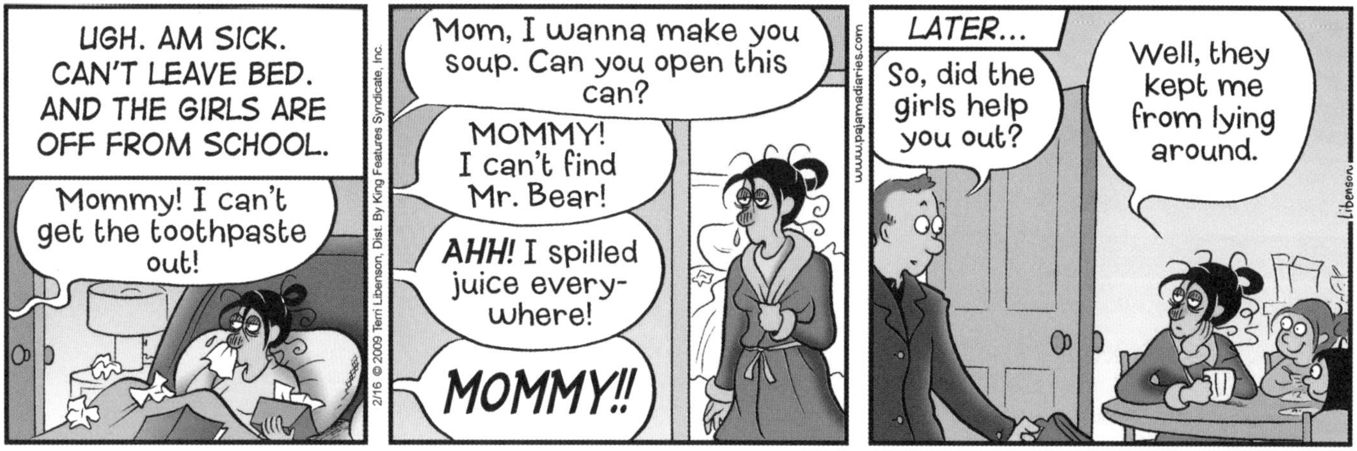
UGH. AM SICK. CAN'T LEAVE BED. AND THE GIRLS ARE OFF FROM SCHOOL.
Mommy! I can't get the toothpaste out!
2/16 © 2009 Terri Libenson, Dist. By King Features Syndicate, Inc.
Mom, I wanna make you soup. Can you open this can?
MOMMY! I can't find Mr. Bear!
AHH! I spilled juice every-where!
MOMMY!!
www.pajamadiaries.com
LATER...
So, did the girls help you out?
Well, they kept me from lying around.
Libenson

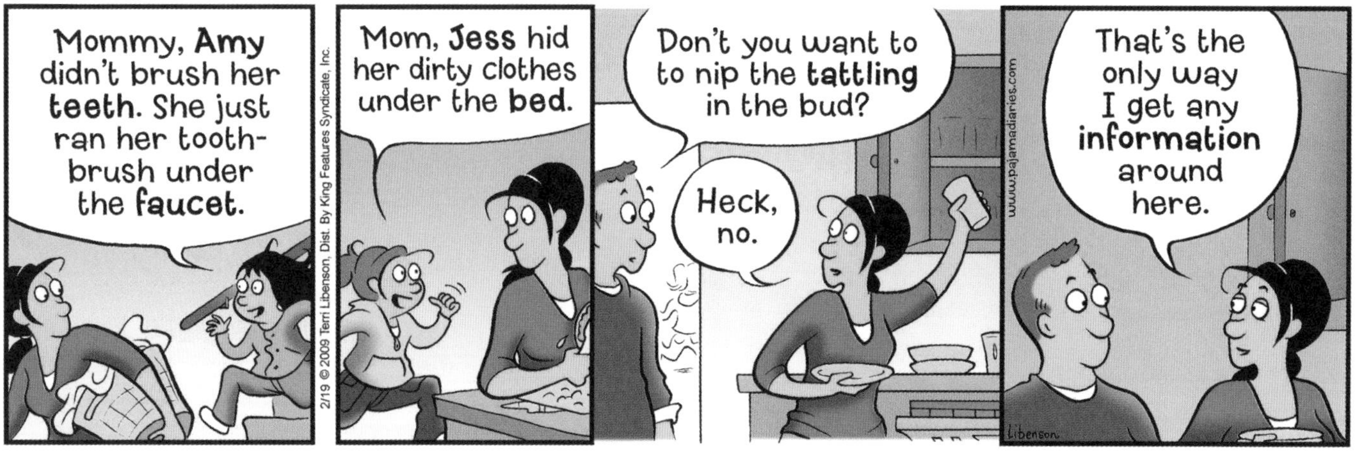
Mommy, Amy didn't brush her teeth. She just ran her tooth-brush under the faucet.
2/19 © 2009 Terri Libenson, Dist. By King Features Syndicate, Inc.
Mom, Jess hid her dirty clothes under the bed.
Don't you want to to nip the tattling in the bud?
Heck, no.
www.pajamadiaries.com
That's the only way I get any information around here.
Libenson

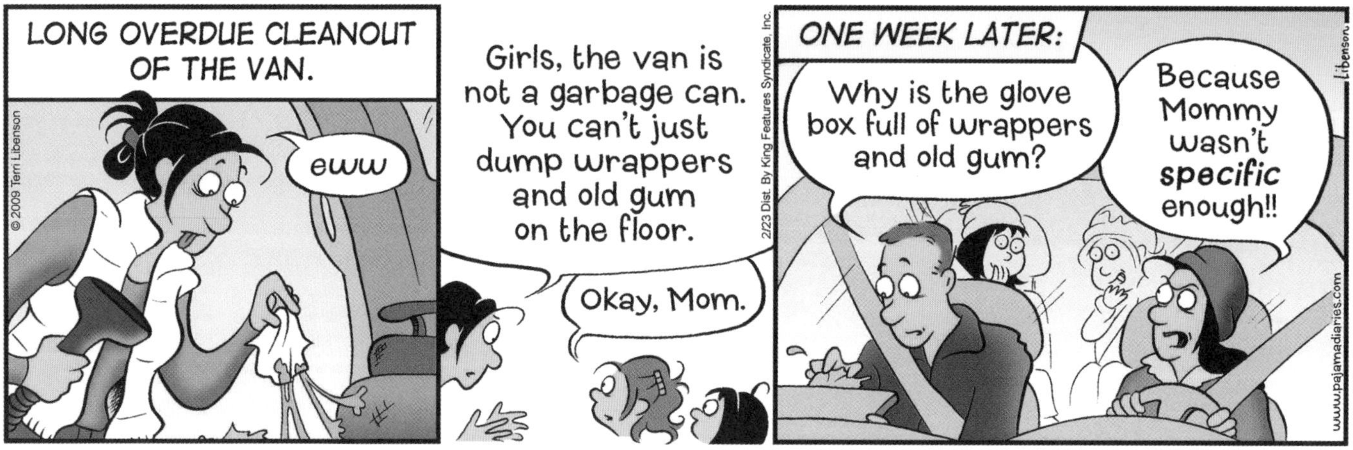
LONG OVERDUE CLEANOUT OF THE VAN.
© 2009 Terri Libenson
eww
Girls, the van is not a garbage can. You can't just dump wrappers and old gum on the floor.
Okay, Mom.
2/23 Dist. By King Features Syndicate, Inc.
ONE WEEK LATER:
Why is the glove box full of wrappers and old gum?
Because Mommy wasn't specific enough!!
Libenson
www.pajamadiaries.com

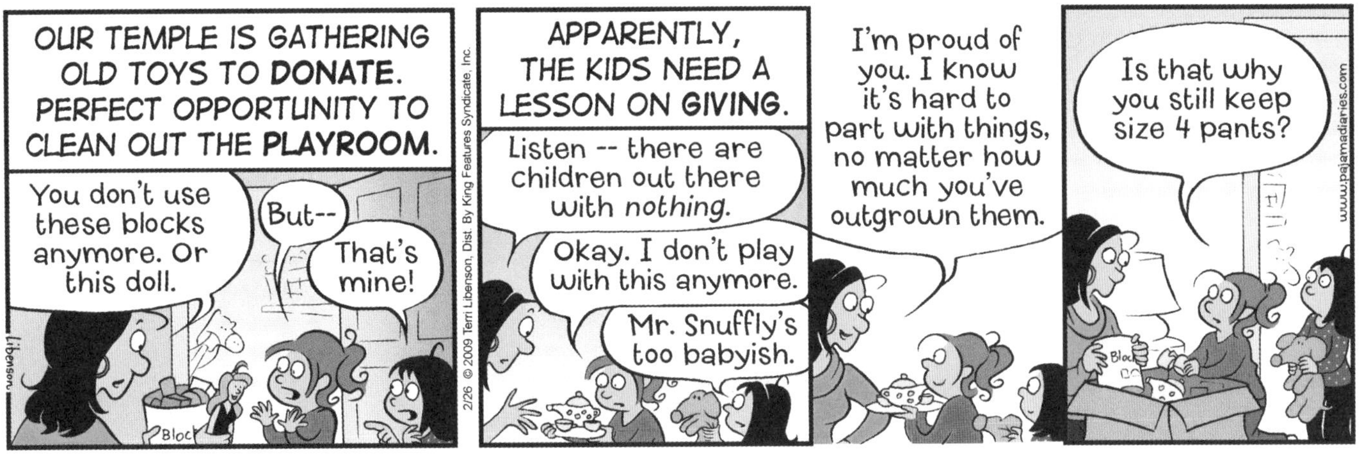
OUR TEMPLE IS GATHERING OLD TOYS TO **DONATE**. PERFECT OPPORTUNITY TO CLEAN OUT THE **PLAYROOM**.
You don't use these blocks anymore. Or this doll.
But--
That's mine!
Block
Libenson
2/26 © 2009 Terri Libenson, Dist. By King Features Syndicate, Inc.
APPARENTLY, THE KIDS NEED A LESSON ON **GIVING**.
Listen -- there are children out there with *nothing*.
Okay. I don't play with this anymore.
Mr. Snuffly's too babyish.
I'm proud of you. I know it's hard to part with things, no matter how much you've outgrown them.
Is that why you still keep size 4 pants?
www.pajamadiaries.com

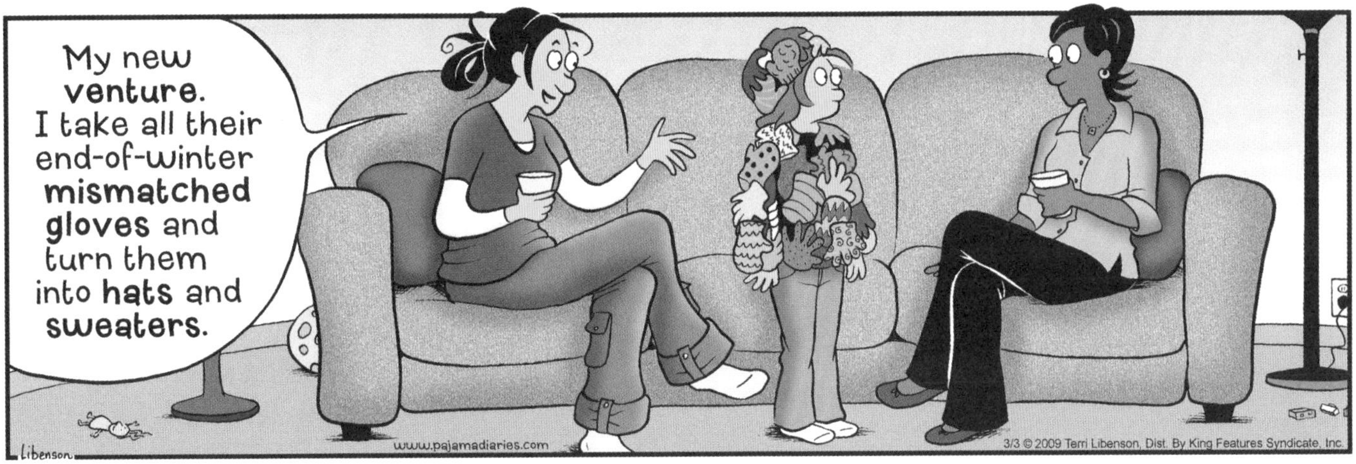
My new **venture**. I take all their end-of-winter **mismatched gloves** and turn them into **hats** and **sweaters**.
Libenson
www.pajamadiaries.com
3/3 © 2009 Terri Libenson, Dist. By King Features Syndicate, Inc.

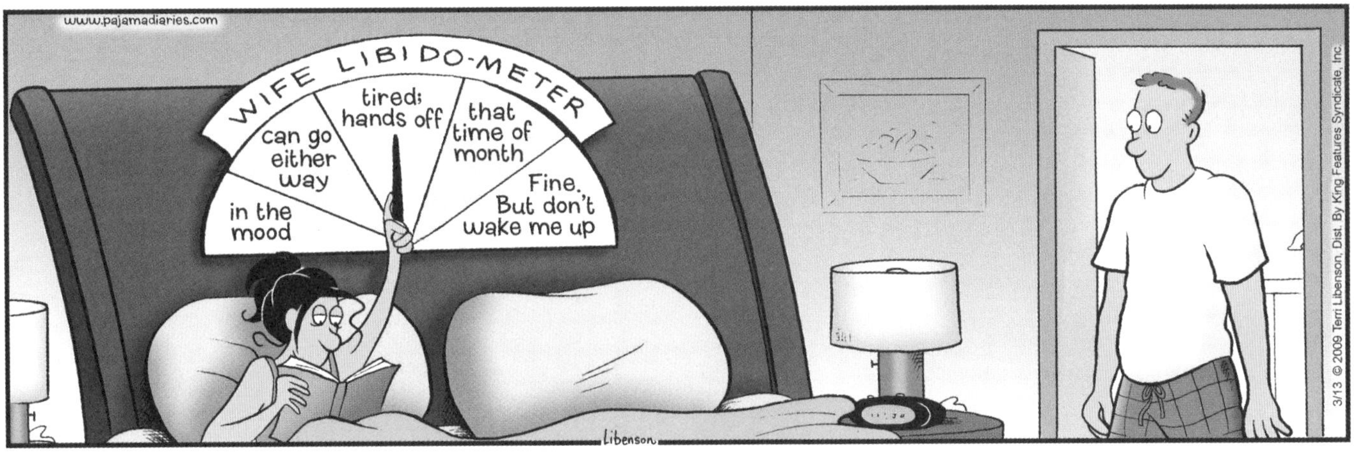
www.pajamadiaries.com
WIFE LIBIDO-METER
in the mood
can go either way
tired; hands off
that time of month
Fine. But don't wake me up
Libenson
3/13 © 2009 Terri Libenson, Dist. By King Features Syndicate, Inc.

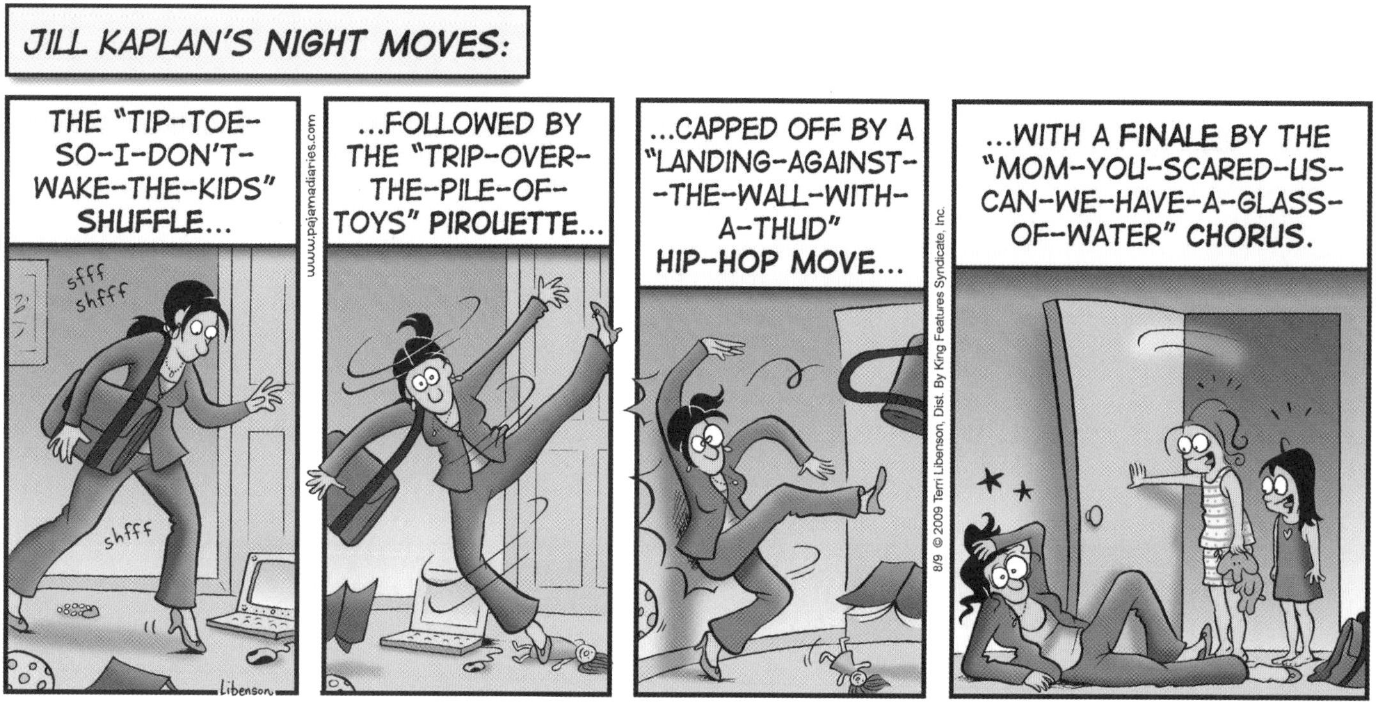
JILL KAPLAN'S NIGHT MOVES:
THE "TIP-TOE-SO-I-DON'T-WAKE-THE-KIDS" SHUFFLE...
sfff
shfff
shfff
Libenson
www.pajamadiaries.com
...FOLLOWED BY THE "TRIP-OVER-THE-PILE-OF-TOYS" PIROUETTE...
...CAPPED OFF BY A "LANDING-AGAINST-THE-WALL-WITH-A-THUD" HIP-HOP MOVE...
8/9 © 2009 Terri Libenson, Dist. By King Features Syndicate, Inc.
...WITH A FINALE BY THE "MOM-YOU-SCARED-US-CAN-WE-HAVE-A-GLASS-OF-WATER" CHORUS.

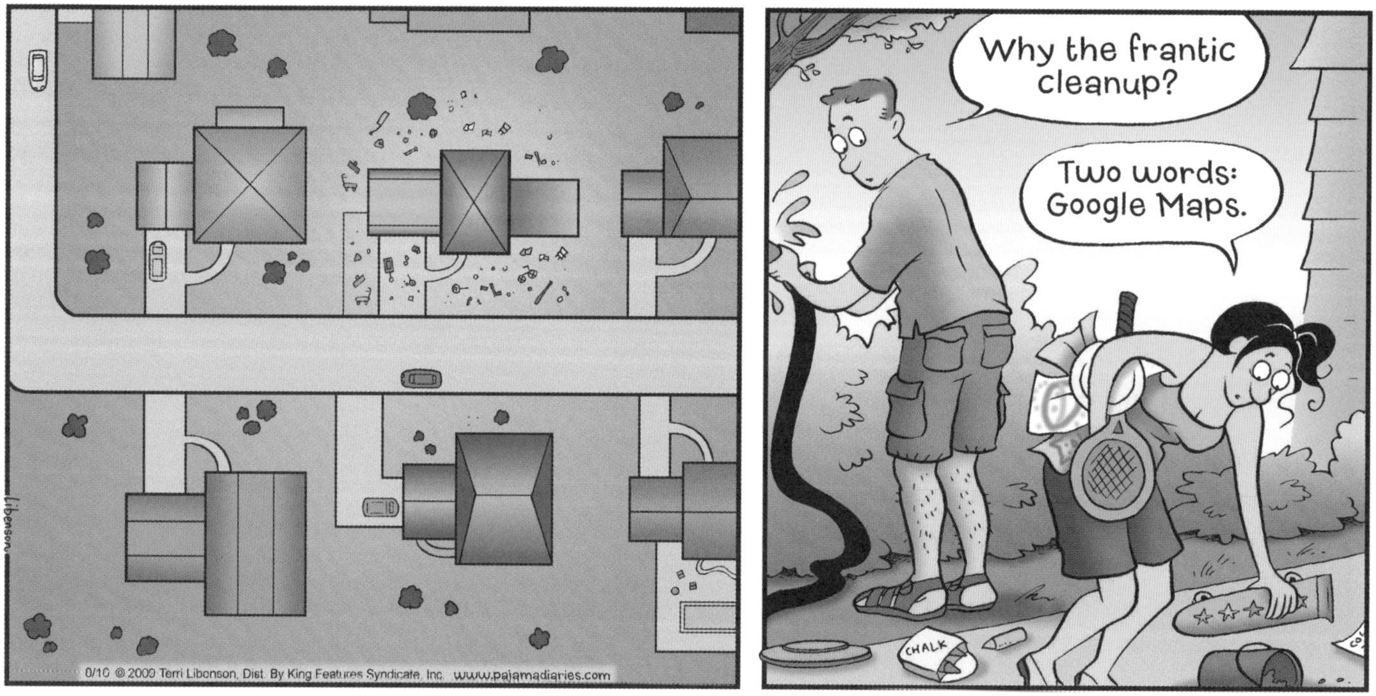
Libenson
0/10 © 2009 Terri Libenson, Dist. By King Features Syndicate, Inc. www.pajamadiaries.com
Why the frantic cleanup?
Two words: Google Maps.
CHALK

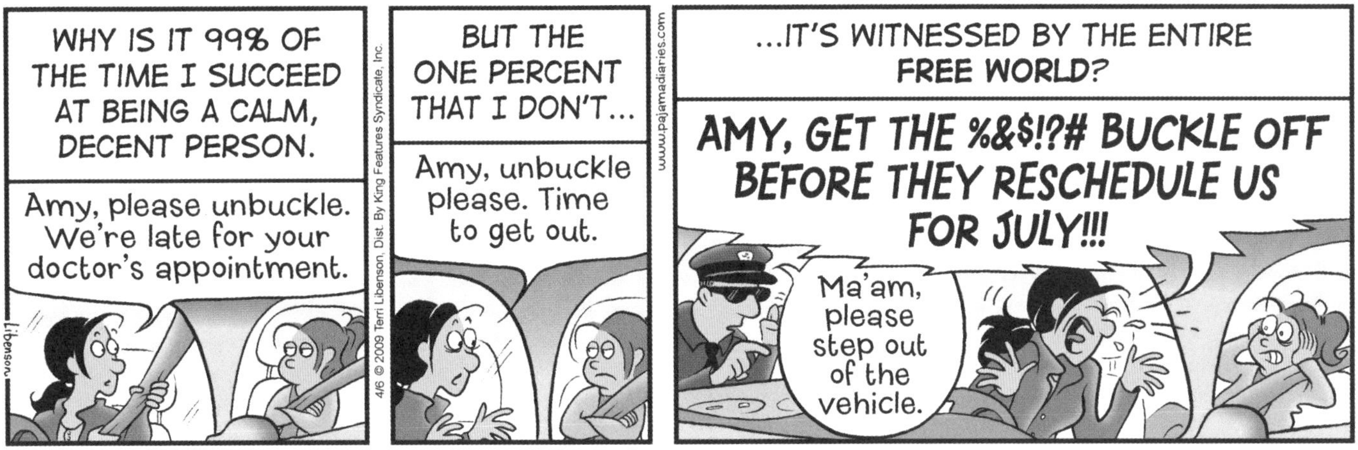
WHY IS IT 99% OF THE TIME I SUCCEED AT BEING A CALM, DECENT PERSON.
Amy, please unbuckle. We're late for your doctor's appointment.
Libenson
4/6 © 2009 Terri Libenson. Dist. By King Features Syndicate, Inc.
BUT THE ONE PERCENT THAT I DON'T...
Amy, unbuckle please. Time to get out.
www.pajamadiaries.com
...IT'S WITNESSED BY THE ENTIRE FREE WORLD?
AMY, GET THE %&$!?# BUCKLE OFF BEFORE THEY RESCHEDULE US FOR JULY!!!
Ma'am, please step out of the vehicle.

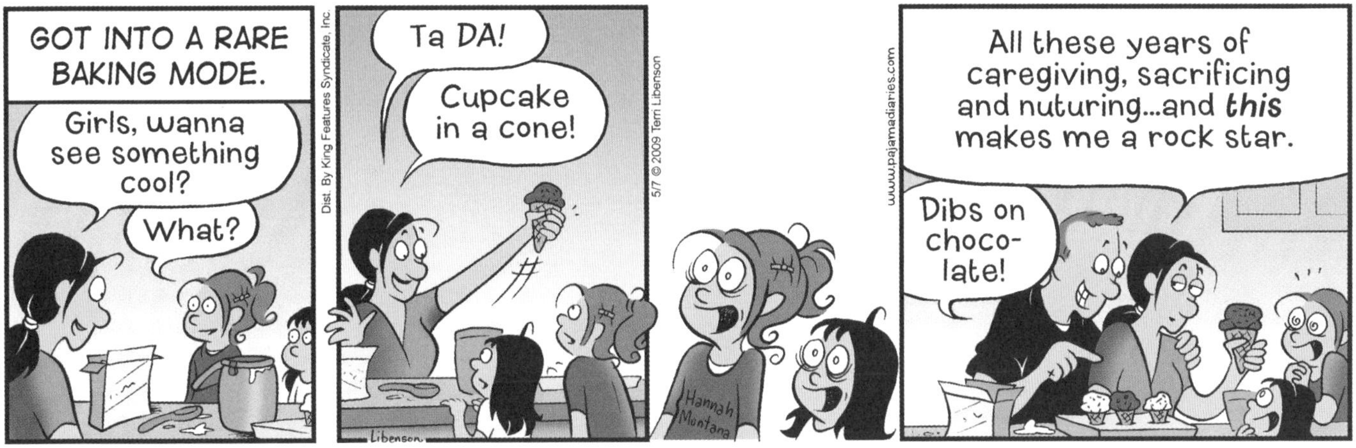
GOT INTO A RARE BAKING MODE.
Girls, wanna see something cool?
What?
Dist. By King Features Syndicate, Inc.
Ta DA!
Cupcake in a cone!
Libenson
5/7 © 2009 Terri Libenson
Hannah Montana
www.pajamadiaries.com
All these years of caregiving, sacrificing and nuturing...and this makes me a rock star.
Dibs on choco-late!

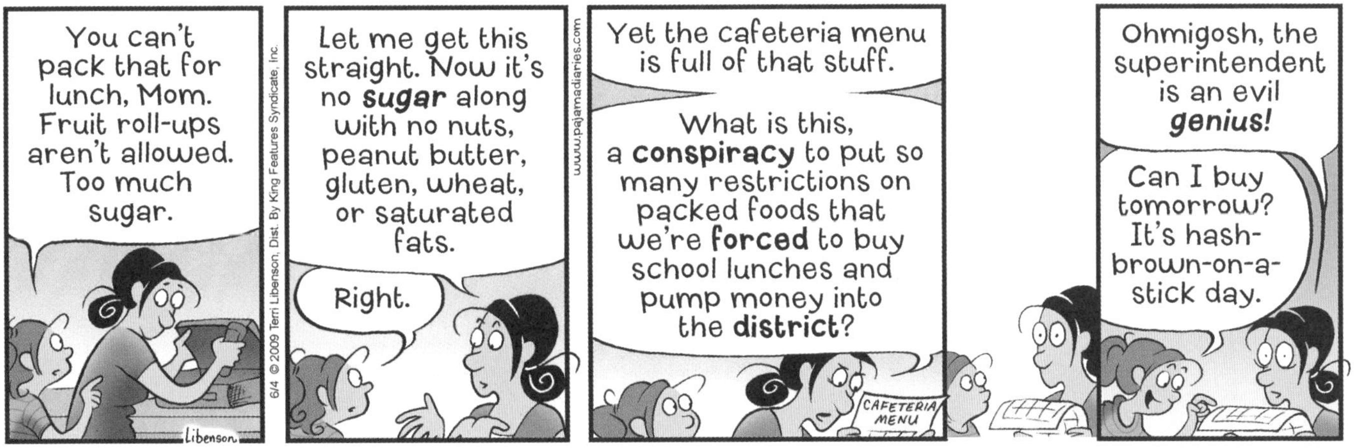
You can't pack that for lunch, Mom. Fruit roll-ups aren't allowed. Too much sugar.
Libenson
6/4 © 2009 Terri Libenson, Dist. By King Features Syndicate, Inc.
Let me get this straight. Now it's no sugar along with no nuts, peanut butter, gluten, wheat, or saturated fats.
Right.
www.pajamadiaries.com
Yet the cafeteria menu is full of that stuff.
What is this, a conspiracy to put so many restrictions on packed foods that we're forced to buy school lunches and pump money into the district?
CAFETERIA MENU
Ohmigosh, the superintendent is an evil genius!
Can I buy tomorrow? It's hash-brown-on-a-stick day.

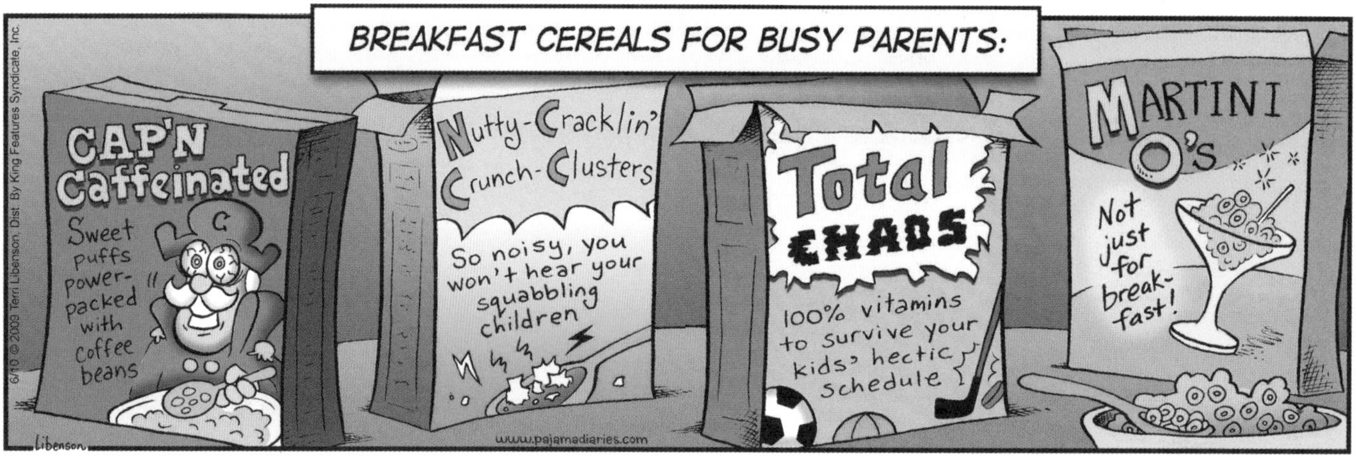
BREAKFAST CEREALS FOR BUSY PARENTS:
CAP'N Caffeinated
Sweet puffs power-packed with coffee beans
Nutty-Cracklin' Crunch-Clusters
So noisy, you won't hear your squabbling children
Total CHAOS
100% vitamins to survive your kids' hectic schedule
MARTINI O's
Not just for break-fast!
6/10 © 2009 Terri Libenson, Dist. By King Features Syndicate, Inc.
Libenson
www.pajamadiaries.com

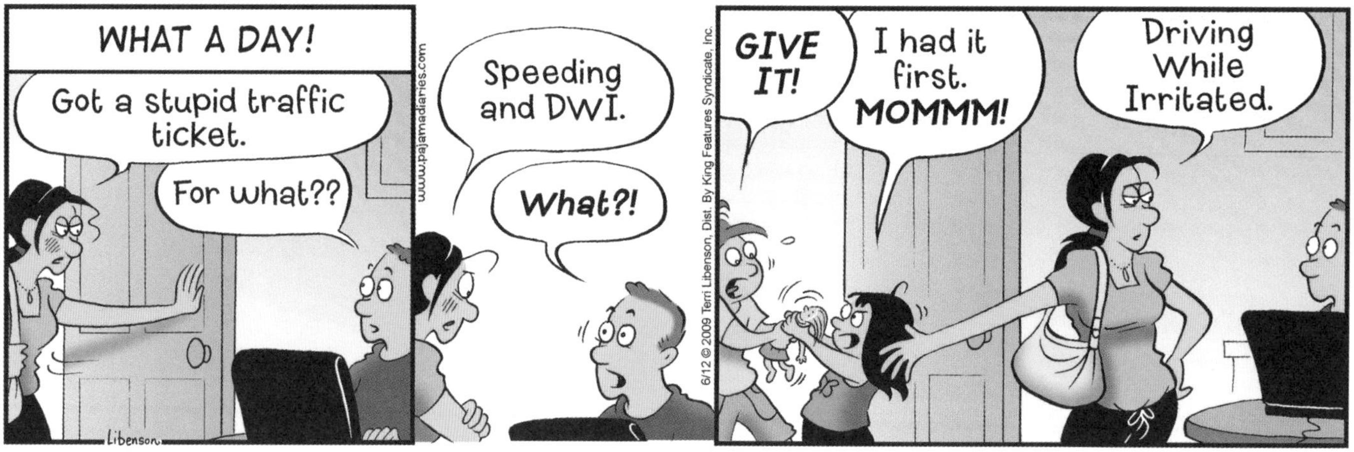
WHAT A DAY!
Got a stupid traffic ticket.
For what??
Speeding and DWI.
What?!
GIVE IT!
I had it first. MOMMM!
Driving While Irritated.
6/12 © 2009 Terri Libenson, Dist. By King Features Syndicate, Inc.
Libenson
www.pajamadiaries.com

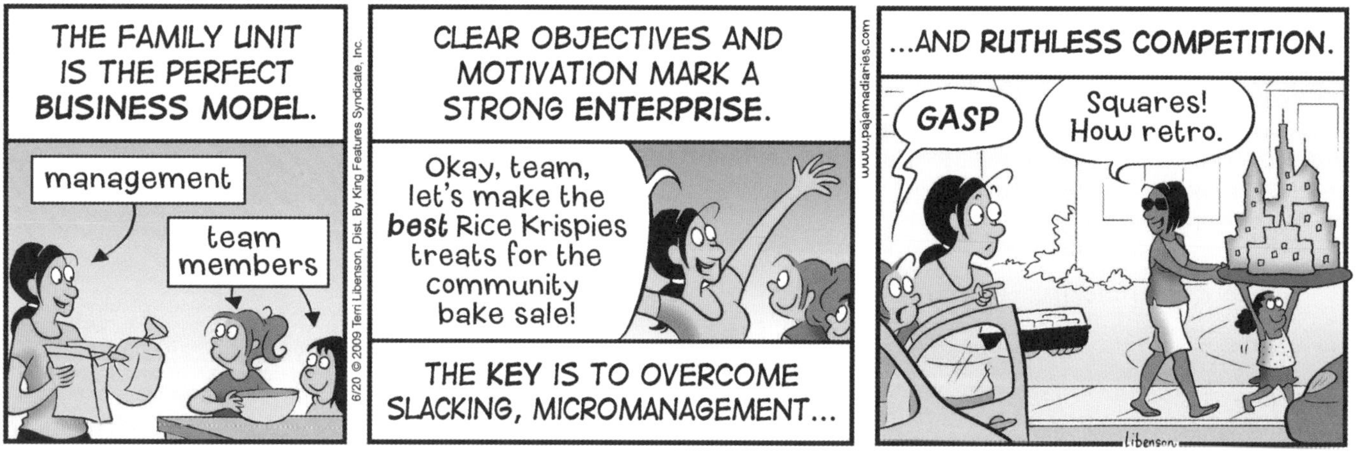
THE FAMILY UNIT IS THE PERFECT BUSINESS MODEL.
management
team members
CLEAR OBJECTIVES AND MOTIVATION MARK A STRONG ENTERPRISE.
Okay, team, let's make the best Rice Krispies treats for the community bake sale!
THE KEY IS TO OVERCOME SLACKING, MICROMANAGEMENT...
...AND RUTHLESS COMPETITION.
GASP
Squares! How retro.
6/20 © 2009 Terri Libenson, Dist. By King Features Syndicate, Inc.
Libenson
www.pajamadiaries.com

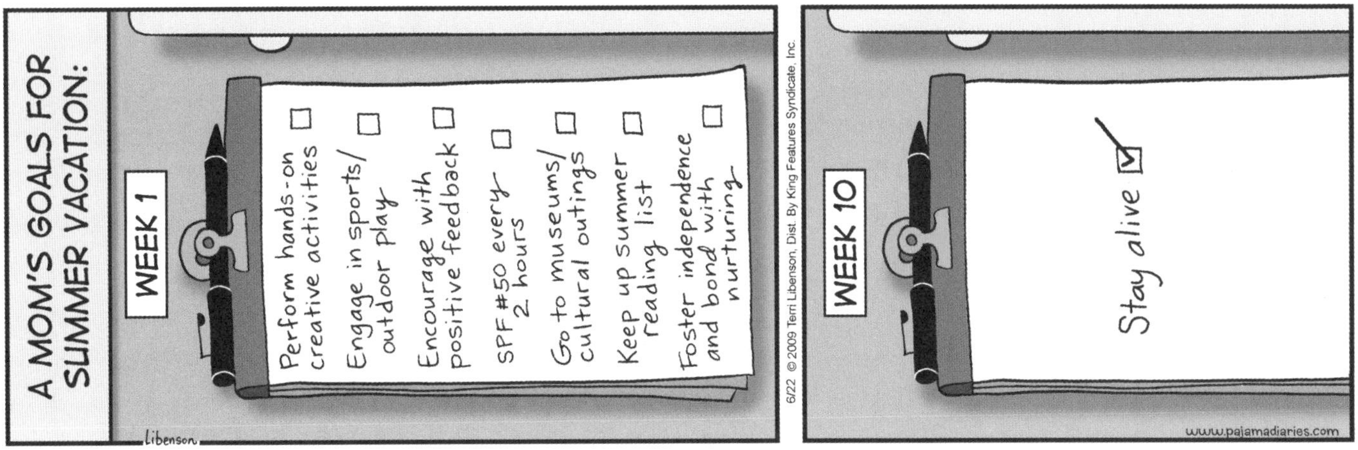
A MOM'S GOALS FOR SUMMER VACATION:
WEEK 1
Perform hands-on creative activities
Engage in sports/outdoor play
Encourage with positive feedback
SPF #50 every 2 hours
Go to museums/cultural outings
Keep up summer reading list
Foster independence and bond with nurturing
Libenson
6/22 © 2009 Terri Libenson, Dist. By King Features Syndicate, Inc.
WEEK 10
Stay alive
www.pajamadiaries.com

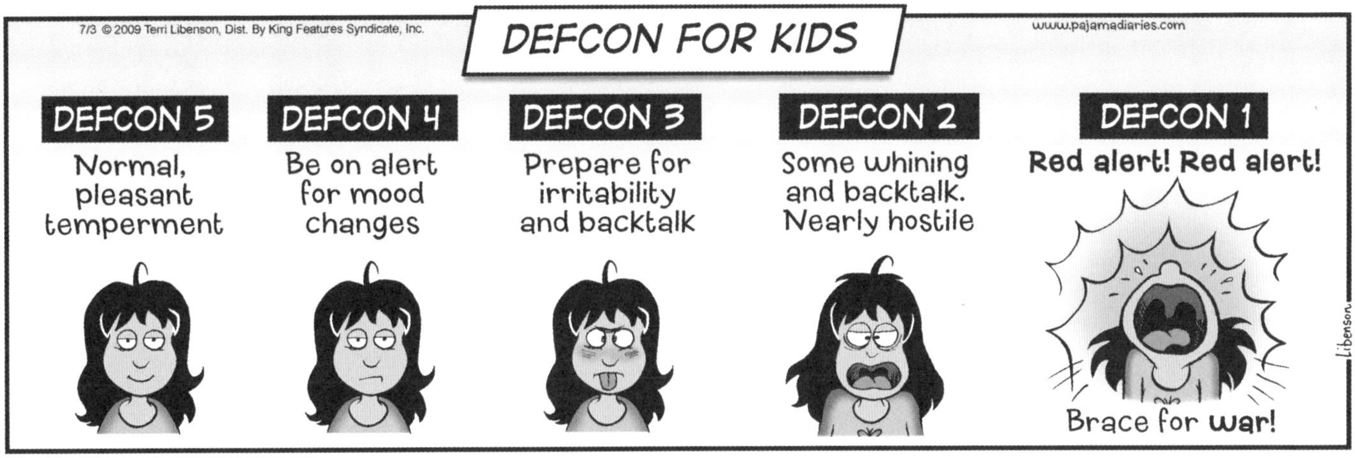
7/3 © 2009 Terri Libenson, Dist. By King Features Syndicate, Inc.
DEFCON FOR KIDS
www.pajamadiaries.com
DEFCON 5
Normal, pleasant temperment
DEFCON 4
Be on alert for mood changes
DEFCON 3
Prepare for irritability and backtalk
DEFCON 2
Some whining and backtalk. Nearly hostile
DEFCON 1
Red alert! Red alert!
Brace for war!
Libenson

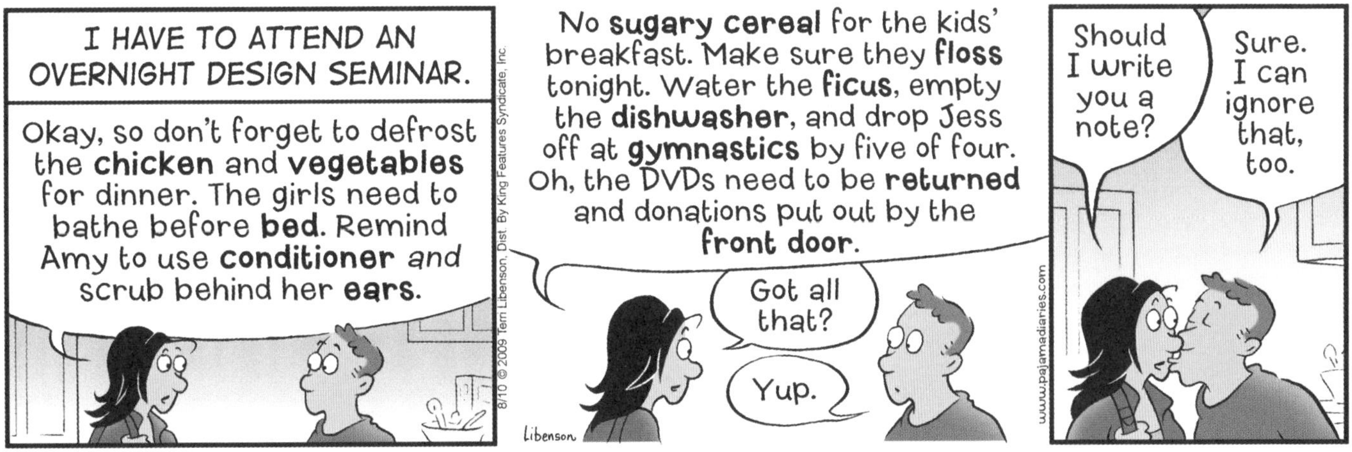
I HAVE TO ATTEND AN OVERNIGHT DESIGN SEMINAR.
Okay, so don't forget to defrost the chicken and vegetables for dinner. The girls need to bathe before bed. Remind Amy to use conditioner and scrub behind her ears.
8/10 © 2009 Terri Libenson, Dist. By King Features Syndicate, Inc.
No sugary cereal for the kids' breakfast. Make sure they floss tonight. Water the ficus, empty the dishwasher, and drop Jess off at gymnastics by five of four. Oh, the DVDs need to be returned and donations put out by the front door.
Got all that?
Yup.
Libenson
www.pajamadiaries.com
Should I write you a note?
Sure. I can ignore that, too.

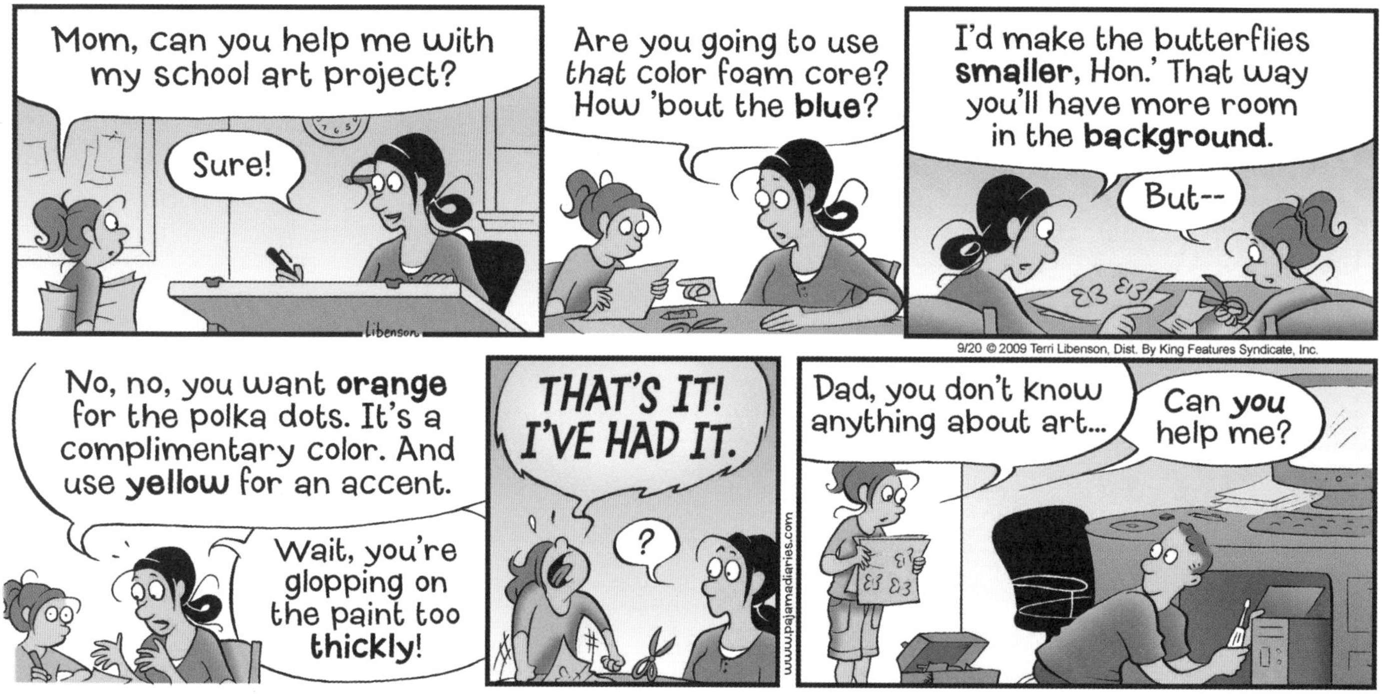
Mom, can you help me with my school art project?
Sure!
Libenson
Are you going to use *that* color foam core? How 'bout the **blue**?
I'd make the butterflies **smaller**, Hon.' That way you'll have more room in the **background**.
But--
9/20 © 2009 Terri Libenson, Dist. By King Features Syndicate, Inc.
No, no, you want **orange** for the polka dots. It's a complimentary color. And use **yellow** for an accent.
Wait, you're glopping on the paint too **thickly**!
THAT'S IT! I'VE HAD IT.
?
www.pajamadiaries.com
Dad, you don't know anything about art...
Can **you** help me?

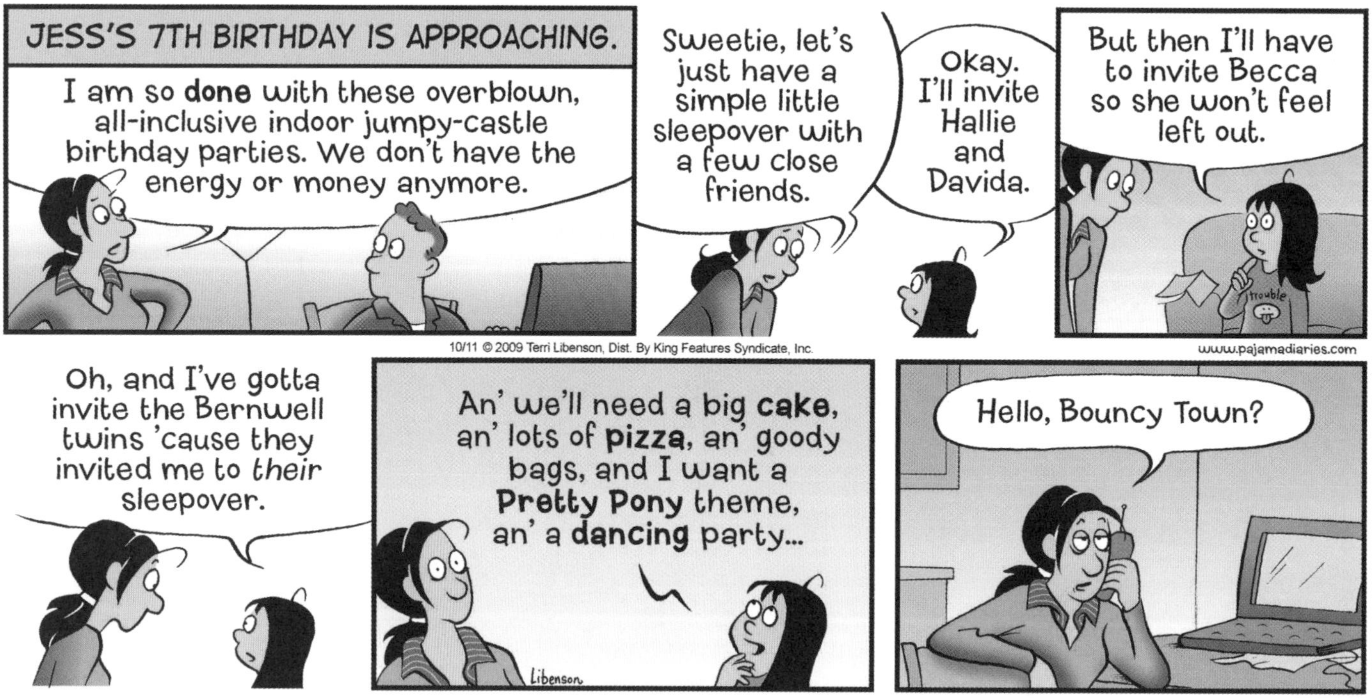
JESS'S 7TH BIRTHDAY IS APPROACHING.
I am so **done** with these overblown, all-inclusive indoor jumpy-castle birthday parties. We don't have the energy or money anymore.
Sweetie, let's just have a simple little sleepover with a few close friends.
Okay. I'll invite Hallie and Davida.
But then I'll have to invite Becca so she won't feel left out.
trouble
10/11 © 2009 Terri Libenson, Dist. By King Features Syndicate, Inc.
www.pajamadiaries.com
Oh, and I've gotta invite the Bernwell twins 'cause they invited me to *their* sleepover.
An' we'll need a big **cake**, an' lots of **pizza**, an' goody bags, and I want a **Pretty Pony** theme, an' a **dancing** party...
Libenson
Hello, Bouncy Town?

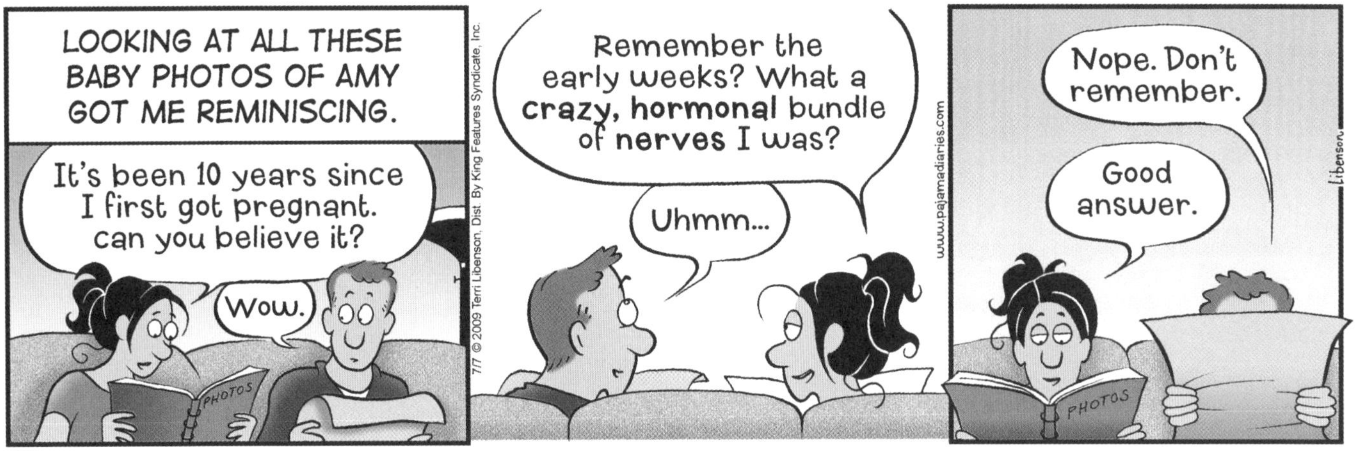
LOOKING AT ALL THESE BABY PHOTOS OF AMY GOT ME REMINISCING.
It's been 10 years since I first got pregnant. can you believe it?
Wow.
PHOTOS
7/7 © 2009 Terri Libenson, Dist. By King Features Syndicate, Inc.
Remember the early weeks? What a **crazy, hormonal** bundle of **nerves** I was?
Uhmm...
www.pajamadiaries.com
Nope. Don't remember.
Good answer.
PHOTOS
Libenson

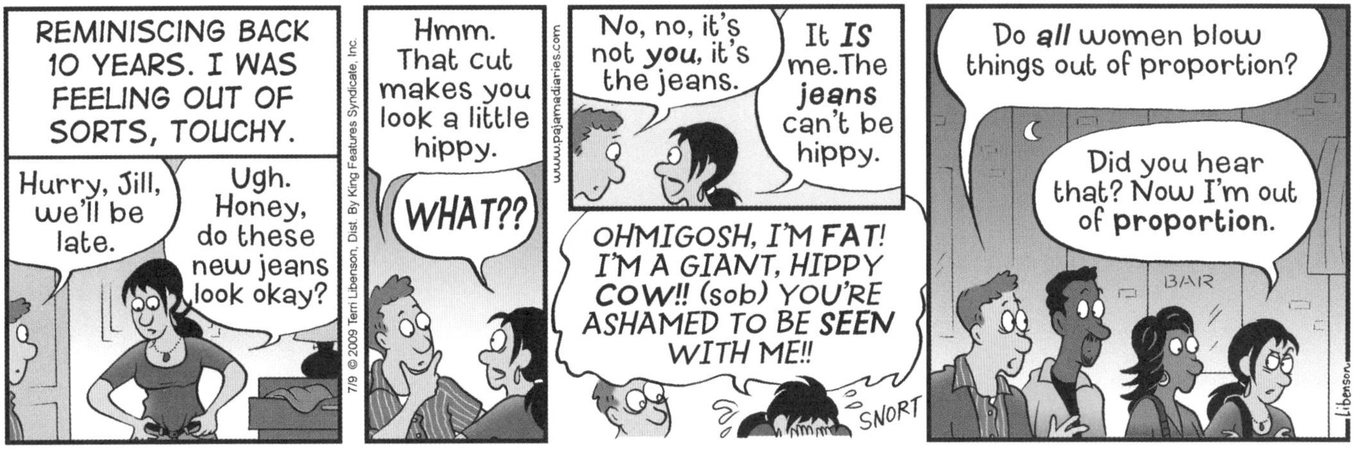
REMINISCING BACK 10 YEARS. I WAS FEELING OUT OF SORTS, TOUCHY.
Hurry, Jill, we'll be late.
Ugh. Honey, do these new jeans look okay?
7/9 © 2009 Terri Libenson, Dist. By King Features Syndicate, Inc.
Hmm. That cut makes you look a little hippy.
WHAT??
www.pajamadiaries.com
No, no, it's not **you**, it's the jeans.
It ***IS*** me. The **jeans** can't be hippy.
OHMIGOSH, I'M **FAT**! I'M A GIANT, HIPPY **COW**!! (sob) YOU'RE ASHAMED TO BE **SEEN** WITH ME!!
SNORT
Do ***all*** women blow things out of proportion?
Did you hear that? Now I'm out of **proportion**.
BAR
Libenson

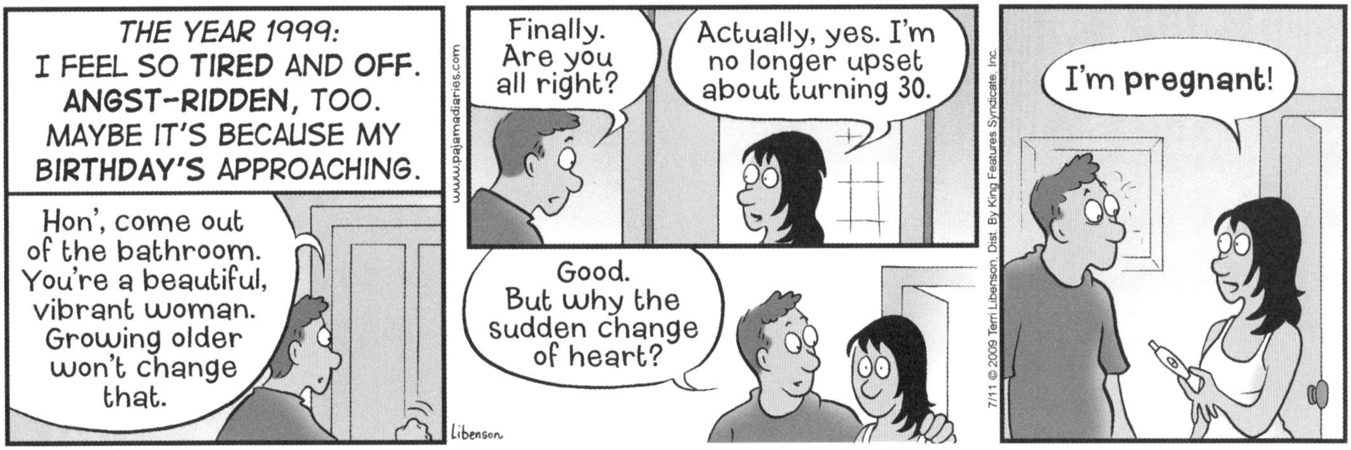
THE YEAR 1999:
I FEEL SO **TIRED** AND **OFF**. **ANGST-RIDDEN**, TOO. MAYBE IT'S BECAUSE MY **BIRTHDAY'S** APPROACHING.
Hon', come out of the bathroom. You're a beautiful, vibrant woman. Growing older won't change that.
Libenson
www.pajamadiaries.com
Finally. Are you all right?
Actually, yes. I'm no longer upset about turning 30.
Good. But why the sudden change of heart?
7/11 © 2009 Terri Libenson, Dist. By King Features Syndicate, Inc.
I'm **pregnant**!

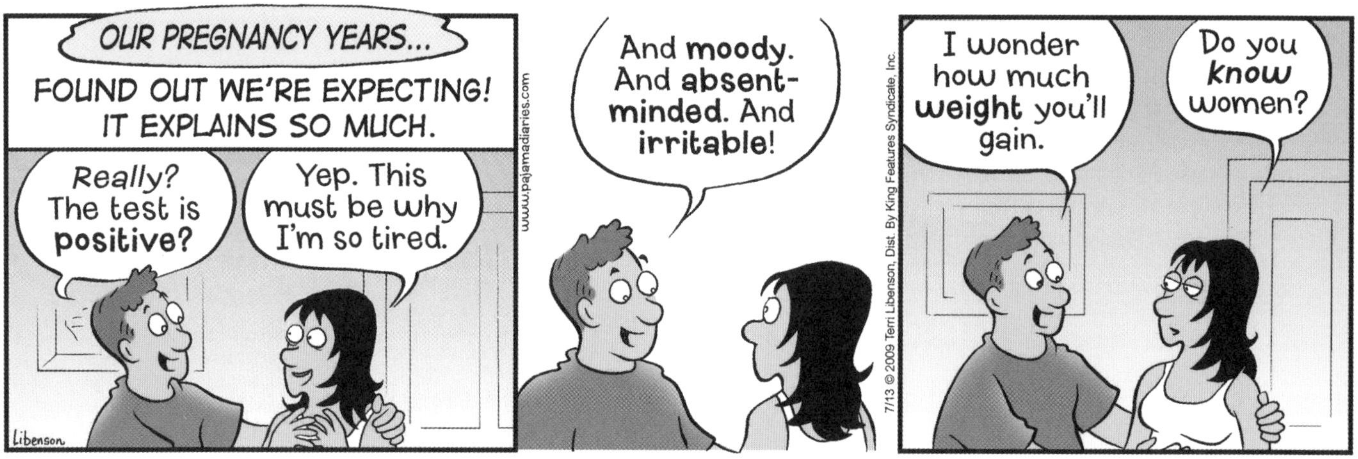
OUR PREGNANCY YEARS...
FOUND OUT WE'RE EXPECTING! IT EXPLAINS SO MUCH.
Really? The test is **positive**?
Yep. This must be why I'm so tired.
Libenson
www.pajamadiaries.com
And **moody**. And **absent-minded**. And **irritable**!
7/13 © 2009 Terri Libenson, Dist. By King Features Syndicate, Inc.
I wonder how much **weight** you'll gain.
Do you **know** women?

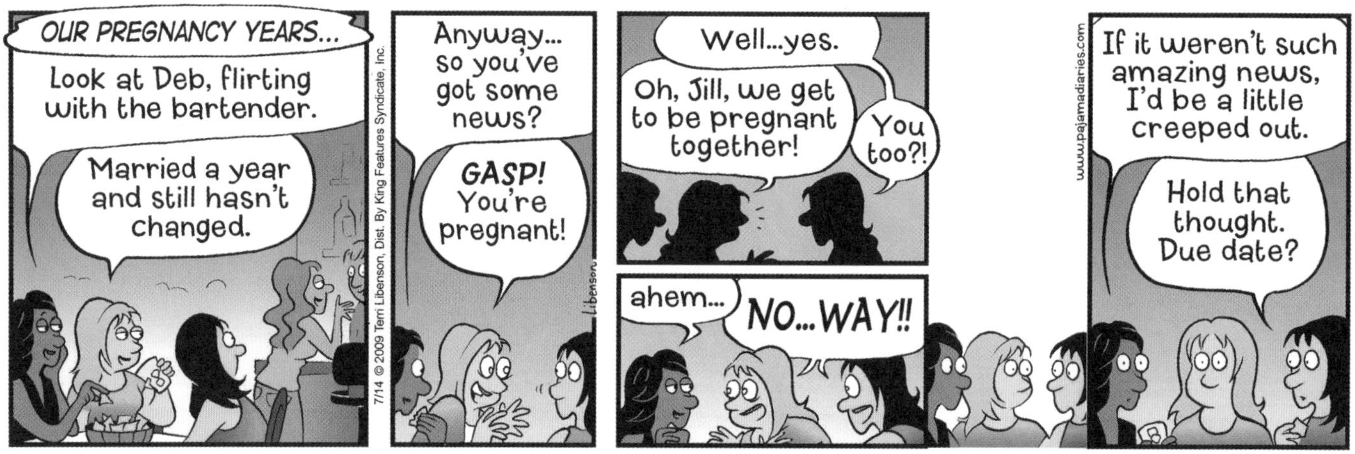
OUR PREGNANCY YEARS...
Look at Deb, flirting with the bartender.
Married a year and still hasn't changed.
7/14 © 2009 Terri Libenson, Dist. By King Features Syndicate, Inc.
Anyway... so you've got some news?
GASP! You're pregnant!
Libenson
Well...yes.
Oh, Jill, we get to be pregnant together!
You too?!
ahem...
NO...WAY!!
www.pajamadiaries.com
If it weren't such amazing news, I'd be a little creeped out.
Hold that thought. Due date?

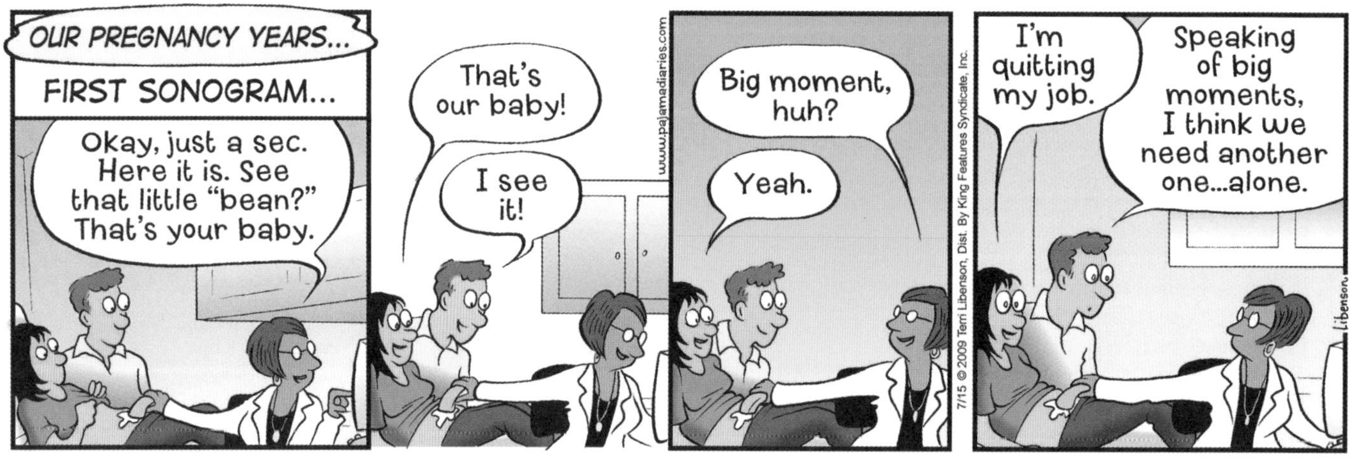
OUR PREGNANCY YEARS...
FIRST SONOGRAM...
Okay, just a sec. Here it is. See that little "bean?" That's your baby.
That's our baby!
I see it!
www.pajamadiaries.com
Big moment, huh?
Yeah.
7/15 © 2009 Terri Libenson, Dist. By King Features Syndicate, Inc.
I'm quitting my job.
Speaking of big moments, I think we need another one...alone.
Libenson

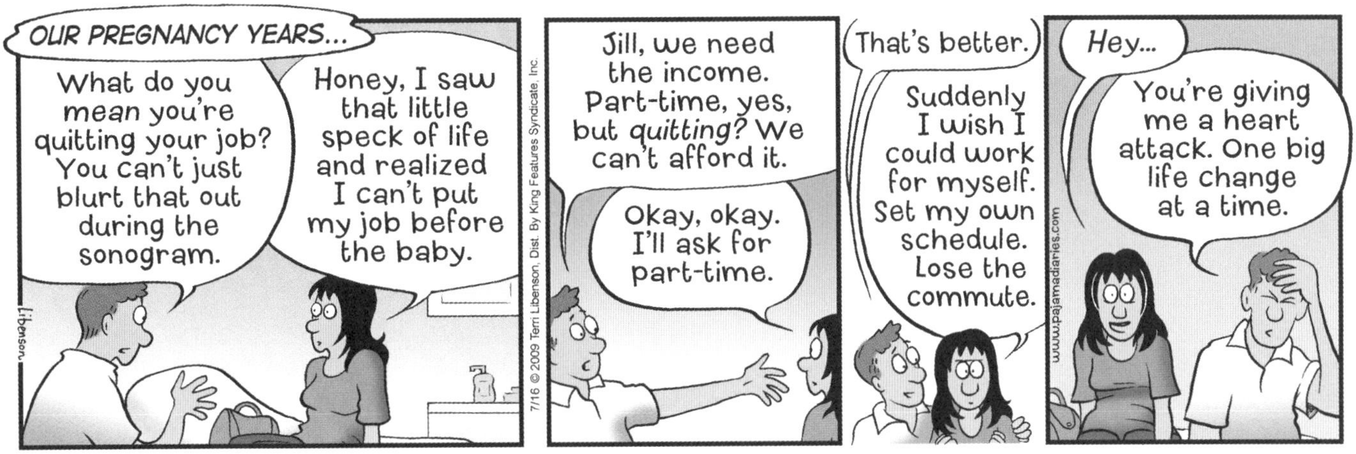
OUR PREGNANCY YEARS...
What do you mean you're quitting your job? You can't just blurt that out during the sonogram.
Honey, I saw that little speck of life and realized I can't put my job before the baby.
Jill, we need the income. Part-time, yes, but *quitting*? We can't afford it.
Okay, okay. I'll ask for part-time.
That's better.
Suddenly I wish I could work for myself. Set my own schedule. Lose the commute.
Hey...
You're giving me a heart attack. One big life change at a time.
7/16 © 2009 Terri Libenson. Dist. By King Features Syndicate, Inc.
www.pajamadiaries.com
Libenson

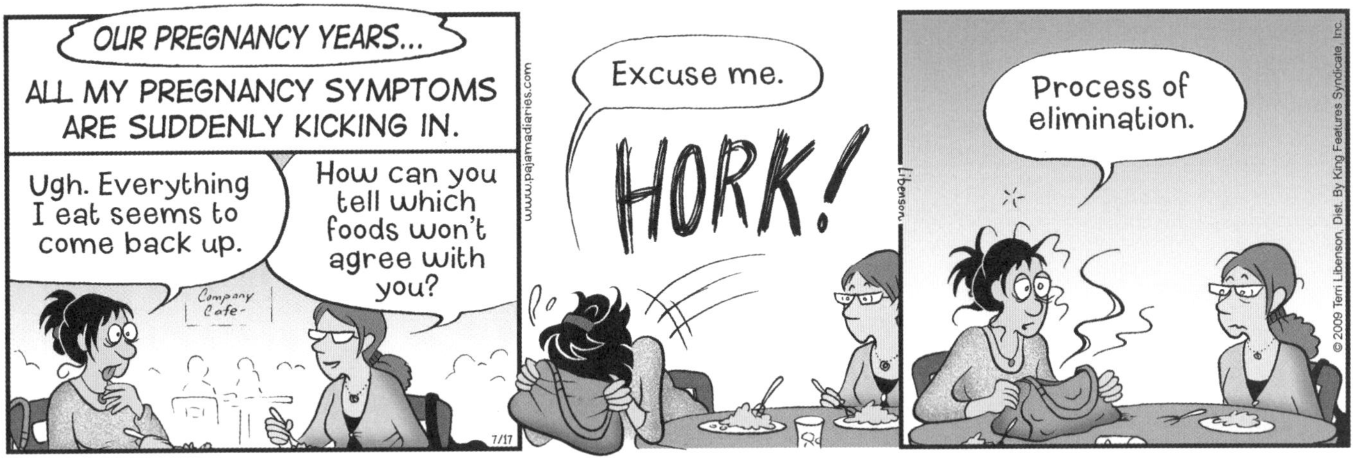
OUR PREGNANCY YEARS...
ALL MY PREGNANCY SYMPTOMS ARE SUDDENLY KICKING IN.
Ugh. Everything I eat seems to come back up.
How can you tell which foods won't agree with you?
Company Cafe
Excuse me.
HORK!
Process of elimination.
www.pajamadiaries.com
7/17
© 2009 Terri Libenson. Dist. By King Features Syndicate, Inc.
Libenson

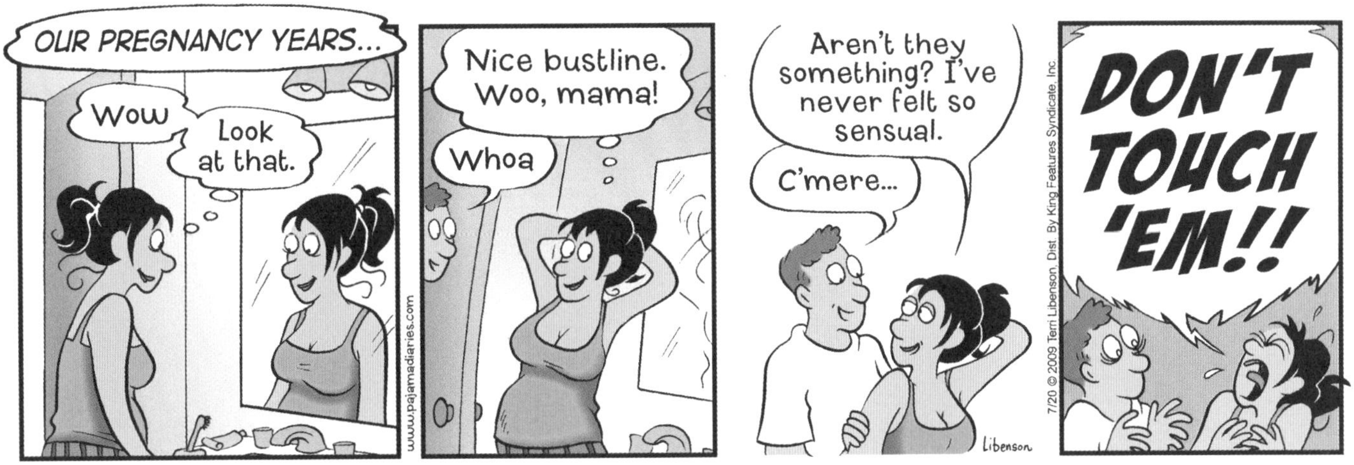
OUR PREGNANCY YEARS...
Wow
Look at that.
Nice bustline. Woo, mama!
Whoa
Aren't they something? I've never felt so sensual.
C'mere...
DON'T TOUCH 'EM!!
www.pajamadiaries.com
7/20 © 2009 Terri Libenson. Dist. By King Features Syndicate, Inc.
Libenson

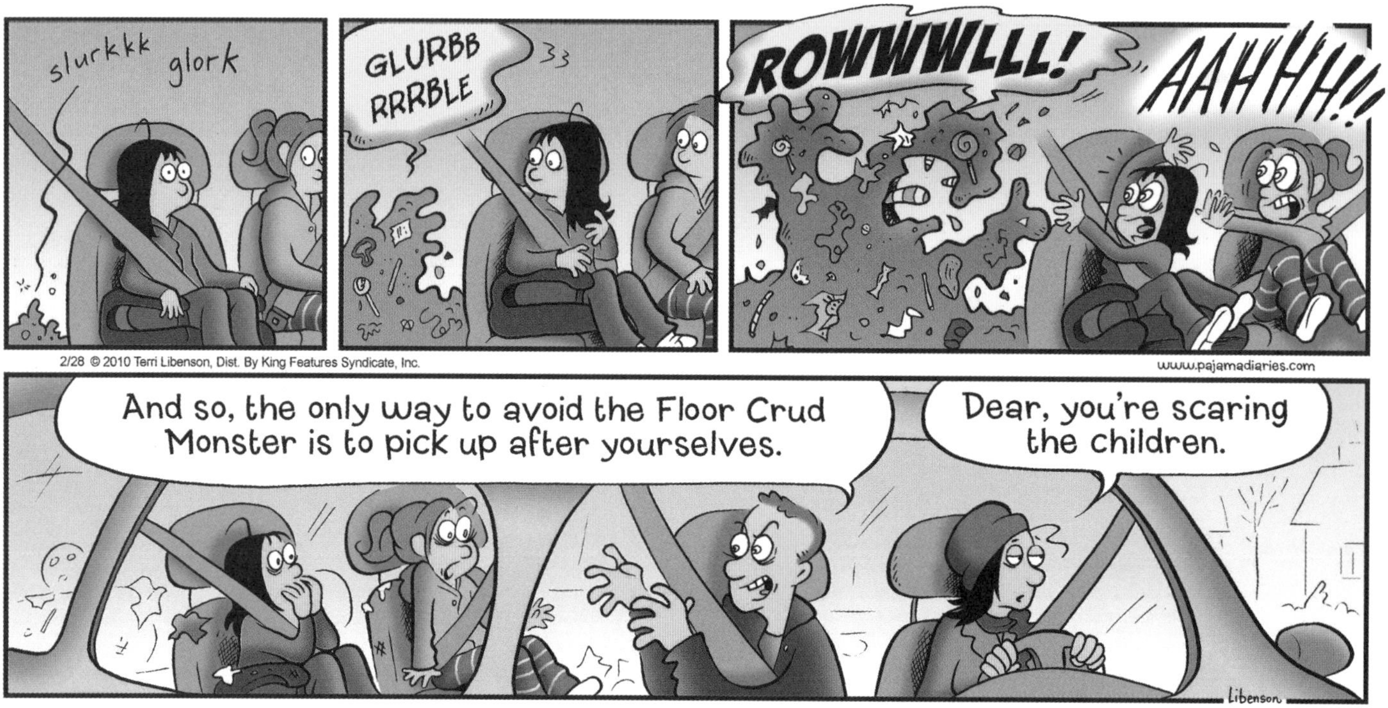
slurkkk
glork
GLURBB RRRBLE
ROWWWLLL!
AAHHH!!
And so, the only way to avoid the Floor Crud Monster is to pick up after yourselves.
Dear, you're scaring the children.
Libenson

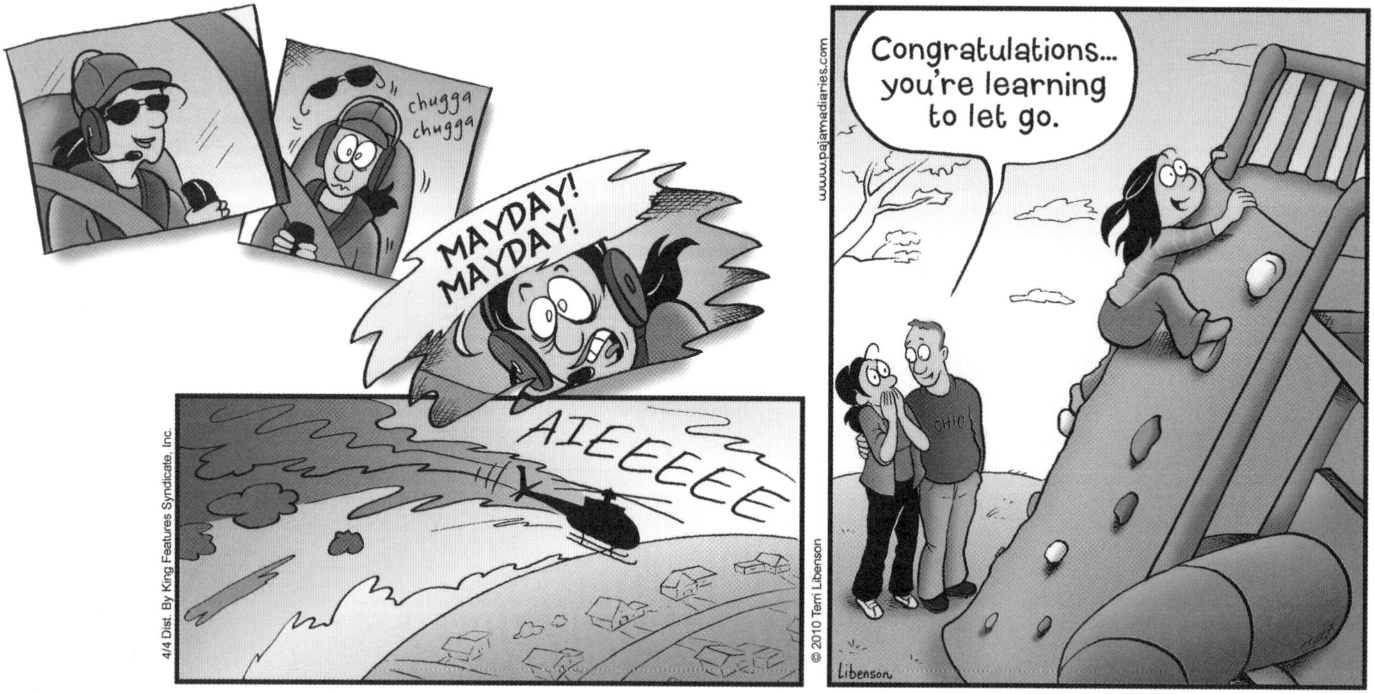
chugga chugga
MAYDAY! MAYDAY!
AIEEEEEE
Congratulations... you're learning to let go.
OHIO
Libenson

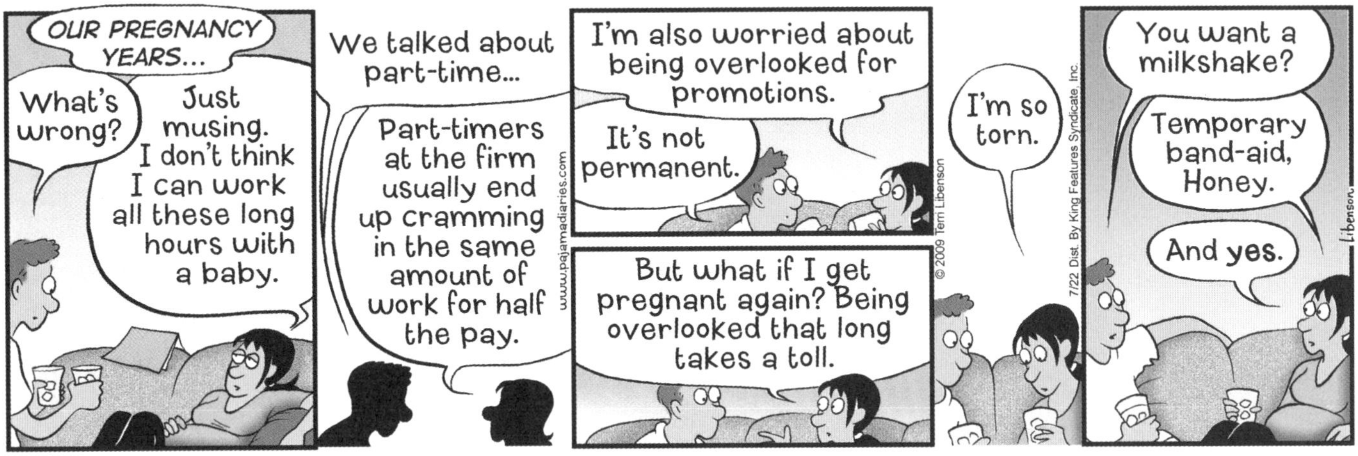
OUR PREGNANCY YEARS...
What's wrong?
Just musing. I don't think I can work all these long hours with a baby.
We talked about part-time...
Part-timers at the firm usually end up cramming in the same amount of work for half the pay.
www.pajamadiaries.com
I'm also worried about being overlooked for promotions.
It's not permanent.
But what if I get pregnant again? Being overlooked that long takes a toll.
© 2009 Terri Libenson
I'm so torn.
7/22 Dist. By King Features Syndicate, Inc.
You want a milkshake?
Temporary band-aid, Honey.
And yes.
Libenson

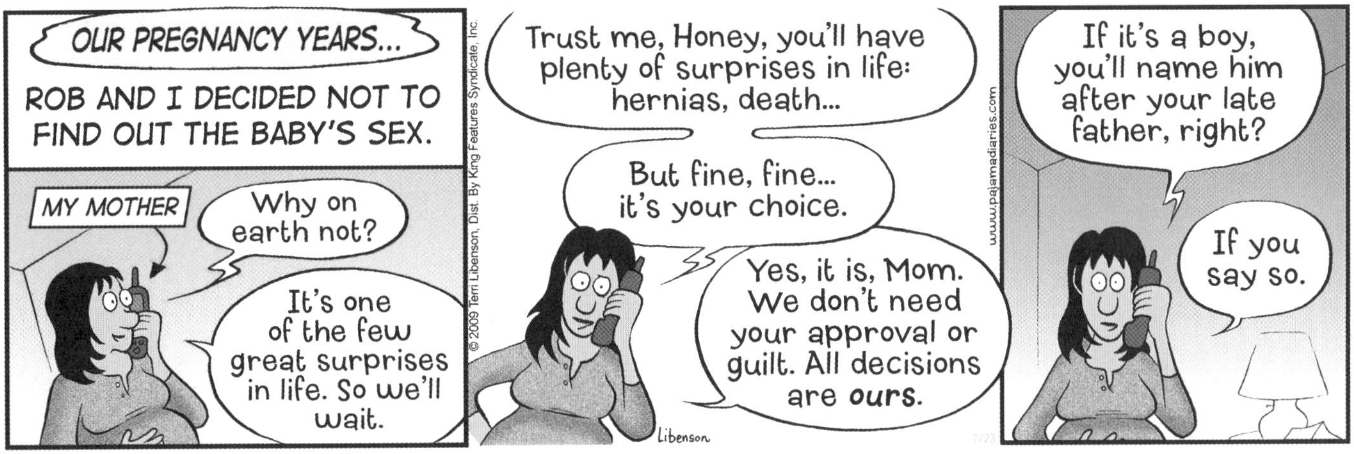
OUR PREGNANCY YEARS...
ROB AND I DECIDED NOT TO FIND OUT THE BABY'S SEX.
MY MOTHER
Why on earth not?
It's one of the few great surprises in life. So we'll wait.
© 2009 Terri Libenson, Dist. By King Features Syndicate, Inc.
Trust me, Honey, you'll have plenty of surprises in life: hernias, death...
But fine, fine... it's your choice.
Yes, it is, Mom. We don't need your approval or guilt. All decisions are ours.
Libenson
www.pajamadiaries.com
If it's a boy, you'll name him after your late father, right?
If you say so.

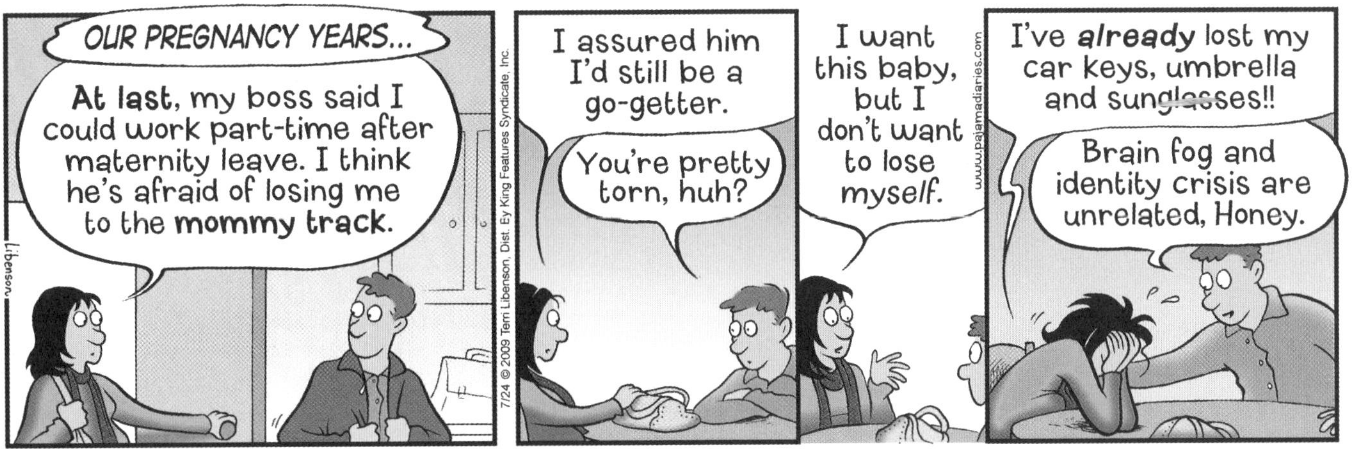
OUR PREGNANCY YEARS...
At last, my boss said I could work part-time after maternity leave. I think he's afraid of losing me to the mommy track.
Libenson
7/24 © 2009 Terri Libenson, Dist. By King Features Syndicate, Inc.
I assured him I'd still be a go-getter.
You're pretty torn, huh?
I want this baby, but I don't want to lose myself.
www.pajamadiaries.com
I've already lost my car keys, umbrella and sunglasses!!
Brain fog and identity crisis are unrelated, Honey.

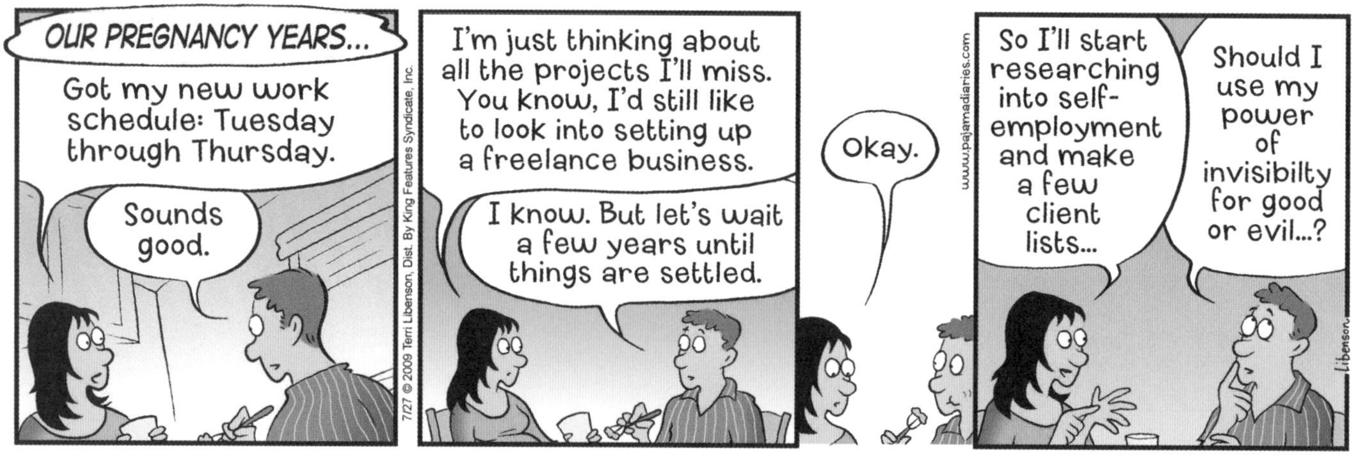
OUR PREGNANCY YEARS...
Got my new work schedule: Tuesday through Thursday.
Sounds good.
7/27 © 2009 Terri Libenson, Dist. By King Features Syndicate, Inc.
I'm just thinking about all the projects I'll miss. You know, I'd still like to look into setting up a freelance business.
I know. But let's wait a few years until things are settled.
Okay.
www.pajamadiaries.com
So I'll start researching into self-employment and make a few client lists...
Should I use my power of invisibilty for good or evil...?
Libenson

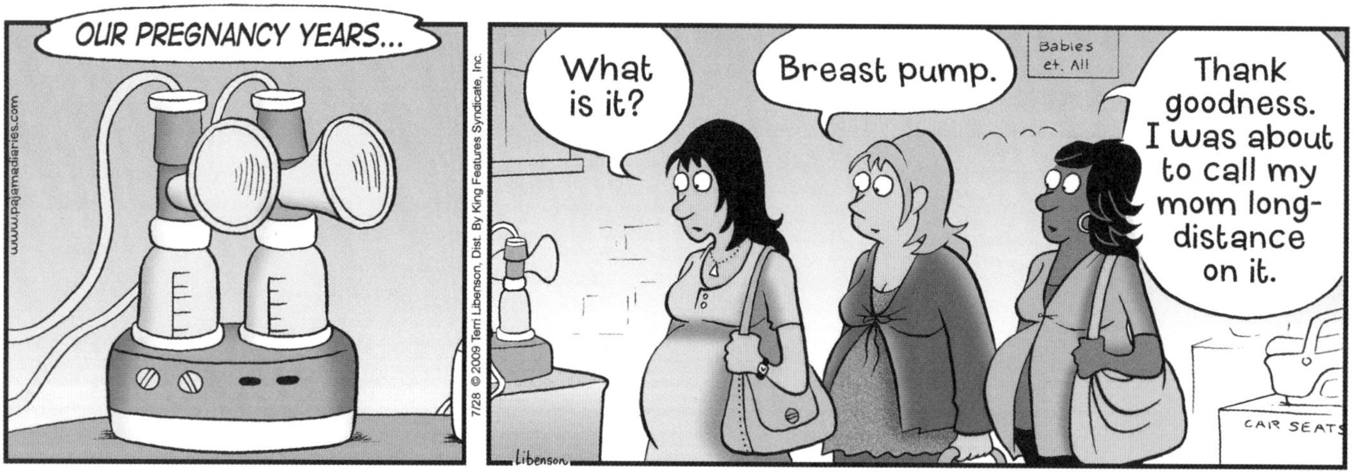
OUR PREGNANCY YEARS...
www.pajamadiaries.com
7/28 © 2009 Terri Libenson, Dist. By King Features Syndicate, Inc.
What is it?
Breast pump.
Babies et. All
Thank goodness. I was about to call my mom long-distance on it.
CAR SEATS
Libenson

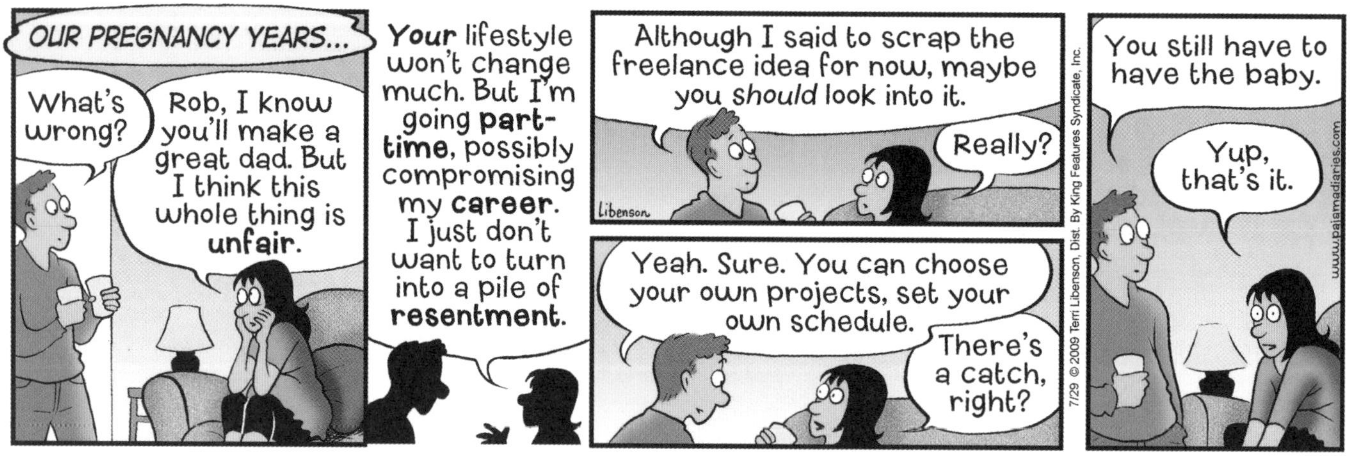
OUR PREGNANCY YEARS...
What's wrong?
Rob, I know you'll make a great dad. But I think this whole thing is **unfair**.
Your lifestyle won't change much. But I'm going **part-time**, possibly compromising my **career**. I just don't want to turn into a pile of **resentment**.
Although I said to scrap the freelance idea for now, maybe you *should* look into it.
Really?
Libenson
Yeah. Sure. You can choose your own projects, set your own schedule.
There's a catch, right?
7/29 © 2009 Terri Libenson, Dist. By King Features Syndicate, Inc.
You still have to have the baby.
Yup, that's it.
www.pajamadiaries.com

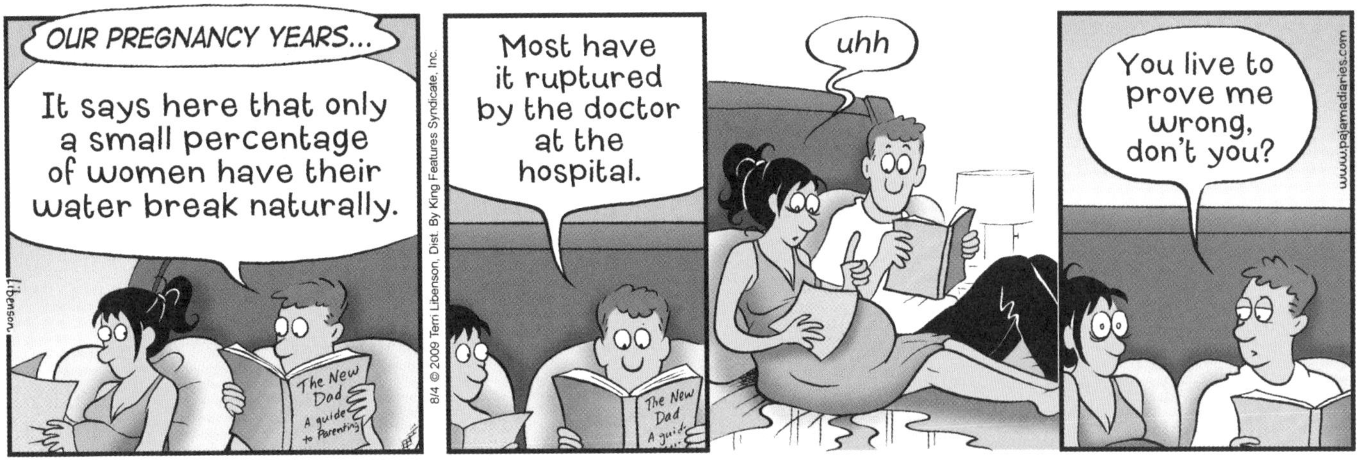
OUR PREGNANCY YEARS...
It says here that only a small percentage of women have their water break naturally.
Libenson
8/4 © 2009 Terri Libenson, Dist. By King Features Syndicate, Inc.
The New Dad A guide to Parenting
Most have it ruptured by the doctor at the hospital.
uhh
You live to prove me wrong, don't you?
www.pajamadiaries.com

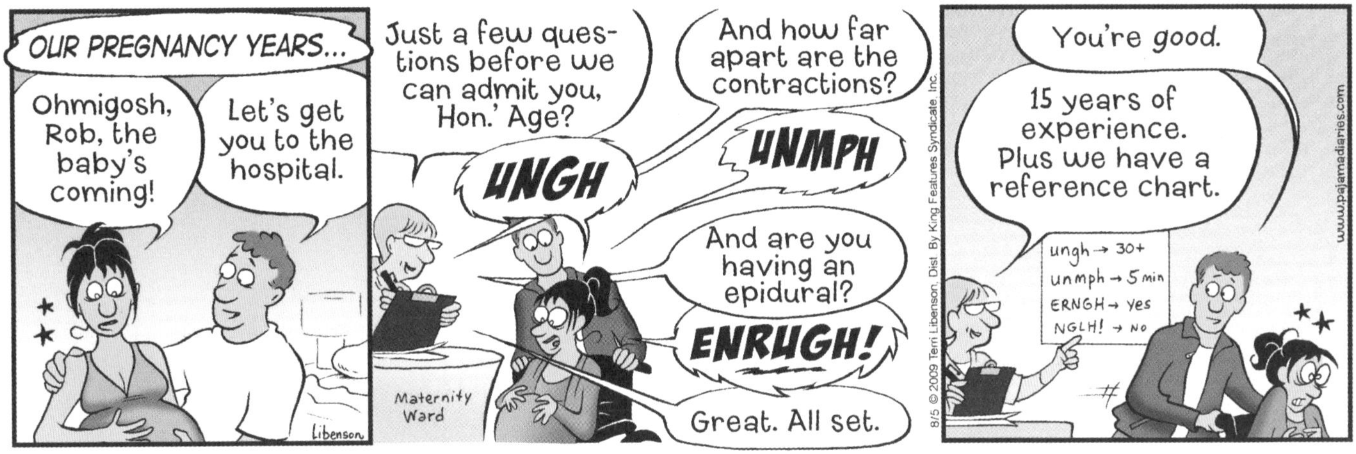
OUR PREGNANCY YEARS...
Ohmigosh, Rob, the baby's coming!
Let's get you to the hospital.
Libenson
Just a few questions before we can admit you, Hon.' Age?
UNGH
And how far apart are the contractions?
UNMPH
And are you having an epidural?
ENRUGH!
Great. All set.
Maternity Ward
8/5 © 2009 Terri Libenson, Dist. By King Features Syndicate, Inc.
You're *good*.
15 years of experience. Plus we have a reference chart.
ungh → 30+
unmph → 5 min
ERNGH → yes
NGLH! → no
www.pajamadiaries.com

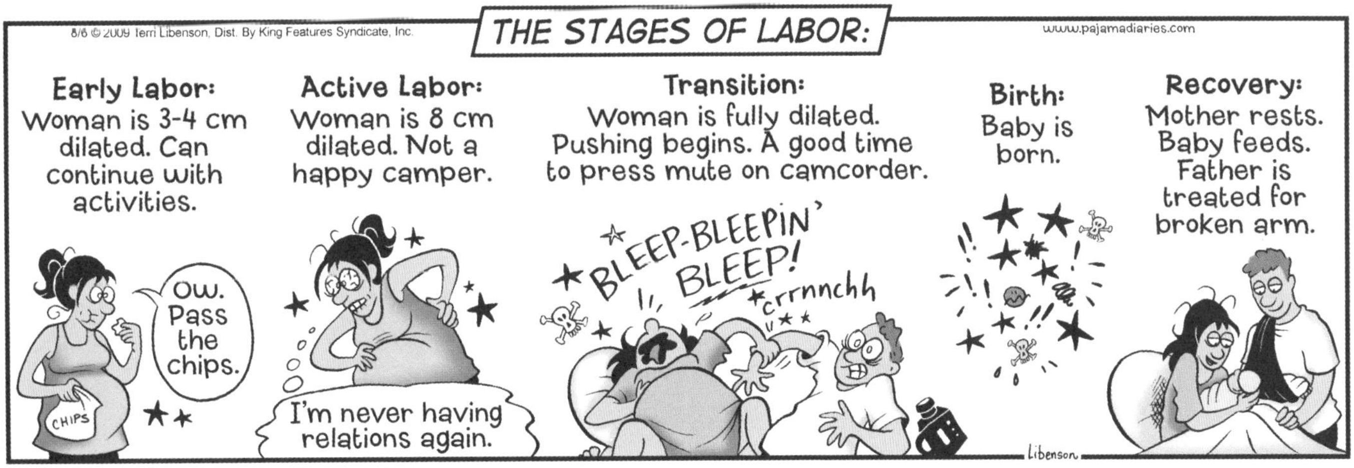
8/6 © 2009 Terri Libenson, Dist. By King Features Syndicate, Inc.
THE STAGES OF LABOR:
www.pajamadiaries.com
Early Labor:
Woman is 3-4 cm dilated. Can continue with activities.
Ow. Pass the chips.
CHIPS
Active Labor:
Woman is 8 cm dilated. Not a happy camper.
I'm never having relations again.
Transition:
Woman is fully dilated. Pushing begins. A good time to press mute on camcorder.
BLEEP-BLEEPIN' BLEEP!
crrnnchh
Birth:
Baby is born.
Recovery:
Mother rests. Baby feeds. Father is treated for broken arm.
Libenson

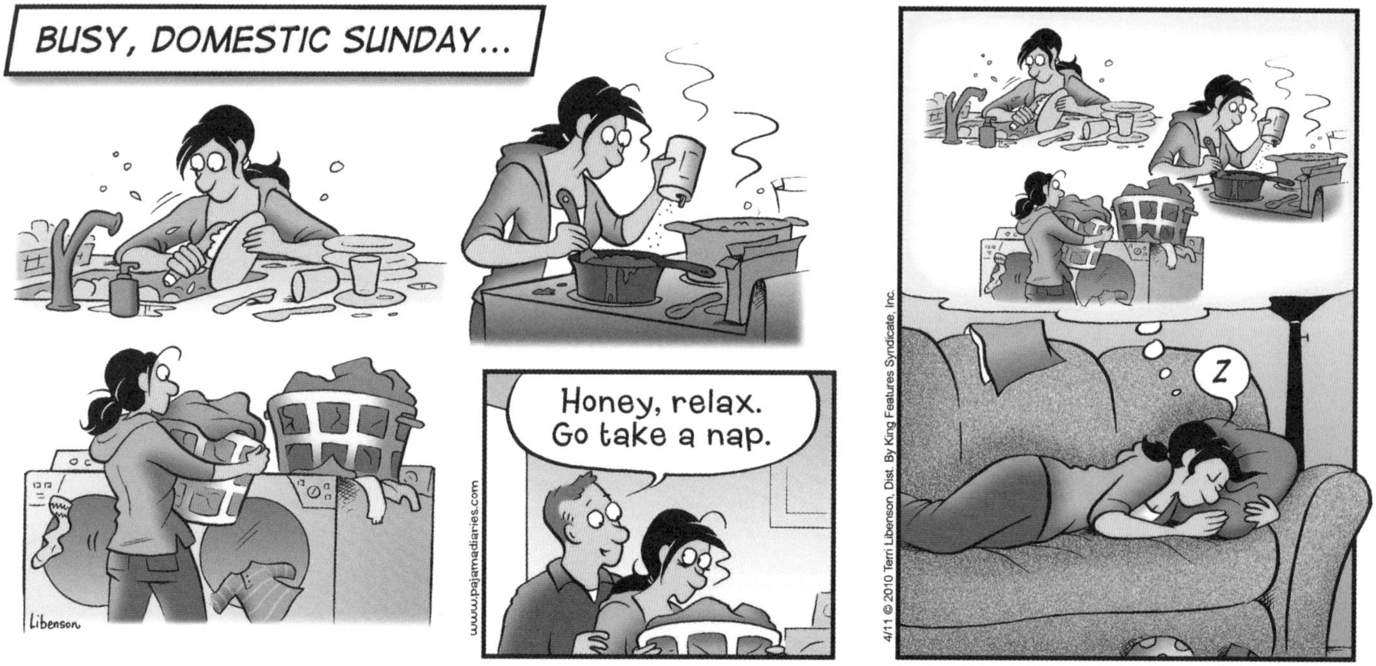
BUSY, DOMESTIC SUNDAY...
Honey, relax. Go take a nap.
Z
www.pajamadiaries.com
4/11 © 2010 Terri Libenson, Dist. By King Features Syndicate, Inc.
Libenson

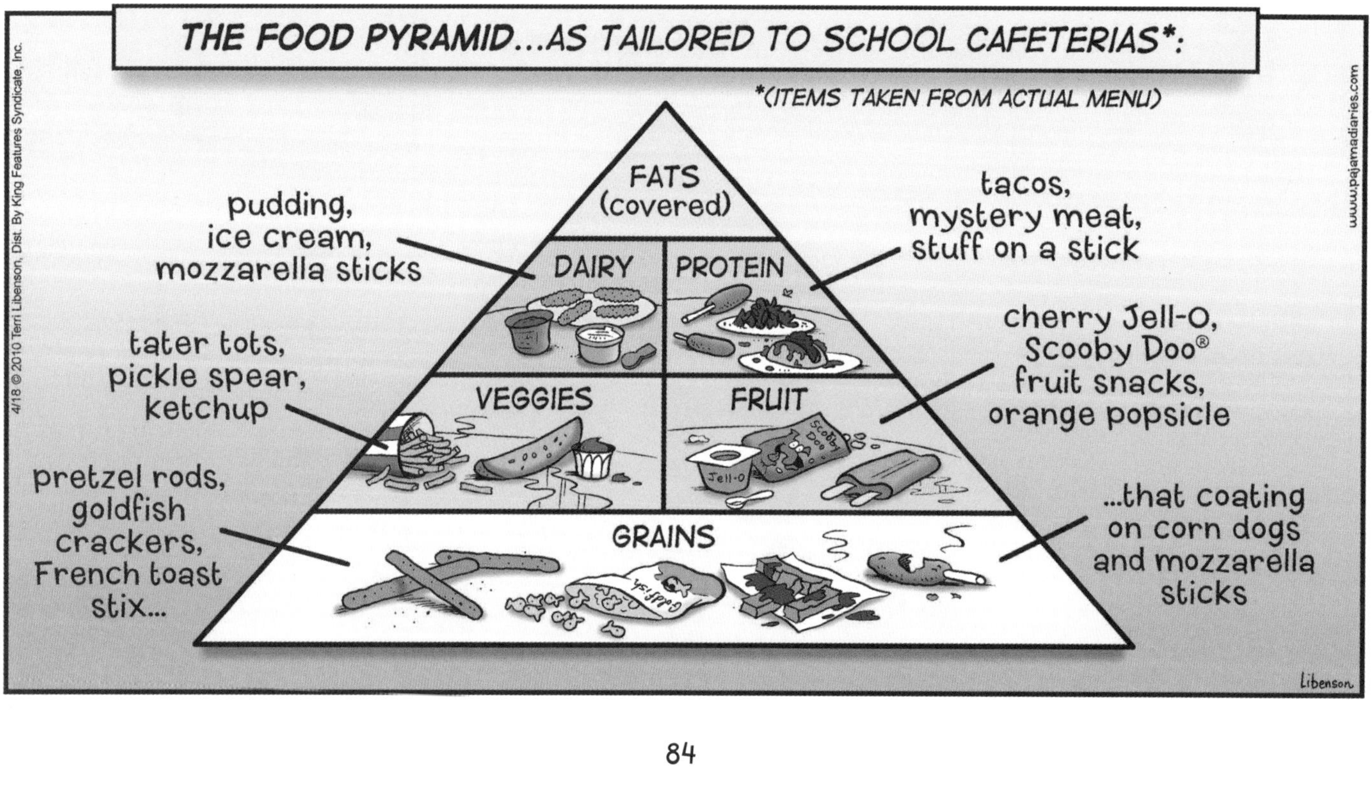
THE FOOD PYRAMID...AS TAILORED TO SCHOOL CAFETERIAS*:
*(ITEMS TAKEN FROM ACTUAL MENU)
FATS (covered)
DAIRY
PROTEIN
VEGGIES
FRUIT
GRAINS
pudding, ice cream, mozzarella sticks
tacos, mystery meat, stuff on a stick
tater tots, pickle spear, ketchup
cherry Jell-O, Scooby Doo® fruit snacks, orange popsicle
pretzel rods, goldfish crackers, French toast stix...
...that coating on corn dogs and mozzarella sticks
4/18 © 2010 Terri Libenson, Dist. By King Features Syndicate, Inc.
www.pajamadiaries.com
Libenson

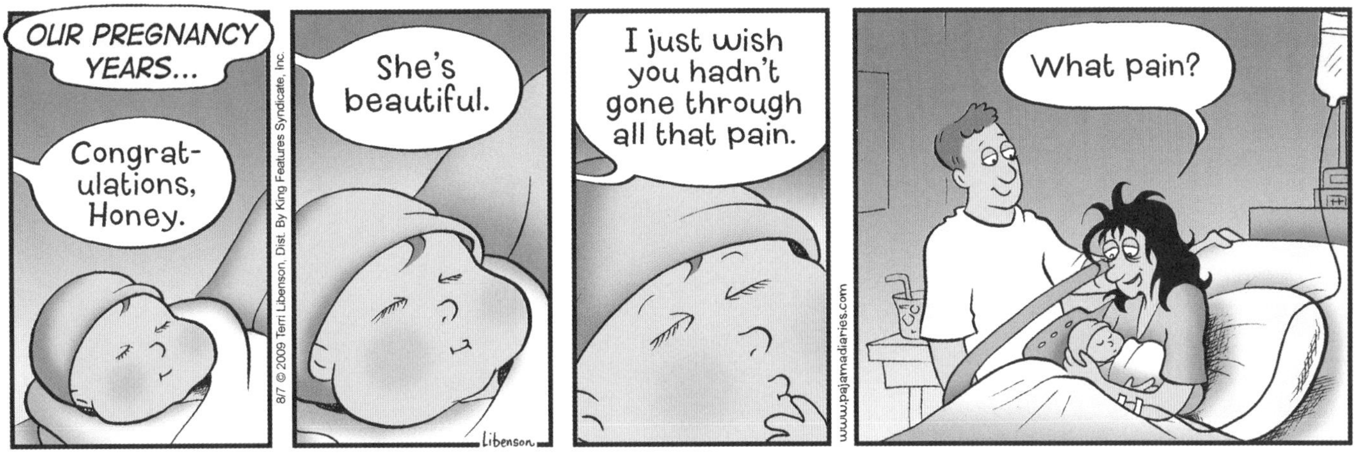
OUR PREGNANCY YEARS...
Congrat-ulations, Honey.
She's beautiful.
I just wish you hadn't gone through all that pain.
What pain?
8/7 © 2009 Terri Libenson, Dist. By King Features Syndicate, Inc.
Libenson
www.pajamadiaries.com

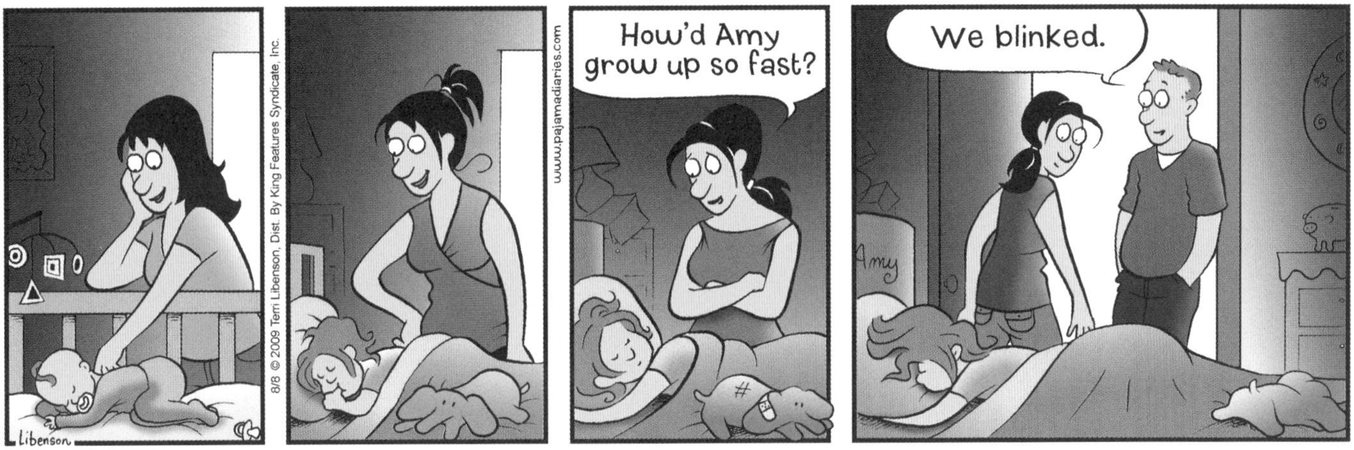
8/8 © 2009 Terri Libenson, Dist. By King Features Syndicate, Inc.
Libenson
www.pajamadiaries.com
How'd Amy grow up so fast?
We blinked.
Amy

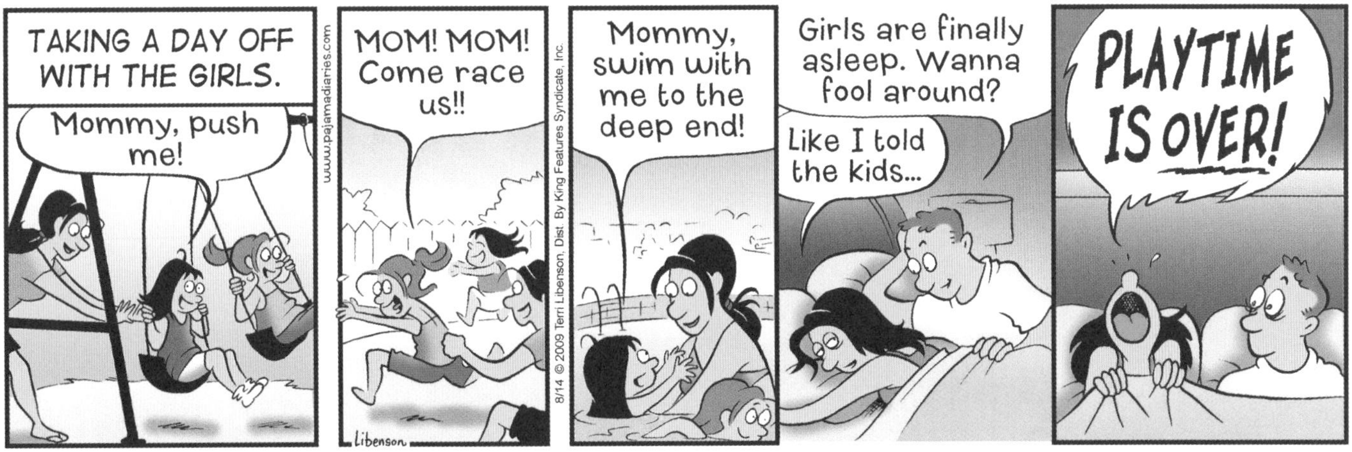
TAKING A DAY OFF WITH THE GIRLS.
Mommy, push me!
www.pajamadiaries.com
MOM! MOM! Come race us!!
Libenson
8/14 © 2009 Terri Libenson, Dist. By King Features Syndicate, Inc.
Mommy, swim with me to the deep end!
Girls are finally asleep. Wanna fool around?
Like I told the kids...
PLAYTIME IS OVER!

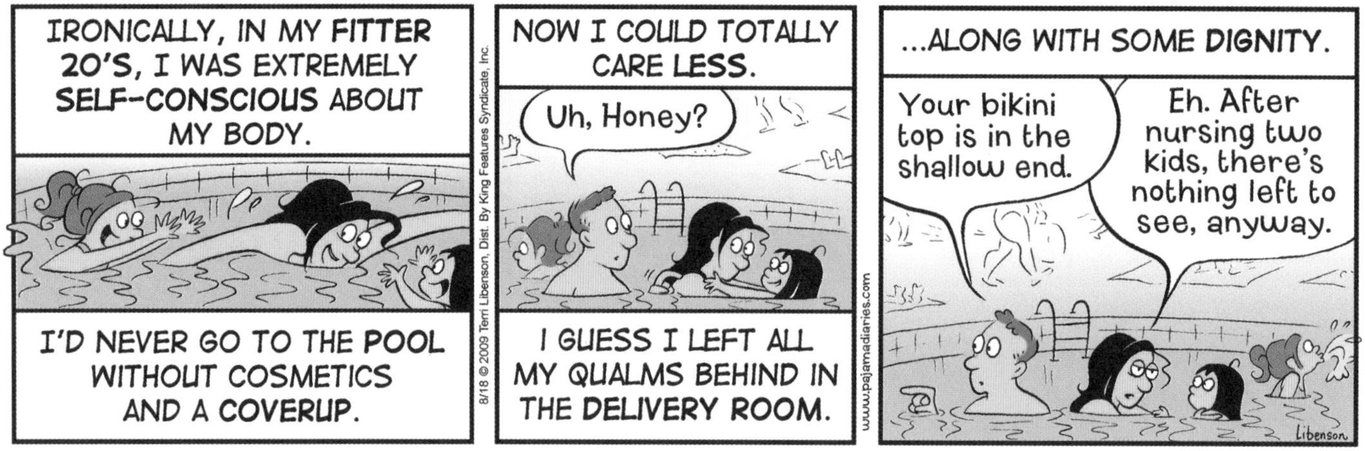
IRONICALLY, IN MY FITTER 20'S, I WAS EXTREMELY SELF-CONSCIOUS ABOUT MY BODY.
I'D NEVER GO TO THE POOL WITHOUT COSMETICS AND A COVERUP.
8/18 © 2009 Terri Libenson, Dist. By King Features Syndicate, Inc.
NOW I COULD TOTALLY CARE LESS.
Uh, Honey?
I GUESS I LEFT ALL MY QUALMS BEHIND IN THE DELIVERY ROOM.
www.pajamadiaries.com
...ALONG WITH SOME DIGNITY.
Your bikini top is in the shallow end.
Eh. After nursing two kids, there's nothing left to see, anyway.
Libenson

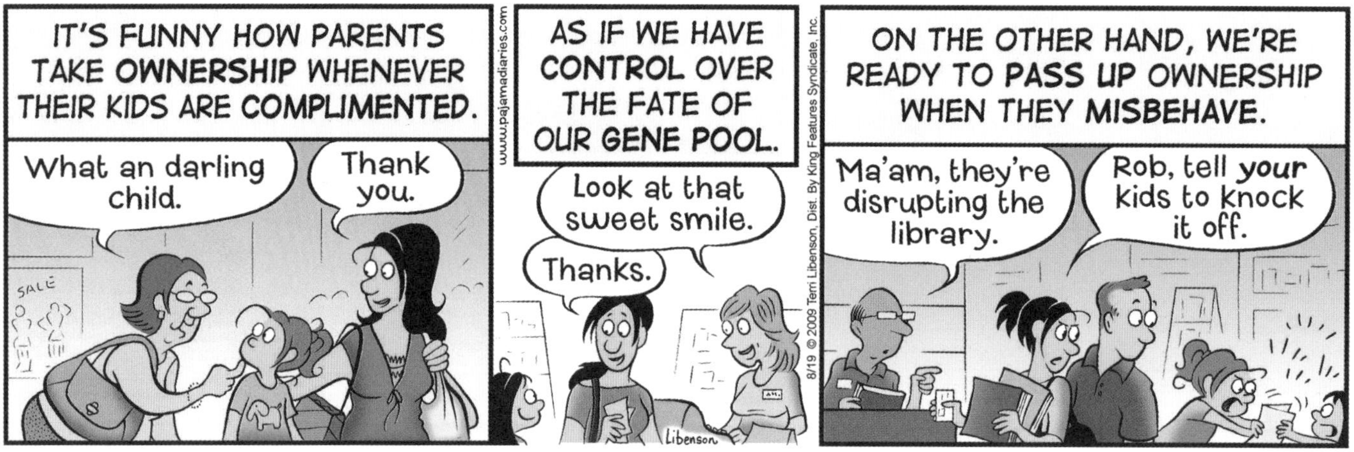
IT'S FUNNY HOW PARENTS TAKE OWNERSHIP WHENEVER THEIR KIDS ARE COMPLIMENTED.
What an darling child.
Thank you.
SALE
www.pajamadiaries.com
AS IF WE HAVE CONTROL OVER THE FATE OF OUR GENE POOL.
Look at that sweet smile.
Thanks.
Libenson
8/19 © 2009 Terri Libenson, Dist. By King Features Syndicate, Inc.
ON THE OTHER HAND, WE'RE READY TO PASS UP OWNERSHIP WHEN THEY MISBEHAVE.
Ma'am, they're disrupting the library.
Rob, tell your kids to knock it off.

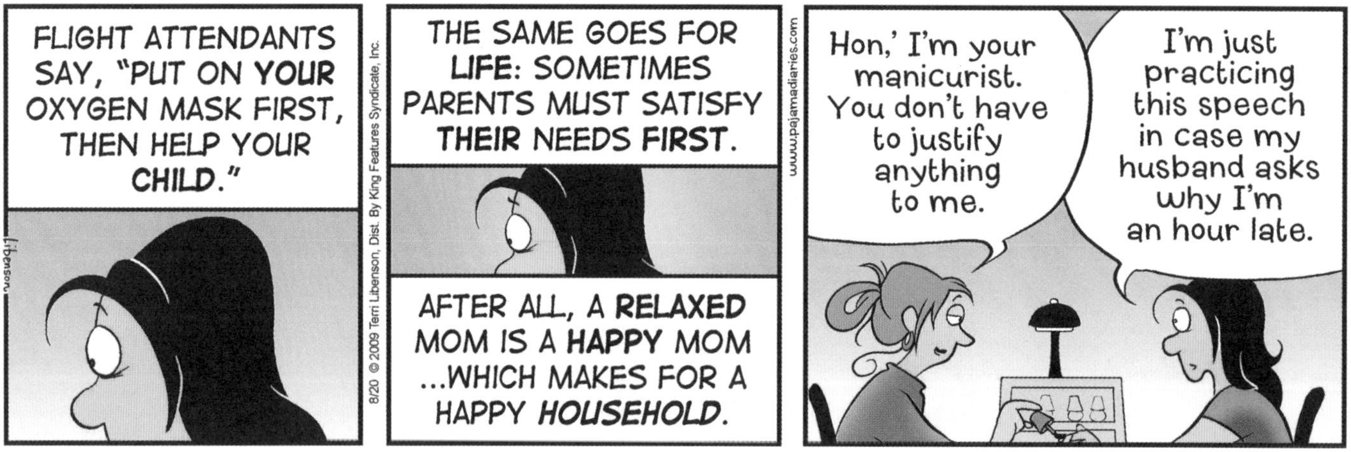
FLIGHT ATTENDANTS SAY, "PUT ON YOUR OXYGEN MASK FIRST, THEN HELP YOUR CHILD."
Libenson
8/20 © 2009 Terri Libenson, Dist. By King Features Syndicate, Inc.
THE SAME GOES FOR LIFE: SOMETIMES PARENTS MUST SATISFY THEIR NEEDS FIRST.
AFTER ALL, A RELAXED MOM IS A HAPPY MOM ...WHICH MAKES FOR A HAPPY HOUSEHOLD.
www.pajamadiaries.com
Hon,' I'm your manicurist. You don't have to justify anything to me.
I'm just practicing this speech in case my husband asks why I'm an hour late.

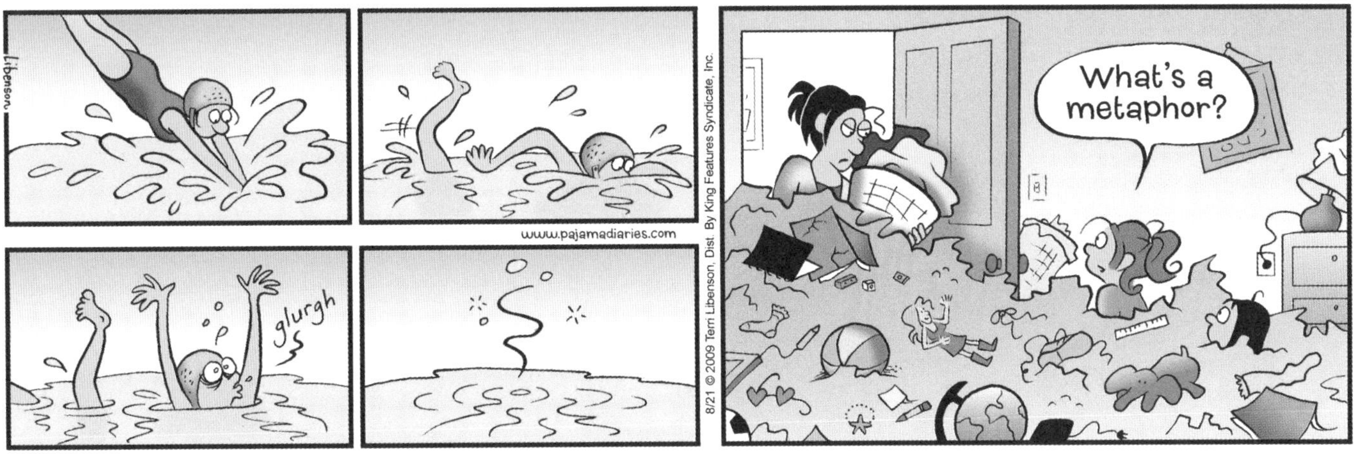
Libenson
www.pajamadiaries.com
glurgh
8/21 © 2009 Terri Libenson, Dist. By King Features Syndicate, Inc.
What's a metaphor?

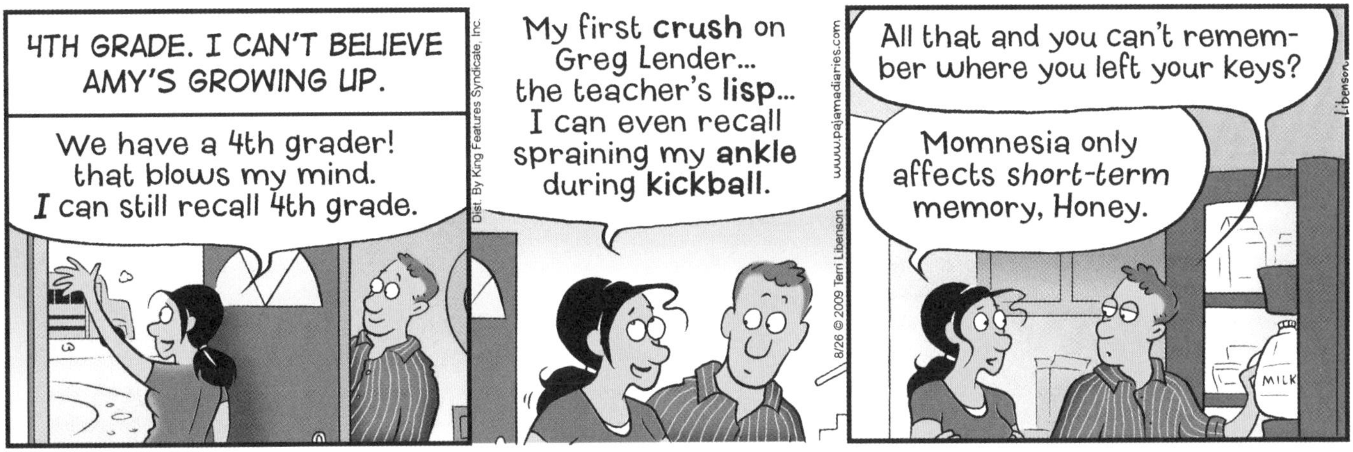
4TH GRADE. I CAN'T BELIEVE AMY'S GROWING UP.
We have a 4th grader! that blows my mind. I can still recall 4th grade.
Dist. By King Features Syndicate, Inc.
My first crush on Greg Lender... the teacher's lisp... I can even recall spraining my ankle during kickball.
www.pajamadiaries.com
8/26 © 2009 Terri Libenson
All that and you can't remember where you left your keys?
Momnesia only affects short-term memory, Honey.
Libenson
MILK

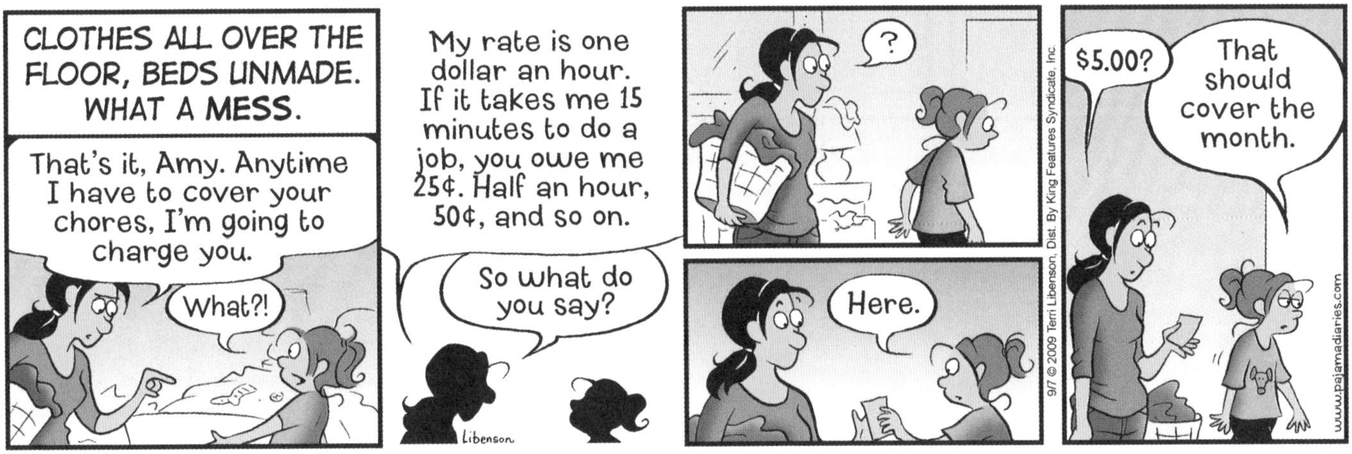
CLOTHES ALL OVER THE FLOOR, BEDS UNMADE. WHAT A MESS.
That's it, Amy. Anytime I have to cover your chores, I'm going to charge you.
What?!
My rate is one dollar an hour. If it takes me 15 minutes to do a job, you owe me 25¢. Half an hour, 50¢, and so on.
So what do you say?
Libenson
?
Here.
9/7 © 2009 Terri Libenson, Dist. By King Features Syndicate, Inc.
$5.00?
That should cover the month.
www.pajamadiaries.com

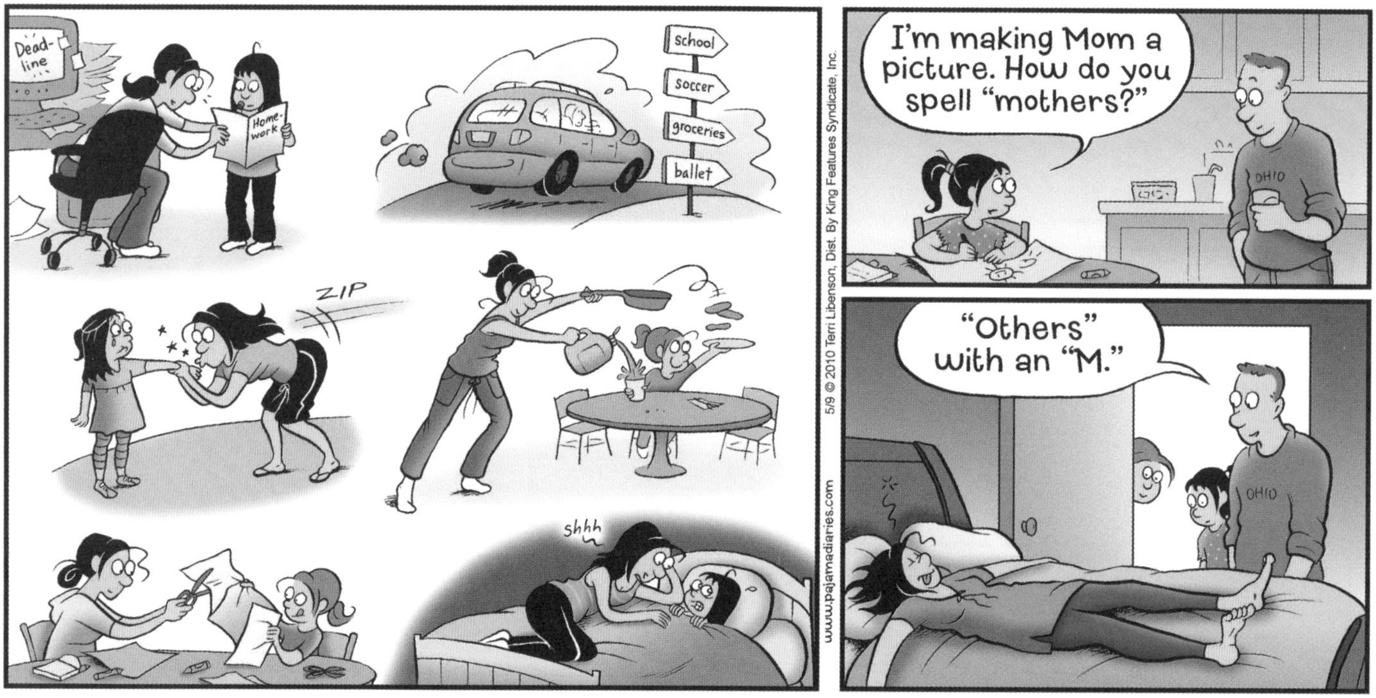
Dead-line
Home-work
school
soccer
groceries
ballet
ZIP
shhh
I'm making Mom a picture. How do you spell "mothers?"
OHIO
"Others" with an "M."
OHIO
5/9 © 2010 Terri Libenson, Dist. By King Features Syndicate, Inc.
www.pajamadiaries.com

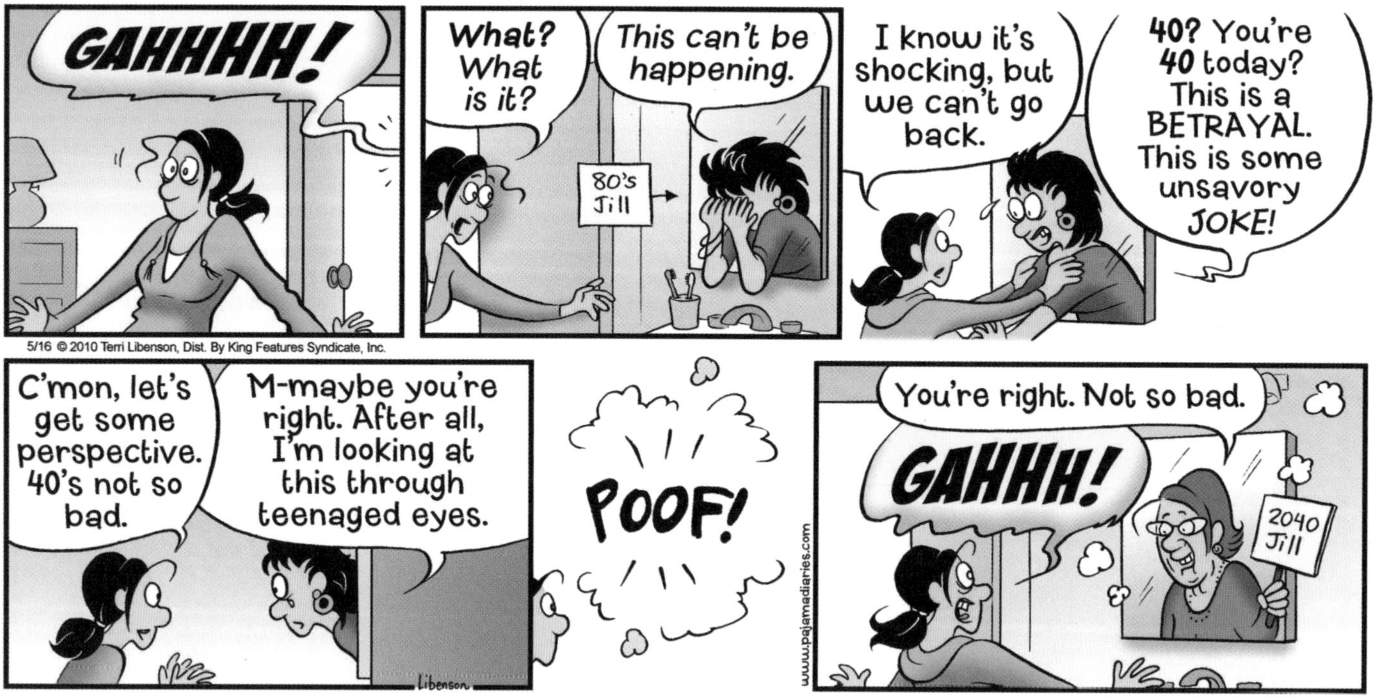
GAHHHH!
What? What is it?
This can't be happening.
80's Jill
I know it's shocking, but we can't go back.
40? You're 40 today? This is a BETRAYAL. This is some unsavory JOKE!
C'mon, let's get some perspective. 40's not so bad.
M-maybe you're right. After all, I'm looking at this through teenaged eyes.
Libenson
POOF!
You're right. Not so bad.
GAHHH!
2040 Jill
5/16 © 2010 Terri Libenson, Dist. By King Features Syndicate, Inc.
www.pajamadiaries.com

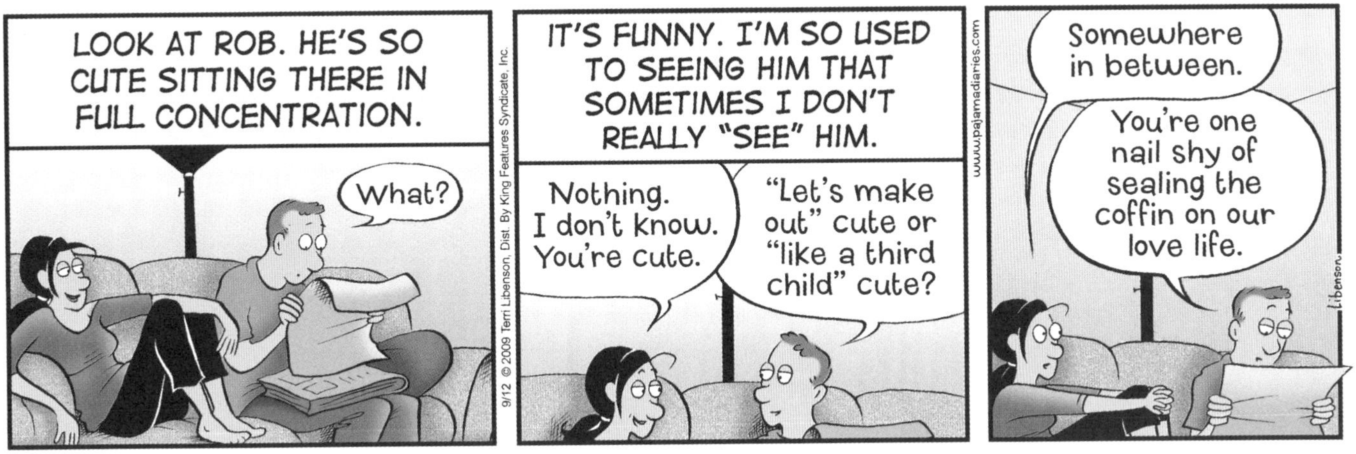
LOOK AT ROB. HE'S SO CUTE SITTING THERE IN FULL CONCENTRATION.
What?
IT'S FUNNY. I'M SO USED TO SEEING HIM THAT SOMETIMES I DON'T REALLY "SEE" HIM.
Nothing. I don't know. You're cute.
"Let's make out" cute or "like a third child" cute?
Somewhere in between.
You're one nail shy of sealing the coffin on our love life.
9/12 © 2009 Terri Libenson, Dist. By King Features Syndicate, Inc.
www.pajamadiaries.com
Libenson

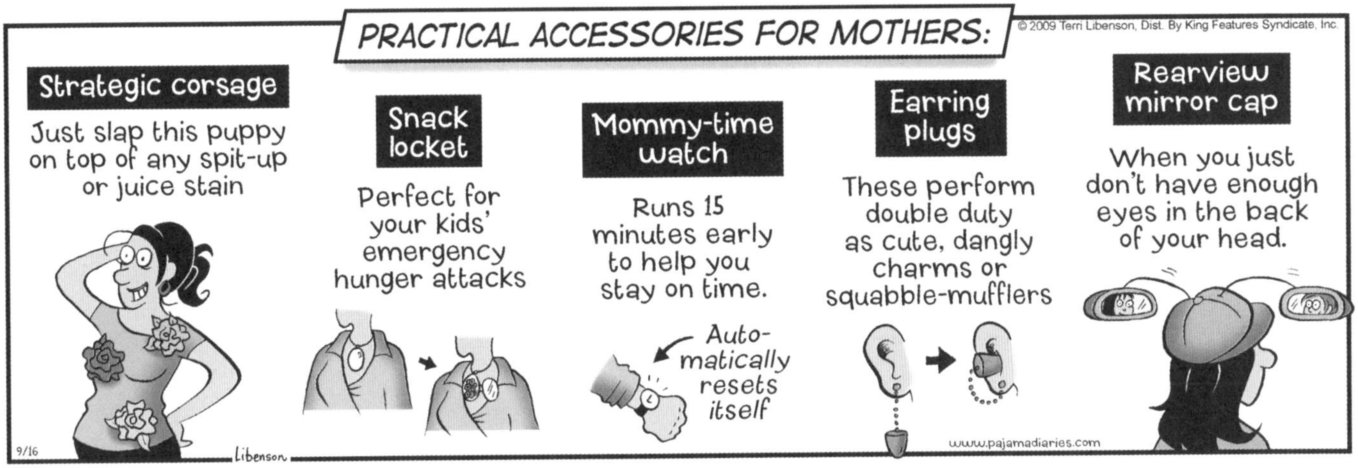
PRACTICAL ACCESSORIES FOR MOTHERS:
© 2009 Terri Libenson, Dist. By King Features Syndicate, Inc.
Strategic corsage
Just slap this puppy on top of any spit-up or juice stain
Snack locket
Perfect for your kids' emergency hunger attacks
Mommy-time watch
Runs 15 minutes early to help you stay on time.
Auto-matically resets itself
Earring plugs
These perform double duty as cute, dangly charms or squabble-mufflers
Rearview mirror cap
When you just don't have enough eyes in the back of your head.
9/16
Libenson
www.pajamadiaries.com

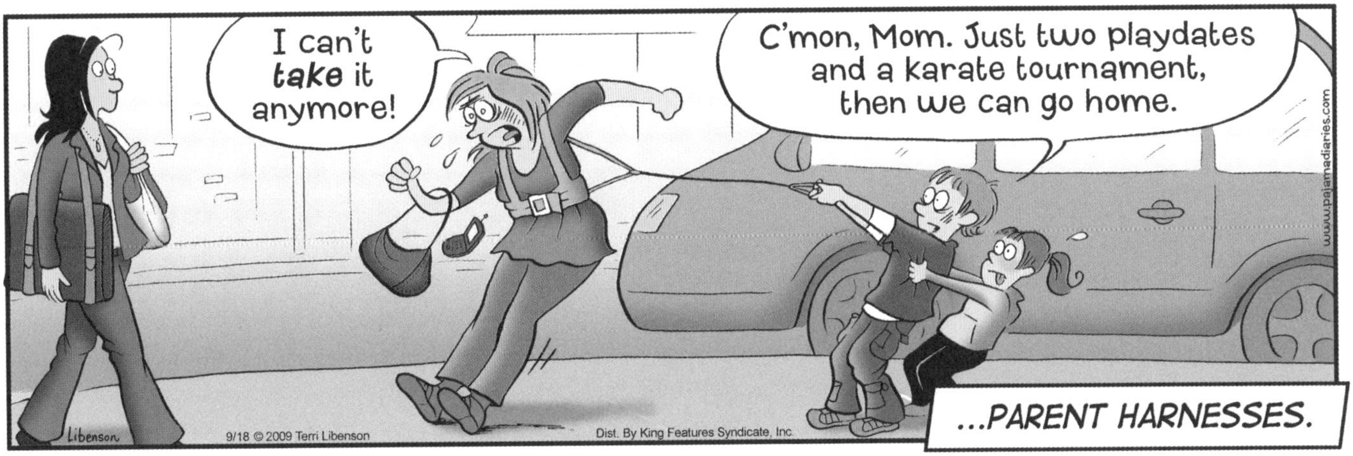
I can't take it anymore!
C'mon, Mom. Just two playdates and a karate tournament, then we can go home.
...PARENT HARNESSES.
Libenson
9/18 © 2009 Terri Libenson
Dist. By King Features Syndicate, Inc.
www.pajamadiaries.com

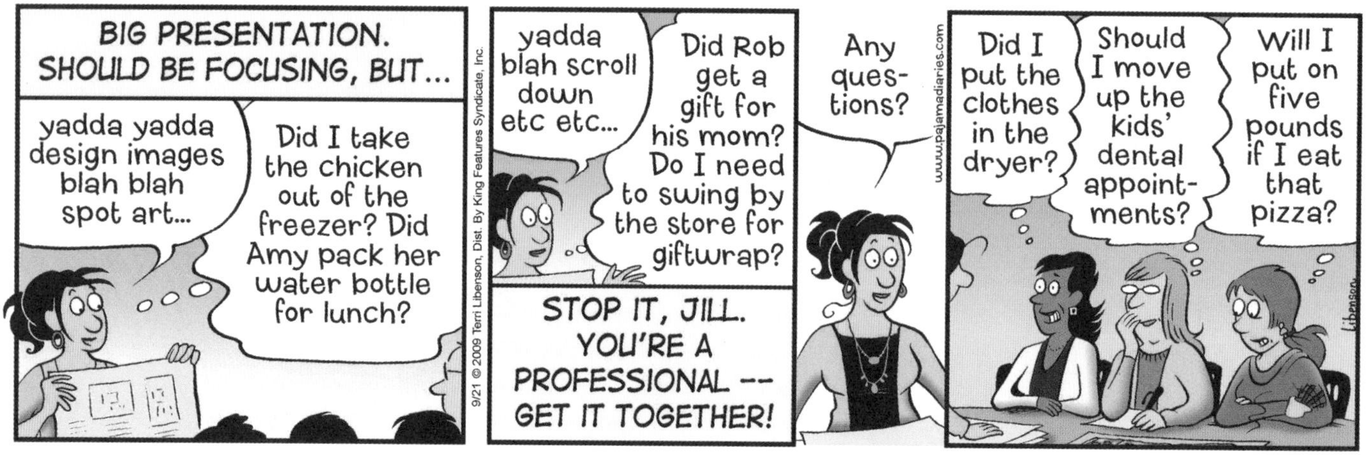
BIG PRESENTATION. SHOULD BE FOCUSING, BUT...
yadda yadda design images blah blah spot art...
Did I take the chicken out of the freezer? Did Amy pack her water bottle for lunch?
9/21 © 2009 Terri Libenson, Dist. By King Features Syndicate, Inc.
yadda blah scroll down etc etc...
Did Rob get a gift for his mom? Do I need to swing by the store for giftwrap?
STOP IT, JILL. YOU'RE A PROFESSIONAL -- GET IT TOGETHER!
Any ques-tions?
www.pajamadiaries.com
Did I put the clothes in the dryer?
Should I move up the kids' dental appoint-ments?
Will I put on five pounds if I eat that pizza?
Libenson

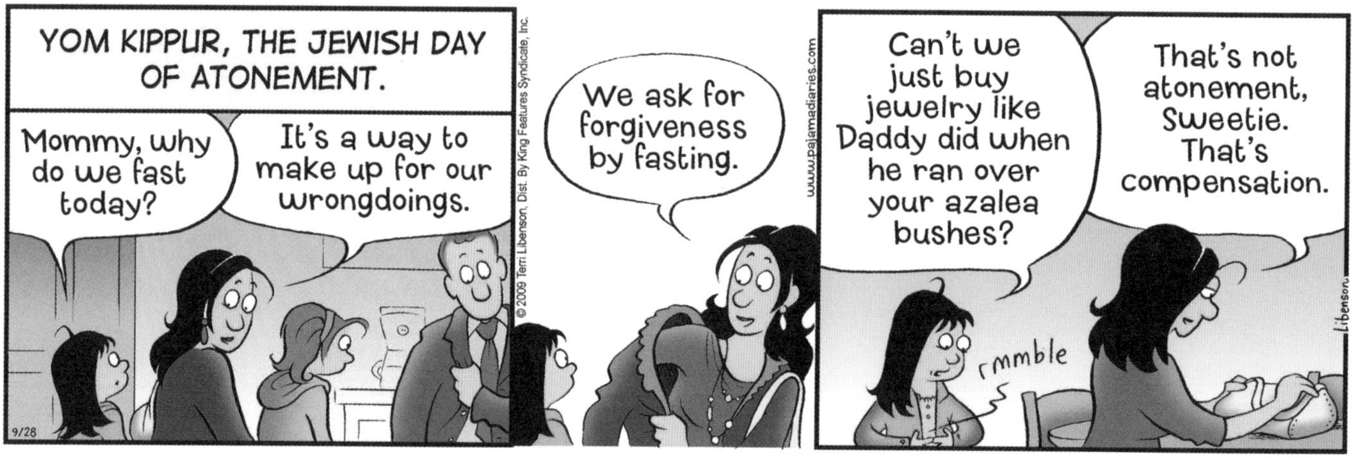
YOM KIPPUR, THE JEWISH DAY OF ATONEMENT.
Mommy, why do we fast today?
It's a way to make up for our wrongdoings.
9/28
© 2009 Terri Libenson, Dist. By King Features Syndicate, Inc.
We ask for forgiveness by fasting.
www.pajamadiaries.com
Can't we just buy jewelry like Daddy did when he ran over your azalea bushes?
That's not atonement, Sweetie. That's compensation.
rmmble
Libenson

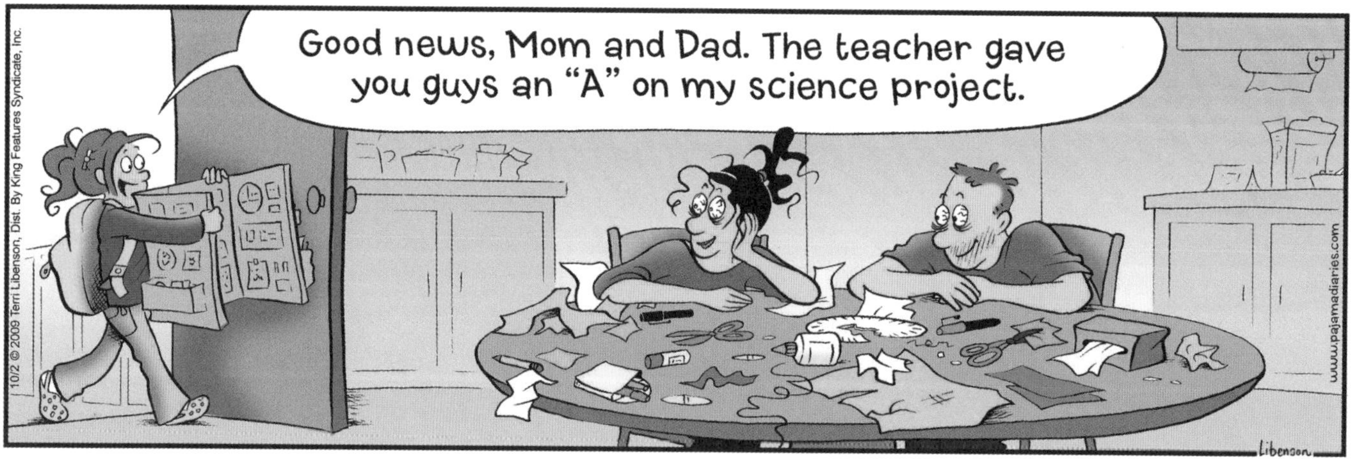
Good news, Mom and Dad. The teacher gave you guys an "A" on my science project.
10/2 © 2009 Terri Libenson, Dist. By King Features Syndicate, Inc.
www.pajamadiaries.com
Libenson

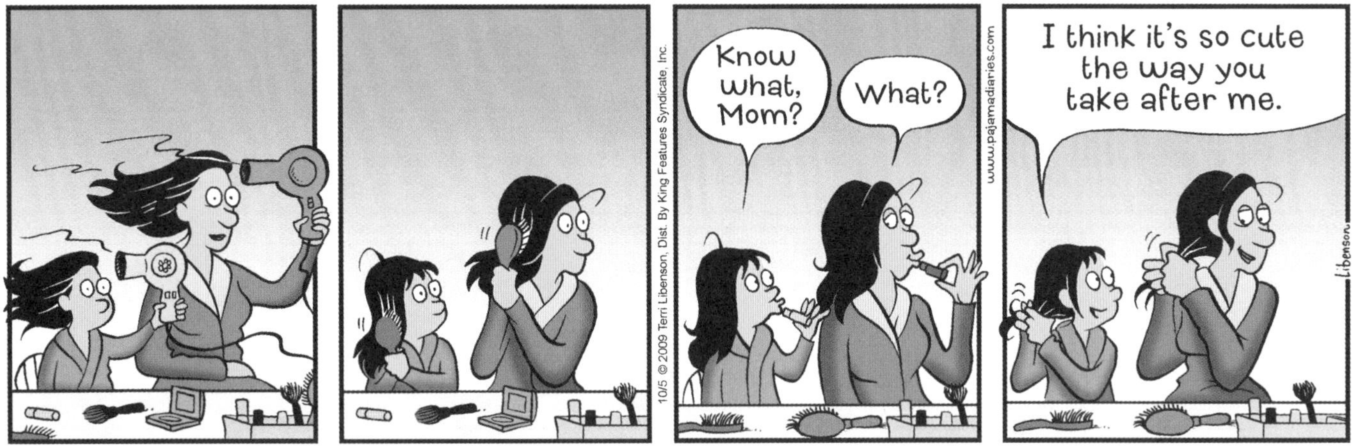
Know what, Mom?
What?
I think it's so cute the way you take after me.
10/5 © 2009 Terri Libenson, Dist. By King Features Syndicate, Inc.
www.pajamadiaries.com
Libenson

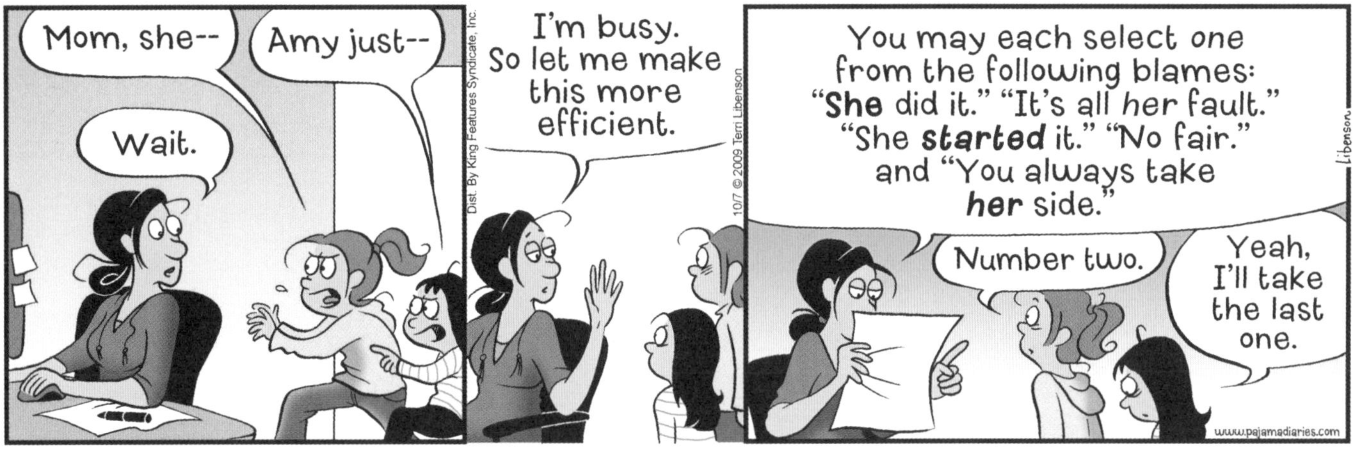
Mom, she--
Amy just--
Wait.
I'm busy. So let me make this more efficient.
You may each select *one* from the following blames: "**She** did it." "It's all *her* fault." "She **started** it." "No fair." and "You always take **her** side."
Number two.
Yeah, I'll take the last one.
10/7 © 2009 Terri Libenson
Dist. By King Features Syndicate, Inc.
www.pajamadiaries.com
Libenson

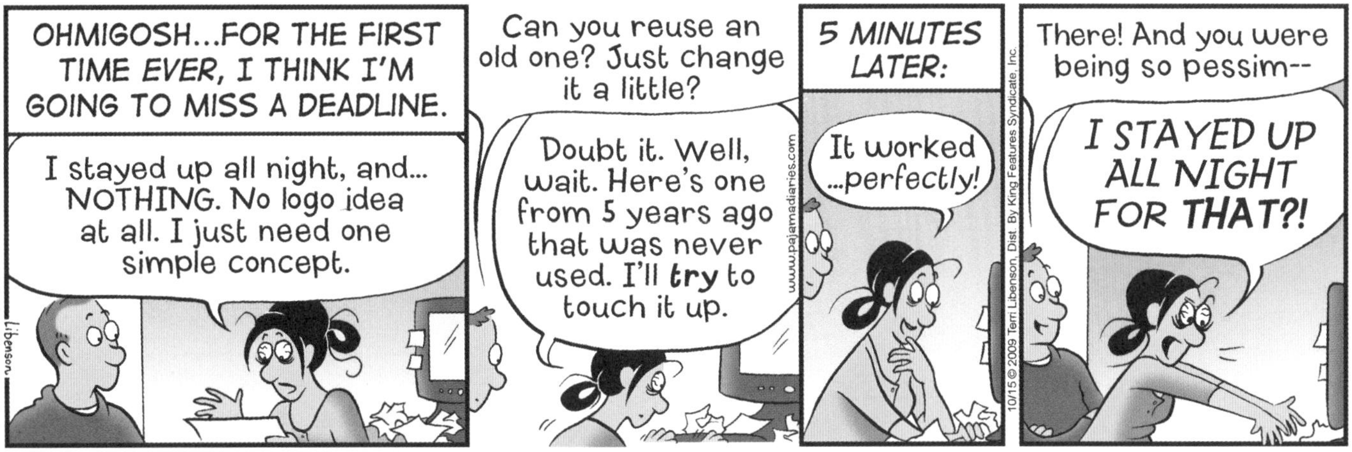
OHMIGOSH...FOR THE FIRST TIME *EVER*, I THINK I'M GOING TO MISS A DEADLINE.
I stayed up all night, and... NOTHING. No logo idea at all. I just need one simple concept.
Can you reuse an old one? Just change it a little?
Doubt it. Well, wait. Here's one from 5 years ago that was never used. I'll **try** to touch it up.
5 MINUTES LATER:
It worked ...*perfectly!*
There! And you were being so pessim--
*I STAYED UP ALL NIGHT FOR **THAT**?!*
Libenson
www.pajamadiaries.com
10/15 © 2009 Terri Libenson, Dist. By King Features Syndicate, Inc.

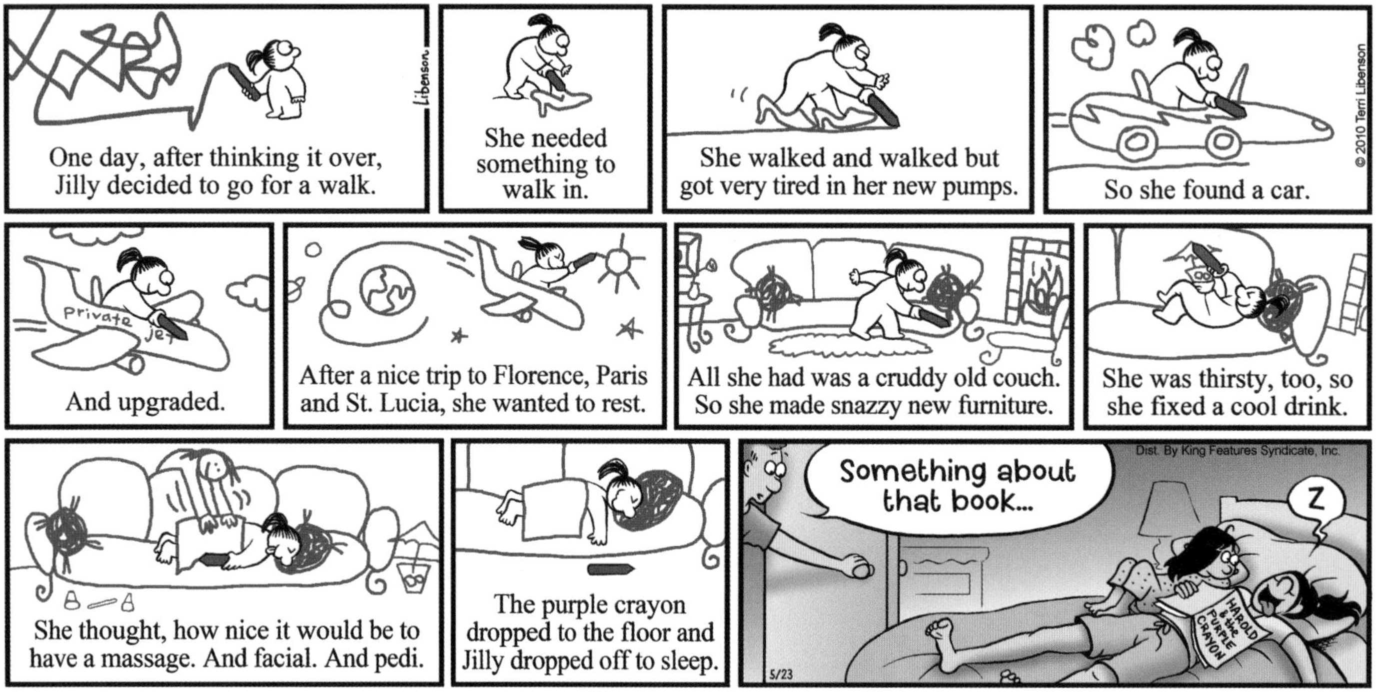
Libenson
One day, after thinking it over, Jilly decided to go for a walk.
She needed something to walk in.
She walked and walked but got very tired in her new pumps.
So she found a car.
© 2010 Terri Libenson
Private Jet
And upgraded.
After a nice trip to Florence, Paris and St. Lucia, she wanted to rest.
All she had was a cruddy old couch. So she made snazzy new furniture.
She was thirsty, too, so she fixed a cool drink.
She thought, how nice it would be to have a massage. And facial. And pedi.
The purple crayon dropped to the floor and Jilly dropped off to sleep.
Dist. By King Features Syndicate, Inc.
Something about that book...
Z
HAROLD & the PURPLE CRAYON
5/23

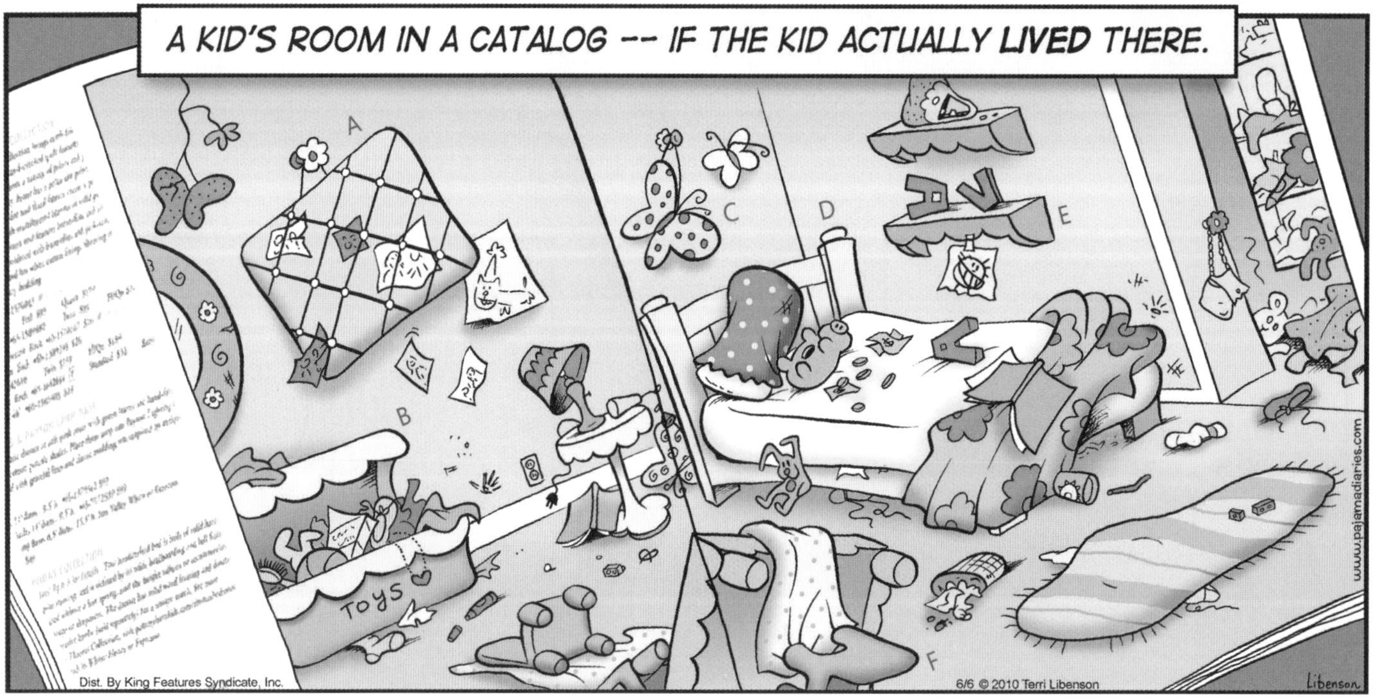
A KID'S ROOM IN A CATALOG -- IF THE KID ACTUALLY LIVED THERE.
A
B
C
D
E
F
TOYS
www.pajamadiaries.com
Dist. By King Features Syndicate, Inc.
6/6 © 2010 Terri Libenson
Libenson

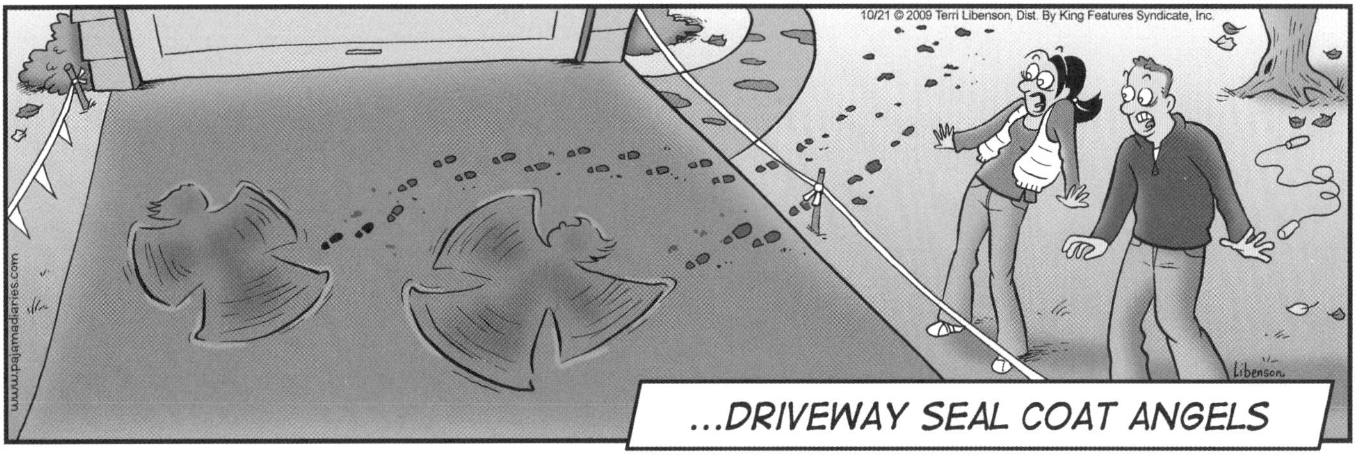
10/21 © 2009 Terri Libenson, Dist. By King Features Syndicate, Inc.
www.pajamadiaries.com
Libenson
...DRIVEWAY SEAL COAT ANGELS

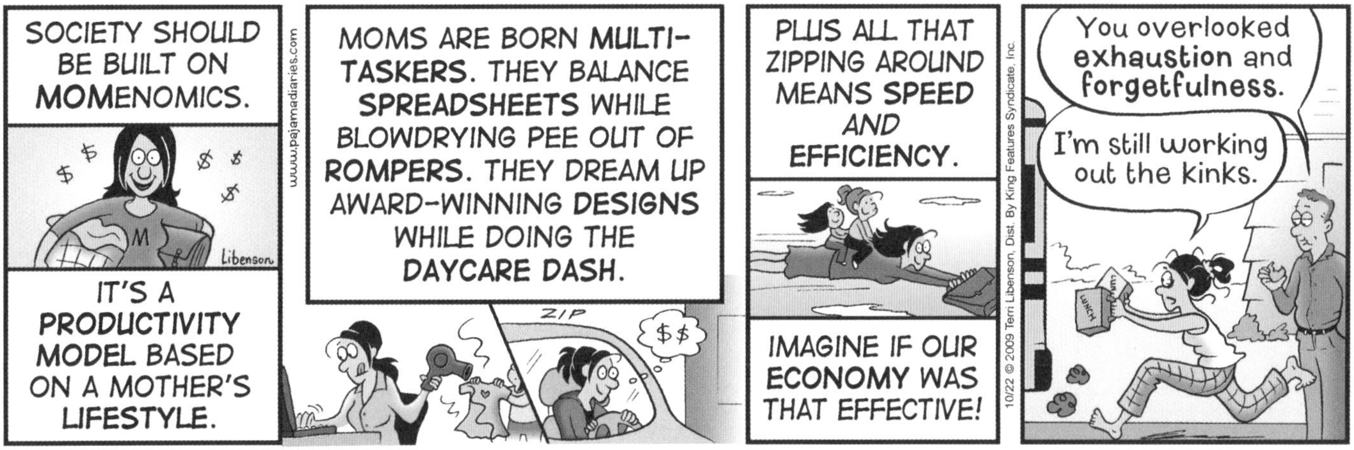
SOCIETY SHOULD BE BUILT ON **MOM**ENOMICS.
Libenson
IT'S A **PRODUCTIVITY** MODEL BASED ON A MOTHER'S **LIFESTYLE**.
www.pajamadiaries.com
MOMS ARE BORN **MULTI-TASKERS**. THEY BALANCE **SPREADSHEETS** WHILE BLOWDRYING PEE OUT OF **ROMPERS**. THEY DREAM UP AWARD-WINNING **DESIGNS** WHILE DOING THE **DAYCARE DASH**.
ZIP
$$
PLUS ALL THAT ZIPPING AROUND MEANS **SPEED** *AND* **EFFICIENCY**.
IMAGINE IF OUR **ECONOMY** WAS THAT EFFECTIVE!
10/22 © 2009 Terri Libenson, Dist. By King Features Syndicate, Inc.
You overlooked **exhaustion** and **forgetfulness**.
I'm still working out the kinks.
LUNCH

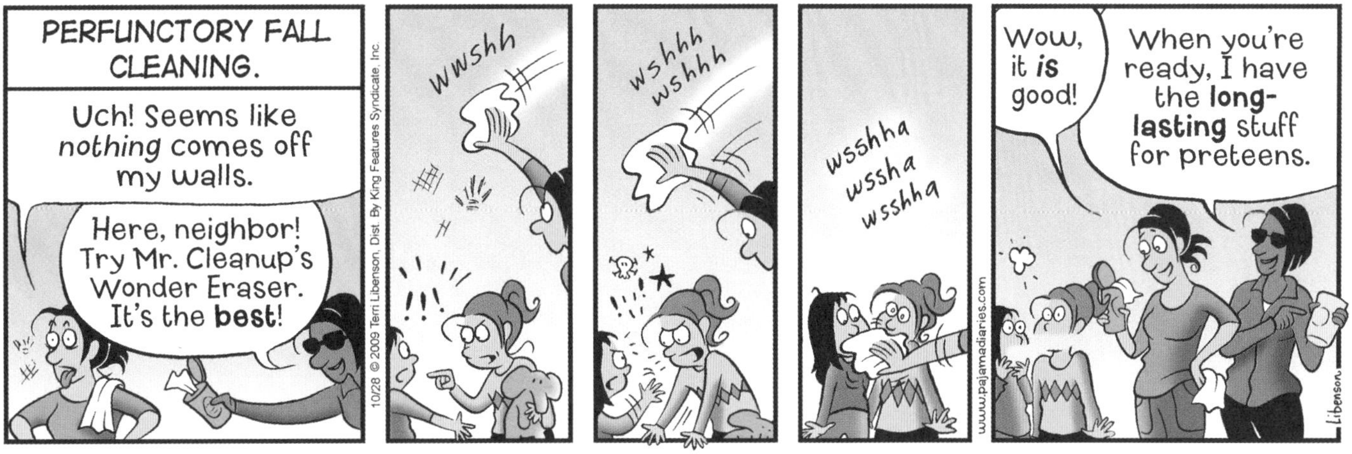
PERFUNCTORY FALL CLEANING.
Uch! Seems like *nothing* comes off my walls.
Here, neighbor! Try Mr. Cleanup's Wonder Eraser. It's the **best**!
10/28 © 2009 Terri Libenson, Dist. By King Features Syndicate, Inc.
wwshh
!!!
wshhh
wshhh
wsshha
wssha
wsshha
www.pajamadiaries.com
Wow, it *is* good!
When you're ready, I have the **long-lasting** stuff for preteens.
Libenson

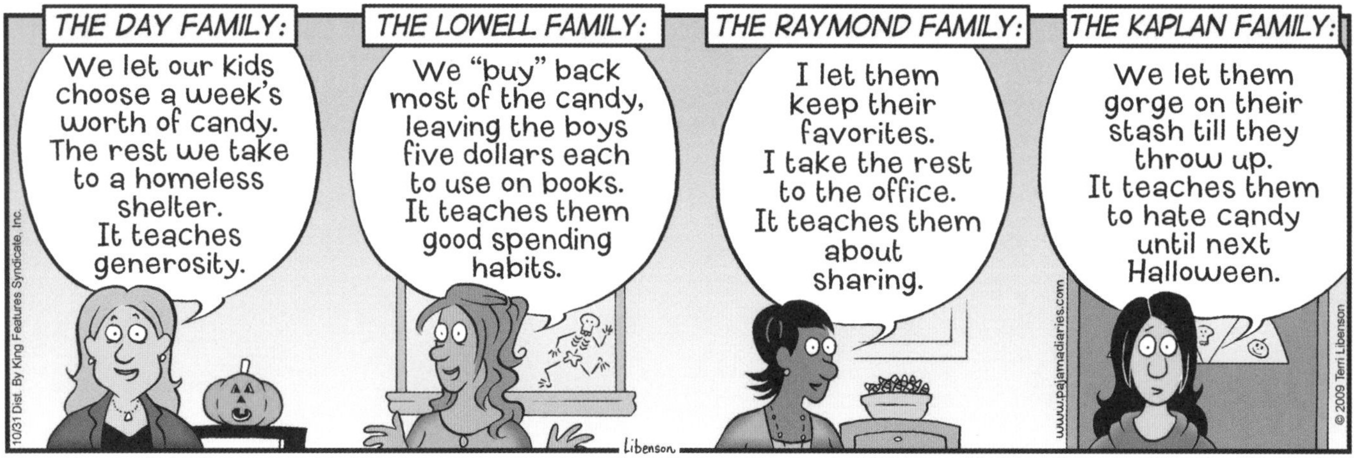
THE DAY FAMILY:
We let our kids choose a week's worth of candy. The rest we take to a homeless shelter. It teaches generosity.
THE LOWELL FAMILY:
We "buy" back most of the candy, leaving the boys five dollars each to use on books. It teaches them good spending habits.
THE RAYMOND FAMILY:
I let them keep their favorites. I take the rest to the office. It teaches them about sharing.
THE KAPLAN FAMILY:
We let them gorge on their stash till they throw up. It teaches them to hate candy until next Halloween.
10/31 Dist. By King Features Syndicate, Inc.
Libenson
www.pajamadiaries.com
© 2009 Terri Libenson

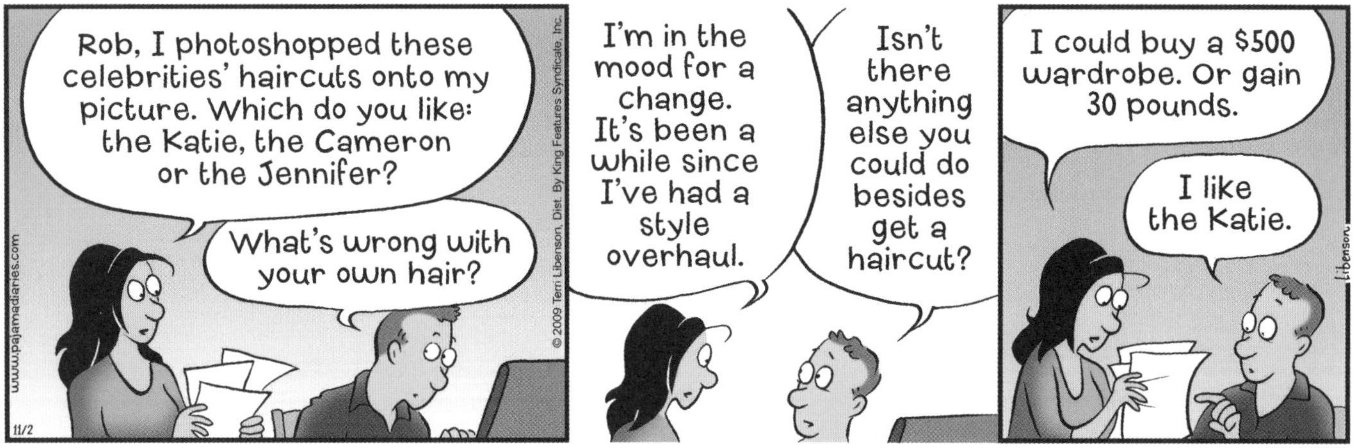
Rob, I photoshopped these celebrities' haircuts onto my picture. Which do you like: the Katie, the Cameron or the Jennifer?
What's wrong with your own hair?
www.pajamadiaries.com
11/2
© 2009 Terri Libenson, Dist. By King Features Syndicate, Inc.
I'm in the mood for a change. It's been a while since I've had a style overhaul.
Isn't there anything else you could do besides get a haircut?
I could buy a $500 wardrobe. Or gain 30 pounds.
I like the Katie.
Libenson

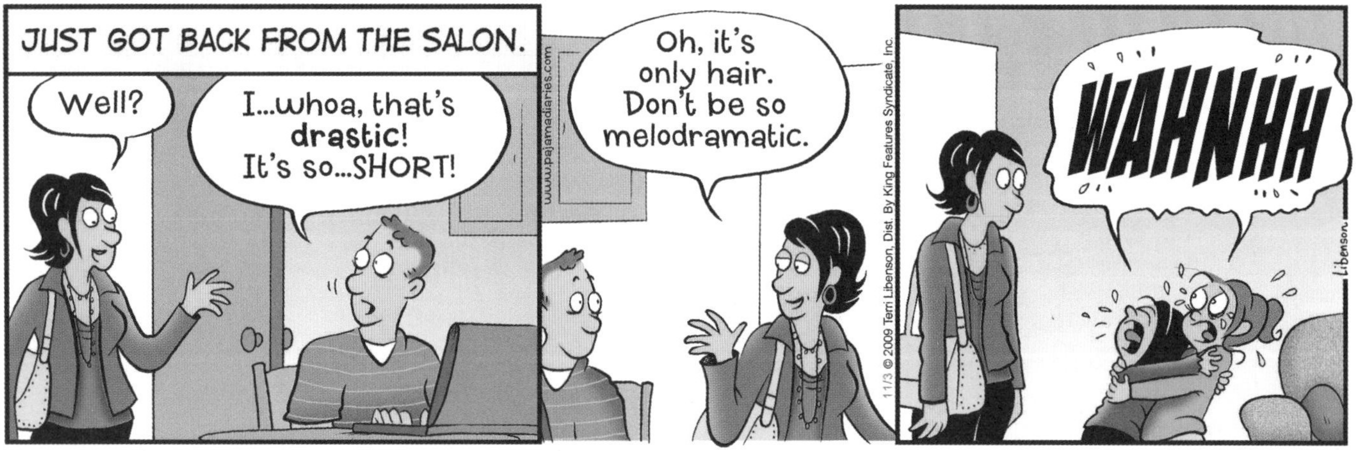
JUST GOT BACK FROM THE SALON.
Well?
I...whoa, that's **drastic**! It's so...SHORT!
www.pajamadiaries.com
Oh, it's only hair. Don't be so melodramatic.
11/3 © 2009 Terri Libenson, Dist. By King Features Syndicate, Inc.
WAHNHH
Libenson

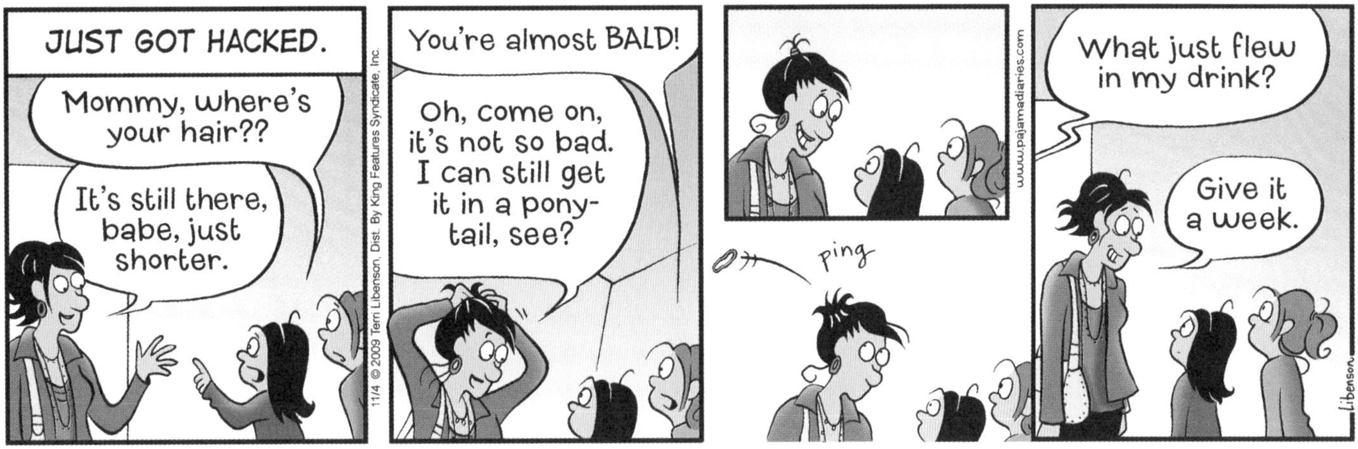
JUST GOT HACKED.
Mommy, where's your hair??
It's still there, babe, just shorter.
11/4 © 2009 Terri Libenson, Dist. By King Features Syndicate, Inc.
You're almost BALD!
Oh, come on, it's not so bad. I can still get it in a pony-tail, see?
ping
www.pajamadiaries.com
What just flew in my drink?
Give it a week.
Libenson

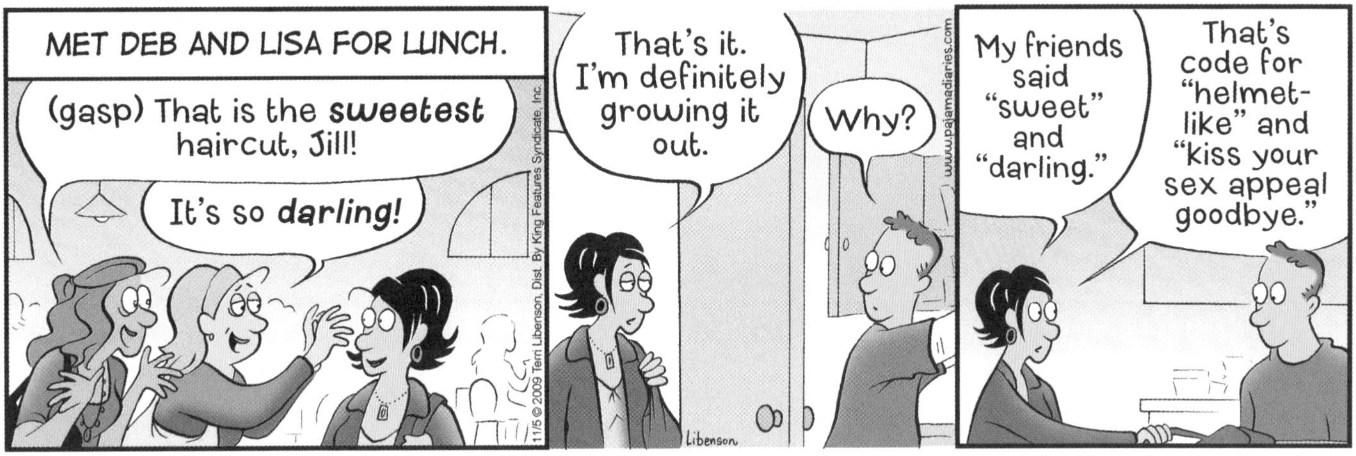
MET DEB AND LISA FOR LUNCH.
(gasp) That is the **sweetest** haircut, Jill!
It's so **darling!**
11/5 © 2009 Terri Libenson, Dist. By King Features Syndicate, Inc.
That's it. I'm definitely growing it out.
Why?
Libenson
www.pajamadiaries.com
My friends said "sweet" and "darling."
That's code for "helmet-like" and "kiss your sex appeal goodbye."

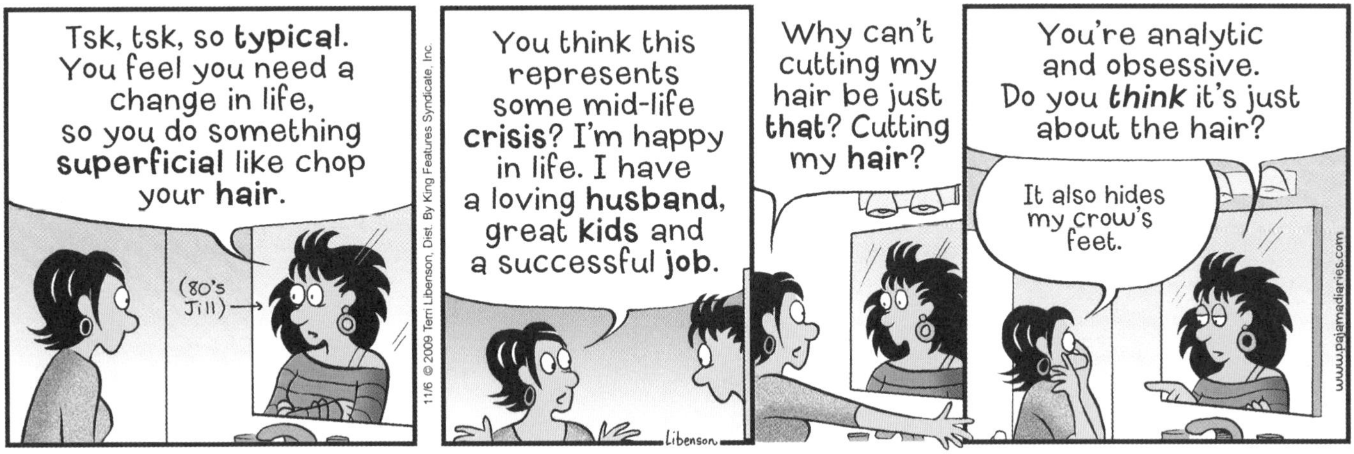
Tsk, tsk, so **typical**. You feel you need a change in life, so you do something **superficial** like chop your **hair**.
(80's Jill)
11/6 © 2009 Terri Libenson, Dist. By King Features Syndicate, Inc.
You think this represents some mid-life **crisis**? I'm happy in life. I have a loving **husband**, great **kids** and a successful **job**.
Why can't cutting my hair be just **that**? Cutting my **hair**?
Libenson
You're analytic and obsessive. Do you ***think*** it's just about the hair?
It also hides my crow's feet.
www.pajamadiaries.com

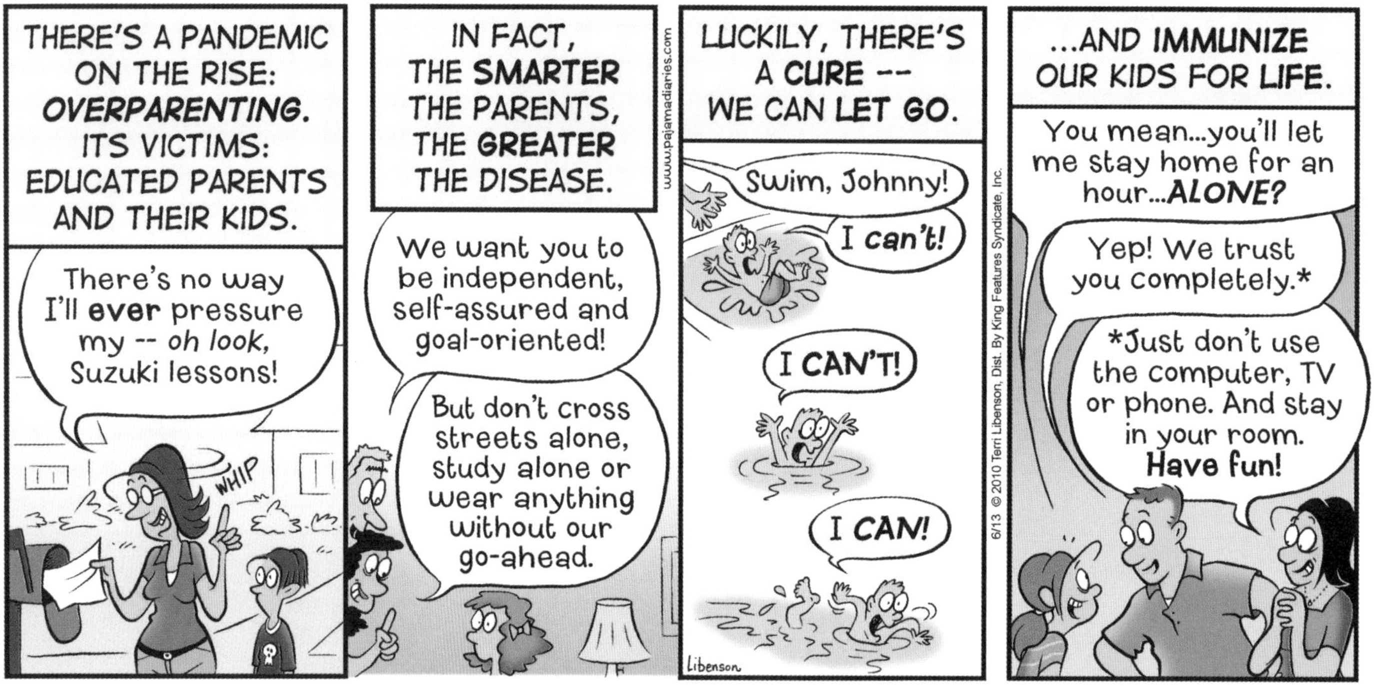
THERE'S A PANDEMIC ON THE RISE: OVERPARENTING. ITS VICTIMS: EDUCATED PARENTS AND THEIR KIDS.
There's no way I'll ever pressure my -- oh look, Suzuki lessons!
WHIP
IN FACT, THE SMARTER THE PARENTS, THE GREATER THE DISEASE.
We want you to be independent, self-assured and goal-oriented!
But don't cross streets alone, study alone or wear anything without our go-ahead.
www.pajamadiaries.com
LUCKILY, THERE'S A CURE -- WE CAN LET GO.
Swim, Johnny!
I can't!
I CAN'T!
I CAN!
Libenson
6/13 © 2010 Terri Libenson, Dist. By King Features Syndicate, Inc.
...AND IMMUNIZE OUR KIDS FOR LIFE.
You mean...you'll let me stay home for an hour...ALONE?
Yep! We trust you completely.*
*Just don't use the computer, TV or phone. And stay in your room. Have fun!

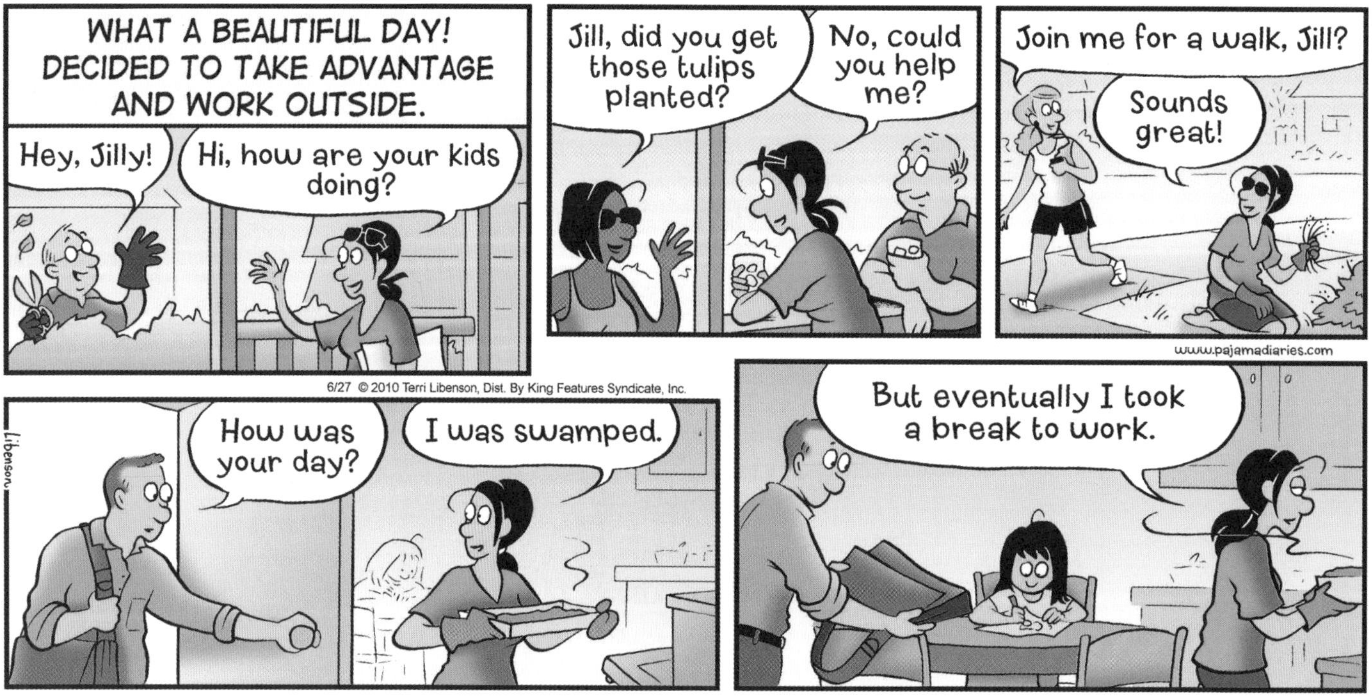
WHAT A BEAUTIFUL DAY! DECIDED TO TAKE ADVANTAGE AND WORK OUTSIDE.
Hey, Jilly!
Hi, how are your kids doing?
Jill, did you get those tulips planted?
No, could you help me?
Join me for a walk, Jill?
Sounds great!
www.pajamadiaries.com
6/27 © 2010 Terri Libenson, Dist. By King Features Syndicate, Inc.
Libenson
How was your day?
I was swamped.
But eventually I took a break to work.

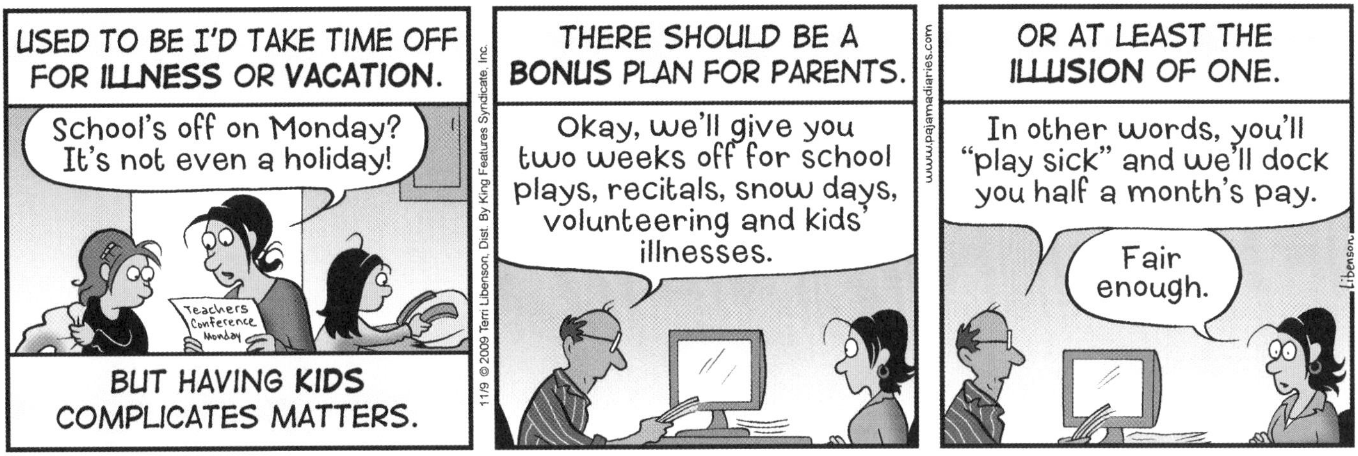
USED TO BE I'D TAKE TIME OFF FOR **ILLNESS** OR **VACATION**.
School's off on Monday? It's not even a holiday!
Teachers Conference Monday
BUT HAVING **KIDS** COMPLICATES MATTERS.
11/9 © 2009 Terri Libenson, Dist. By King Features Syndicate, Inc.
THERE SHOULD BE A **BONUS** PLAN FOR PARENTS.
Okay, we'll give you two weeks off for school plays, recitals, snow days, volunteering and kids' illnesses.
www.pajamadiaries.com
OR AT LEAST THE **ILLUSION** OF ONE.
In other words, you'll "play sick" and we'll dock you half a month's pay.
Fair enough.
Libenson

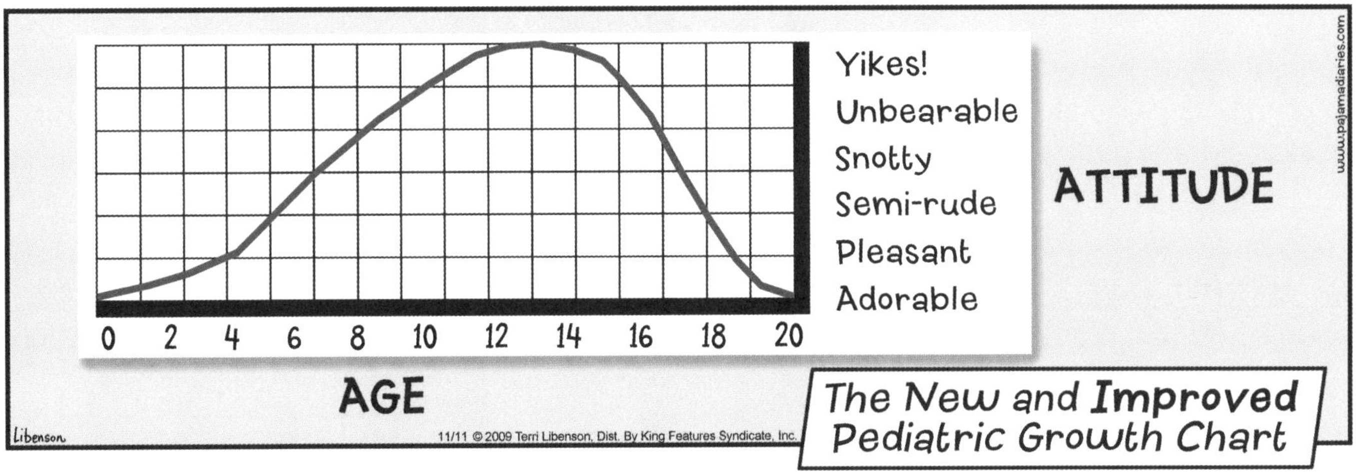
Yikes!
Unbearable
Snotty
Semi-rude
Pleasant
Adorable
ATTITUDE
0 2 4 6 8 10 12 14 16 18 20
AGE
The New and **Improved** Pediatric Growth Chart
Libenson
11/11 © 2009 Terri Libenson, Dist. By King Features Syndicate, Inc.
www.pajamadiaries.com

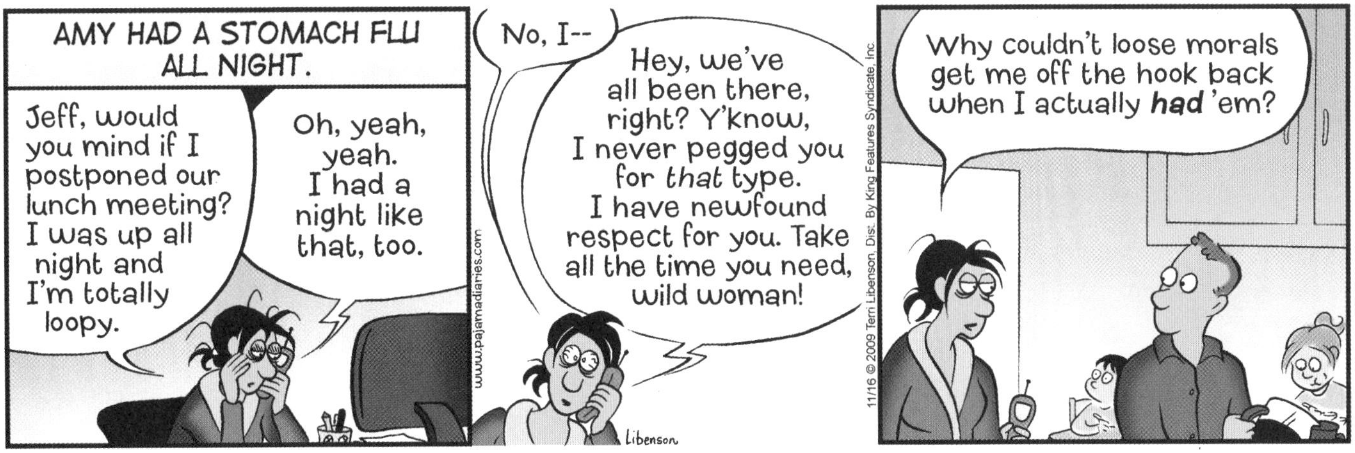
AMY HAD A STOMACH FLU ALL NIGHT.
Jeff, would you mind if I postponed our lunch meeting? I was up all night and I'm totally loopy.
Oh, yeah, yeah. I had a night like that, too.
www.pajamadiaries.com
No, I--
Hey, we've all been there, right? Y'know, I never pegged you for *that* type. I have newfound respect for you. Take all the time you need, wild woman!
Libenson
11/16 © 2009 Terri Libenson, Dist. By King Features Syndicate, Inc.
Why couldn't loose morals get me off the hook back when I actually ***had*** 'em?

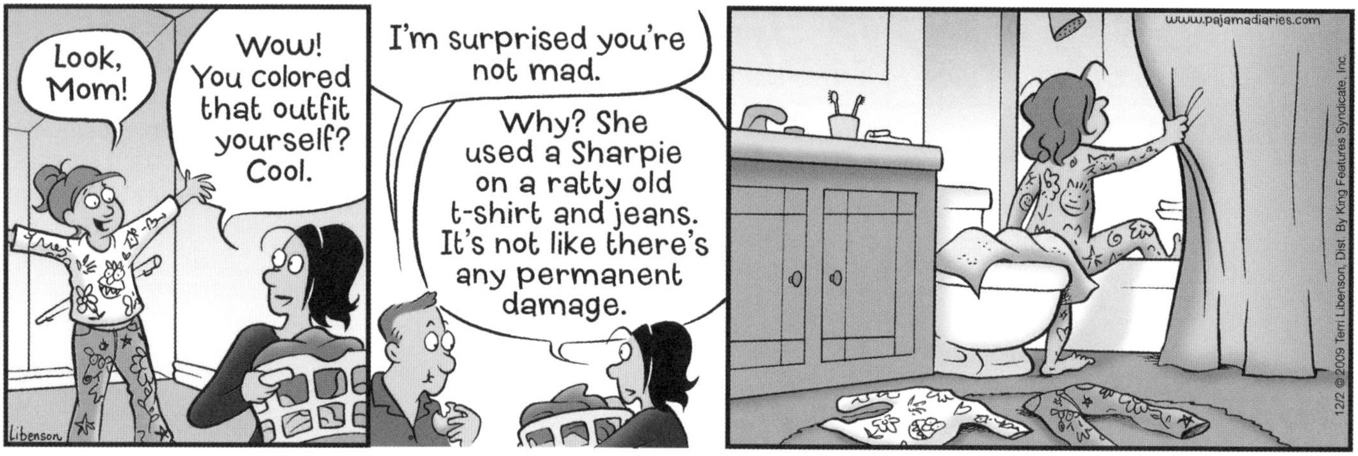
Look, Mom!
Wow! You colored that outfit yourself? Cool.
I'm surprised you're not mad.
Why? She used a Sharpie on a ratty old t-shirt and jeans. It's not like there's any permanent damage.
Libenson
www.pajamadiaries.com
12/2 © 2009 Terri Libenson, Dist. By King Features Syndicate, Inc.

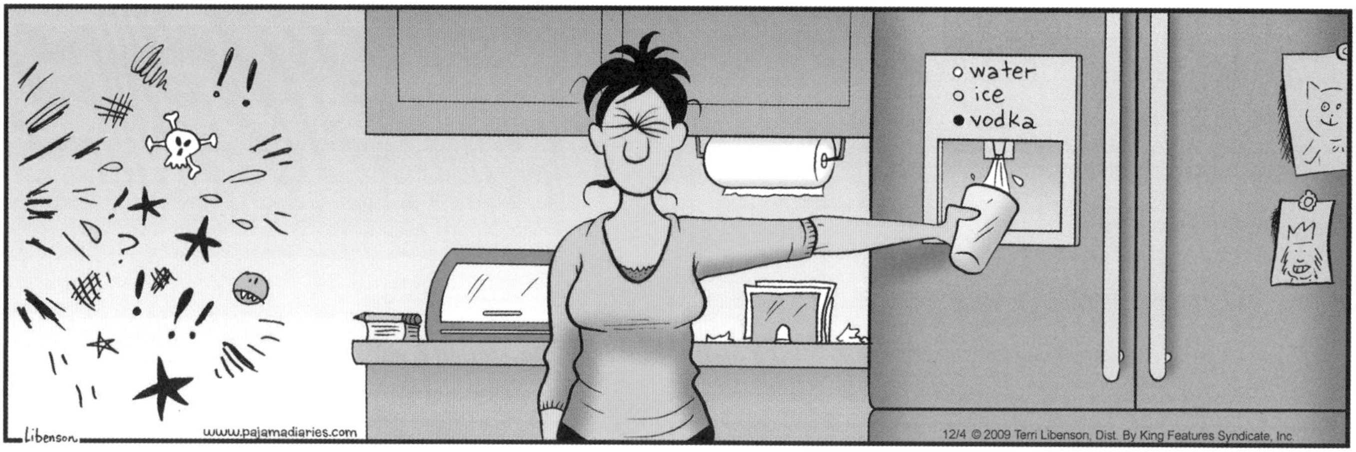
o water
o ice
● vodka
Libenson
www.pajamadiaries.com
12/4 © 2009 Terri Libenson, Dist. By King Features Syndicate, Inc.

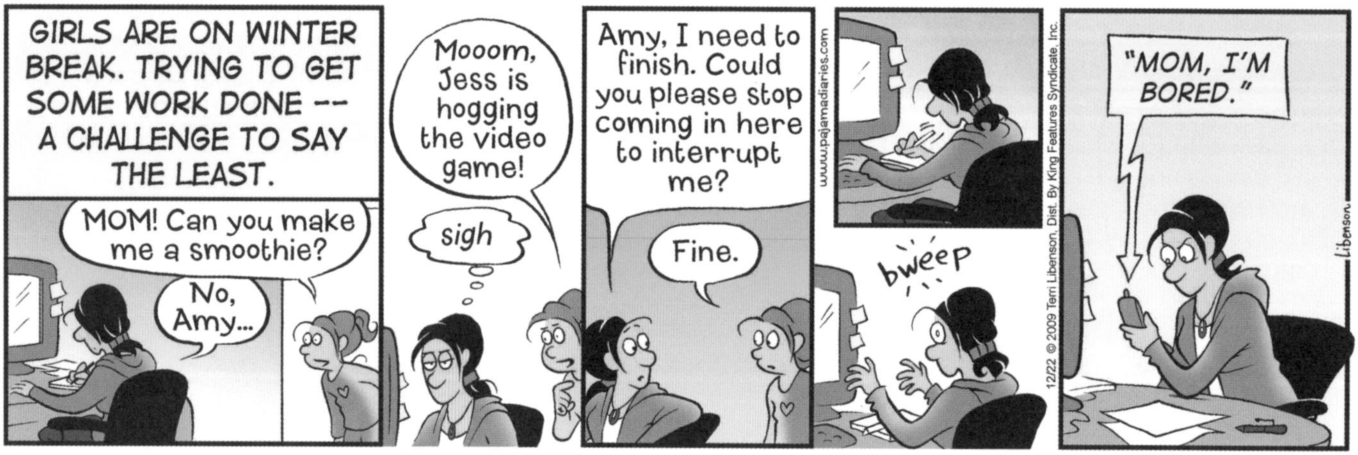
GIRLS ARE ON WINTER BREAK. TRYING TO GET SOME WORK DONE -- A CHALLENGE TO SAY THE LEAST.
MOM! Can you make me a smoothie?
No, Amy...
Mooom, Jess is hogging the video game!
sigh
Amy, I need to finish. Could you please stop coming in here to interrupt me?
Fine.
www.pajamadiaries.com
bweep
12/22 © 2009 Terri Libenson, Dist. By King Features Syndicate, Inc.
"MOM, I'M BORED."
Libenson

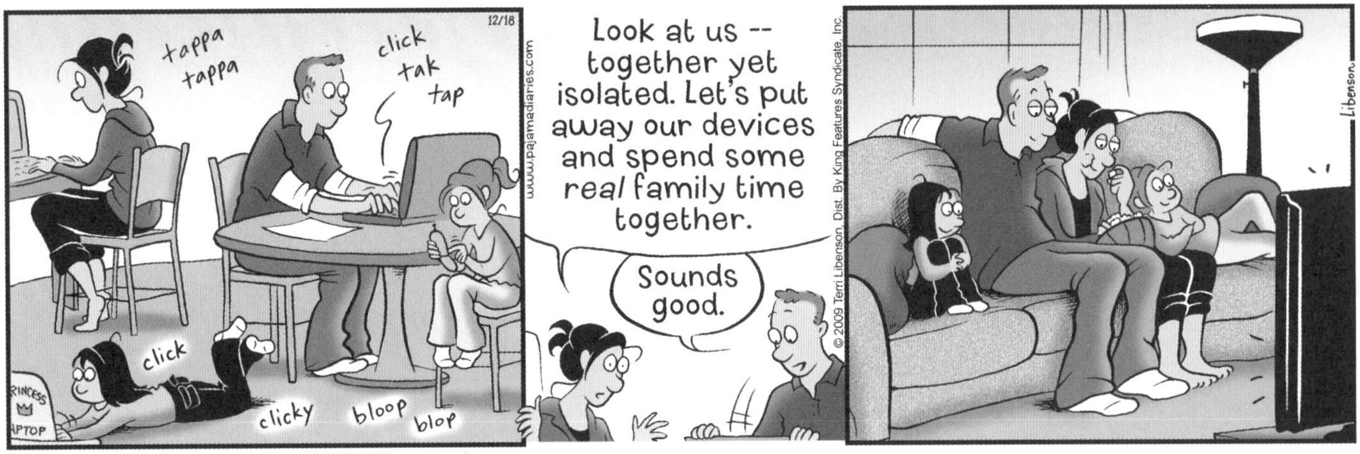
12/18
tappa tappa
click tak tap
click
clicky
bloop
blop
PRINCESS LAPTOP
www.pajamadiaries.com
Look at us -- together yet isolated. Let's put away our devices and spend some *real* family time together.
Sounds good.
© 2009 Terri Libenson, Dist. By King Features Syndicate, Inc.
Libenson

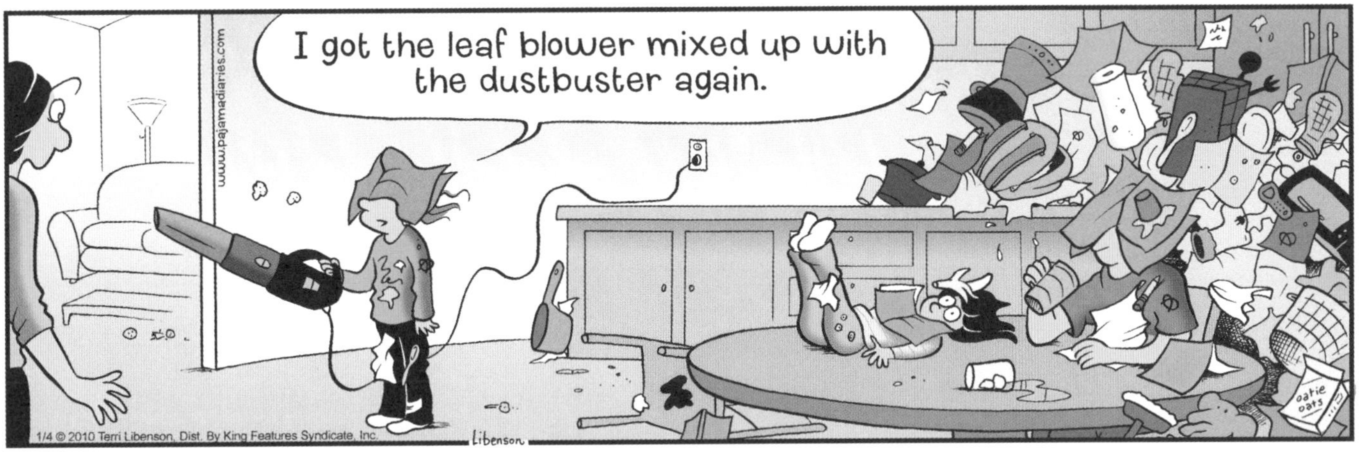
www.pajamadiaries.com
I got the leaf blower mixed up with the dustbuster again.
oatie oats
1/4 © 2010 Terri Libenson, Dist. By King Features Syndicate, Inc.
Libenson

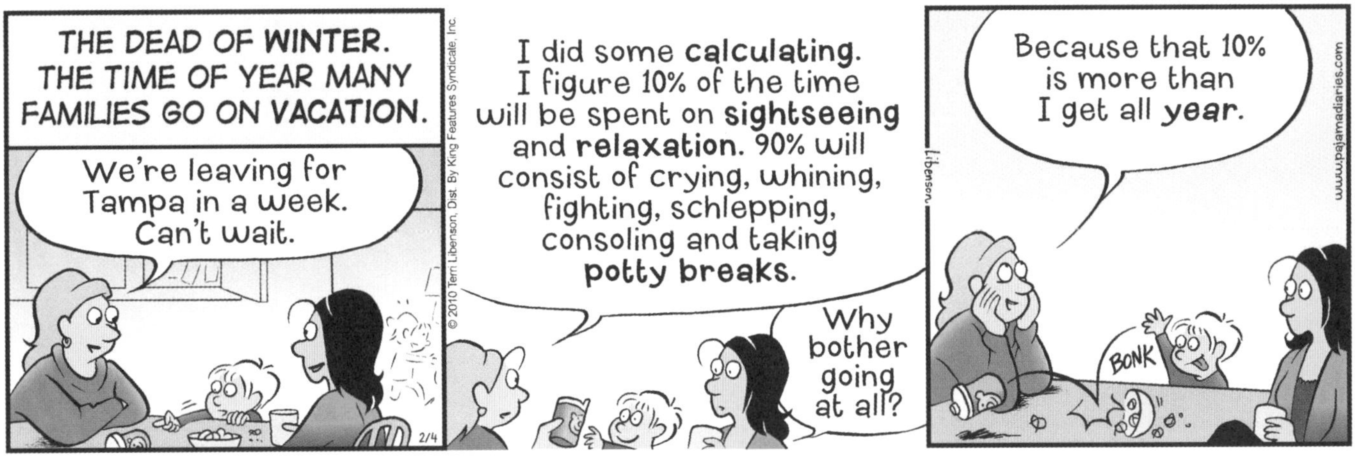
THE DEAD OF WINTER. THE TIME OF YEAR MANY FAMILIES GO ON VACATION.
We're leaving for Tampa in a week. Can't wait.
2/4
© 2010 Terri Libenson, Dist. By King Features Syndicate, Inc.
I did some **calculating**. I figure 10% of the time will be spent on **sightseeing** and **relaxation**. 90% will consist of crying, whining, fighting, schlepping, consoling and taking **potty breaks**.
Why bother going at all?
Libenson
Because that 10% is more than I get all **year**.
BONK
www.pajamadiaries.com

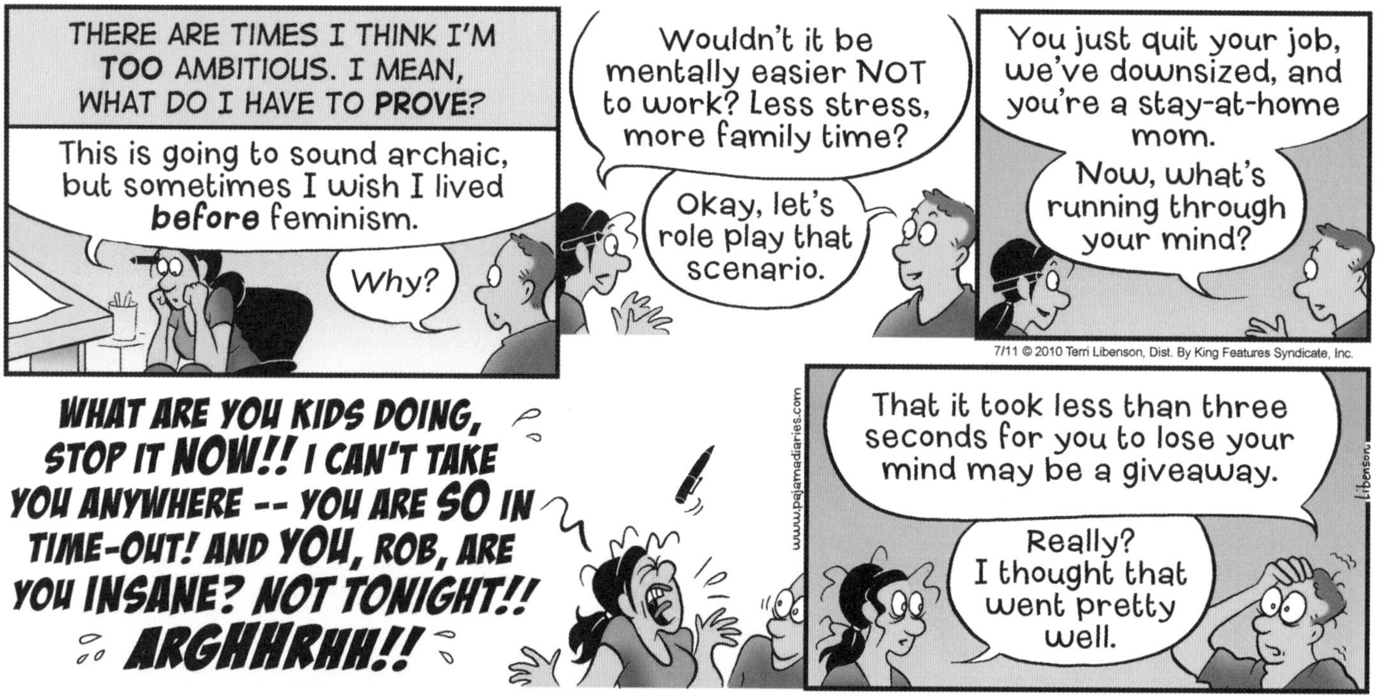
THERE ARE TIMES I THINK I'M TOO AMBITIOUS. I MEAN, WHAT DO I HAVE TO PROVE?
This is going to sound archaic, but sometimes I wish I lived before feminism.
Why?
Wouldn't it be mentally easier NOT to work? Less stress, more family time?
Okay, let's role play that scenario.
You just quit your job, we've downsized, and you're a stay-at-home mom.
Now, what's running through your mind?
7/11 © 2010 Terri Libenson, Dist. By King Features Syndicate, Inc.
WHAT ARE YOU KIDS DOING, STOP IT NOW!! I CAN'T TAKE YOU ANYWHERE -- YOU ARE SO IN TIME-OUT! AND YOU, ROB, ARE YOU INSANE? NOT TONIGHT!!
ARGHHRHH!!
www.pajamadiaries.com
That it took less than three seconds for you to lose your mind may be a giveaway.
Really? I thought that went pretty well.
Libenson

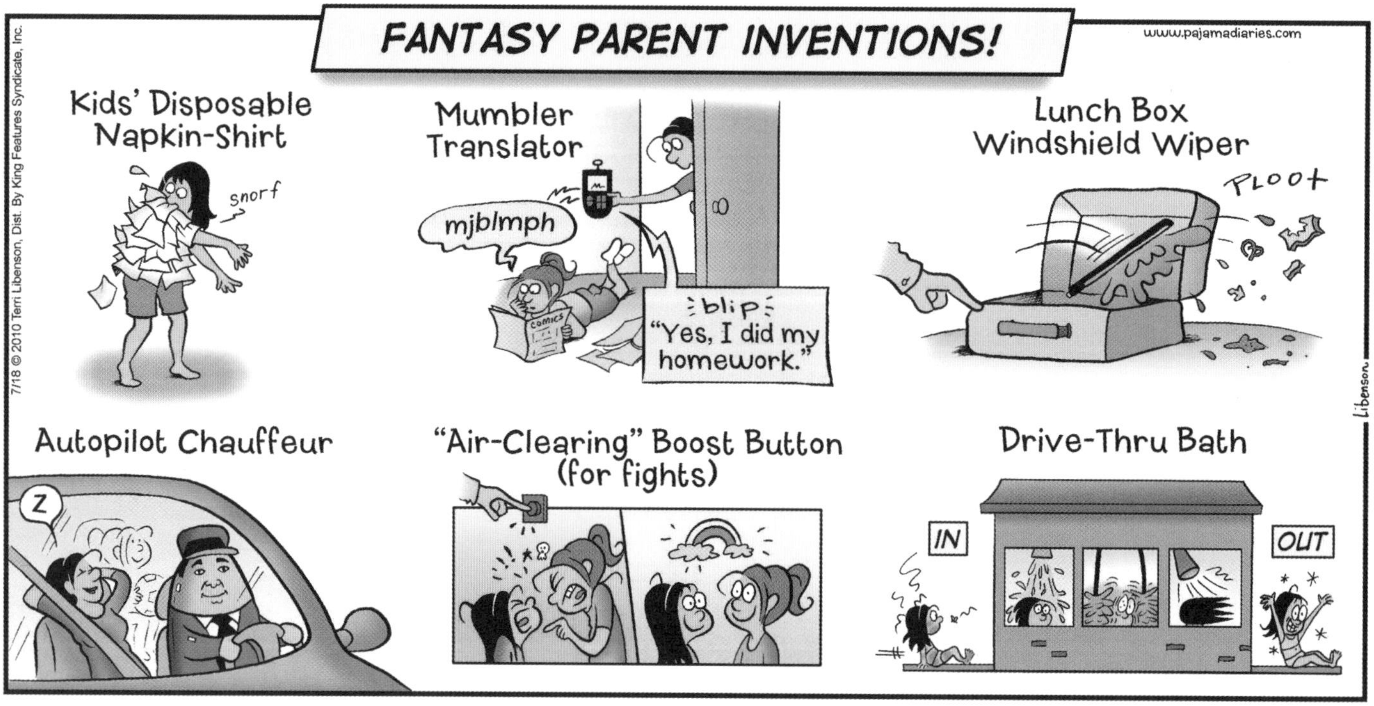
FANTASY PARENT INVENTIONS!
www.pajamadiaries.com
7/18 © 2010 Terri Libenson, Dist. By King Features Syndicate, Inc.
Kids' Disposable Napkin-Shirt
snorf
Mumbler Translator
mjblmph
blip
"Yes, I did my homework."
COMICS
Lunch Box Windshield Wiper
PLOOT
Libenson
Autopilot Chauffeur
Z
"Air-Clearing" Boost Button (for fights)
Drive-Thru Bath
IN
OUT

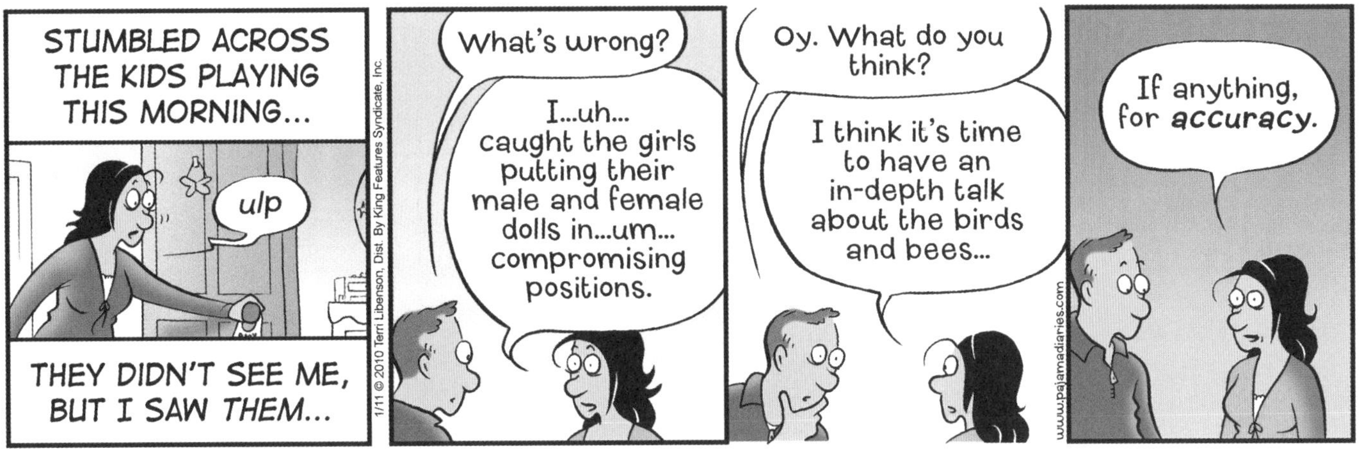
STUMBLED ACROSS THE KIDS PLAYING THIS MORNING...
u/p
THEY DIDN'T SEE ME, BUT I SAW THEM...
1/11 © 2010 Terri Libenson, Dist. By King Features Syndicate, Inc.
What's wrong?
I...uh... caught the girls putting their male and female dolls in...um... compromising positions.
Oy. What do you think?
I think it's time to have an in-depth talk about the birds and bees...
www.pajamadiaries.com
If anything, for **accuracy**.

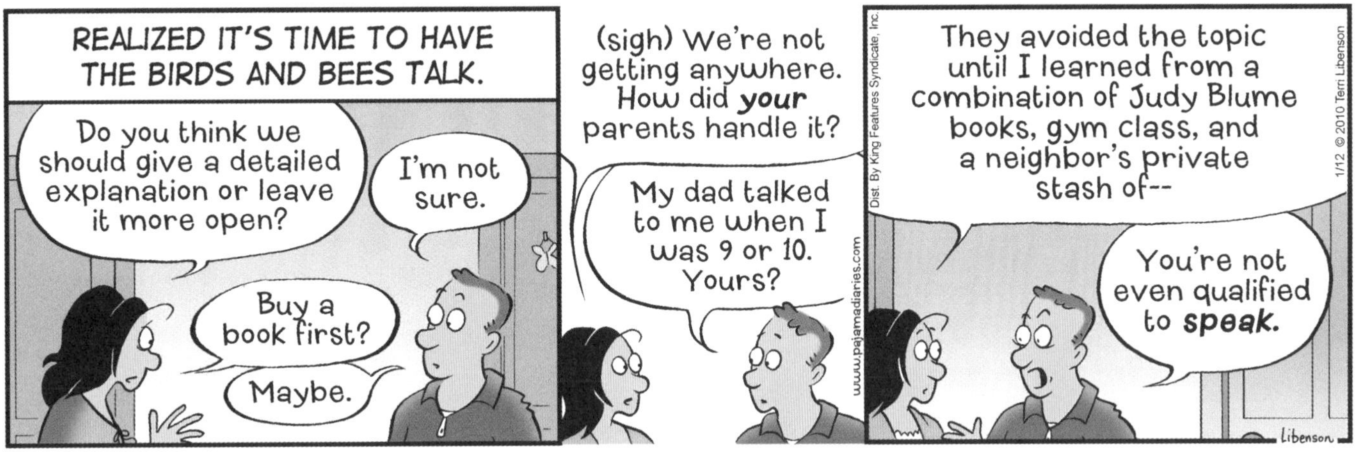
REALIZED IT'S TIME TO HAVE THE BIRDS AND BEES TALK.
Do you think we should give a detailed explanation or leave it more open?
I'm not sure.
Buy a book first?
Maybe.
(sigh) We're not getting anywhere. How did **your** parents handle it?
My dad talked to me when I was 9 or 10. Yours?
www.pajamadiaries.com
Dist. By King Features Syndicate, Inc.
They avoided the topic until I learned from a combination of Judy Blume books, gym class, and a neighbor's private stash of--
You're not even qualified to **speak**.
1/12 © 2010 Terri Libenson
Libenson

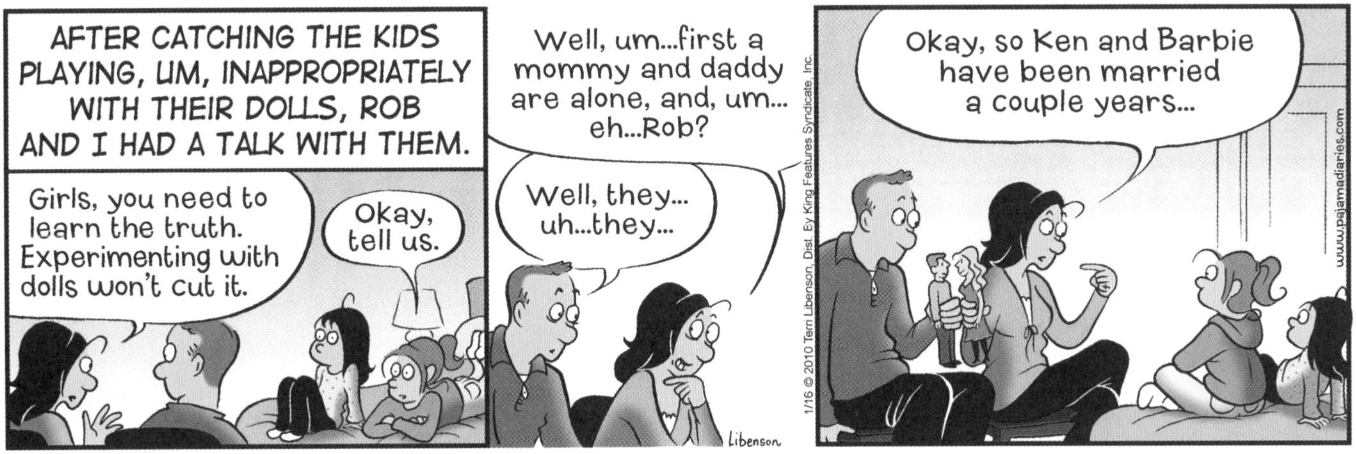
AFTER CATCHING THE KIDS PLAYING, UM, INAPPROPRIATELY WITH THEIR DOLLS, ROB AND I HAD A TALK WITH THEM.
Girls, you need to learn the truth. Experimenting with dolls won't cut it.
Okay, tell us.
Well, um...first a mommy and daddy are alone, and, um... eh...Rob?
Well, they... uh...they...
Libenson
1/16 © 2010 Terri Libenson, Dist. By King Features Syndicate, Inc.
Okay, so Ken and Barbie have been married a couple years...
www.pajamadiaries.com

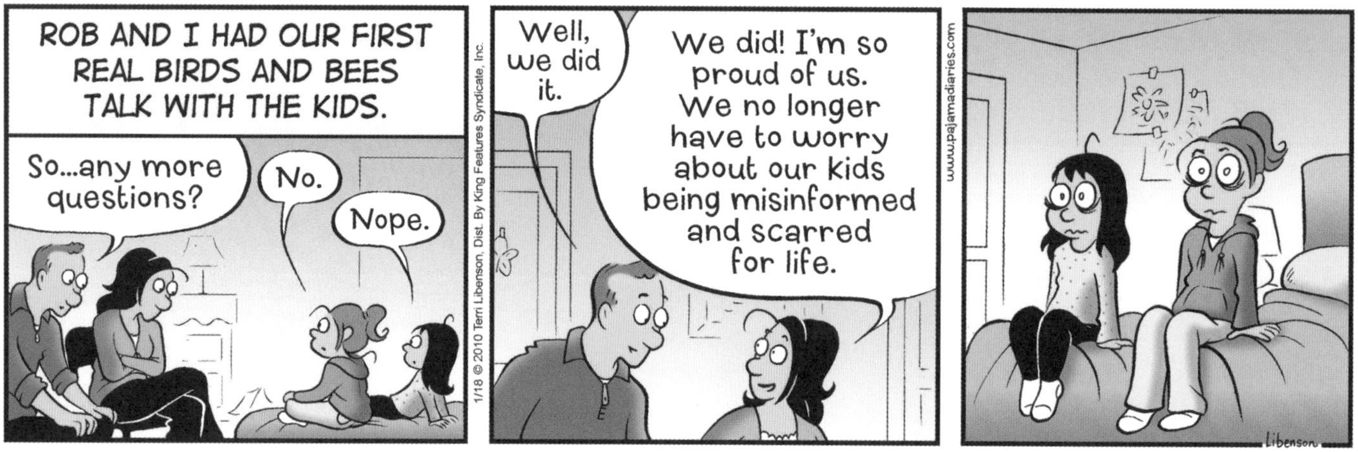
ROB AND I HAD OUR FIRST REAL BIRDS AND BEES TALK WITH THE KIDS.
So...any more questions?
No.
Nope.
1/18 © 2010 Terri Libenson, Dist. By King Features Syndicate, Inc.
Well, we did it.
We did! I'm so proud of us. We no longer have to worry about our kids being misinformed and scarred for life.
www.pajamadiaries.com
Libenson

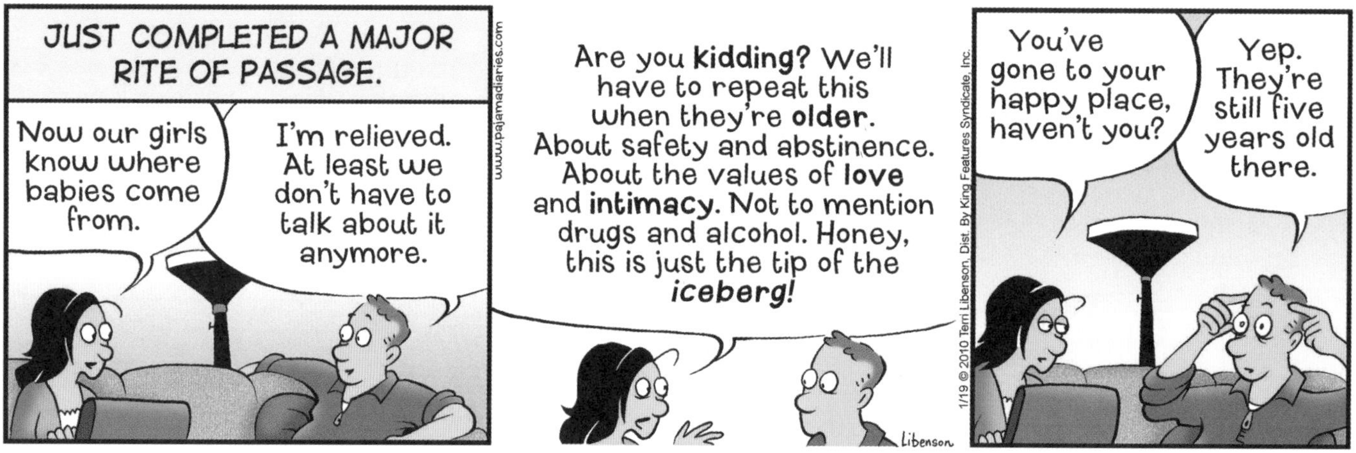
JUST COMPLETED A MAJOR RITE OF PASSAGE.
Now our girls know where babies come from.
I'm relieved. At least we don't have to talk about it anymore.
www.pajamadiaries.com
Are you **kidding?** We'll have to repeat this when they're **older**. About safety and abstinence. About the values of **love** and **intimacy**. Not to mention drugs and alcohol. Honey, this is just the tip of the ***iceberg!***
Libenson
1/19 © 2010 Terri Libenson, Dist. By King Features Syndicate, Inc.
You've gone to your happy place, haven't you?
Yep. They're still five years old there.

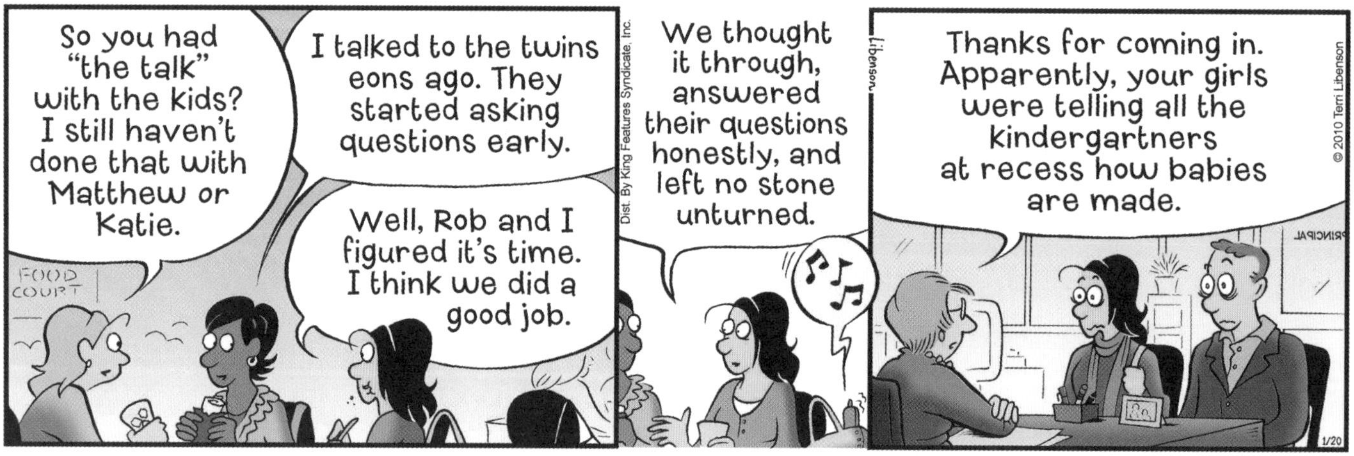
So you had "the talk" with the kids? I still haven't done that with Matthew or Katie.
I talked to the twins eons ago. They started asking questions early.
FOOD COURT
Well, Rob and I figured it's time. I think we did a good job.
Dist. By King Features Syndicate, Inc.
We thought it through, answered their questions honestly, and left no stone unturned.
Libenson
Thanks for coming in. Apparently, your girls were telling all the kindergartners at recess how babies are made.
© 2010 Terri Libenson
PRINCIPAL
1/20

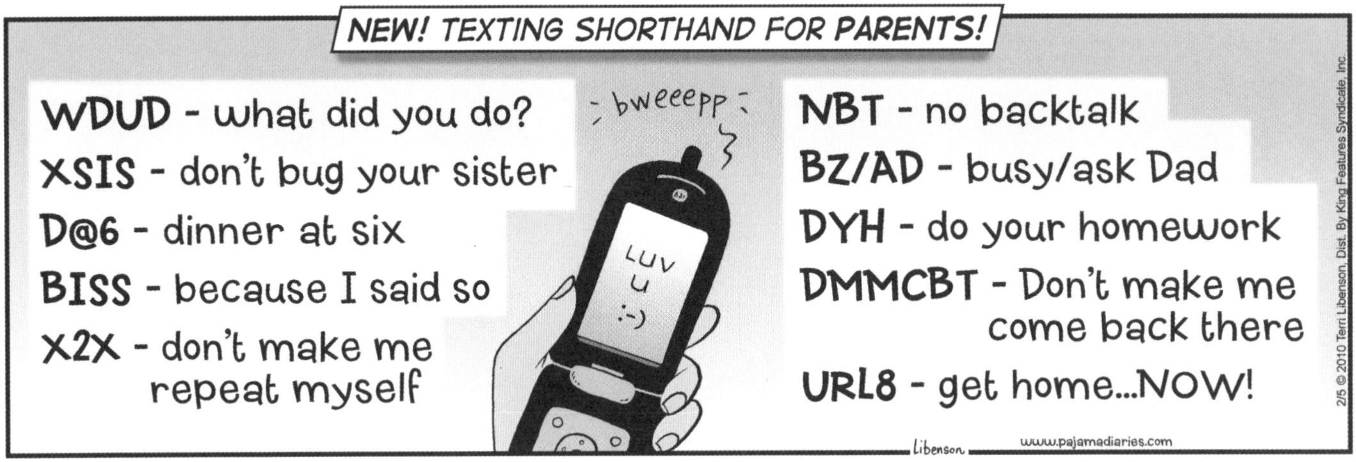

NEW! TEXTING SHORTHAND FOR PARENTS!
WDUD - what did you do?
XSIS - don't bug your sister
D@6 - dinner at six
BISS - because I said so
X2X - don't make me repeat myself
bweeepp
LUV U :-)
NBT - no backtalk
BZ/AD - busy/ask Dad
DYH - do your homework
DMMCBT - Don't make me come back there
URL8 - get home...NOW!
2/5 © 2010 Terri Libenson, Dist. By King Features Syndicate, Inc.
Libenson
www.pajamadiaries.com

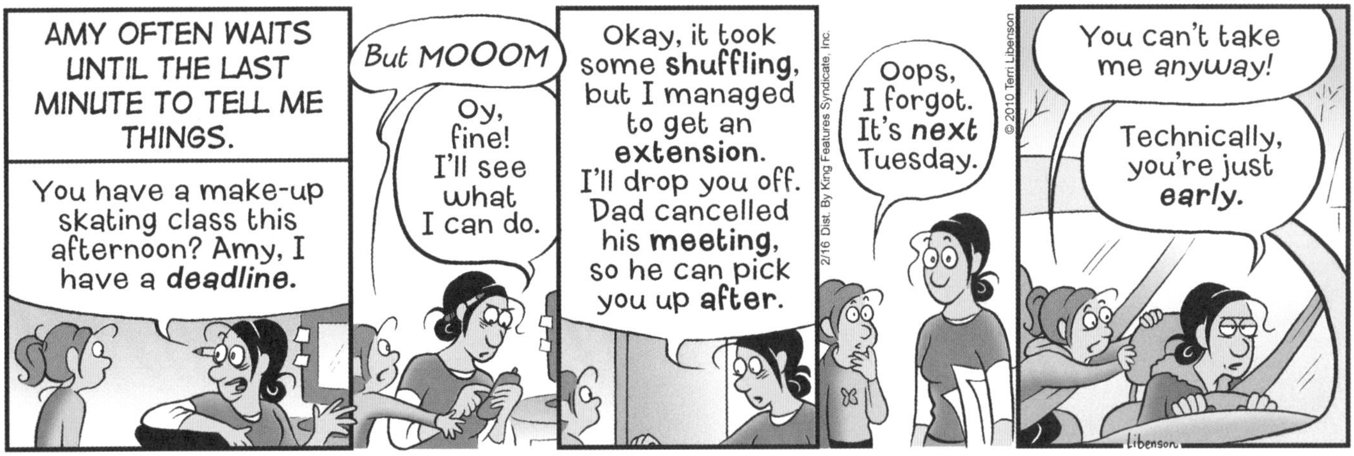

AMY OFTEN WAITS UNTIL THE LAST MINUTE TO TELL ME THINGS.
You have a make-up skating class this afternoon? Amy, I have a *deadline*.
But MOOOM
Oy, fine! I'll see what I can do.
Okay, it took some **shuffling**, but I managed to get an **extension**. I'll drop you off. Dad cancelled his **meeting**, so he can pick you up **after**.
2/16 Dist. By King Features Syndicate, Inc.
Oops, I forgot. It's *next* Tuesday.
© 2010 Terri Libenson
You can't take me *anyway!*
Technically, you're just *early*.
Libenson

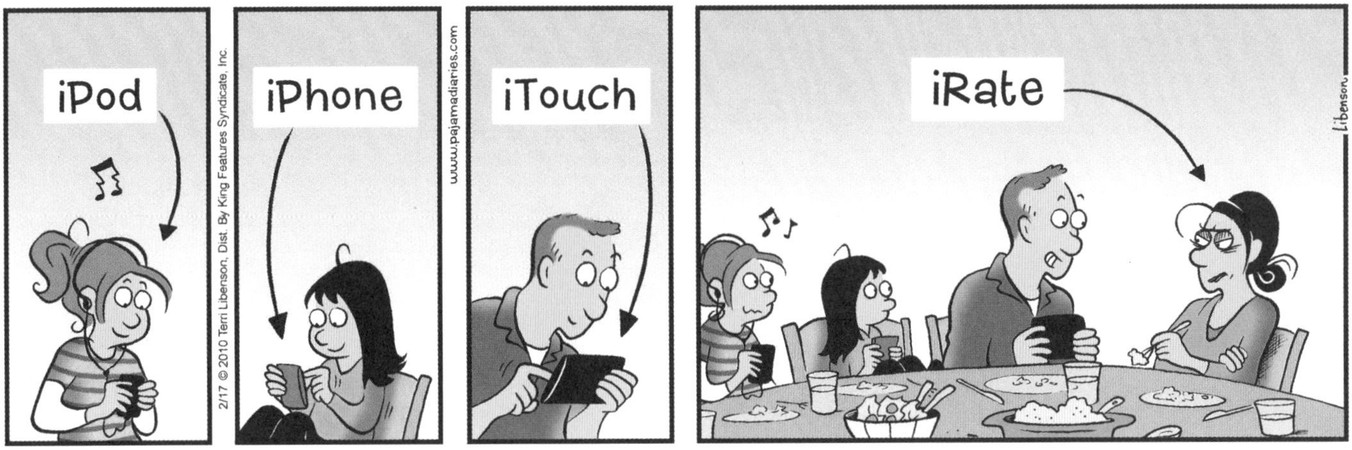

iPod
2/17 © 2010 Terri Libenson, Dist. By King Features Syndicate, Inc.
iPhone
www.pajamadiaries.com
iTouch
iRate
Libenson

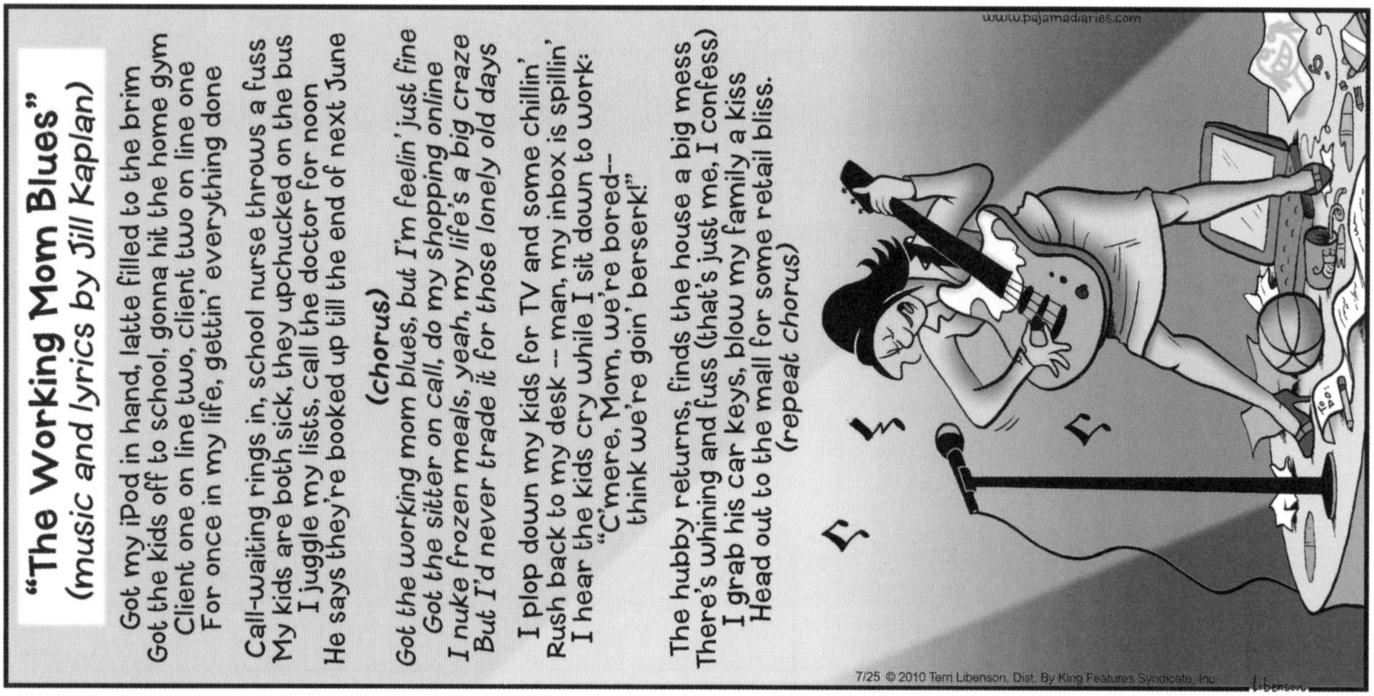
"The Working Mom Blues"
(music and lyrics by Jill Kaplan)
Got my iPod in hand, latte filled to the brim
Got the kids off to school, gonna hit the home gym
Client one on line two, client two on line one
For once in my life, gettin' everything done
Call-waiting rings in, school nurse throws a fuss
My kids are both sick, they upchucked on the bus
I juggle my lists, call the doctor for noon
He says they're booked up till the end of next June
(chorus)
Got the working mom blues, but I'm feelin' just fine
Got the sitter on call, do my shopping online
I nuke frozen meals, yeah, my life's a big craze
But I'd never trade it for those lonely old days
I plop down my kids for TV and some chillin'
Rush back to my desk -- man, my inbox is spillin'
I hear the kids cry while I sit down to work:
"C'mere, Mom, we're bored--
think we're goin' berserk!"
The hubby returns, finds the house a big mess
There's whining and fuss (that's just me, I confess)
I grab his car keys, blow my family a kiss
Head out to the mall for some retail bliss.
(repeat chorus)
www.pajamadiaries.com
7/25 © 2010 Terri Libenson, Dist. By King Features Syndicate, Inc.
Libenson

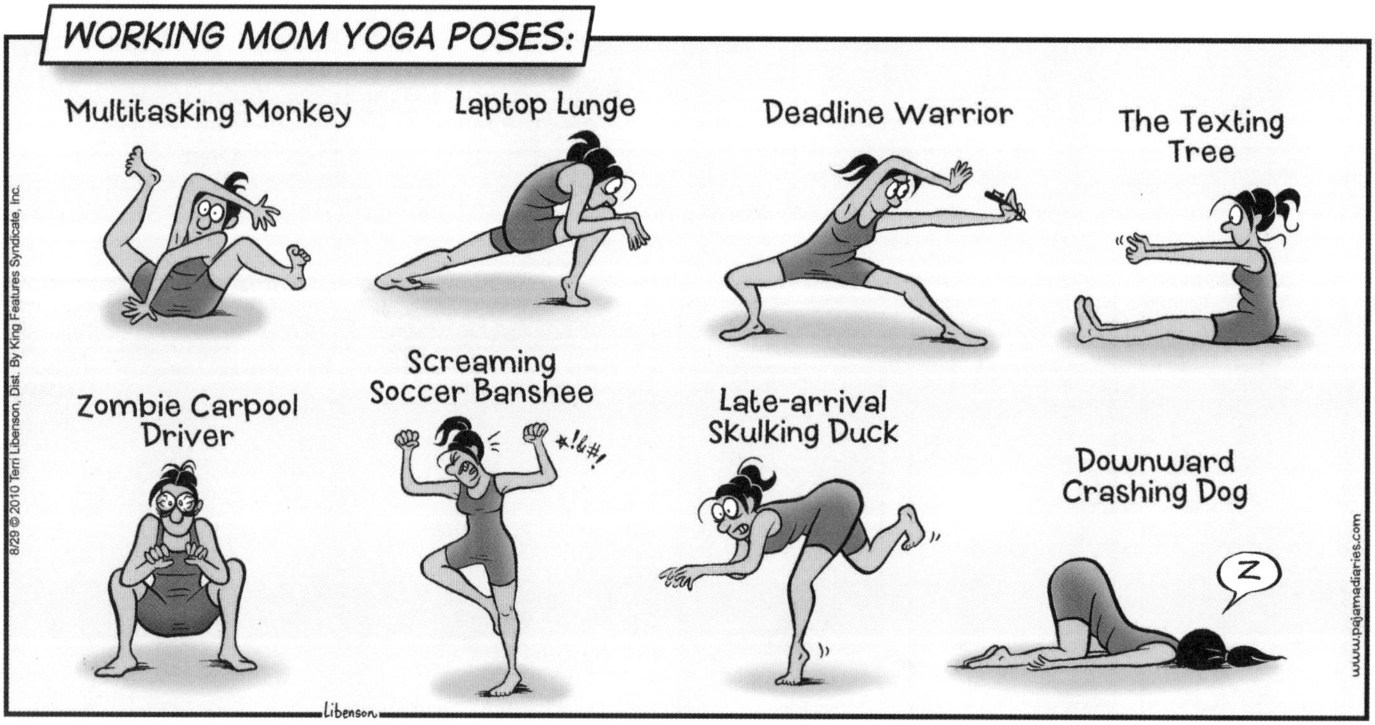
WORKING MOM YOGA POSES:
Multitasking Monkey
Laptop Lunge
Deadline Warrior
The Texting Tree
Zombie Carpool Driver
Screaming Soccer Banshee
*!&#!
Late-arrival Skulking Duck
Downward Crashing Dog
Z
8/29 © 2010 Terri Libenson, Dist. By King Features Syndicate, Inc.
www.pajamadiaries.com
Libenson

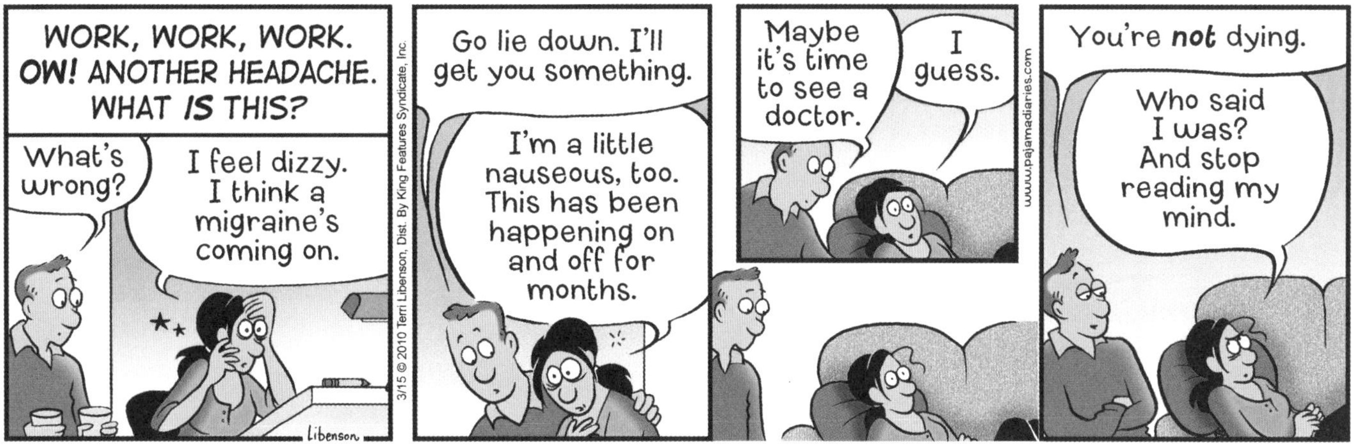

WORK, WORK, WORK. OW! ANOTHER HEADACHE. WHAT IS THIS?
What's wrong?
I feel dizzy. I think a migraine's coming on.
Libenson
3/15 © 2010 Terri Libenson, Dist. By King Features Syndicate, Inc.
Go lie down. I'll get you something.
I'm a little nauseous, too. This has been happening on and off for months.
Maybe it's time to see a doctor.
I guess.
www.pajamadiaries.com
You're not dying.
Who said I was? And stop reading my mind.

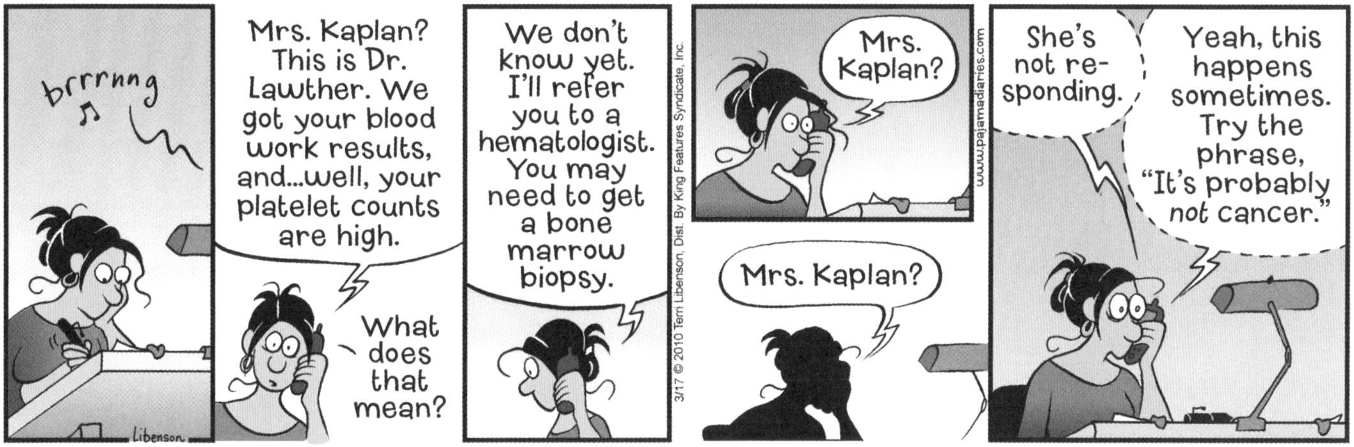

brrrnng
Mrs. Kaplan? This is Dr. Lawther. We got your blood work results, and...well, your platelet counts are high.
What does that mean?
Libenson
We don't know yet. I'll refer you to a hematologist. You may need to get a bone marrow biopsy.
3/17 © 2010 Terri Libenson, Dist. By King Features Syndicate, Inc.
Mrs. Kaplan?
Mrs. Kaplan?
www.pajamadiaries.com
She's not re-sponding.
Yeah, this happens sometimes. Try the phrase, "It's probably not cancer."

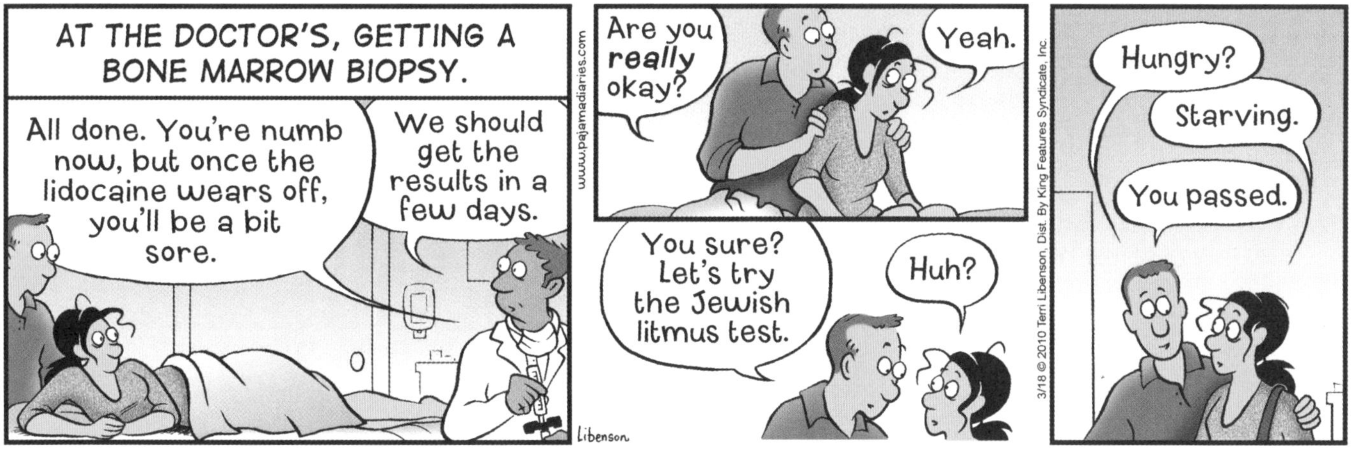

AT THE DOCTOR'S, GETTING A BONE MARROW BIOPSY.
All done. You're numb now, but once the lidocaine wears off, you'll be a bit sore.
We should get the results in a few days.
Libenson
www.pajamadiaries.com
Are you really okay?
Yeah.
You sure? Let's try the Jewish litmus test.
Huh?
3/18 © 2010 Terri Libenson, Dist. By King Features Syndicate, Inc.
Hungry?
Starving.
You passed.

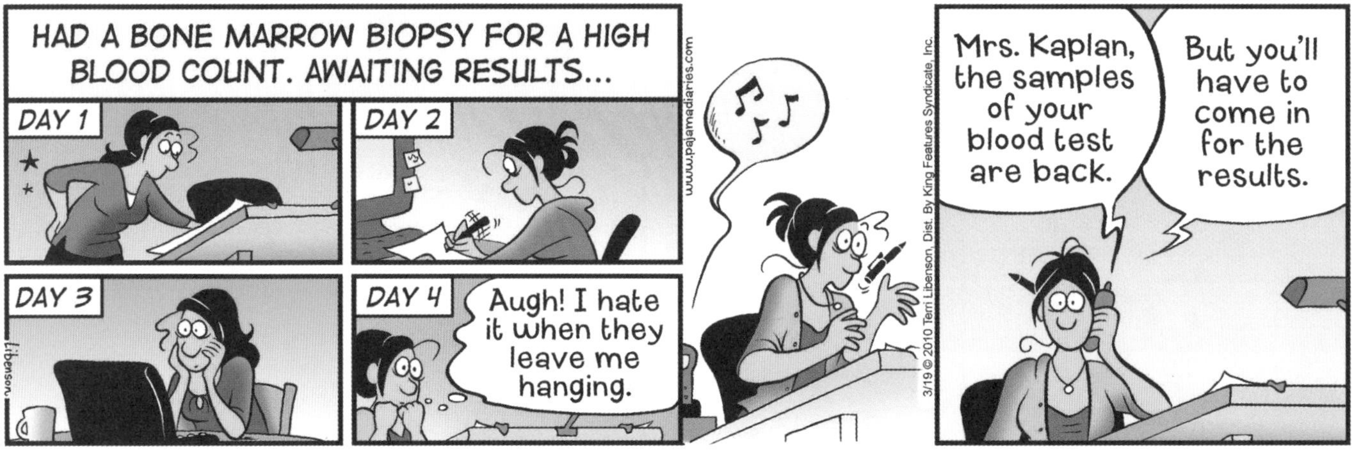
HAD A BONE MARROW BIOPSY FOR A HIGH BLOOD COUNT. AWAITING RESULTS...
DAY 1
DAY 2
DAY 3
DAY 4
Augh! I hate it when they leave me hanging.
Libenson
www.pajamadiaries.com
Mrs. Kaplan, the samples of your blood test are back.
But you'll have to come in for the results.
3/19 © 2010 Terri Libenson, Dist. By King Features Syndicate, Inc.

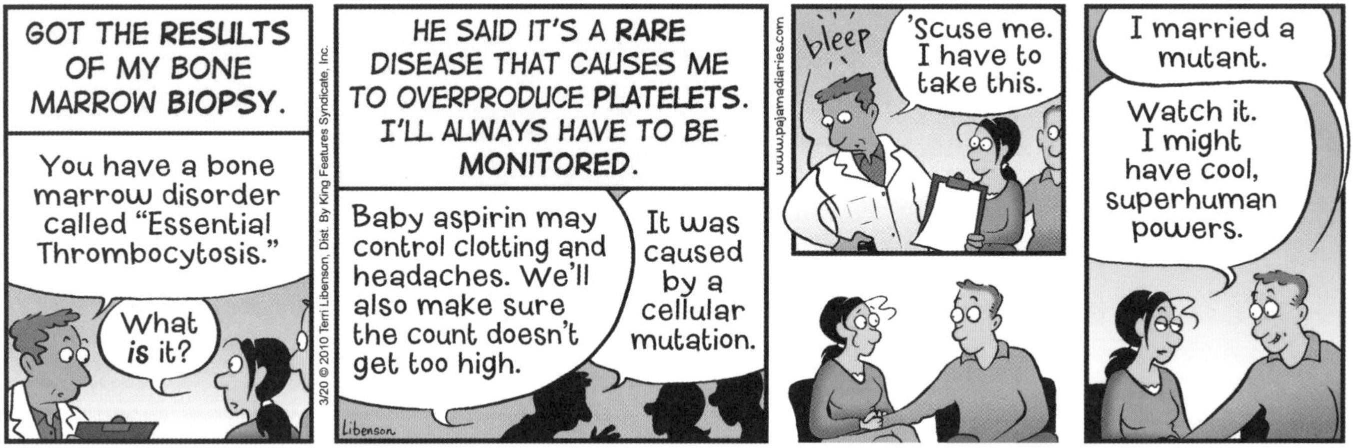
GOT THE RESULTS OF MY BONE MARROW BIOPSY.
You have a bone marrow disorder called "Essential Thrombocytosis."
What is it?
3/20 © 2010 Terri Libenson, Dist. By King Features Syndicate, Inc.
HE SAID IT'S A RARE DISEASE THAT CAUSES ME TO OVERPRODUCE PLATELETS. I'LL ALWAYS HAVE TO BE MONITORED.
Baby aspirin may control clotting and headaches. We'll also make sure the count doesn't get too high.
It was caused by a cellular mutation.
Libenson
www.pajamadiaries.com
bleep
'Scuse me. I have to take this.
I married a mutant.
Watch it. I might have cool, superhuman powers.

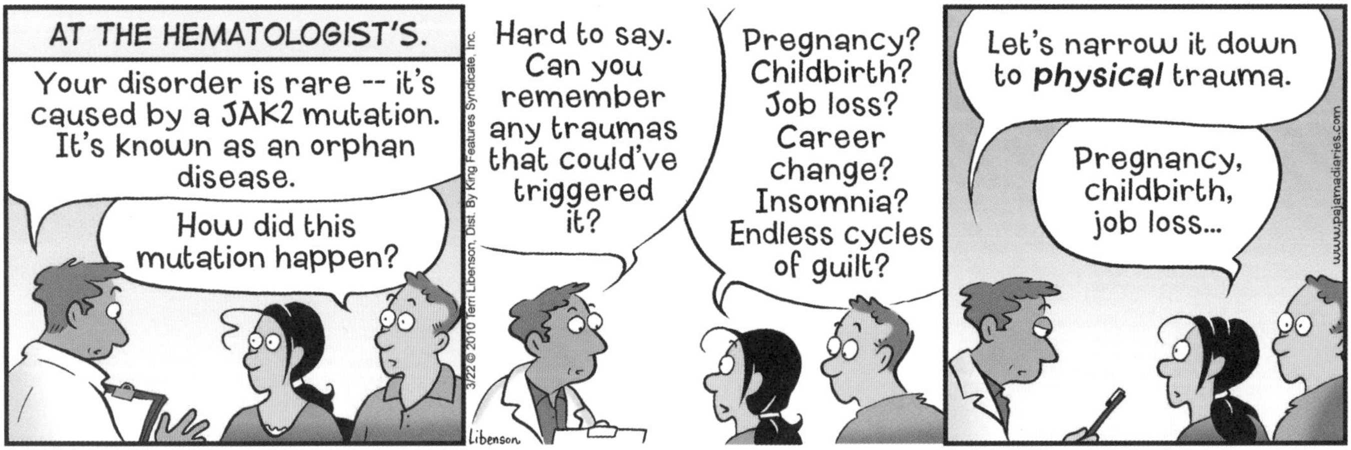
AT THE HEMATOLOGIST'S.
Your disorder is rare -- it's caused by a JAK2 mutation. It's known as an orphan disease.
How did this mutation happen?
3/22 © 2010 Terri Libenson, Dist. By King Features Syndicate, Inc.
Hard to say. Can you remember any traumas that could've triggered it?
Libenson
Pregnancy? Childbirth? Job loss? Career change? Insomnia? Endless cycles of guilt?
Let's narrow it down to physical trauma.
Pregnancy, childbirth, job loss...
www.pajamadiaries.com

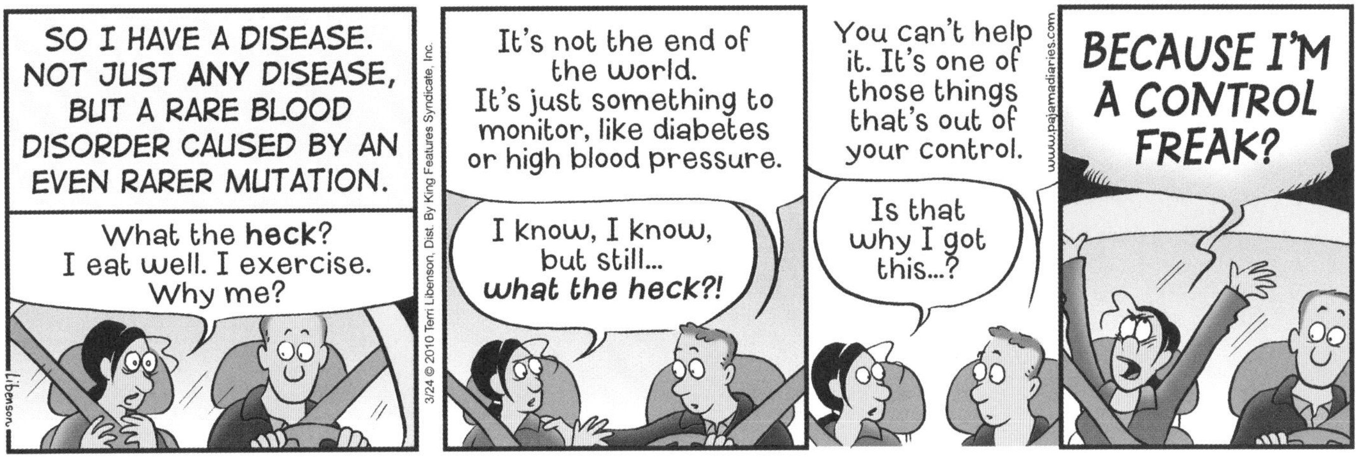
SO I HAVE A DISEASE. NOT JUST ANY DISEASE, BUT A RARE BLOOD DISORDER CAUSED BY AN EVEN RARER MUTATION.
What the **heck**? I eat well. I exercise. Why me?
Libenson
3/24 © 2010 Terri Libenson, Dist. By King Features Syndicate, Inc.
It's not the end of the world. It's just something to monitor, like diabetes or high blood pressure.
I know, I know, but still... ***what the heck?!***
You can't help it. It's one of those things that's out of your control.
Is that why I got this...?
www.pajamadiaries.com
BECAUSE I'M A CONTROL FREAK?

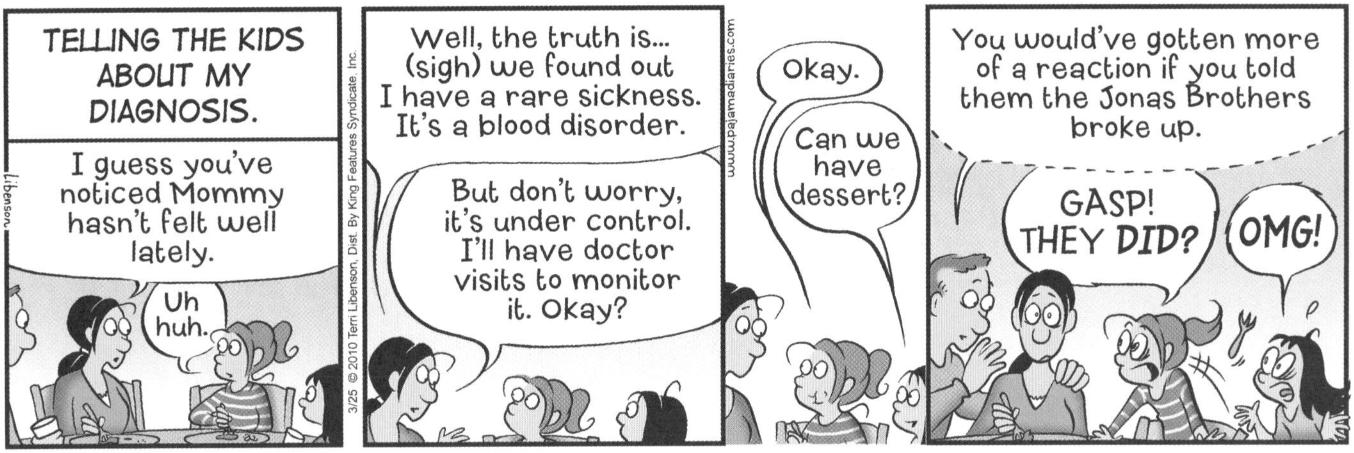
TELLING THE KIDS ABOUT MY DIAGNOSIS.
I guess you've noticed Mommy hasn't felt well lately.
Uh huh.
Libenson
3/25 © 2010 Terri Libenson, Dist. By King Features Syndicate, Inc.
Well, the truth is... (sigh) we found out I have a rare sickness. It's a blood disorder.
But don't worry, it's under control. I'll have doctor visits to monitor it. Okay?
www.pajamadiaries.com
Okay.
Can we have dessert?
You would've gotten more of a reaction if you told them the Jonas Brothers broke up.
GASP! THEY **DID?**
OMG!

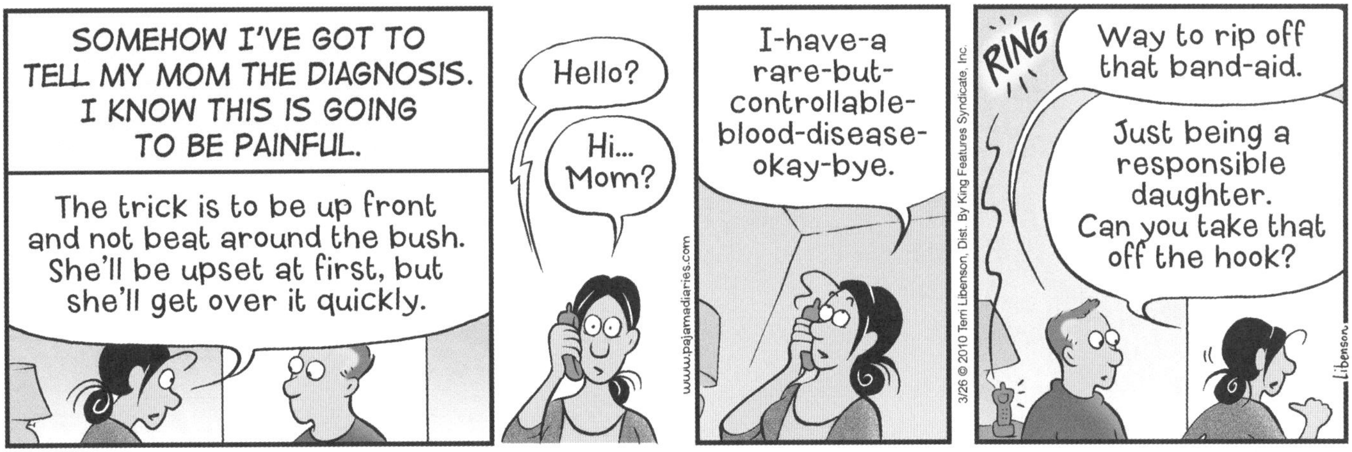
SOMEHOW I'VE GOT TO TELL MY MOM THE DIAGNOSIS. I KNOW THIS IS GOING TO BE PAINFUL.
The trick is to be up front and not beat around the bush. She'll be upset at first, but she'll get over it quickly.
Hello?
Hi... Mom?
www.pajamadiaries.com
I-have-a rare-but-controllable-blood-disease-okay-bye.
3/26 © 2010 Terri Libenson, Dist. By King Features Syndicate, Inc.
RING
Way to rip off that band-aid.
Just being a responsible daughter. Can you take that off the hook?
Libenson

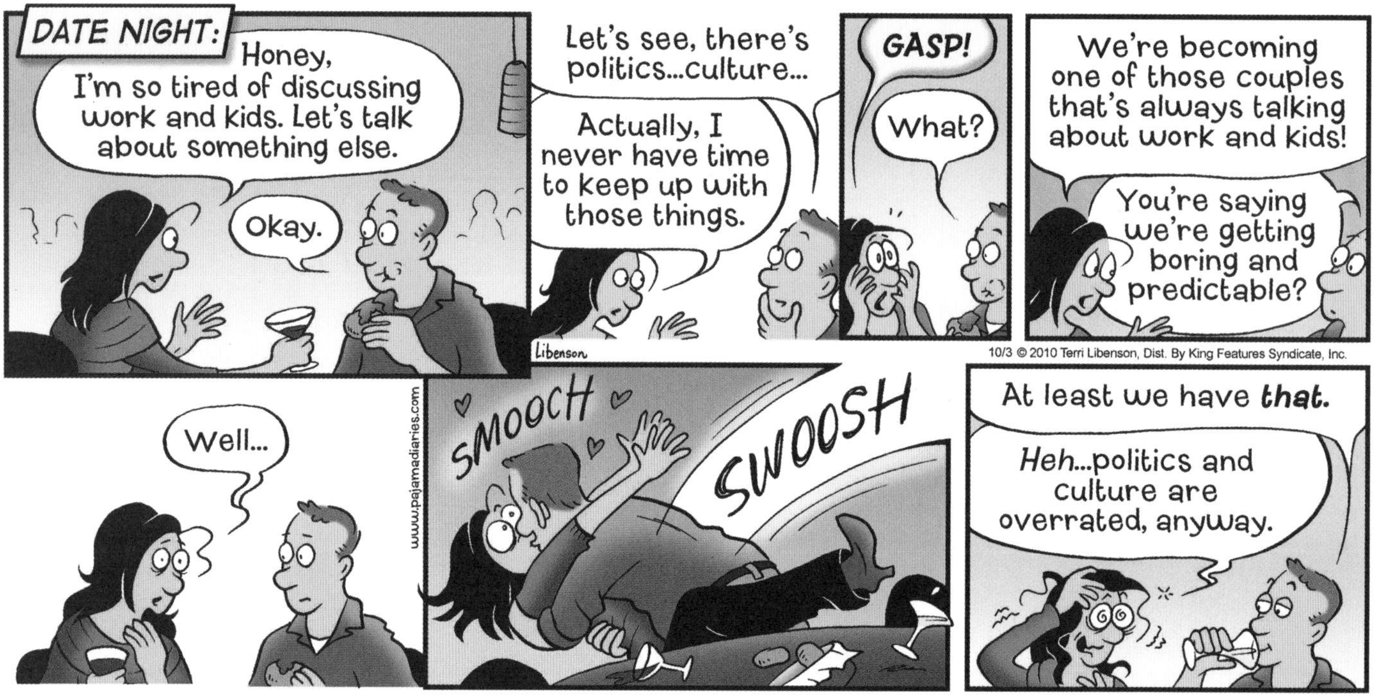
DATE NIGHT:
Honey, I'm so tired of discussing work and kids. Let's talk about something else.
Okay.
Let's see, there's politics...culture...
Actually, I never have time to keep up with those things.
GASP!
What?
We're becoming one of those couples that's always talking about work and kids!
You're saying we're getting boring and predictable?
Libenson
10/3 © 2010 Terri Libenson, Dist. By King Features Syndicate, Inc.
Well...
www.pajamadiaries.com
SMOOCH
SWOOSH
At least we have *that.*
Heh...politics and culture are overrated, anyway.

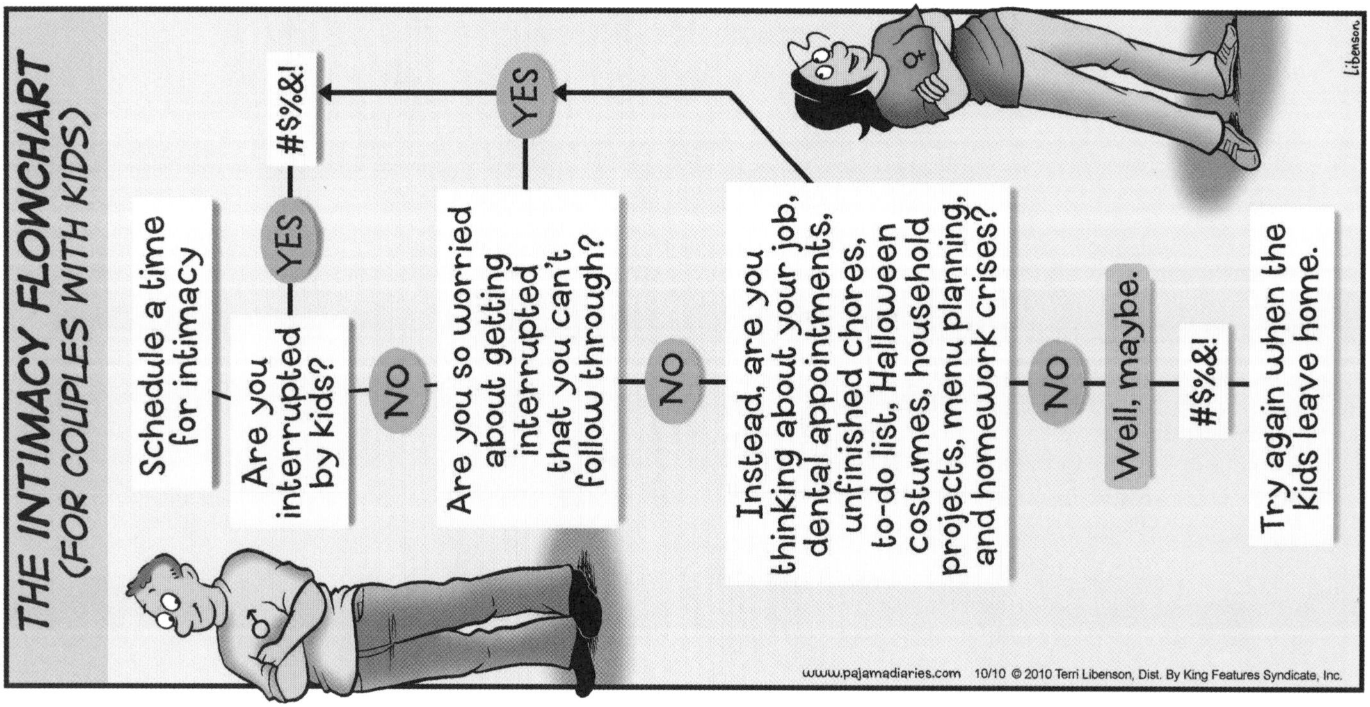
THE INTIMACY FLOWCHART
(FOR COUPLES WITH KIDS)
Schedule a time for intimacy
Are you interrupted by kids?
YES
#$%&!
NO
Are you so worried about getting interrupted that you can't follow through?
YES
NO
Instead, are you thinking about your job, dental appointments, unfinished chores, to-do list, Halloween costumes, household projects, menu planning, and homework crises?
NO
Well, maybe.
#$%&!
Try again when the kids leave home.
Libenson
www.pajamadiaries.com 10/10 © 2010 Terri Libenson, Dist. By King Features Syndicate, Inc.

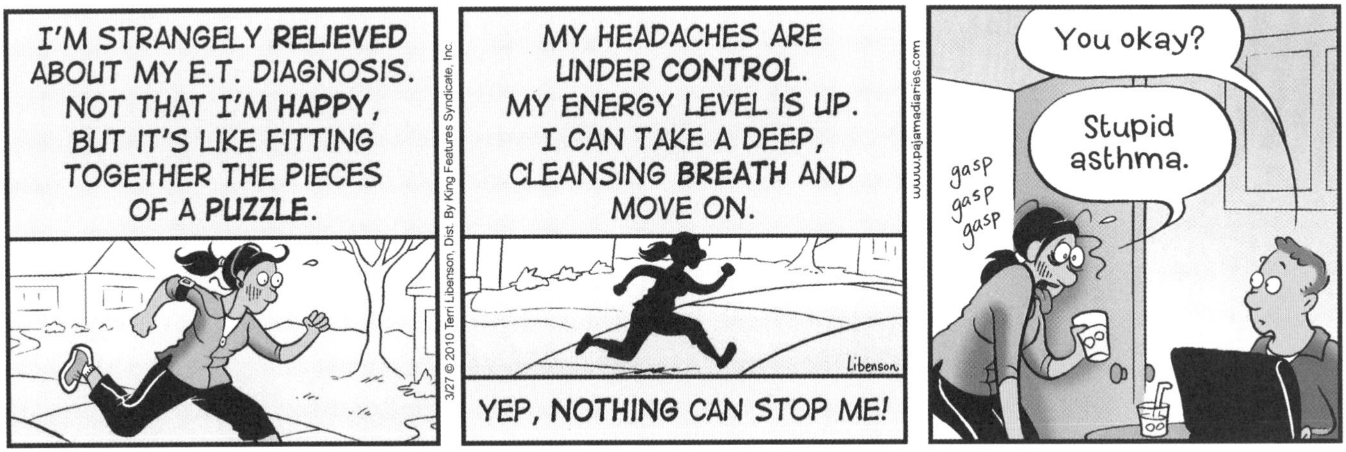
I'M STRANGELY RELIEVED ABOUT MY E.T. DIAGNOSIS. NOT THAT I'M HAPPY, BUT IT'S LIKE FITTING TOGETHER THE PIECES OF A PUZZLE.
MY HEADACHES ARE UNDER CONTROL. MY ENERGY LEVEL IS UP. I CAN TAKE A DEEP, CLEANSING BREATH AND MOVE ON.
YEP, NOTHING CAN STOP ME!
gasp gasp gasp
You okay?
Stupid asthma.
3/27 © 2010 Terri Libenson, Dist. By King Features Syndicate, Inc.
www.pajamadiaries.com
Libenson

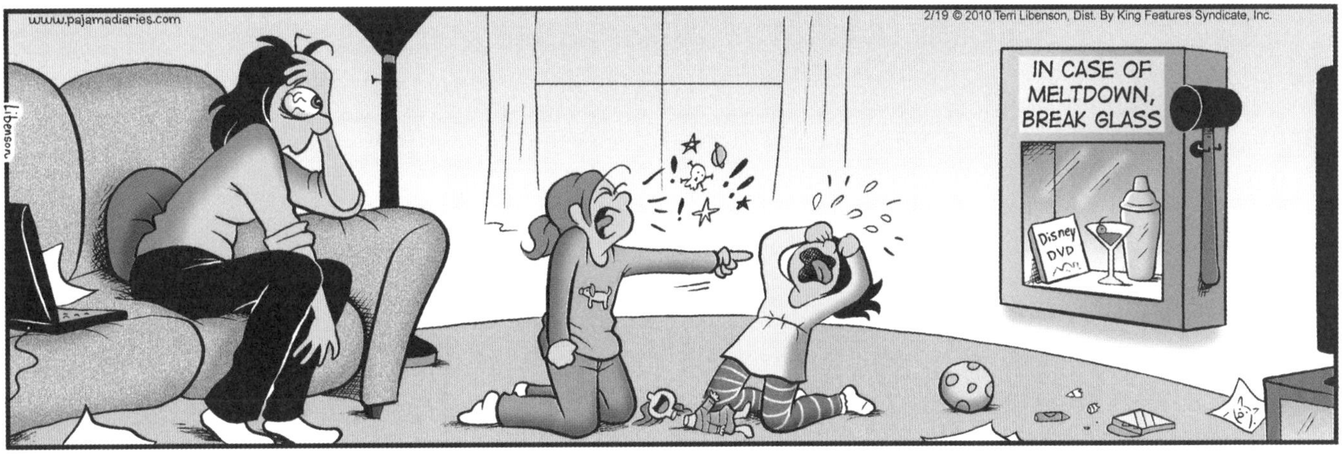
www.pajamadiaries.com
2/19 © 2010 Terri Libenson, Dist. By King Features Syndicate, Inc.
IN CASE OF MELTDOWN, BREAK GLASS
Disney DVD
Libenson

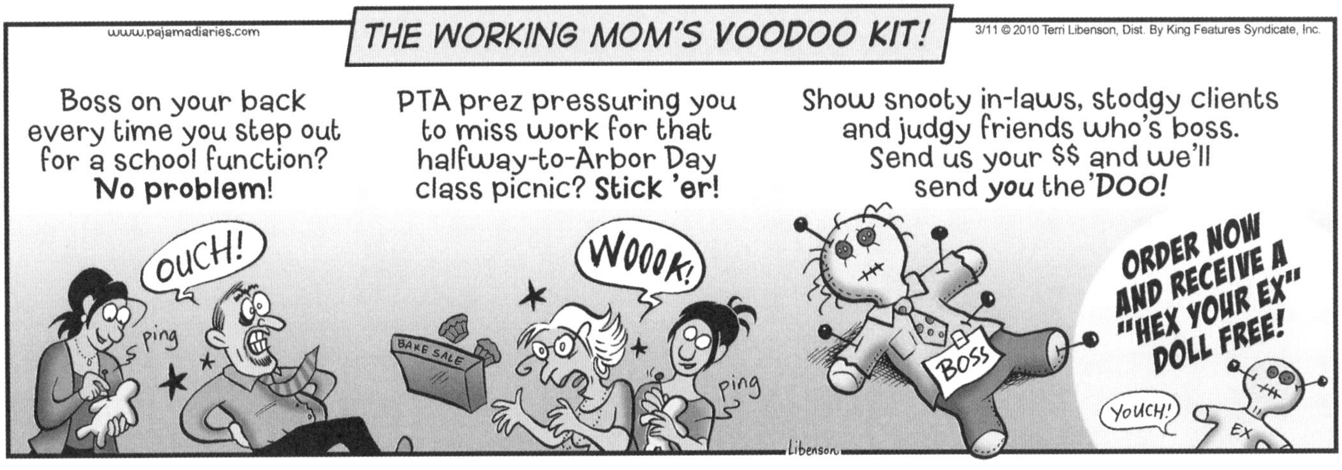
THE WORKING MOM'S VOODOO KIT!
www.pajamadiaries.com
3/11 © 2010 Terri Libenson, Dist. By King Features Syndicate, Inc.
Boss on your back every time you step out for a school function? No problem!
PTA prez pressuring you to miss work for that halfway-to-Arbor Day class picnic? Stick 'er!
Show snooty in-laws, stodgy clients and judgy friends who's boss. Send us your $$ and we'll send you the 'DOO!
OUCH!
ping
WOOOK!
BAKE SALE
ping
BOSS
ORDER NOW AND RECEIVE A "HEX YOUR EX" DOLL FREE!
YOUCH!
EX
Libenson

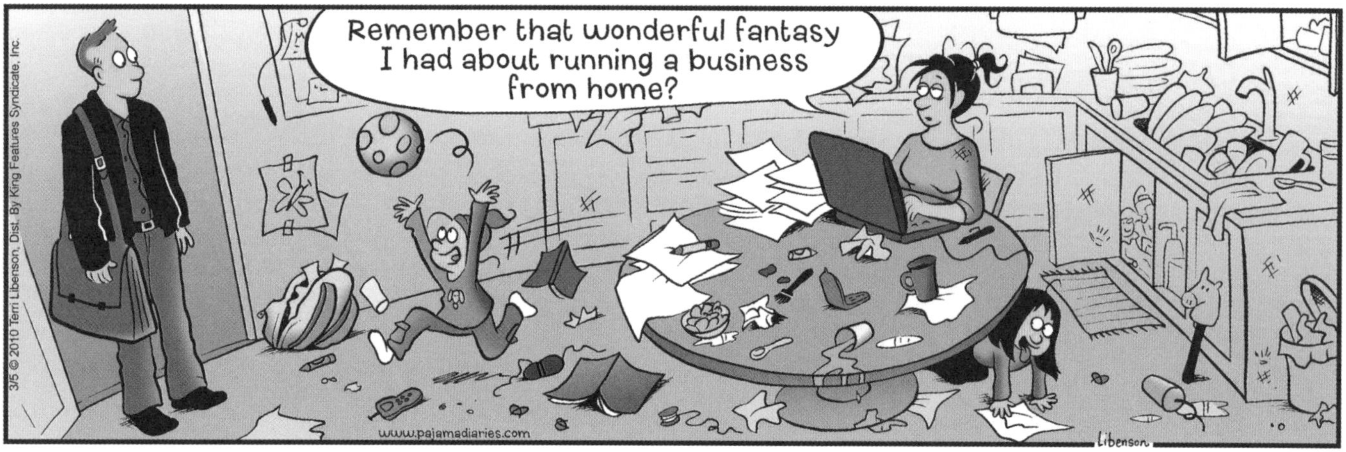
Remember that wonderful fantasy I had about running a business from home?
3/5 © 2010 Terri Libenson, Dist. By King Features Syndicate, Inc.
www.pajamadiaries.com
Libenson

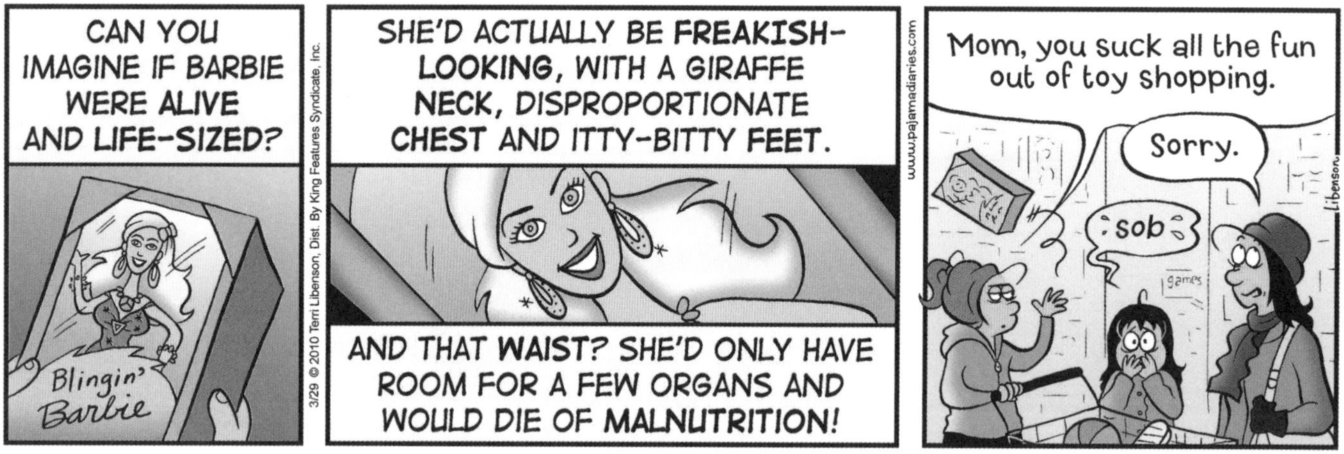
CAN YOU IMAGINE IF BARBIE WERE ALIVE AND LIFE-SIZED?
Blingin' Barbie
3/29 © 2010 Terri Libenson, Dist. By King Features Syndicate, Inc.
SHE'D ACTUALLY BE FREAKISH-LOOKING, WITH A GIRAFFE NECK, DISPROPORTIONATE CHEST AND ITTY-BITTY FEET.
AND THAT WAIST? SHE'D ONLY HAVE ROOM FOR A FEW ORGANS AND WOULD DIE OF MALNUTRITION!
www.pajamadiaries.com
Mom, you suck all the fun out of toy shopping.
Sorry.
sob
games
Libenson

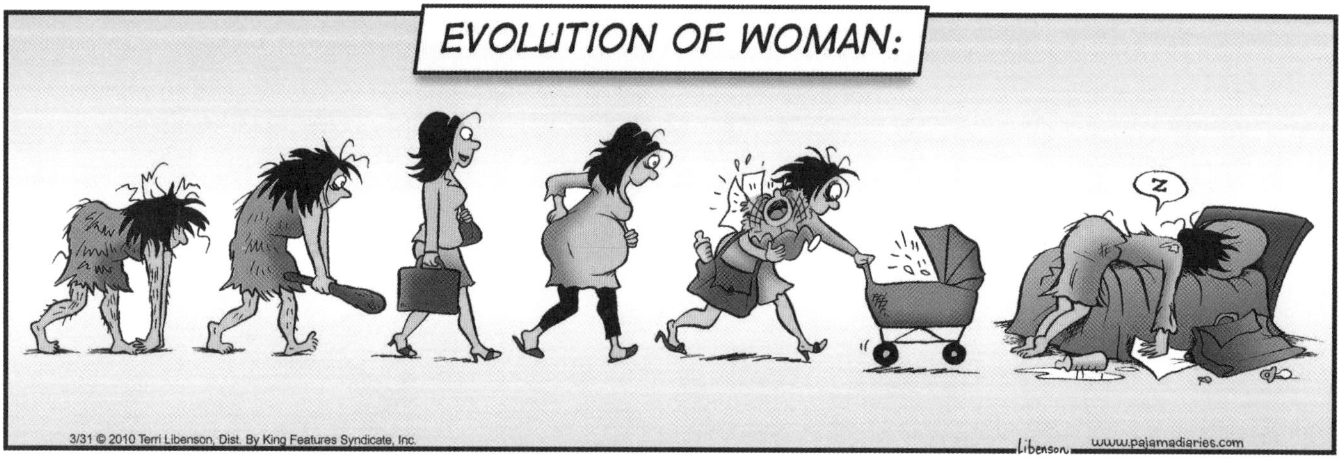
EVOLUTION OF WOMAN:
z
3/31 © 2010 Terri Libenson, Dist. By King Features Syndicate, Inc.
Libenson
www.pajamadiaries.com

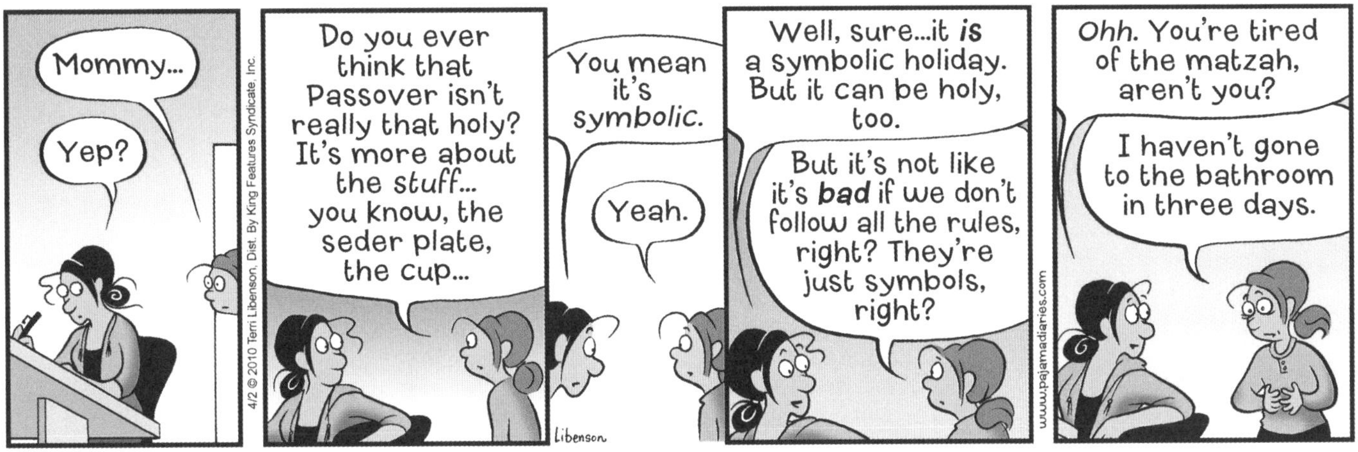
Mommy...
Yep?
4/2 © 2010 Terri Libenson, Dist. By King Features Syndicate, Inc.
Do you ever think that Passover isn't really that holy? It's more about the *stuff*... you know, the seder plate, the cup...
You mean it's *symbolic*.
Yeah.
Libenson
Well, sure...it ***is*** a symbolic holiday. But it can be holy, too.
But it's not like it's ***bad*** if we don't follow all the rules, right? They're just symbols, right?
www.pajamadiaries.com
Ohh. You're tired of the matzah, aren't you?
I haven't gone to the bathroom in three days.

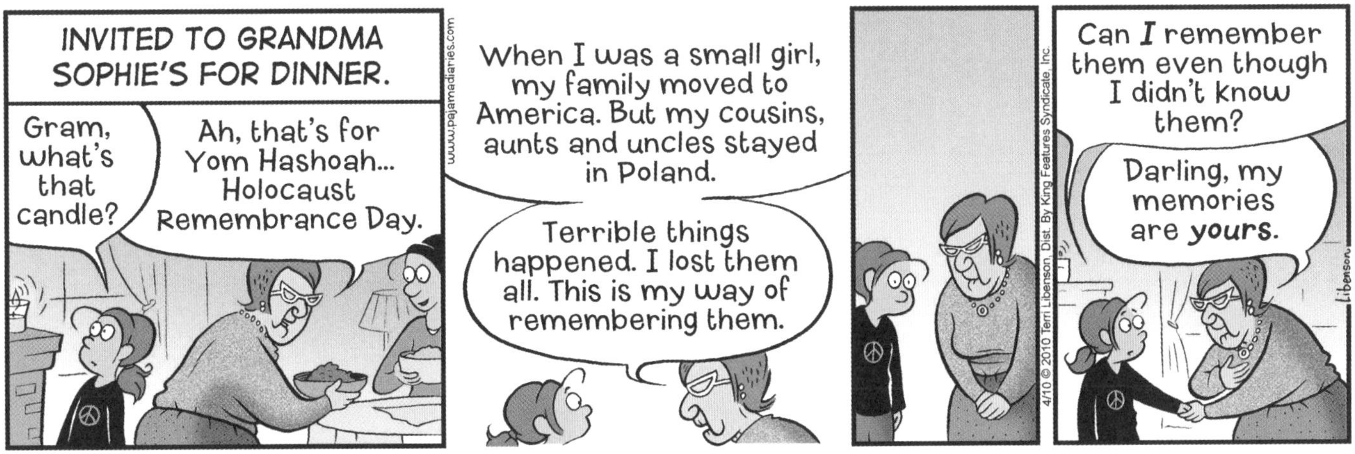
INVITED TO GRANDMA SOPHIE'S FOR DINNER.
Gram, what's that candle?
Ah, that's for Yom Hashoah... Holocaust Remembrance Day.
www.pajamadiaries.com
When I was a small girl, my family moved to America. But my cousins, aunts and uncles stayed in Poland.
Terrible things happened. I lost them all. This is my way of remembering them.
4/10 © 2010 Terri Libenson, Dist. By King Features Syndicate, Inc.
Can ***I*** remember them even though I didn't know them?
Darling, my memories are ***yours***.
Libenson

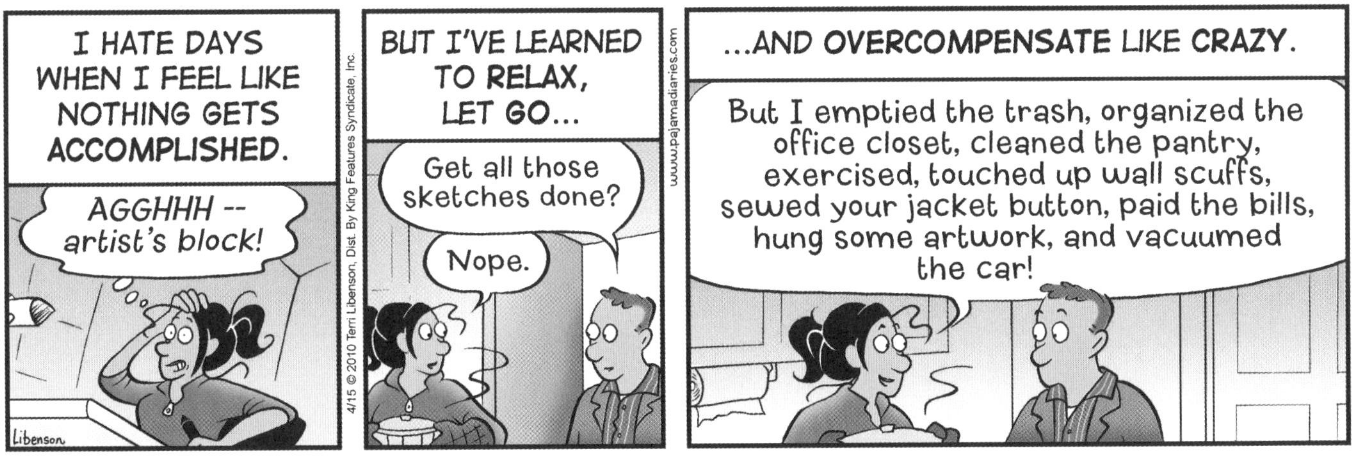
I HATE DAYS WHEN I FEEL LIKE NOTHING GETS **ACCOMPLISHED**.
AGGHHH -- artist's block!
Libenson
4/15 © 2010 Terri Libenson, Dist. By King Features Syndicate, Inc.
BUT I'VE LEARNED TO **RELAX**, LET GO...
Get all those sketches done?
Nope.
www.pajamadiaries.com
...AND **OVERCOMPENSATE** LIKE **CRAZY**.
But I emptied the trash, organized the office closet, cleaned the pantry, exercised, touched up wall scuffs, sewed your jacket button, paid the bills, hung some artwork, and vacuumed the car!

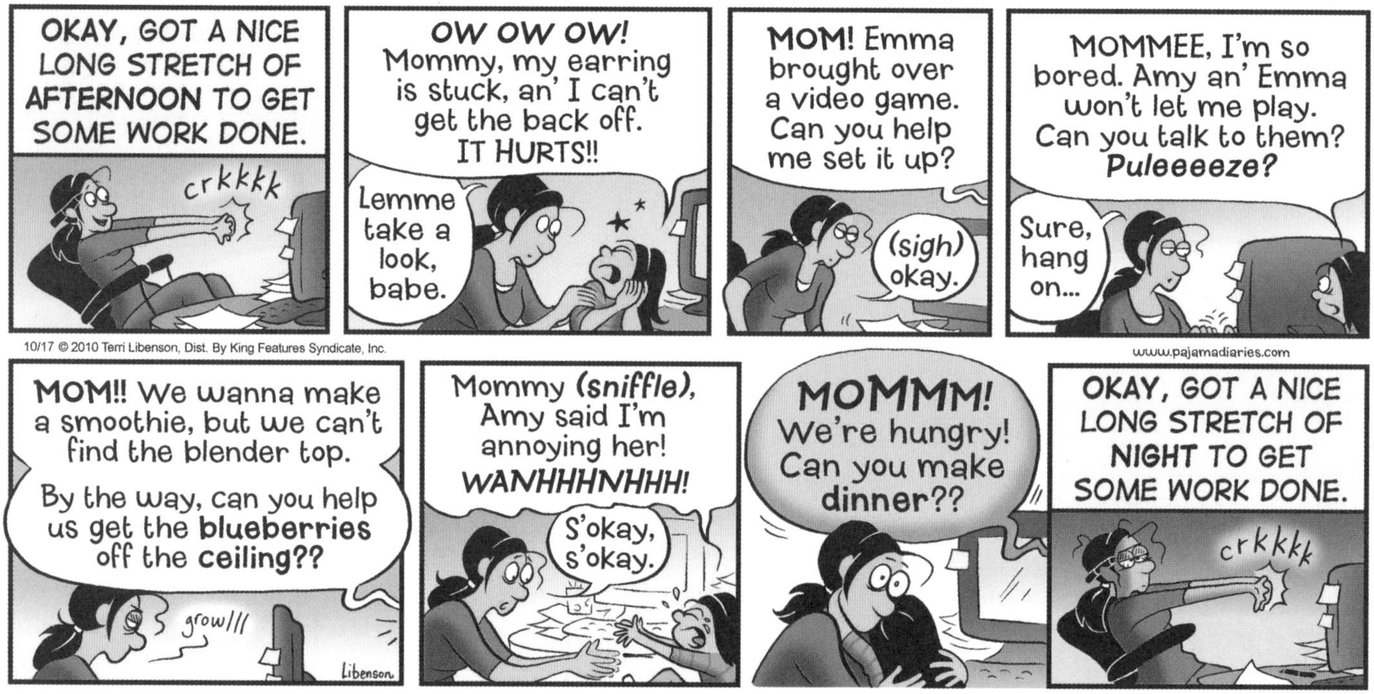
OKAY, GOT A NICE LONG STRETCH OF AFTERNOON TO GET SOME WORK DONE.
crkkkk
OW OW OW! Mommy, my earring is stuck, an' I can't get the back off. IT HURTS!!
Lemme take a look, babe.
MOM! Emma brought over a video game. Can you help me set it up?
(sigh) okay.
MOMMEE, I'm so bored. Amy an' Emma won't let me play. Can you talk to them? Puleeeeze?
Sure, hang on...
10/17 © 2010 Terri Libenson, Dist. By King Features Syndicate, Inc.
www.pajamadiaries.com
MOM!! We wanna make a smoothie, but we can't find the blender top.
By the way, can you help us get the blueberries off the ceiling??
growl//
Mommy (sniffle), Amy said I'm annoying her! WANHHHNHHH!
S'okay, s'okay.
MOMMM! We're hungry! Can you make dinner??
OKAY, GOT A NICE LONG STRETCH OF NIGHT TO GET SOME WORK DONE.
crkkkk
Libenson

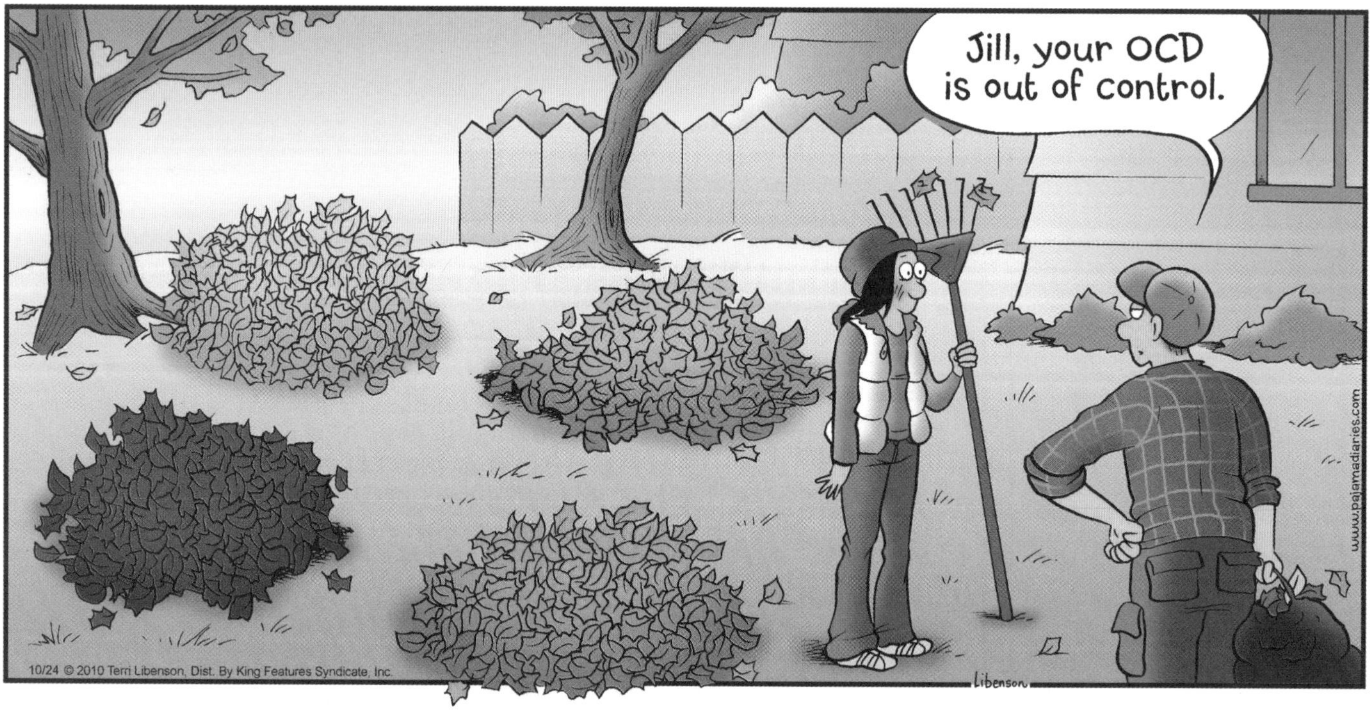
Jill, your OCD is out of control.
www.pajamadiaries.com
10/24 © 2010 Terri Libenson, Dist. By King Features Syndicate, Inc.
Libenson

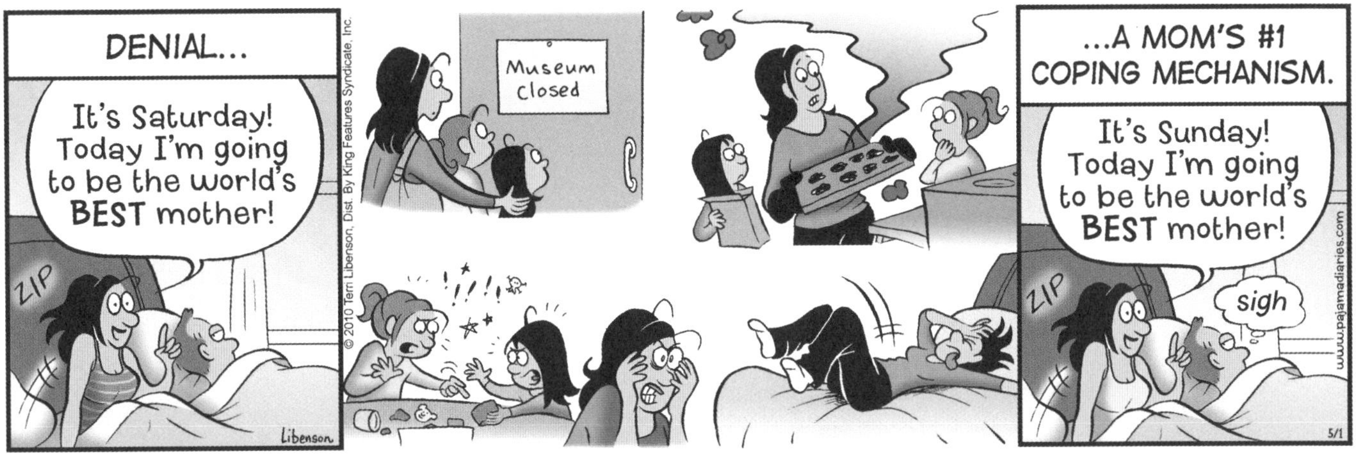
DENIAL...
It's Saturday! Today I'm going to be the world's BEST mother!
ZIP
Libenson
© 2010 Terri Libenson, Dist. By King Features Syndicate, Inc.
Museum Closed
...A MOM'S #1 COPING MECHANISM.
It's Sunday! Today I'm going to be the world's BEST mother!
ZIP
sigh
www.pajamadiaries.com
5/1

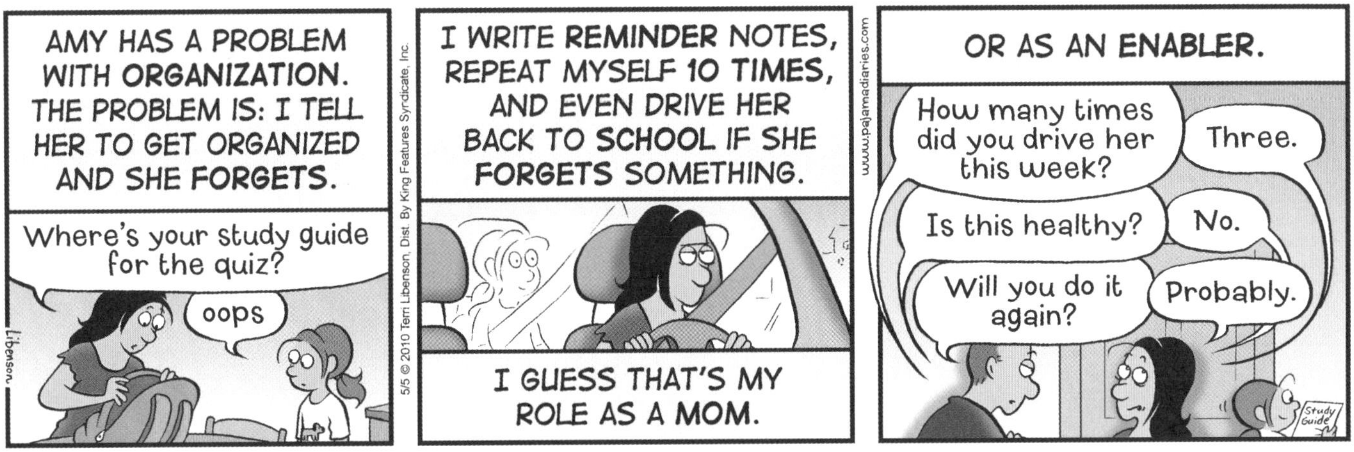
AMY HAS A PROBLEM WITH ORGANIZATION. THE PROBLEM IS: I TELL HER TO GET ORGANIZED AND SHE FORGETS.
Where's your study guide for the quiz?
oops
Libenson
5/5 © 2010 Terri Libenson, Dist. By King Features Syndicate, Inc.
I WRITE REMINDER NOTES, REPEAT MYSELF 10 TIMES, AND EVEN DRIVE HER BACK TO SCHOOL IF SHE FORGETS SOMETHING.
I GUESS THAT'S MY ROLE AS A MOM.
www.pajamadiaries.com
OR AS AN ENABLER.
How many times did you drive her this week?
Three.
Is this healthy?
No.
Will you do it again?
Probably.
Study Guide

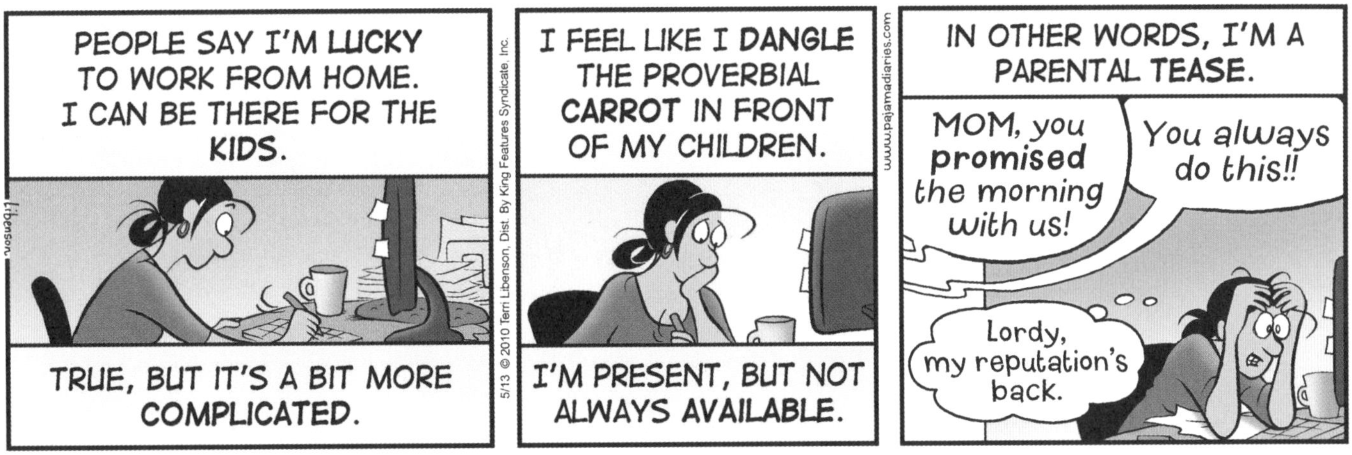
PEOPLE SAY I'M LUCKY TO WORK FROM HOME. I CAN BE THERE FOR THE KIDS.
TRUE, BUT IT'S A BIT MORE COMPLICATED.
Libenson
5/13 © 2010 Terri Libenson, Dist. By King Features Syndicate, Inc.
I FEEL LIKE I DANGLE THE PROVERBIAL CARROT IN FRONT OF MY CHILDREN.
I'M PRESENT, BUT NOT ALWAYS AVAILABLE.
www.pajamadiaries.com
IN OTHER WORDS, I'M A PARENTAL TEASE.
MOM, you promised the morning with us!
You always do this!!
Lordy, my reputation's back.

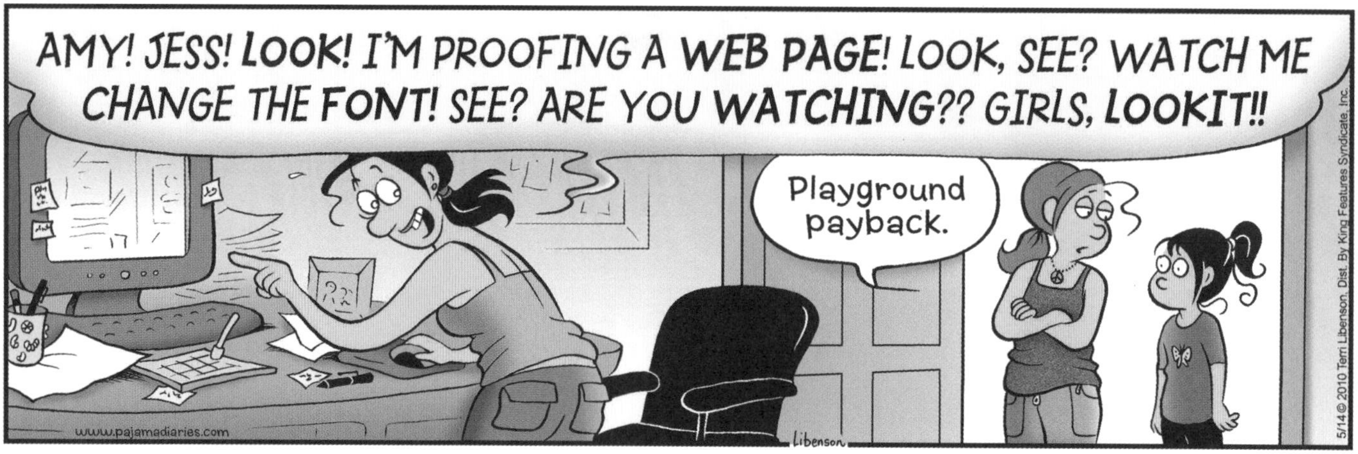
AMY! JESS! LOOK! I'M PROOFING A WEB PAGE! LOOK, SEE? WATCH ME CHANGE THE FONT! SEE? ARE YOU WATCHING?? GIRLS, LOOKIT!!
Playground payback.
www.pajamadiaries.com
Libenson
5/14 © 2010 Terri Libenson. Dist. By King Features Syndicate, Inc.

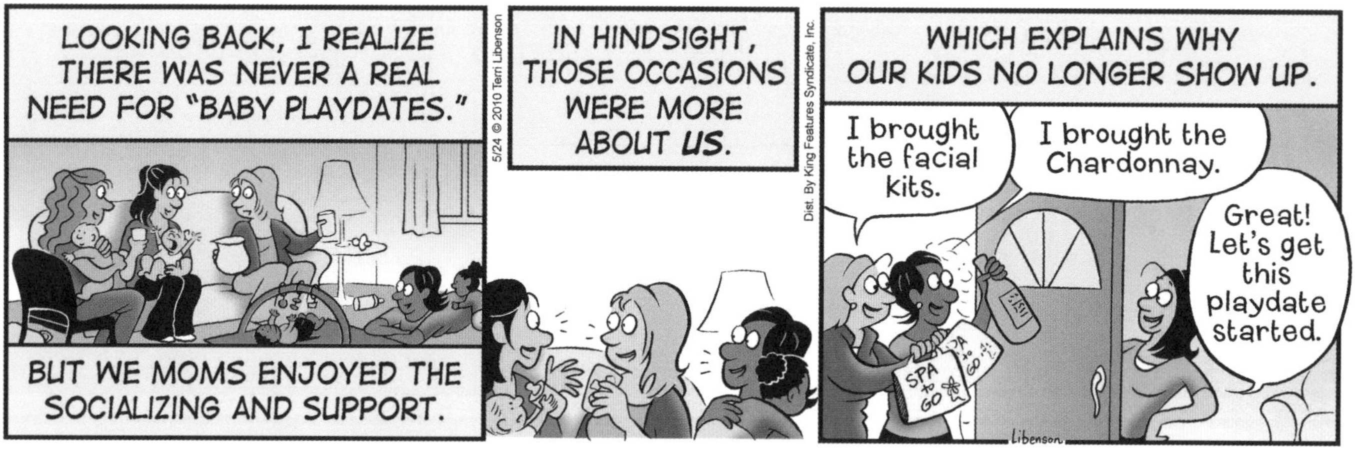
LOOKING BACK, I REALIZE THERE WAS NEVER A REAL NEED FOR "BABY PLAYDATES."
BUT WE MOMS ENJOYED THE SOCIALIZING AND SUPPORT.
5/24 © 2010 Terri Libenson
IN HINDSIGHT, THOSE OCCASIONS WERE MORE ABOUT US.
Dist. By King Features Syndicate, Inc.
WHICH EXPLAINS WHY OUR KIDS NO LONGER SHOW UP.
I brought the facial kits.
I brought the Chardonnay.
Great! Let's get this playdate started.
SPA to GO
Libenson

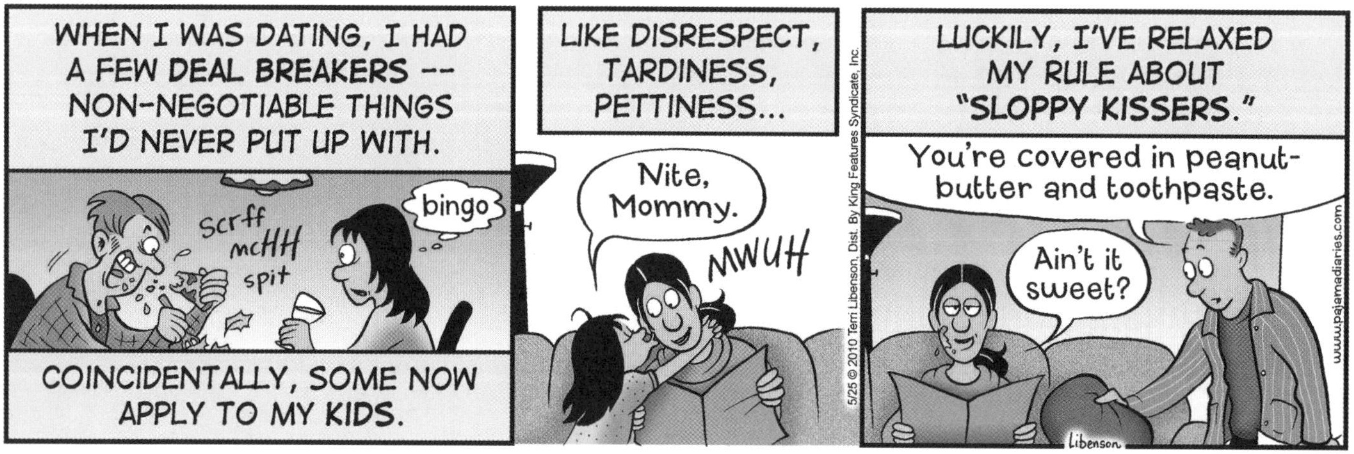
WHEN I WAS DATING, I HAD A FEW DEAL BREAKERS -- NON-NEGOTIABLE THINGS I'D NEVER PUT UP WITH.
bingo
scrff
mcHH
spit
COINCIDENTALLY, SOME NOW APPLY TO MY KIDS.
LIKE DISRESPECT, TARDINESS, PETTINESS...
Nite, Mommy.
MWUH
5/25 © 2010 Terri Libenson, Dist. By King Features Syndicate, Inc.
LUCKILY, I'VE RELAXED MY RULE ABOUT "SLOPPY KISSERS."
You're covered in peanut-butter and toothpaste.
Ain't it sweet?
www.pajamadiaries.com
Libenson

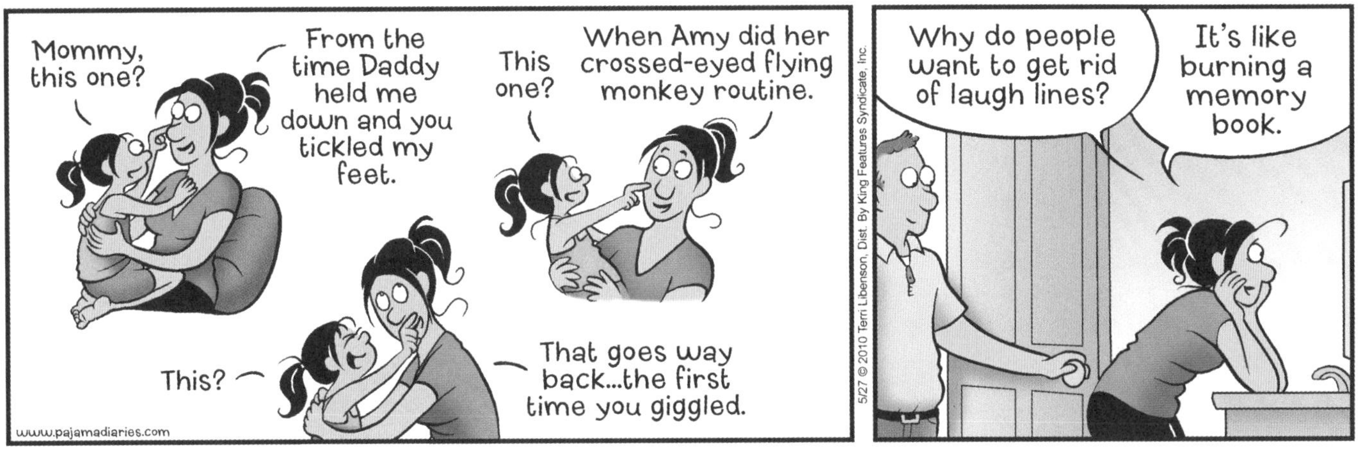
Mommy, this one?
From the time Daddy held me down and you tickled my feet.
This?
That goes way back...the first time you giggled.
This one?
When Amy did her crossed-eyed flying monkey routine.
www.pajamadiaries.com
5/27 © 2010 Terri Libenson, Dist. By King Features Syndicate, Inc.
Why do people want to get rid of laugh lines?
It's like burning a memory book.

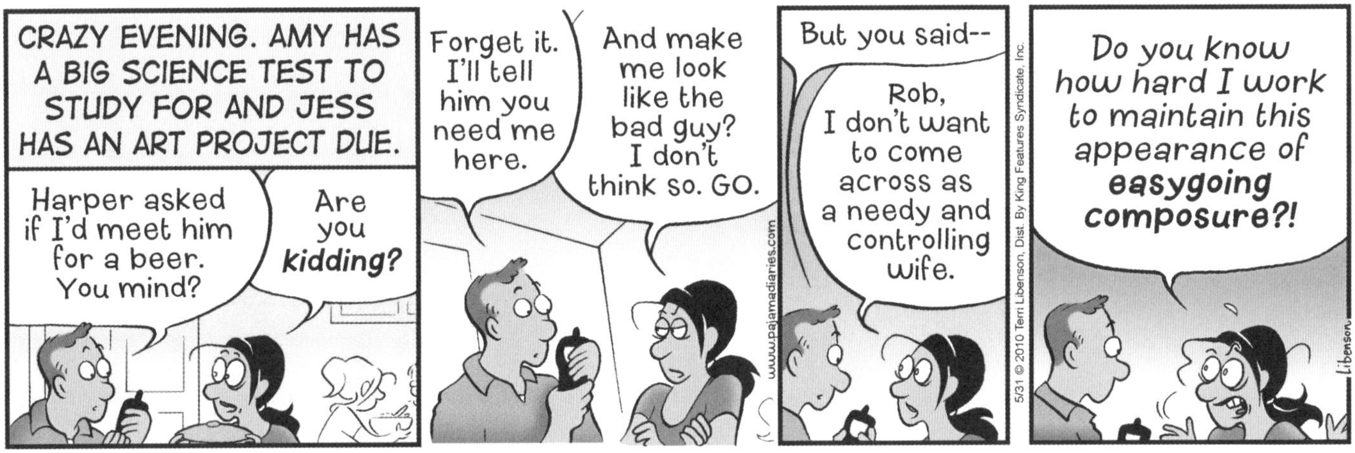
CRAZY EVENING. AMY HAS A BIG SCIENCE TEST TO STUDY FOR AND JESS HAS AN ART PROJECT DUE.
Harper asked if I'd meet him for a beer. You mind?
Are you kidding?
Forget it. I'll tell him you need me here.
And make me look like the bad guy? I don't think so. GO.
www.pajamadiaries.com
But you said--
Rob, I don't want to come across as a needy and controlling wife.
5/31 © 2010 Terri Libenson, Dist. By King Features Syndicate, Inc.
Do you know how hard I work to maintain this appearance of easygoing composure?!
Libenson

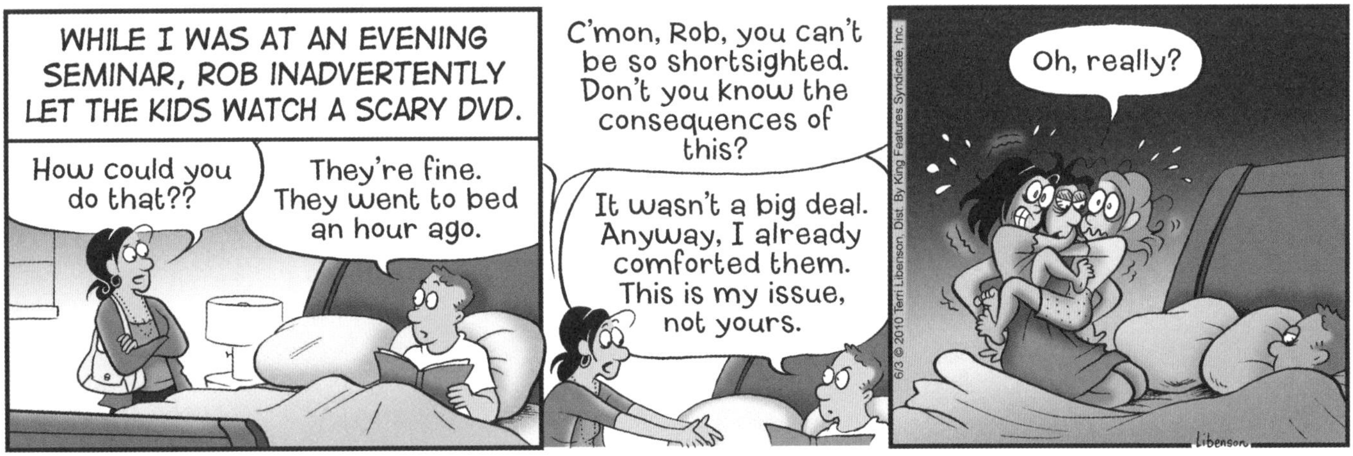
WHILE I WAS AT AN EVENING SEMINAR, ROB INADVERTENTLY LET THE KIDS WATCH A SCARY DVD.
How could you do that??
They're fine. They went to bed an hour ago.
C'mon, Rob, you can't be so shortsighted. Don't you know the consequences of this?
It wasn't a big deal. Anyway, I already comforted them. This is my issue, not yours.
6/3 © 2010 Terri Libenson, Dist. By King Features Syndicate, Inc.
Oh, really?
Libenson

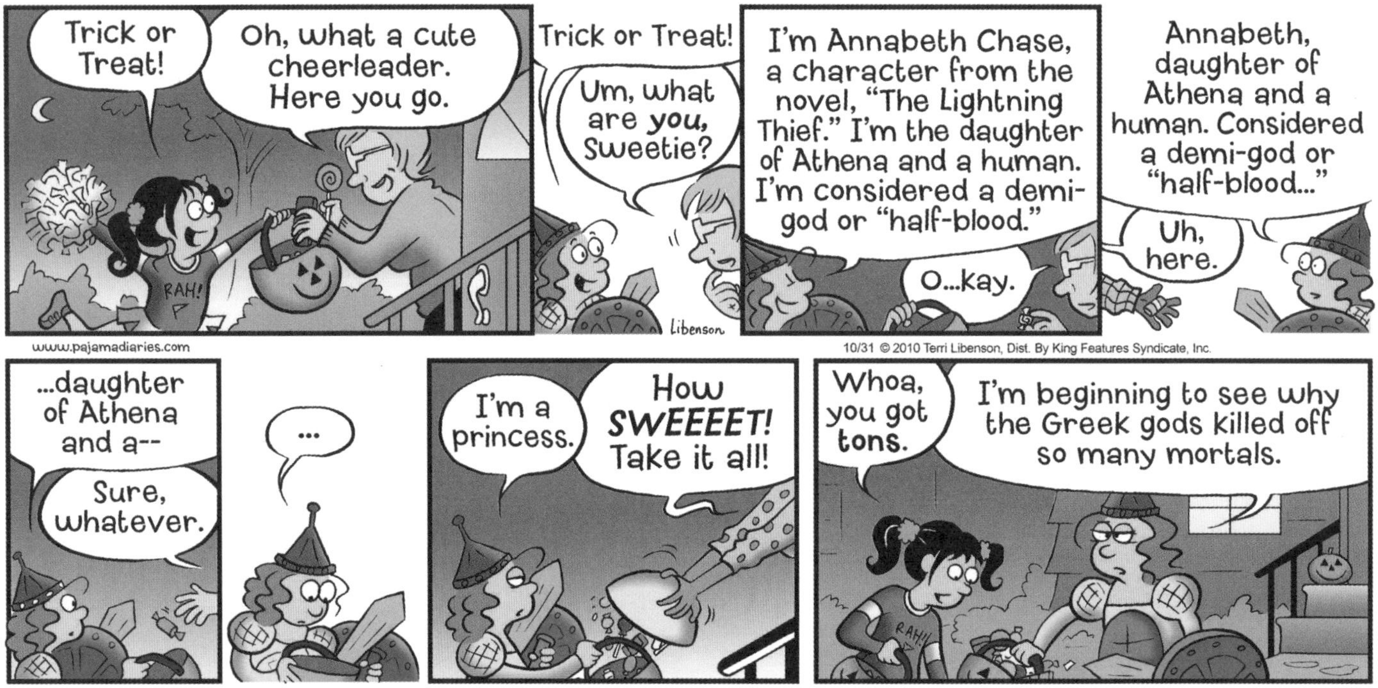
Trick or Treat!
Oh, what a cute cheerleader. Here you go.
RAH!
Trick or Treat!
Um, what are **you,** Sweetie?
Libenson
I'm Annabeth Chase, a character from the novel, "The Lightning Thief." I'm the daughter of Athena and a human. I'm considered a demi-god or "half-blood."
O...kay.
Annabeth, daughter of Athena and a human. Considered a demi-god or "half-blood..."
Uh, here.
www.pajamadiaries.com
10/31 © 2010 Terri Libenson, Dist. By King Features Syndicate, Inc.
...daughter of Athena and a--
Sure, whatever.
...
I'm a princess.
How **SWEEEET!** Take it all!
Whoa, you got **tons.**
I'm beginning to see why the Greek gods killed off so many mortals.
RAH!

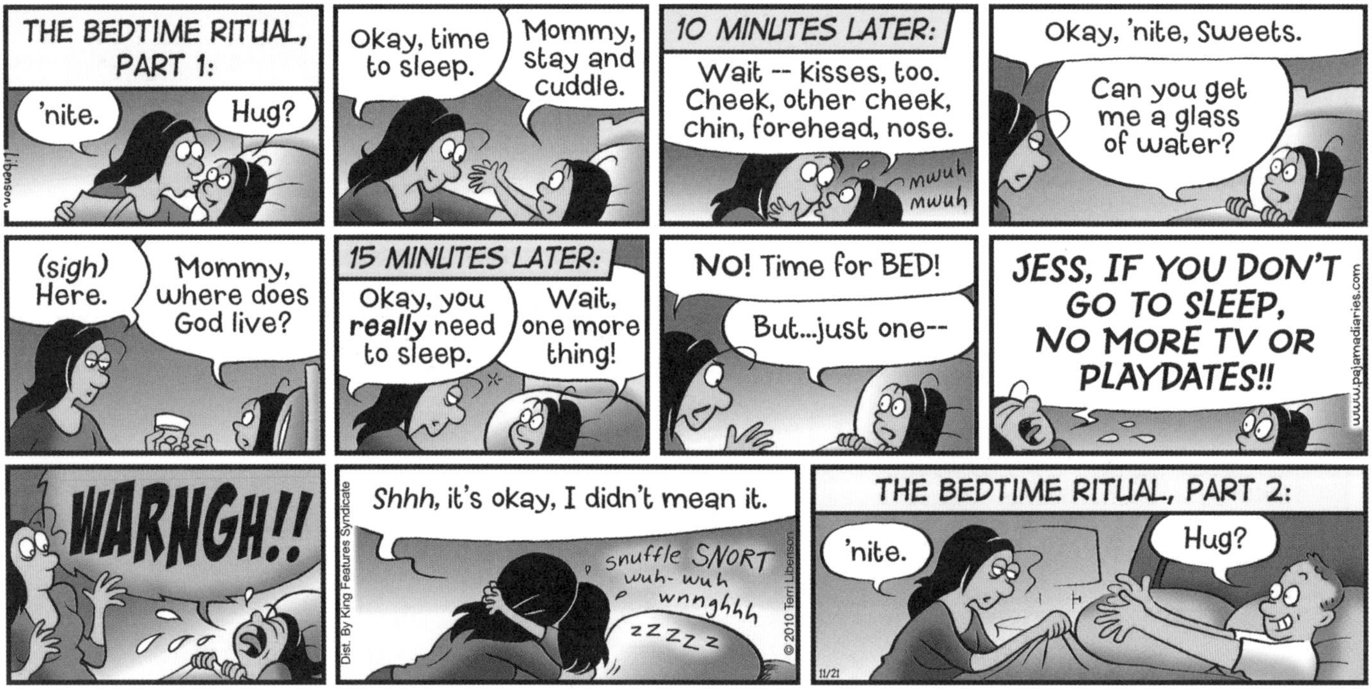
THE BEDTIME RITUAL, PART 1:
'nite.
Hug?
Libenson
Okay, time to sleep.
Mommy, stay and cuddle.
10 MINUTES LATER:
Wait -- kisses, too. Cheek, other cheek, chin, forehead, nose.
mwuh mwuh
Okay, 'nite, Sweets.
Can you get me a glass of water?
(sigh) Here.
Mommy, where does God live?
15 MINUTES LATER:
Okay, you **really** need to sleep.
Wait, one more thing!
NO! Time for BED!
But...just one--
JESS, IF YOU DON'T GO TO SLEEP, NO MORE TV OR PLAYDATES!!
www.pajamadiaries.com
WARNGH!!
Dist. By King Features Syndicate
Shhh, it's okay, I didn't mean it.
snuffle SNORT
wuh-wuh
wnnghhh
zzzzz
© 2010 Terri Libenson
THE BEDTIME RITUAL, PART 2:
'nite.
Hug?
11/21

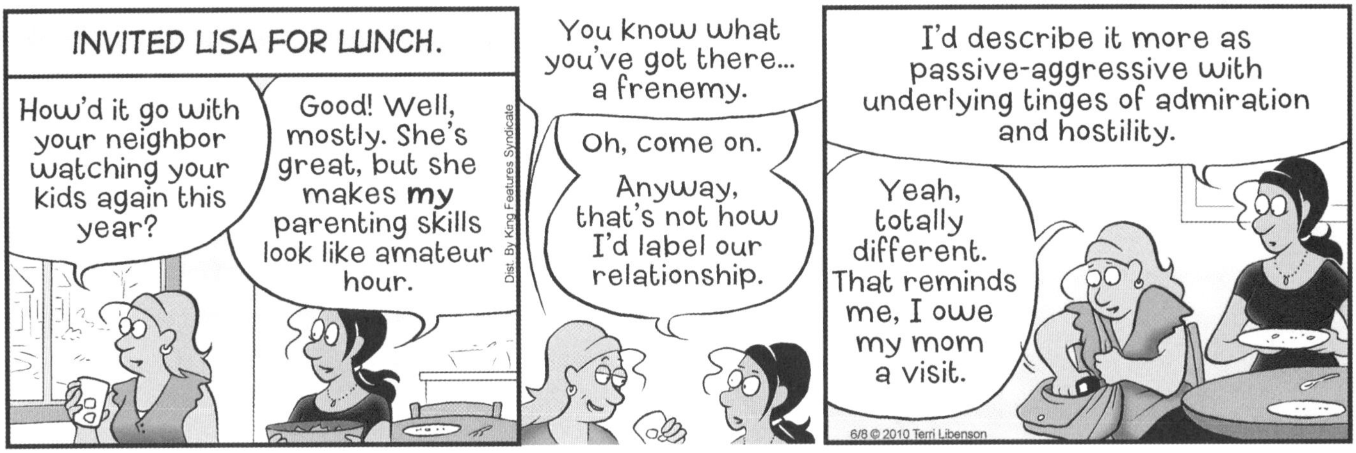
INVITED LISA FOR LUNCH.
How'd it go with your neighbor watching your kids again this year?
Good! Well, mostly. She's great, but she makes **my** parenting skills look like amateur hour.
Dist. By King Features Syndicate
You know what you've got there... a frenemy.
Oh, come on.
Anyway, that's not how I'd label our relationship.
I'd describe it more as passive-aggressive with underlying tinges of admiration and hostility.
Yeah, totally different. That reminds me, I owe my mom a visit.
6/8 © 2010 Terri Libenson

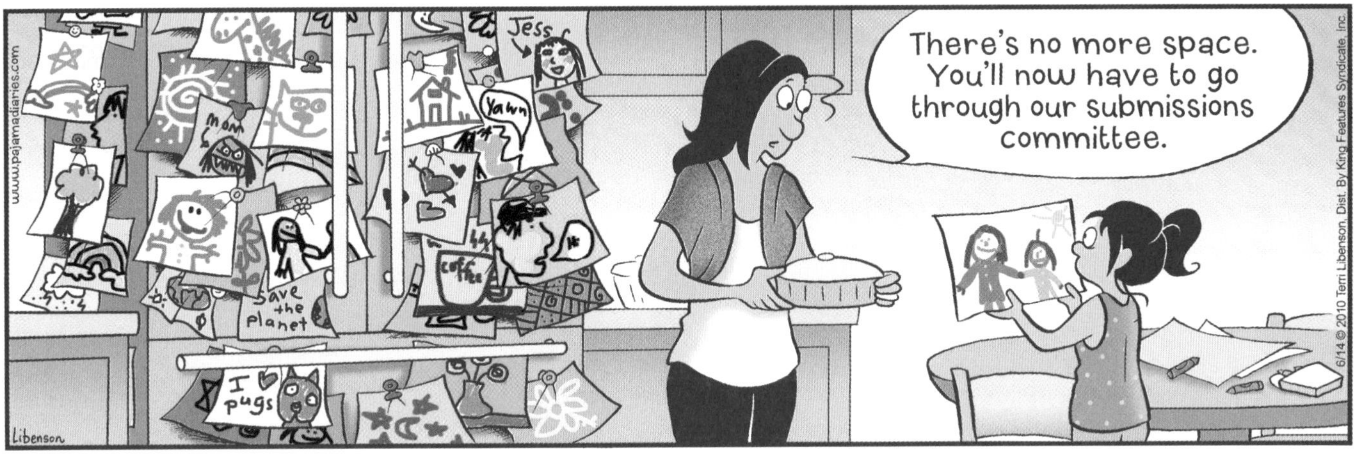
www.pajamadiaries.com
Jess
mom
Yawn
Save the Planet
I ♥ pugs
Libenson
There's no more space. You'll now have to go through our submissions committee.
6/14 © 2010 Terri Libenson, Dist. By King Features Syndicate, Inc.

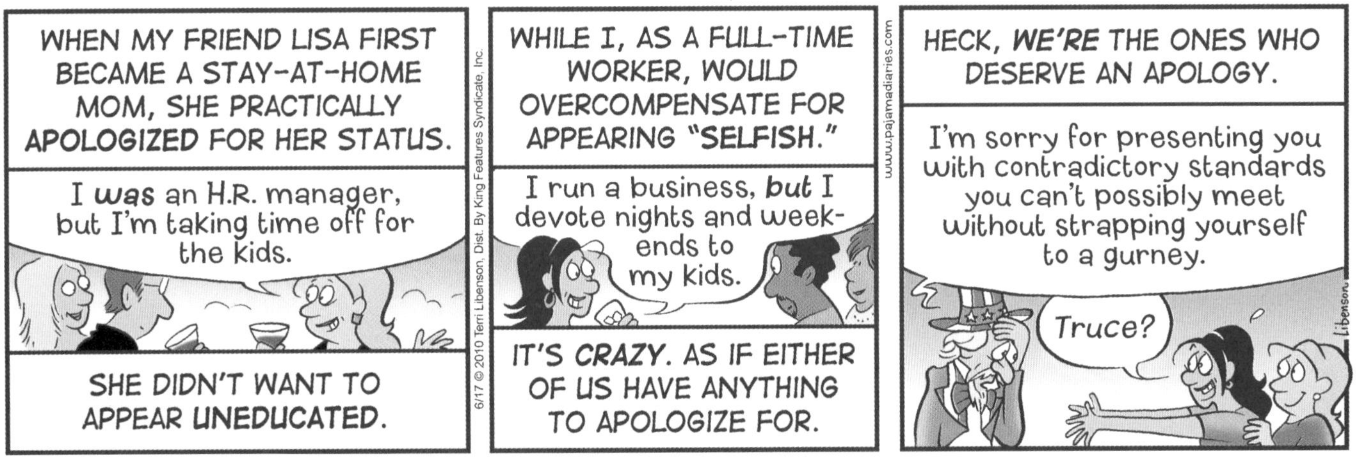
WHEN MY FRIEND LISA FIRST BECAME A STAY-AT-HOME MOM, SHE PRACTICALLY **APOLOGIZED** FOR HER STATUS.
I *was* an H.R. manager, but I'm taking time off for the kids.
SHE DIDN'T WANT TO APPEAR **UNEDUCATED**.
6/17 © 2010 Terri Libenson, Dist. By King Features Syndicate, Inc.
WHILE I, AS A FULL-TIME WORKER, WOULD OVERCOMPENSATE FOR APPEARING **"SELFISH."**
I run a business, ***but*** I devote nights and week-ends to my kids.
IT'S ***CRAZY***. AS IF EITHER OF US HAVE ANYTHING TO APOLOGIZE FOR.
www.pajamadiaries.com
HECK, ***WE'RE*** THE ONES WHO DESERVE AN APOLOGY.
I'm sorry for presenting you with contradictory standards you can't possibly meet without strapping yourself to a gurney.
Truce?
Libenson

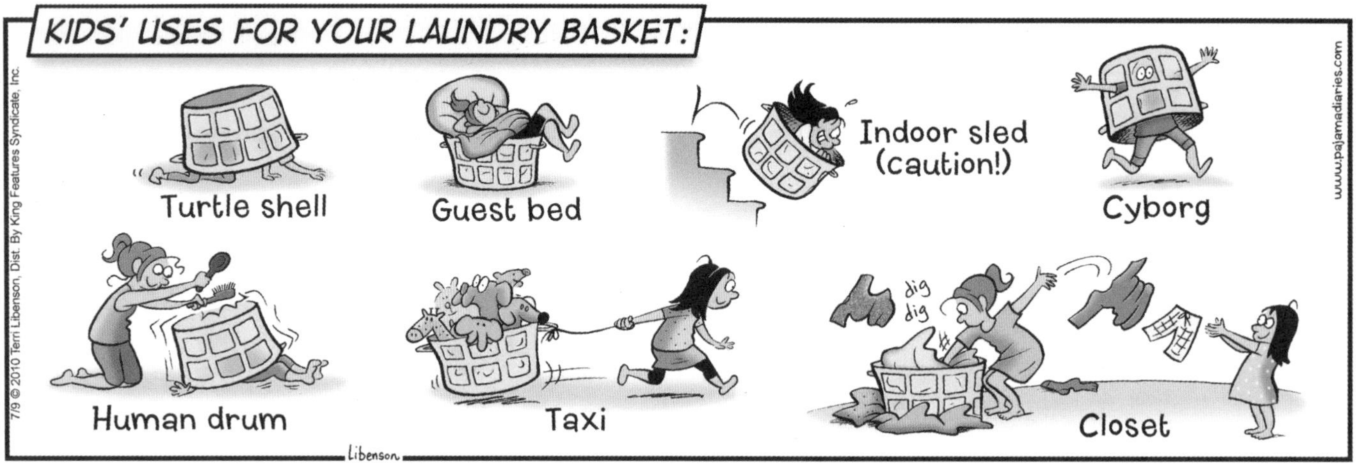
KIDS' USES FOR YOUR LAUNDRY BASKET:
Turtle shell
Guest bed
Indoor sled (caution!)
Cyborg
Human drum
Taxi
dig dig
Closet
7/9 © 2010 Terri Libenson, Dist. By King Features Syndicate, Inc.
www.pajamadiaries.com
Libenson

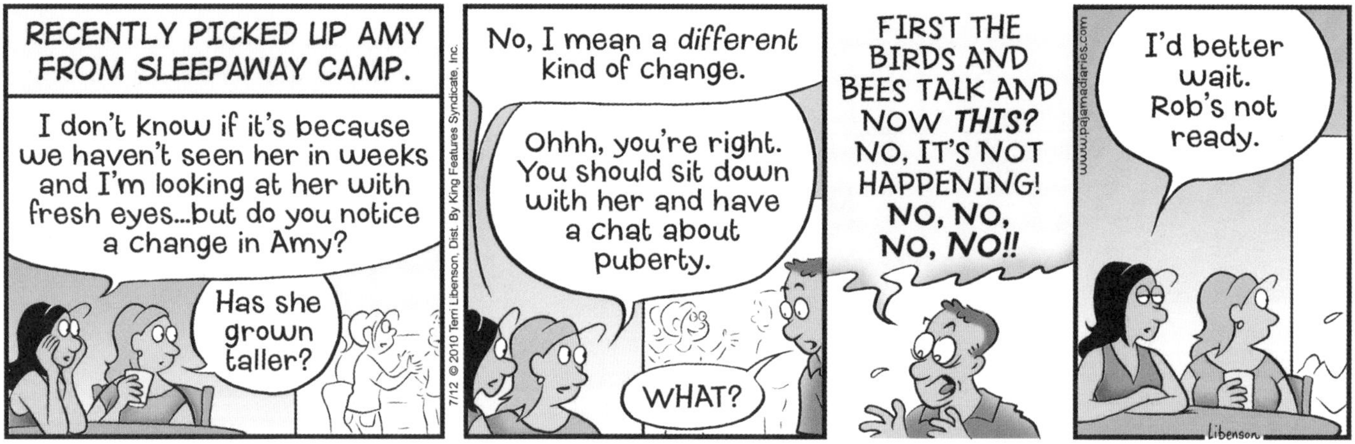
RECENTLY PICKED UP AMY FROM SLEEPAWAY CAMP.
I don't know if it's because we haven't seen her in weeks and I'm looking at her with fresh eyes...but do you notice a change in Amy?
Has she grown taller?
7/12 © 2010 Terri Libenson, Dist. By King Features Syndicate, Inc.
No, I mean a *different* kind of change.
Ohhh, you're right. You should sit down with her and have a chat about puberty.
WHAT?
FIRST THE BIRDS AND BEES TALK AND NOW *THIS?* NO, IT'S NOT HAPPENING! **NO, NO, NO, *NO!!***
www.pajamadiaries.com
I'd better wait. Rob's not ready.
Libenson

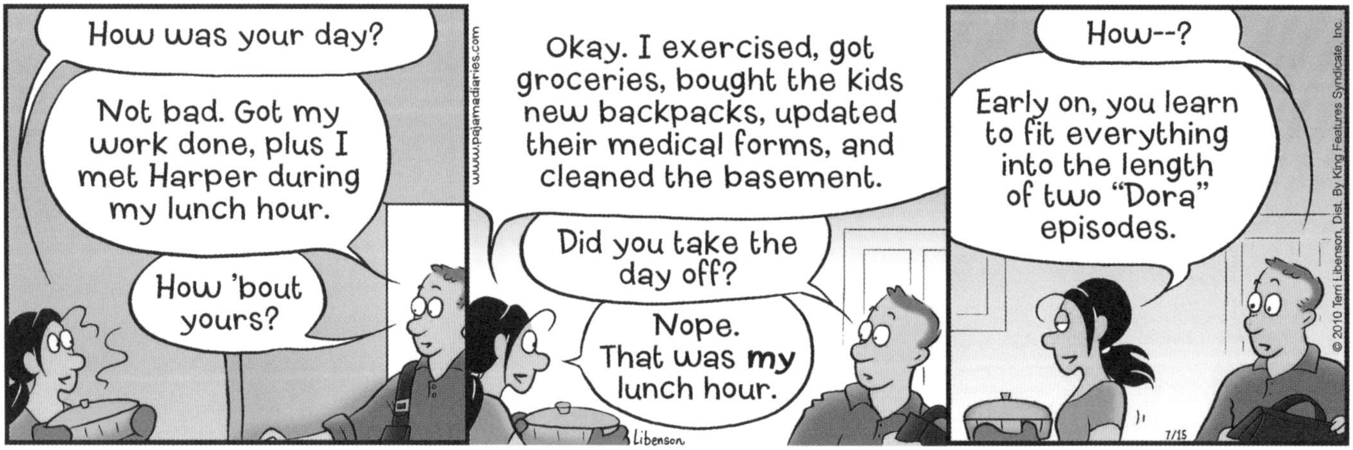
How was your day?
Not bad. Got my work done, plus I met Harper during my lunch hour.
How 'bout yours?
www.pajamadiaries.com
Okay. I exercised, got groceries, bought the kids new backpacks, updated their medical forms, and cleaned the basement.
Did you take the day off?
Nope. That was **my** lunch hour.
Libenson
How--?
Early on, you learn to fit everything into the length of two "Dora" episodes.
7/15
© 2010 Terri Libenson, Dist. By King Features Syndicate, Inc.

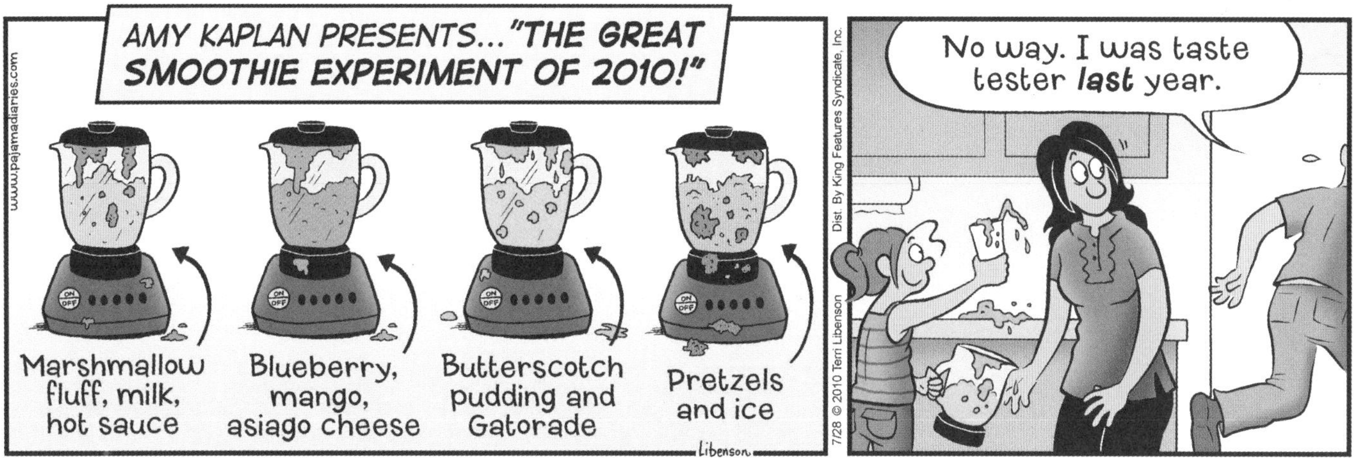
AMY KAPLAN PRESENTS... "THE GREAT SMOOTHIE EXPERIMENT OF 2010!"
Marshmallow fluff, milk, hot sauce
Blueberry, mango, asiago cheese
Butterscotch pudding and Gatorade
Pretzels and ice
Libenson
www.pajamadiaries.com
7/28 © 2010 Terri Libenson Dist. By King Features Syndicate, Inc.
No way. I was taste tester **last** year.

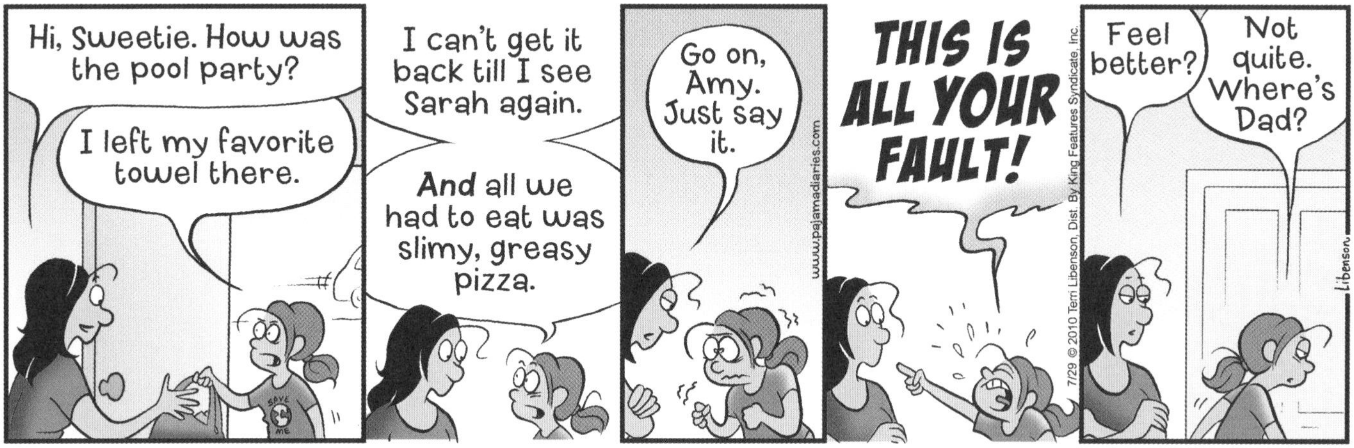
Hi, Sweetie. How was the pool party?
I left my favorite towel there.
I can't get it back till I see Sarah again.
And all we had to eat was slimy, greasy pizza.
Go on, Amy. Just say it.
www.pajamadiaries.com
THIS IS ALL YOUR FAULT!
7/29 © 2010 Terri Libenson. Dist. By King Features Syndicate, Inc.
Feel better?
Not quite. Where's Dad?
Libenson

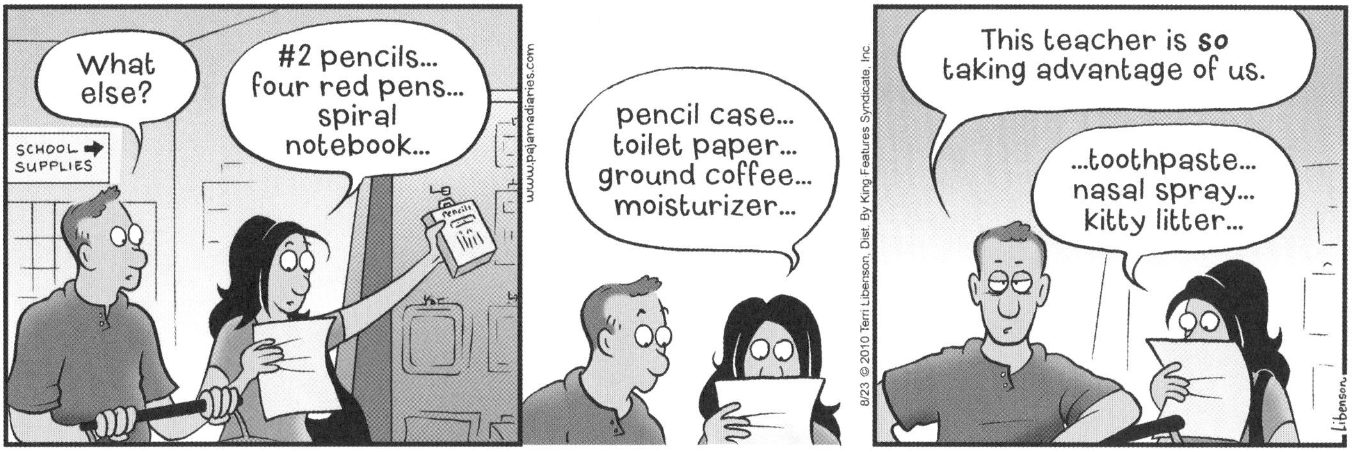
What else?
#2 pencils... four red pens... spiral notebook...
SCHOOL SUPPLIES
www.pajamadiaries.com
pencil case... toilet paper... ground coffee... moisturizer...
8/23 © 2010 Terri Libenson. Dist. By King Features Syndicate, Inc.
This teacher is **so** taking advantage of us.
...toothpaste... nasal spray... kitty litter...
Libenson

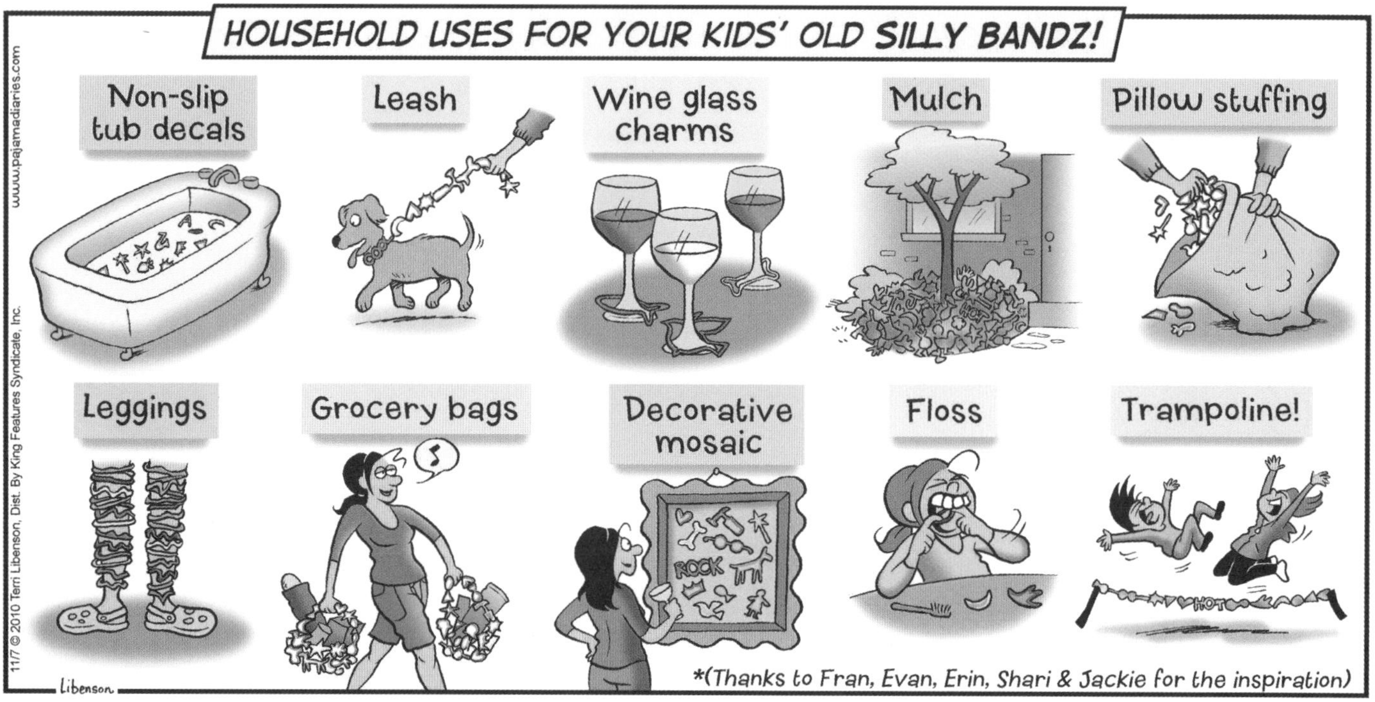
HOUSEHOLD USES FOR YOUR KIDS' OLD SILLY BANDZ!
Non-slip tub decals
Leash
Wine glass charms
Mulch
Pillow stuffing
Leggings
Grocery bags
Decorative mosaic
Floss
Trampoline!
*(Thanks to Fran, Evan, Erin, Shari & Jackie for the inspiration)
11/7 © 2010 Terri Libenson, Dist. By King Features Syndicate, Inc.
www.pajamadiaries.com
Libenson

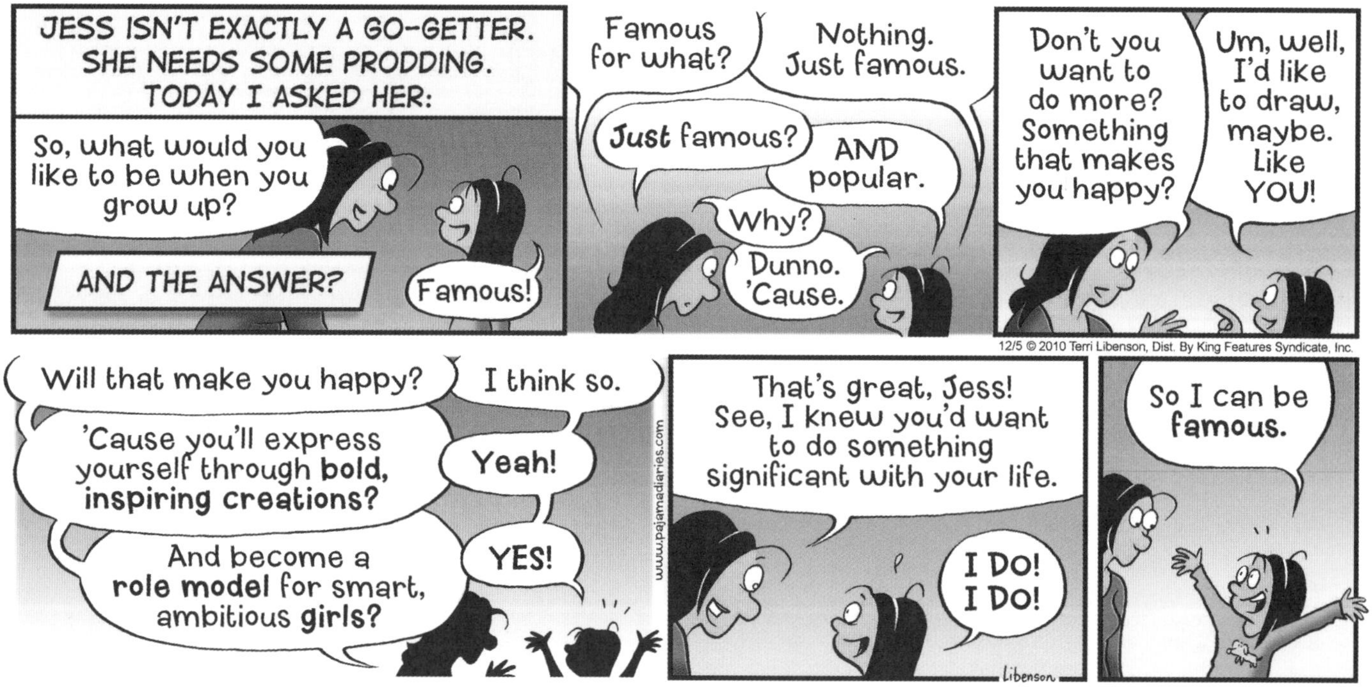
JESS ISN'T EXACTLY A GO-GETTER. SHE NEEDS SOME PRODDING. TODAY I ASKED HER:
So, what would you like to be when you grow up?
AND THE ANSWER?
Famous!
Famous for what?
Nothing. Just famous.
Just famous?
AND popular.
Why?
Dunno. 'Cause.
Don't you want to do more? Something that makes you happy?
Um, well, I'd like to draw, maybe. Like YOU!
12/5 © 2010 Terri Libenson, Dist. By King Features Syndicate, Inc.
Will that make you happy?
I think so.
'Cause you'll express yourself through bold, inspiring creations?
Yeah!
And become a role model for smart, ambitious girls?
YES!
www.pajamadiaries.com
That's great, Jess! See, I knew you'd want to do something significant with your life.
I DO! I DO!
Libenson
So I can be famous.

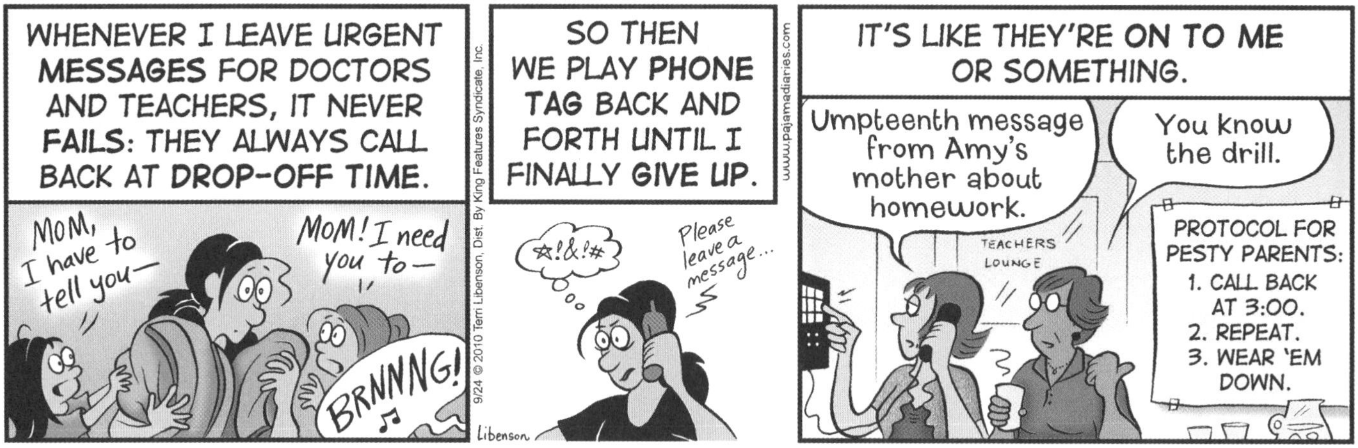
WHENEVER I LEAVE URGENT MESSAGES FOR DOCTORS AND TEACHERS, IT NEVER FAILS: THEY ALWAYS CALL BACK AT DROP-OFF TIME.
MOM, I have to tell you—
MOM! I need you to—
BRNNNG!
9/24 © 2010 Terri Libenson, Dist. By King Features Syndicate, Inc.
SO THEN WE PLAY PHONE TAG BACK AND FORTH UNTIL I FINALLY GIVE UP.
*!&!#
Please leave a message...
Libenson
www.pajamadiaries.com
IT'S LIKE THEY'RE ON TO ME OR SOMETHING.
Umpteenth message from Amy's mother about homework.
You know the drill.
TEACHERS LOUNGE
PROTOCOL FOR PESTY PARENTS:
1. CALL BACK AT 3:00.
2. REPEAT.
3. WEAR 'EM DOWN.

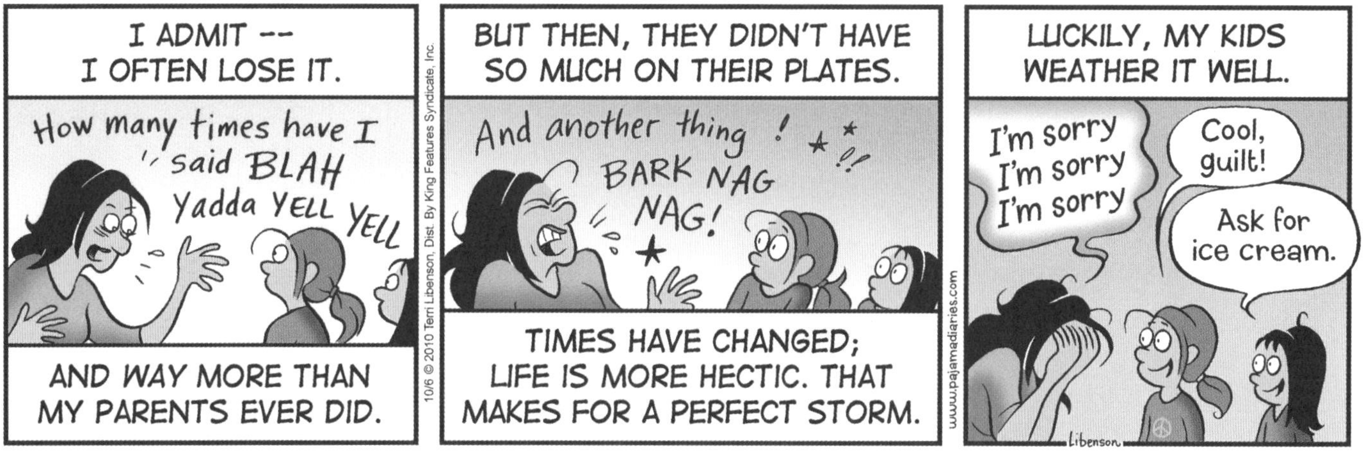
I ADMIT -- I OFTEN LOSE IT.
How many times have I said BLAH Yadda YELL YELL
AND WAY MORE THAN MY PARENTS EVER DID.
10/6 © 2010 Terri Libenson, Dist. By King Features Syndicate, Inc.
BUT THEN, THEY DIDN'T HAVE SO MUCH ON THEIR PLATES.
And another thing!
BARK NAG NAG!
TIMES HAVE CHANGED; LIFE IS MORE HECTIC. THAT MAKES FOR A PERFECT STORM.
www.pajamadiaries.com
LUCKILY, MY KIDS WEATHER IT WELL.
I'm sorry I'm sorry I'm sorry
Cool, guilt!
Ask for ice cream.
Libenson

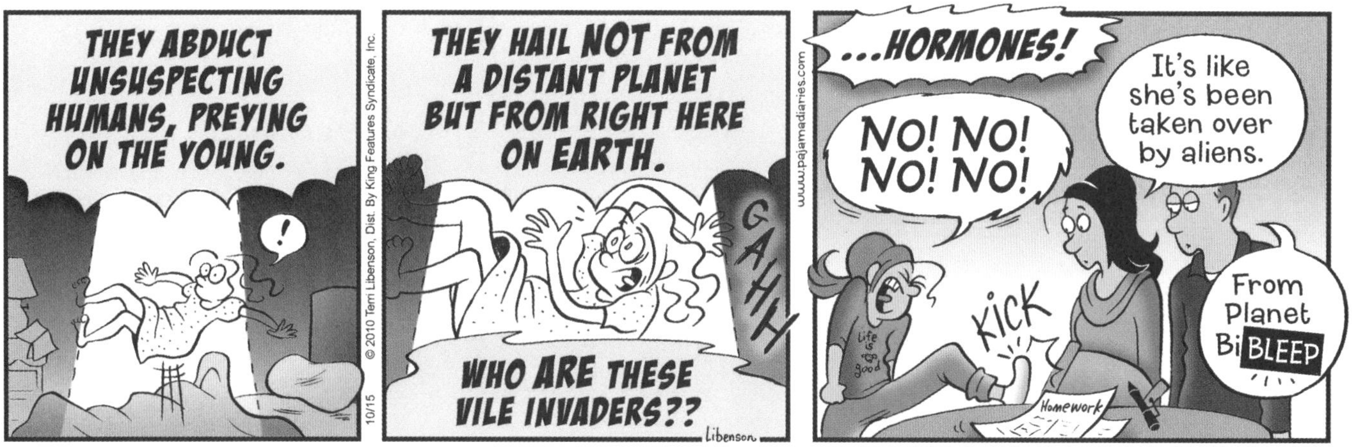
THEY ABDUCT UNSUSPECTING HUMANS, PREYING ON THE YOUNG.
!
10/15 © 2010 Terri Libenson, Dist. By King Features Syndicate, Inc.
THEY HAIL NOT FROM A DISTANT PLANET BUT FROM RIGHT HERE ON EARTH.
GAHHH
WHO ARE THESE VILE INVADERS??
Libenson
www.pajamadiaries.com
...HORMONES!
NO! NO! NO! NO!
It's like she's been taken over by aliens.
From Planet Bi BLEEP
KICK
Life is good
Homework

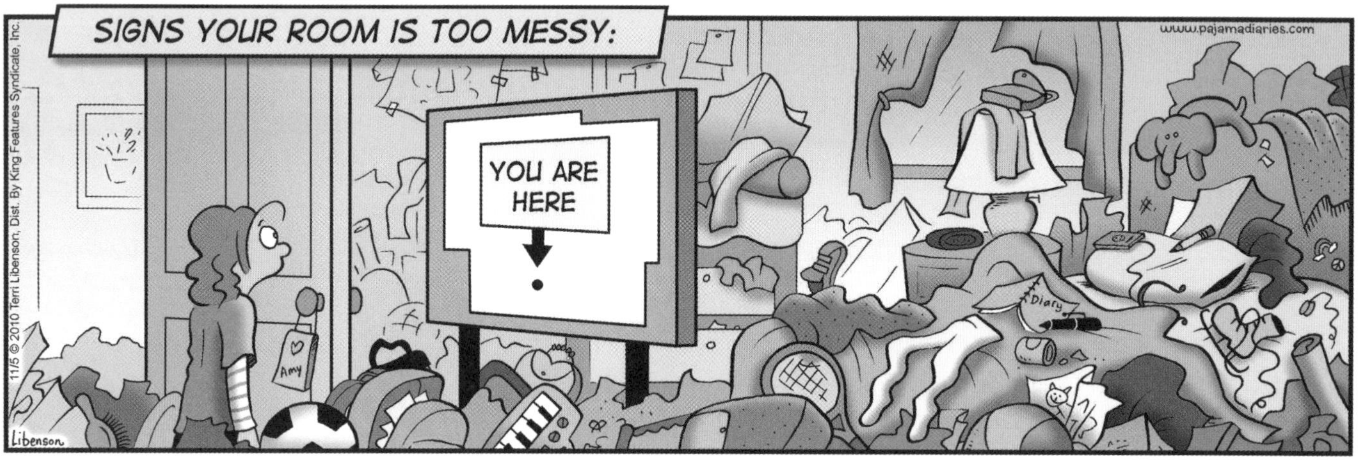
SIGNS YOUR ROOM IS TOO MESSY:
www.pajamadiaries.com
YOU ARE HERE
Diary
Amy
Libenson
11/5 © 2010 Terri Libenson, Dist. By King Features Syndicate, Inc.

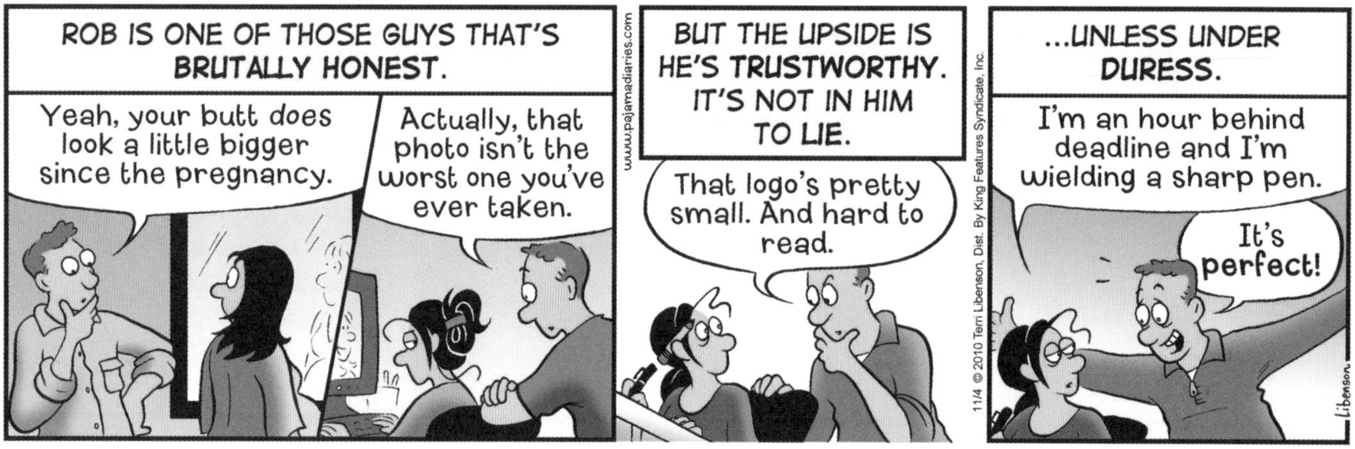
ROB IS ONE OF THOSE GUYS THAT'S **BRUTALLY HONEST.**
Yeah, your butt *does* look a little bigger since the pregnancy.
Actually, that photo isn't the worst one you've ever taken.
www.pajamadiaries.com
BUT THE UPSIDE IS HE'S **TRUSTWORTHY.** IT'S NOT IN HIM TO LIE.
That logo's pretty small. And hard to read.
11/4 © 2010 Terri Libenson, Dist. By King Features Syndicate, Inc.
...UNLESS UNDER **DURESS.**
I'm an hour behind deadline and I'm wielding a sharp pen.
It's **perfect!**
Libenson

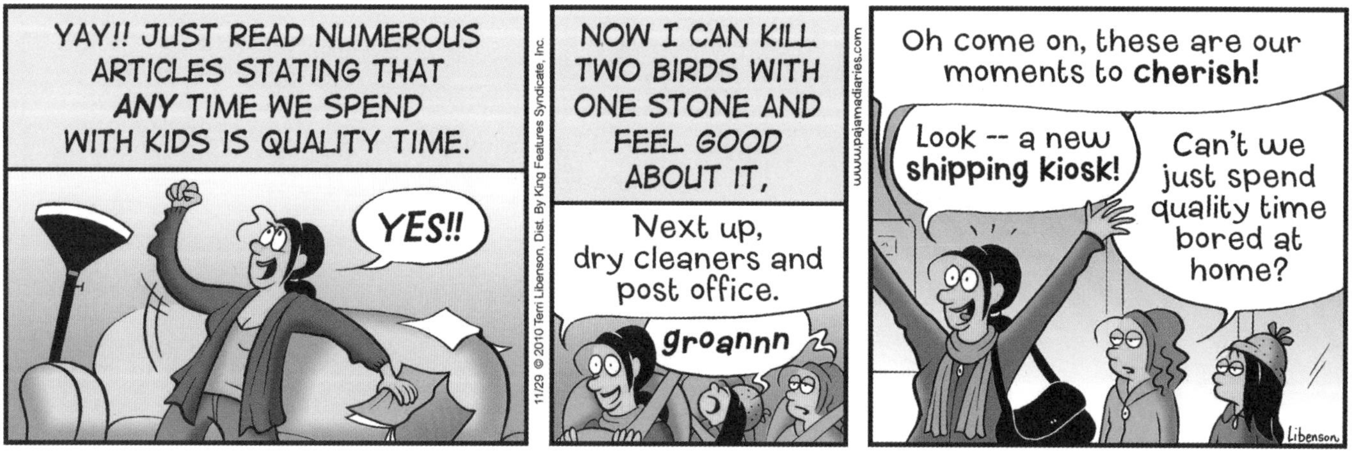
YAY!! JUST READ NUMEROUS ARTICLES STATING THAT ***ANY*** TIME WE SPEND WITH KIDS IS QUALITY TIME.
YES!!
11/29 © 2010 Terri Libenson, Dist. By King Features Syndicate, Inc.
NOW I CAN KILL TWO BIRDS WITH ONE STONE AND FEEL *GOOD* ABOUT IT,
Next up, dry cleaners and post office.
groannn
www.pajamadiaries.com
Oh come on, these are our moments to **cherish!**
Look -- a new **shipping kiosk!**
Can't we just spend quality time bored at home?
Libenson

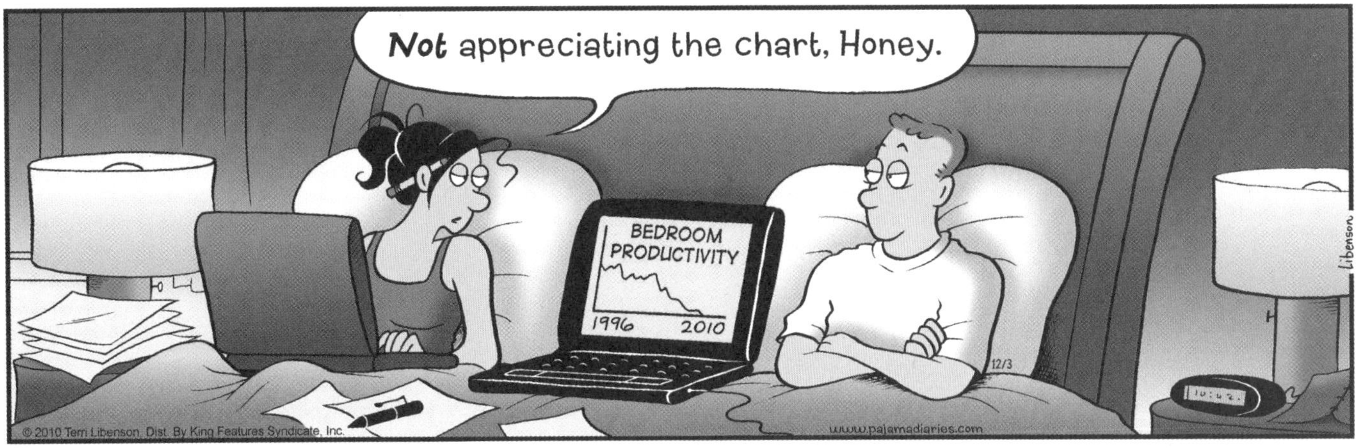
Not appreciating the chart, Honey.
BEDROOM PRODUCTIVITY
1996
2010
12/3
Libenson
© 2010 Terri Libenson. Dist. By King Features Syndicate, Inc.
www.pajamadiaries.com

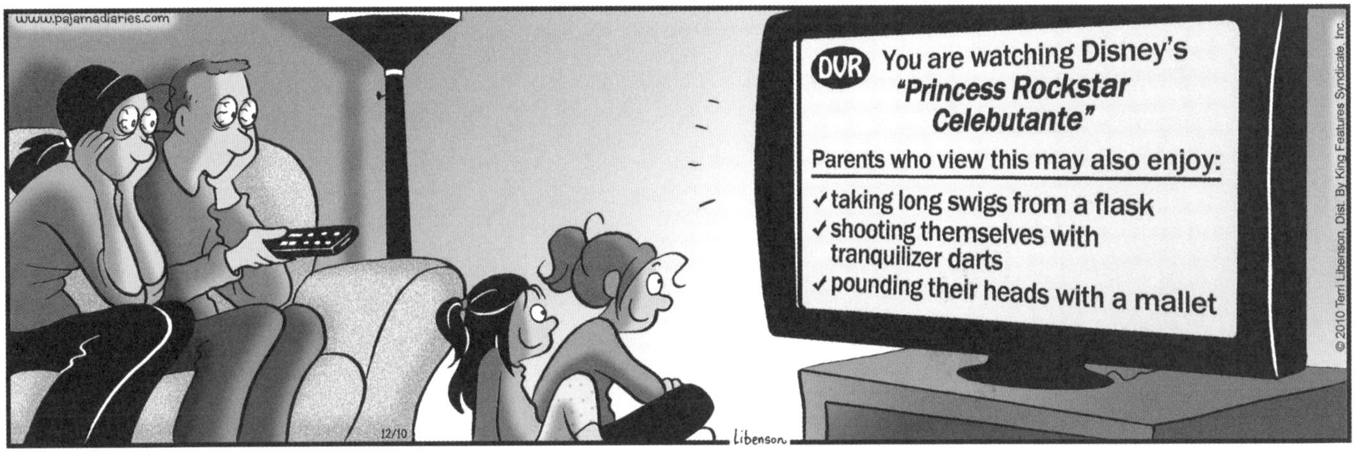
www.pajamadiaries.com
DVR
You are watching Disney's
"Princess Rockstar Celebutante"
Parents who view this may also enjoy:
✓ taking long swigs from a flask
✓ shooting themselves with tranquilizer darts
✓ pounding their heads with a mallet
© 2010 Terri Libenson. Dist. By King Features Syndicate, Inc.
12/10
Libenson

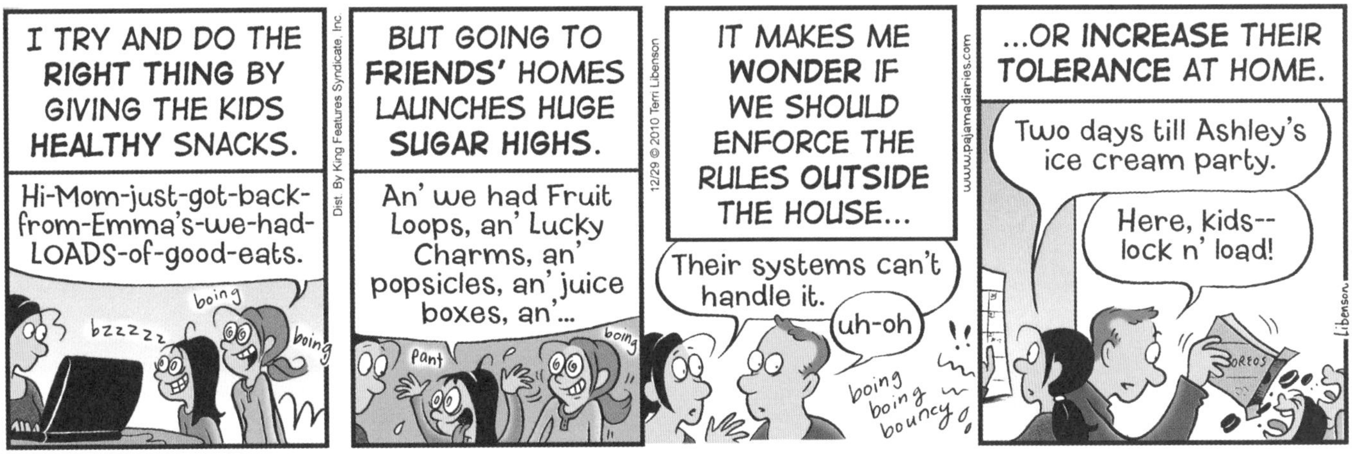
I TRY AND DO THE RIGHT THING BY GIVING THE KIDS HEALTHY SNACKS.
Hi-Mom-just-got-back-from-Emma's-we-had-LOADS-of-good-eats.
bzzzzz
boing
boing
Dist. By King Features Syndicate, Inc.
BUT GOING TO FRIENDS' HOMES LAUNCHES HUGE SUGAR HIGHS.
An' we had Fruit Loops, an' Lucky Charms, an' popsicles, an' juice boxes, an'...
pant
boing
12/29 © 2010 Terri Libenson
IT MAKES ME WONDER IF WE SHOULD ENFORCE THE RULES OUTSIDE THE HOUSE...
Their systems can't handle it.
uh-oh
boing boing bouncy
www.pajamadiaries.com
...OR INCREASE THEIR TOLERANCE AT HOME.
Two days till Ashley's ice cream party.
Here, kids--lock n' load!
OREOS
Libenson

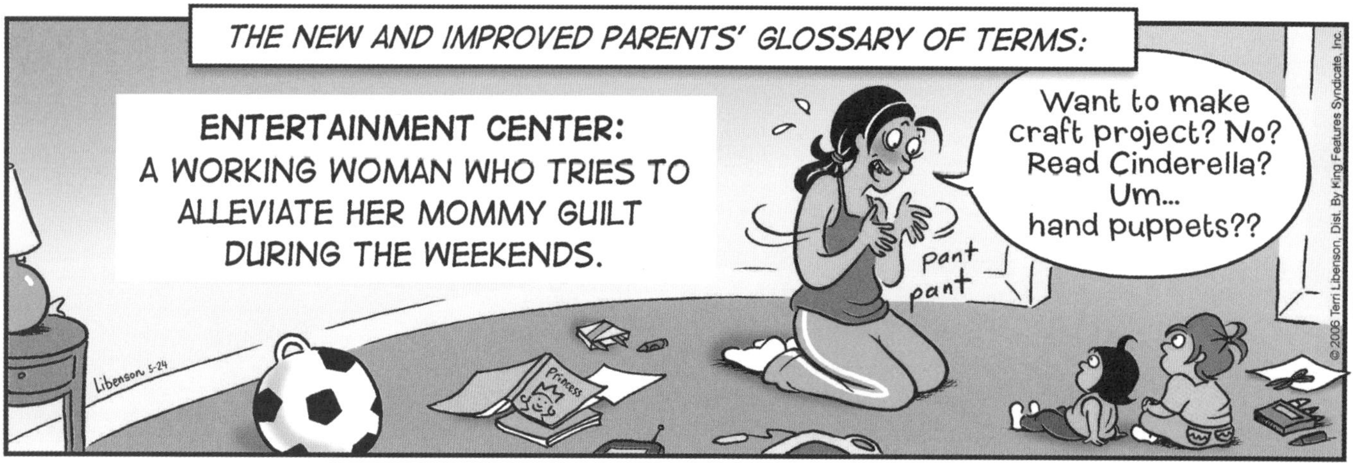
THE NEW AND IMPROVED PARENTS' GLOSSARY OF TERMS:
ENTERTAINMENT CENTER:
A WORKING WOMAN WHO TRIES TO ALLEVIATE HER MOMMY GUILT DURING THE WEEKENDS.
Want to make craft project? No? Read Cinderella? Um... hand puppets??
pant pant
Princess
Libenson 5-24
© 2006 Terri Libenson, Dist. By King Features Syndicate, Inc.

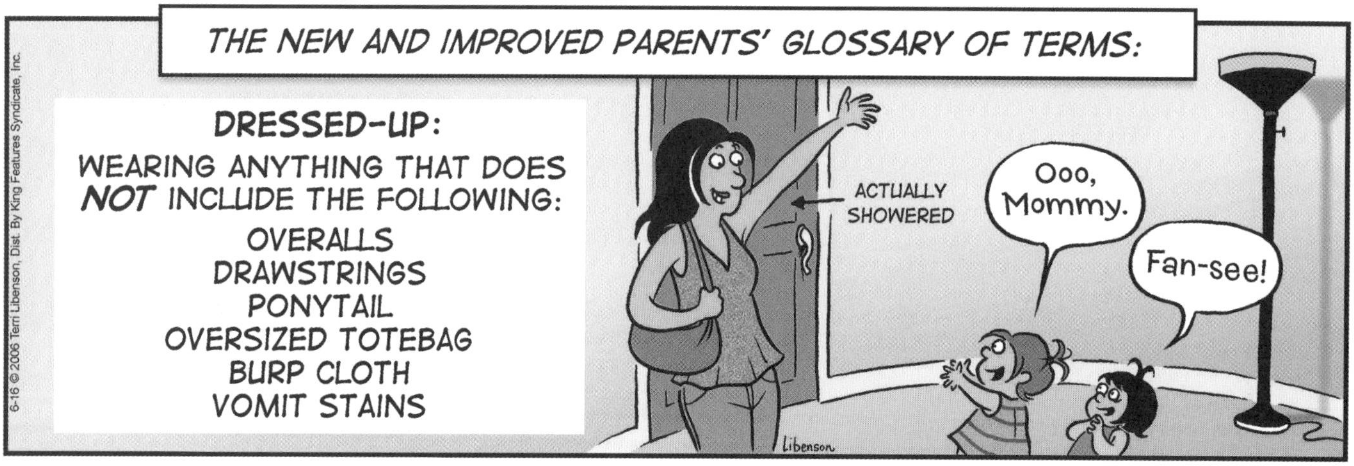
THE NEW AND IMPROVED PARENTS' GLOSSARY OF TERMS:
DRESSED-UP:
WEARING ANYTHING THAT DOES *NOT* INCLUDE THE FOLLOWING:
OVERALLS
DRAWSTRINGS
PONYTAIL
OVERSIZED TOTEBAG
BURP CLOTH
VOMIT STAINS
ACTUALLY SHOWERED
Ooo, Mommy.
Fan-see!
Libenson
6-16 © 2006 Terri Libenson, Dist. By King Features Syndicate, Inc.

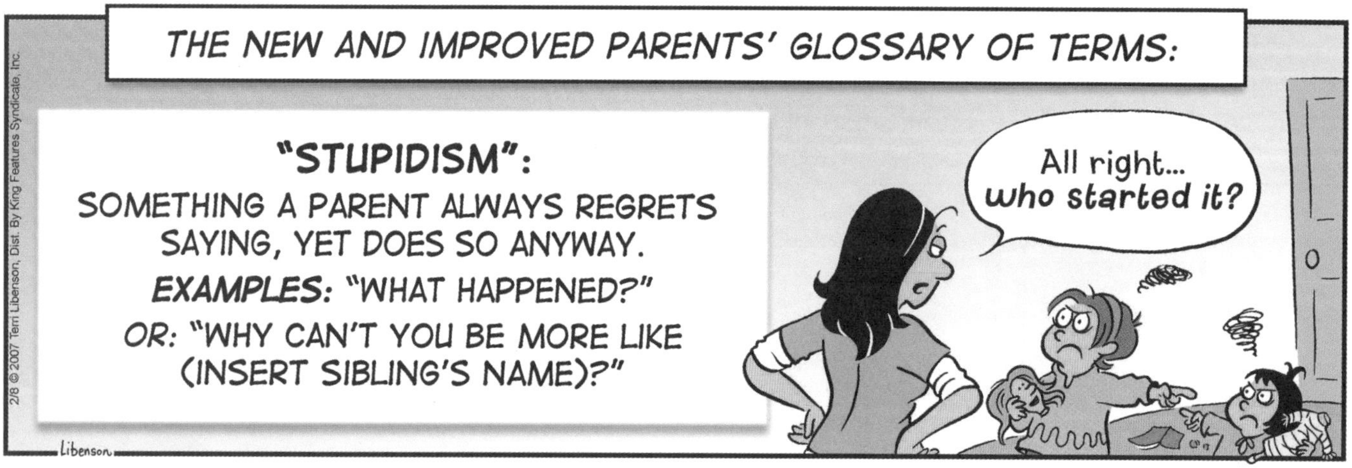
THE NEW AND IMPROVED PARENTS' GLOSSARY OF TERMS:
"STUPIDISM":
SOMETHING A PARENT ALWAYS REGRETS SAYING, YET DOES SO ANYWAY.
EXAMPLES: "WHAT HAPPENED?"
OR: "WHY CAN'T YOU BE MORE LIKE (INSERT SIBLING'S NAME)?"
All right... who started it?
Libenson
2/8 © 2007 Terri Libenson, Dist. By King Features Syndicate, Inc.

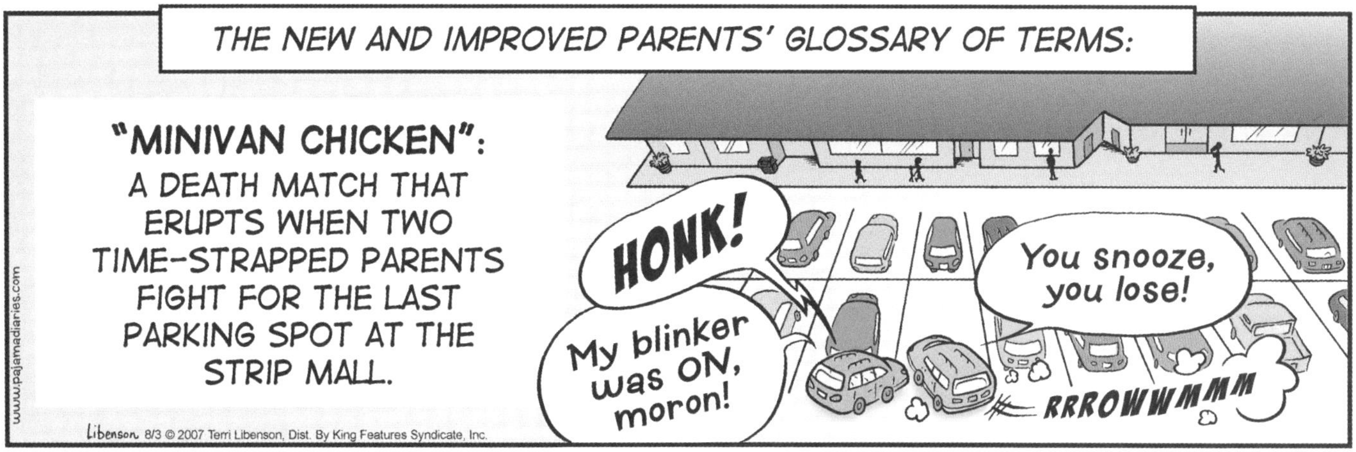
THE NEW AND IMPROVED PARENTS' GLOSSARY OF TERMS:
"MINIVAN CHICKEN": A DEATH MATCH THAT ERUPTS WHEN TWO TIME-STRAPPED PARENTS FIGHT FOR THE LAST PARKING SPOT AT THE STRIP MALL.
HONK!
My blinker was ON, moron!
You snooze, you lose!
RRROWWMMM
www.pajamadiaries.com
Libenson 8/3 © 2007 Terri Libenson, Dist. By King Features Syndicate, Inc.

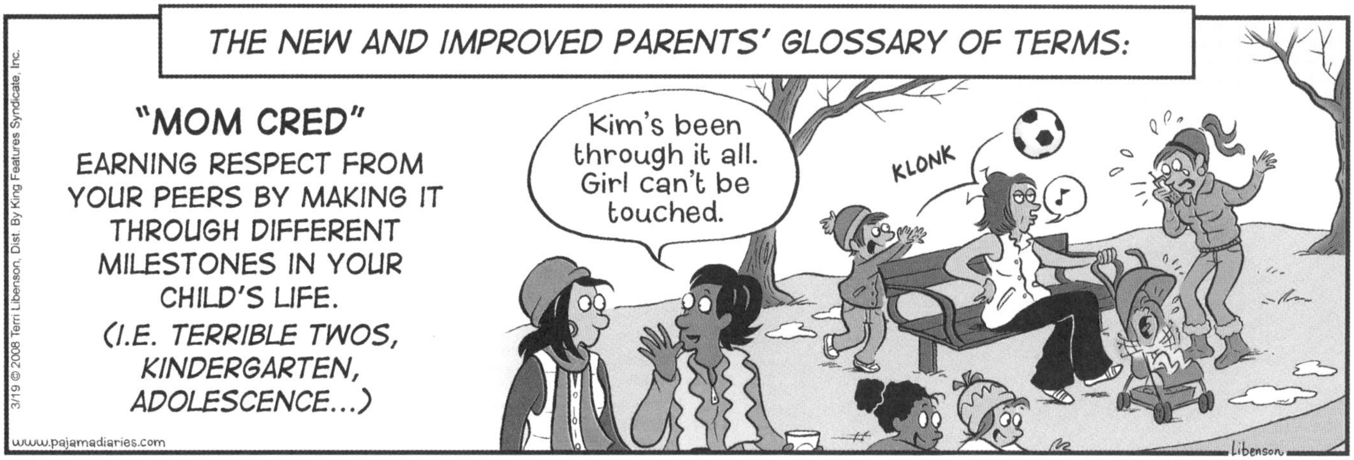
THE NEW AND IMPROVED PARENTS' GLOSSARY OF TERMS:
"MOM CRED"
EARNING RESPECT FROM YOUR PEERS BY MAKING IT THROUGH DIFFERENT MILESTONES IN YOUR CHILD'S LIFE.
(I.E. TERRIBLE TWOS, KINDERGARTEN, ADOLESCENCE...)
Kim's been through it all. Girl can't be touched.
KLONK
3/19 © 2008 Terri Libenson, Dist. By King Features Syndicate, Inc.
www.pajamadiaries.com
Libenson

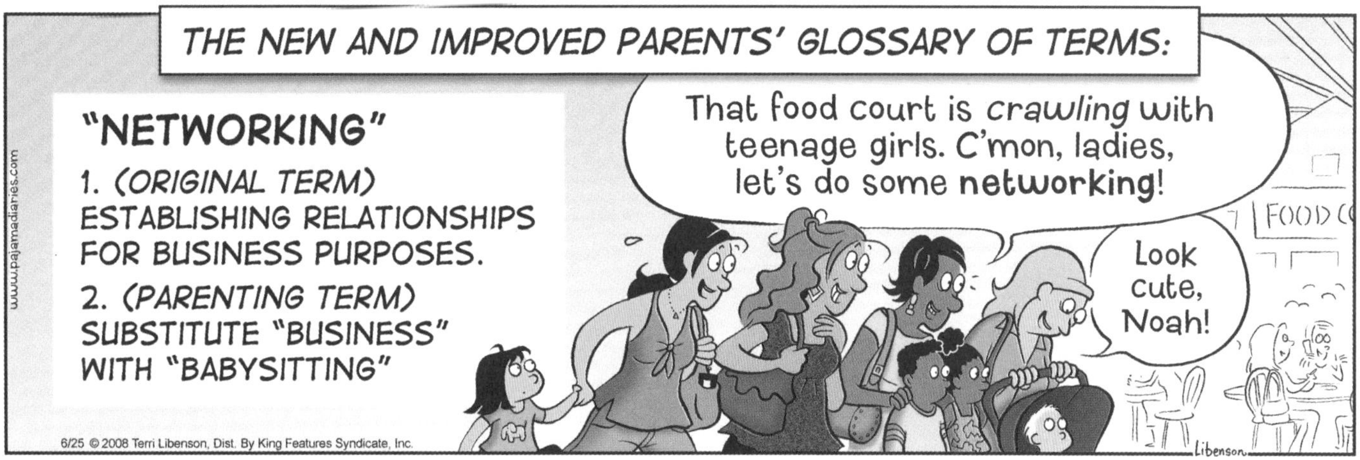
THE NEW AND IMPROVED PARENTS' GLOSSARY OF TERMS:
"NETWORKING"
1. (ORIGINAL TERM) ESTABLISHING RELATIONSHIPS FOR BUSINESS PURPOSES.
2. (PARENTING TERM) SUBSTITUTE "BUSINESS" WITH "BABYSITTING"
That food court is crawling with teenage girls. C'mon, ladies, let's do some networking!
Look cute, Noah!
www.pajamadiaries.com
6/25 © 2008 Terri Libenson, Dist. By King Features Syndicate, Inc.
Libenson

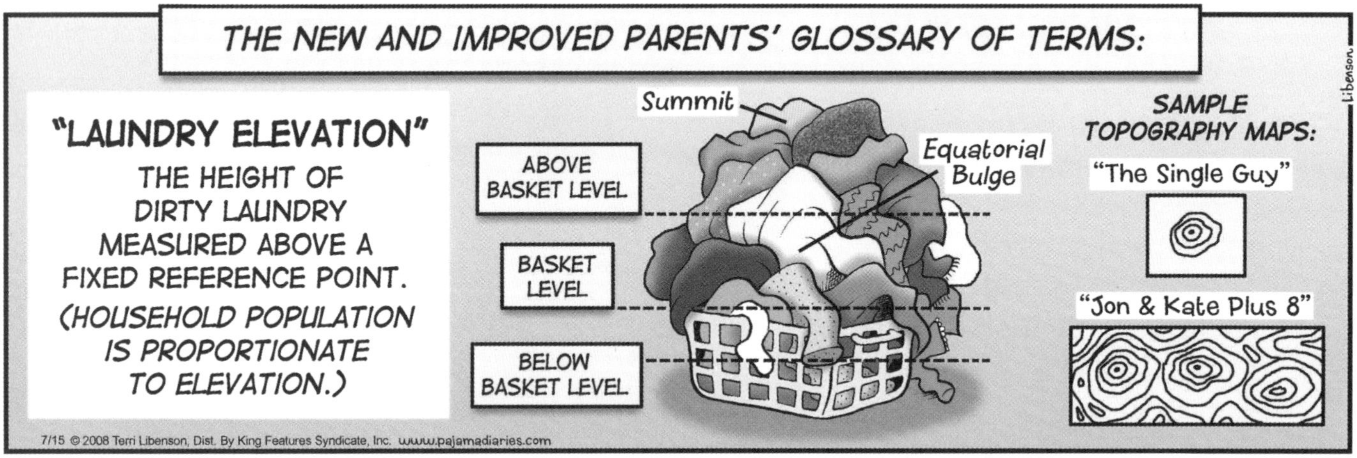
THE NEW AND IMPROVED PARENTS' GLOSSARY OF TERMS:
"LAUNDRY ELEVATION"
THE HEIGHT OF DIRTY LAUNDRY MEASURED ABOVE A FIXED REFERENCE POINT.
(HOUSEHOLD POPULATION IS PROPORTIONATE TO ELEVATION.)
Summit
Equatorial Bulge
ABOVE BASKET LEVEL
BASKET LEVEL
BELOW BASKET LEVEL
SAMPLE TOPOGRAPHY MAPS:
"The Single Guy"
"Jon & Kate Plus 8"
Libenson
7/15 © 2008 Terri Libenson, Dist. By King Features Syndicate, Inc. www.pajamadiaries.com

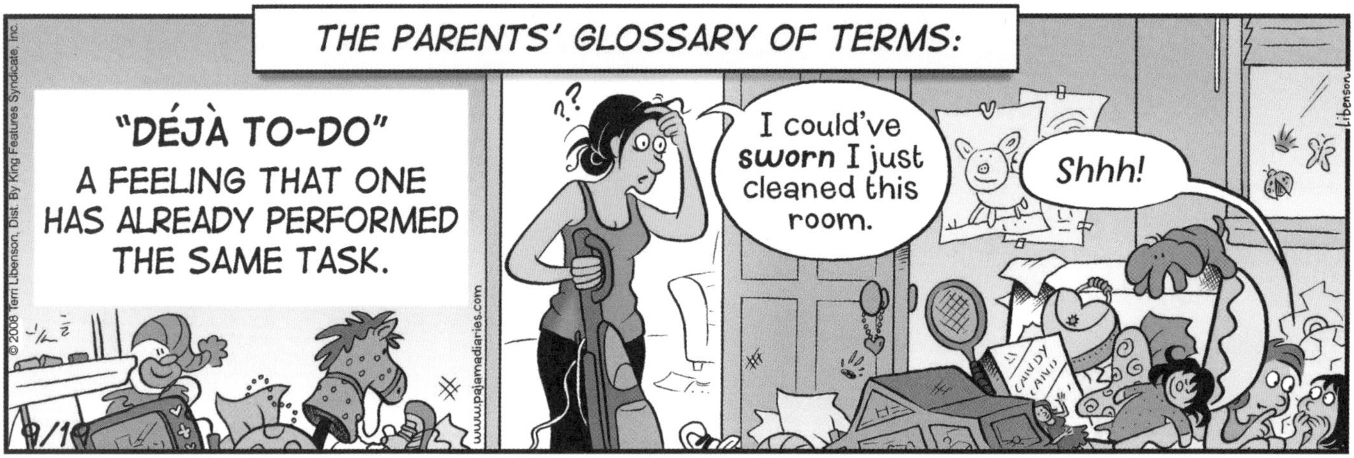
THE PARENTS' GLOSSARY OF TERMS:
"DÉJÀ TO-DO"
A FEELING THAT ONE HAS ALREADY PERFORMED THE SAME TASK.
I could've sworn I just cleaned this room.
Shhh!
9/19
© 2008 Terri Libenson, Dist. By King Features Syndicate, Inc.
www.pajamadiaries.com
Libenson

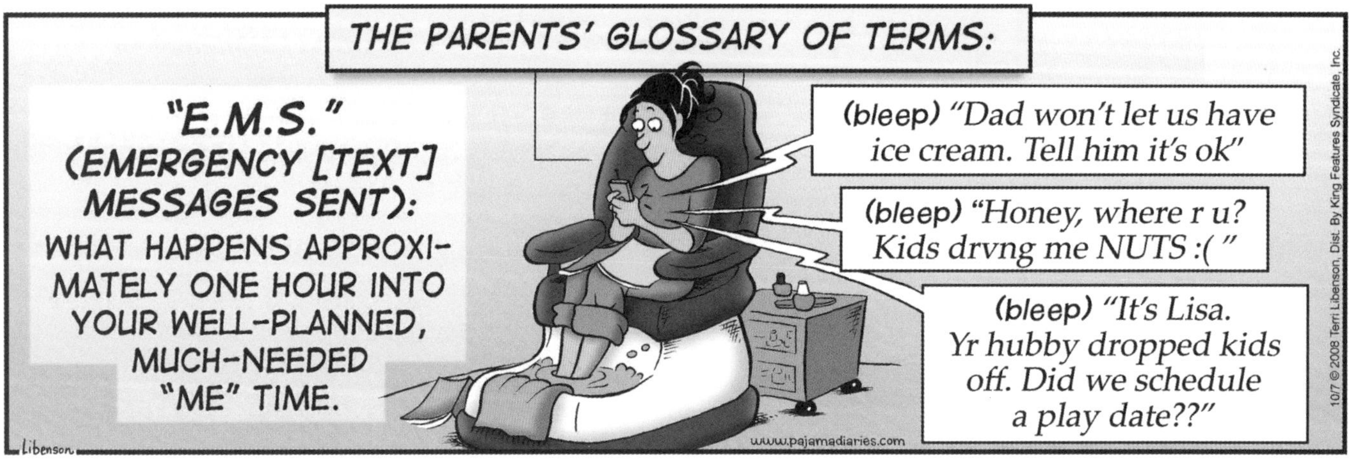
THE PARENTS' GLOSSARY OF TERMS:
"E.M.S."
(EMERGENCY [TEXT] MESSAGES SENT):
WHAT HAPPENS APPROXIMATELY ONE HOUR INTO YOUR WELL-PLANNED, MUCH-NEEDED "ME" TIME.
(bleep) "Dad won't let us have ice cream. Tell him it's ok"
(bleep) "Honey, where r u? Kids drvng me NUTS :("
(bleep) "It's Lisa. Yr hubby dropped kids off. Did we schedule a play date??"
Libenson
www.pajamadiaries.com
10/7 © 2008 Terri Libenson, Dist. By King Features Syndicate, Inc.

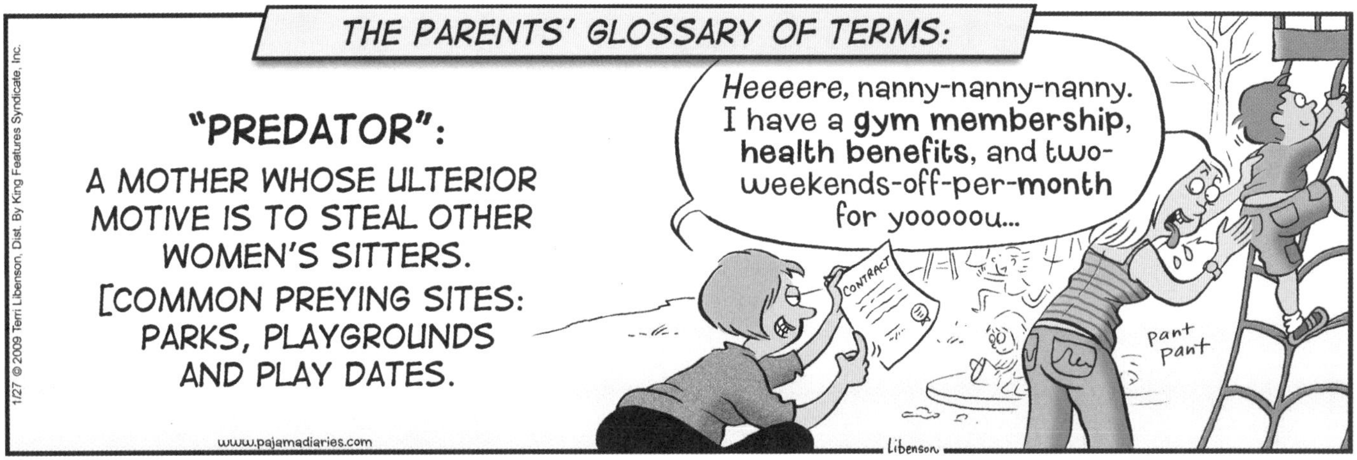
THE PARENTS' GLOSSARY OF TERMS:
"PREDATOR":
A MOTHER WHOSE ULTERIOR MOTIVE IS TO STEAL OTHER WOMEN'S SITTERS.
[COMMON PREYING SITES: PARKS, PLAYGROUNDS AND PLAY DATES.
Heeeere, nanny-nanny-nanny. I have a gym membership, health benefits, and two-weekends-off-per-month for yoooou...
CONTRACT
pant pant
1/27 © 2009 Terri Libenson, Dist. By King Features Syndicate, Inc.
www.pajamadiaries.com
Libenson

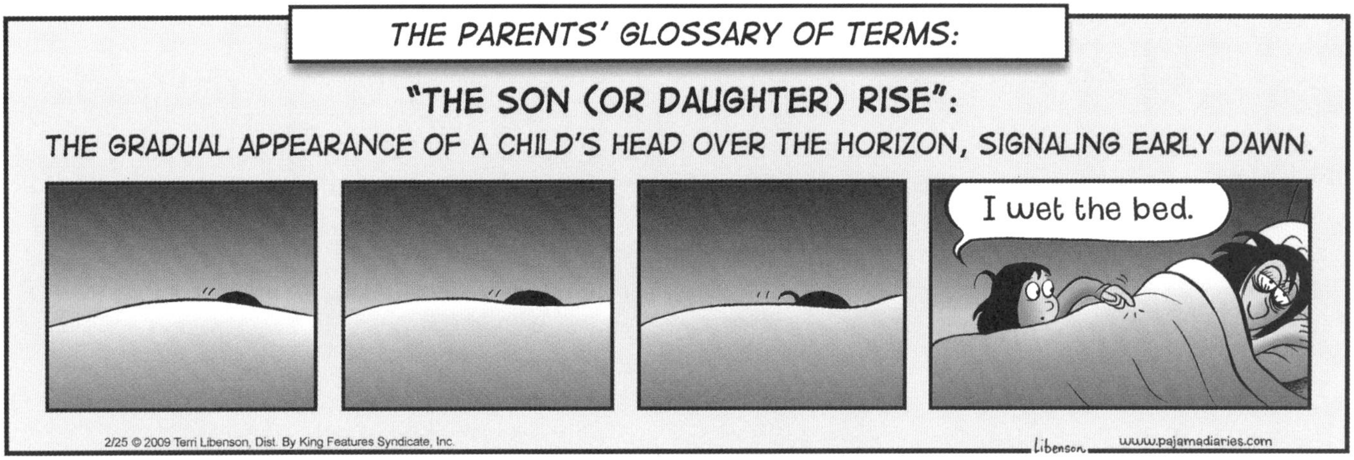
THE PARENTS' GLOSSARY OF TERMS:
"THE SON (OR DAUGHTER) RISE":
THE GRADUAL APPEARANCE OF A CHILD'S HEAD OVER THE HORIZON, SIGNALING EARLY DAWN.
I wet the bed.
2/25 © 2009 Terri Libenson, Dist. By King Features Syndicate, Inc.
Libenson
www.pajamadiaries.com

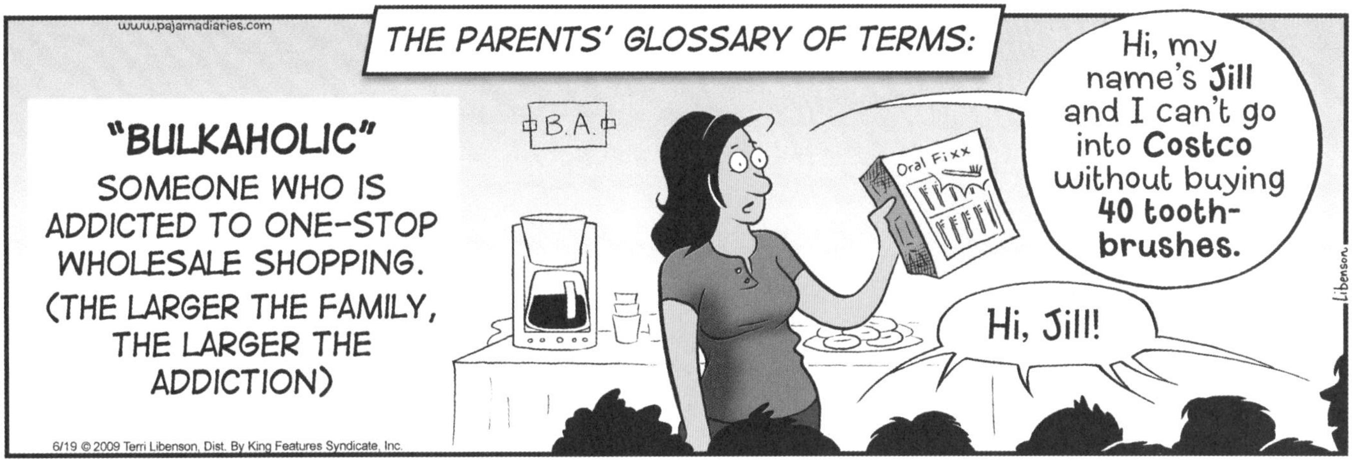
www.pajamadiaries.com
THE PARENTS' GLOSSARY OF TERMS:
"BULKAHOLIC"
SOMEONE WHO IS ADDICTED TO ONE-STOP WHOLESALE SHOPPING.
(THE LARGER THE FAMILY, THE LARGER THE ADDICTION)
B.A.
Oral Fixx
Hi, my name's Jill and I can't go into Costco without buying 40 tooth-brushes.
Hi, Jill!
Libenson
6/19 © 2009 Terri Libenson, Dist. By King Features Syndicate, Inc.

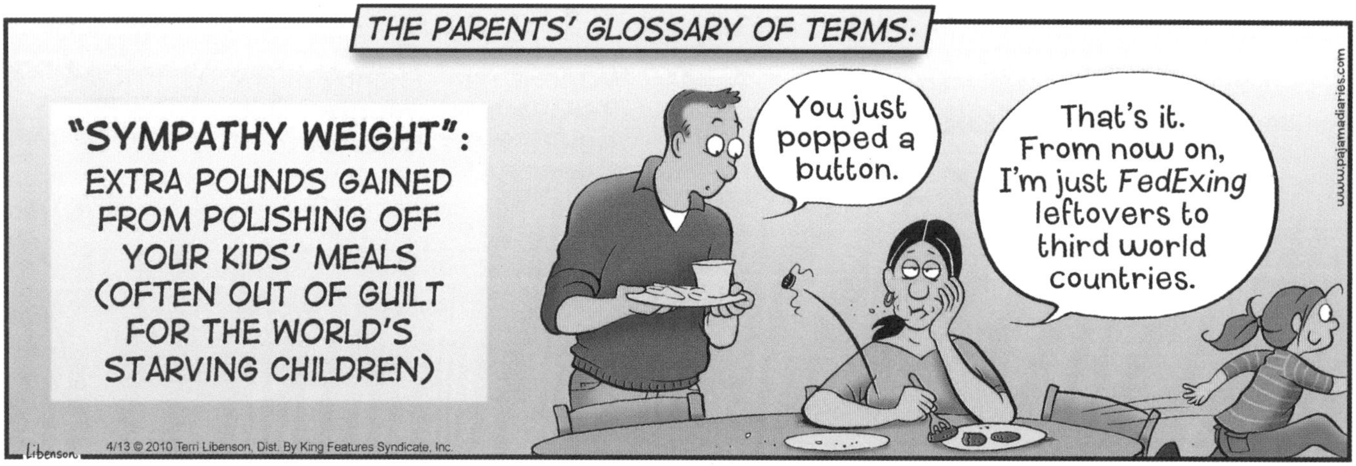
THE PARENTS' GLOSSARY OF TERMS:
"SYMPATHY WEIGHT": EXTRA POUNDS GAINED FROM POLISHING OFF YOUR KIDS' MEALS (OFTEN OUT OF GUILT FOR THE WORLD'S STARVING CHILDREN)
You just popped a button.
That's it. From now on, I'm just FedExing leftovers to third world countries.
www.pajamadiaries.com
4/13 © 2010 Terri Libenson, Dist. By King Features Syndicate, Inc.
Libenson

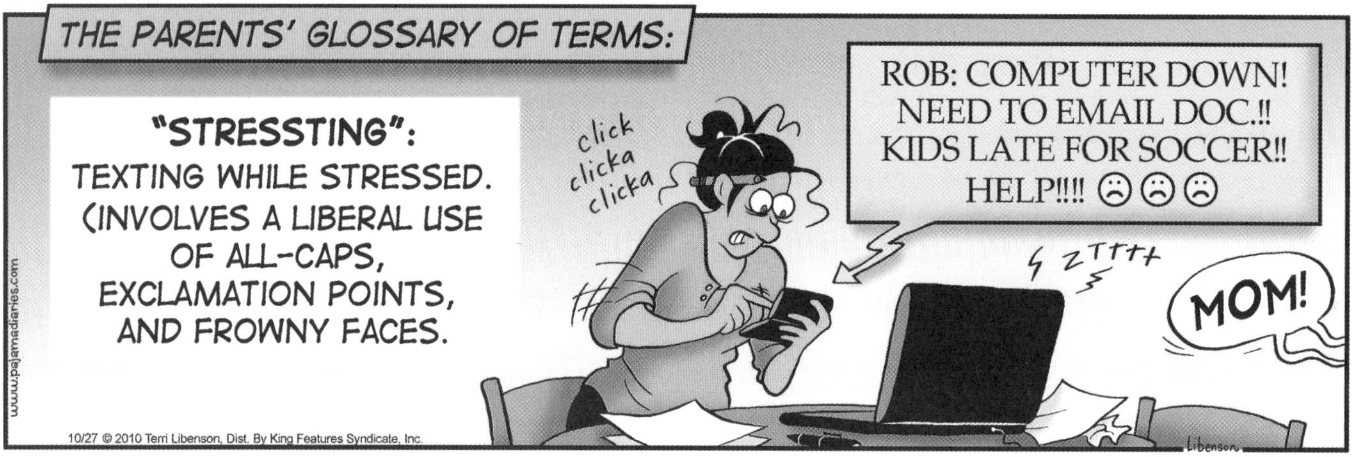
THE PARENTS' GLOSSARY OF TERMS:
"STRESSTING": TEXTING WHILE STRESSED. (INVOLVES A LIBERAL USE OF ALL-CAPS, EXCLAMATION POINTS, AND FROWNY FACES.
click clicka clicka
ROB: COMPUTER DOWN! NEED TO EMAIL DOC.!! KIDS LATE FOR SOCCER!! HELP!!!! ☹☹☹
MOM!
www.pajamadiaries.com
10/27 © 2010 Terri Libenson, Dist. By King Features Syndicate, Inc.
Libenson

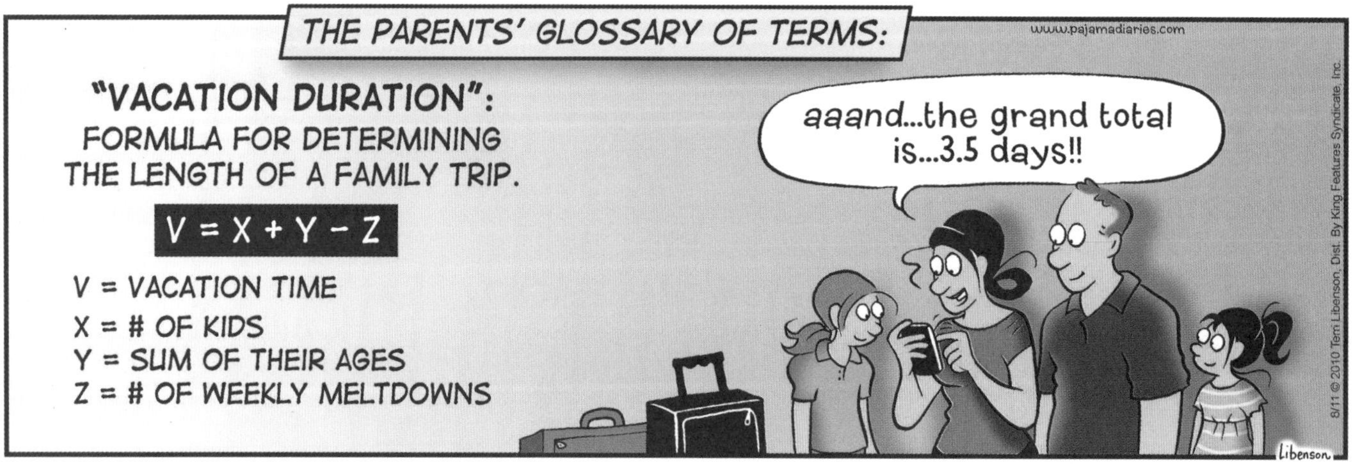
THE PARENTS' GLOSSARY OF TERMS:
"VACATION DURATION": FORMULA FOR DETERMINING THE LENGTH OF A FAMILY TRIP.
V = X + Y – Z
V = VACATION TIME
X = # OF KIDS
Y = SUM OF THEIR AGES
Z = # OF WEEKLY MELTDOWNS
aaand...the grand total is...3.5 days!!
www.pajamadiaries.com
8/11 © 2010 Terri Libenson, Dist. By King Features Syndicate, Inc.
Libenson